ROMA RIGHTS AND CIVIL RIGHTS

Roma Rights and Civil Rights tackles the movements for – and expressions of – equality for Roma in Central and Southeast Europe and African Americans from two complementary perspectives: law and cultural studies. Interdisciplinary in approach, the book engages with comparative law, European studies, cultural studies, and critical race theory. Its central contribution is to compare the experiences of Roma and African Americans regarding racialization, marginalization, and mobilization for equality. Deploying a novel approach, the book challenges conventional notions of civil rights and entrenched paradigms in Romani studies.

Felix B. Chang is Professor of Law at the University of Cincinnati College of Law.

Sunnie T. Rucker-Chang is Assistant Professor of Slavic and East European Studies and Director of European Studies at the University of Cincinnati.

Roma Rights and Civil Rights

A TRANSATLANTIC COMPARISON

FELIX B. CHANG
University of Cincinnati College of Law

SUNNIE T. RUCKER-CHANG
University of Cincinnati (European Studies)

CAMBRIDGE
UNIVERSITY PRESS

CAMBRIDGE
UNIVERSITY PRESS

University Printing House, Cambridge CB2 8BS, United Kingdom

One Liberty Plaza, 20th Floor, New York, NY 10006, USA

477 Williamstown Road, Port Melbourne, VIC 3207, Australia

314–321, 3rd Floor, Plot 3, Splendor Forum, Jasola District Centre, New Delhi – 110025, India

79 Anson Road, #06–04/06, Singapore 079906

Cambridge University Press is part of the University of Cambridge.

It furthers the University's mission by disseminating knowledge in the pursuit of education, learning, and research at the highest international levels of excellence.

www.cambridge.org
Information on this title: www.cambridge.org/9781107158368
DOI: 10.1017/9781316663813

First published 2020

A catalogue record for this publication is available from the British Library.

Library of Congress Cataloging-in-Publication Data
NAMES: Chang, Felix B., editor. | Rucker-Chang, Sunnie T., editor.
TITLE: Roma rights and civil rights : a transatlantic comparison / [edited by] Felix B. Chang, Sunnie T. Rucker-Chang.
DESCRIPTION: 1. | New York : Cambridge University Press, 2020. | Includes bibliographical references and index.
IDENTIFIERS: LCCN 2019046520 (print) | LCCN 2019046521 (ebook) | ISBN 9781107158368 (hardback) | ISBN 9781316663813 (ebook)
SUBJECTS: LCSH: Race discrimination – Law and legislation – United States. | Race discrimination – Law and legislation – Europe. | African Americans – Civil rights. | Romanies – Civil rights – Europe. | Minorities – Legal status, laws, etc. – United States. | Minorities – Legal status, laws, etc. – Europe.
CLASSIFICATION: LCC K3242 .R66 2020 (print) | LCC K3242 (ebook) | DDC 323.1196/073–dc23
LC record available at https://lccn.loc.gov/2019046520
LC ebook record available at https://lccn.loc.gov/2019046521

ISBN 978-1-107-15836-8 Hardback
ISBN 978-1-316-61090-9 Paperback

This book is dedicated to our children, from whom we borrowed much time in the course of this project.

Contents

Acknowledgments

This book benefitted greatly from the generosity and support of many colleagues, friends, and institutions. Without their insights and diverse perspectives, this project could never have moved from conception to print. Sunnie's interest in Romani studies began in a graduate course on nationalism in 2002 with Dr. Katherine David-Fox, who challenged her students to move beyond stereotypes in their engagement with Romani peoples. Felix's interest in comparative law was sparked by James Boyd White, a mentor to generations of students. Since that time, both of us have had the fortune of working with scholars and activists who deepened our comprehension of Roma rights.

We would like to thank the Gypsy Lore Society, whose members provided feedback on the earliest iterations of this project. We were fortunate to count Thomas Acton, Elena Marushiakova, and Carol Silverman among our first commentators and supporters. Conversations with the Roma Access Program, which has now been incorporated into the Romani studies program at Central European University (CEU), were germane to our understanding of the importance of education and civil society. Other members of civil society groups who graciously shared their time include Andrzej Mirga of the Roma Education Fund, Lilla Farkas of the European University Institute, Gábor Daróczi of Romaversitas, Judit Geller and Bernard Rorke of the European Roma Rights Centre, and Jim Goldston and Ostalinda Maya of the Open Society Justice Initiative. This book was made possible by the path-breaking work of Ian Hancock, and, on a personal level, we are grateful for his warmth and encouragement.

Through CEU's Critical Romani Studies conferences, we met a community of scholars engaged in not only the critical turn in Romani studies but also issues of race in Europe. Working alongside them has been one of the great joys of this project; it has challenged our assumptions and pushed us in new directions. Therefore, we thank the organizers of these conferences, especially Iulius Rostas and Márton Rövid, who also launched the journal *Critical Romani Studies* as a forum for like-minded scholars. We benefitted from conversations at other conferences, symposia, and professional meetings, including Duke Law School's conference "The Present and Future of Civil Rights Movements: Race and Reform in 21st Century America"; Ohio State University's Sawyer seminar "Imagining Alternative Modernities: Interventions from the Balkans and South Asia"; the "Antigypsism and Film" conference at the Zentral Rat Deutscher Sinti und Roma; the Younger Scholars Forum in Comparative Law at the Quadrennial Congress of the International Academy of Comparative Law in Fukuoka, Japan; the Gypsy Lore Society annual meetings in Stockholm and Nicosia; the American Society of Comparative Law Younger Comparativists Conference at Florida State; and various Midwest Slavic conferences. We are also grateful to the following participants of the "Transatlantic Approaches to Racial Equality" conference that we organized at the University of Cincinnati, who broadened our comparisons of minorities, race, and racialization: Amna Akbar, Cengiz Barskanmaz, Eddie Bruce-Jones, Gregor Fischer, Tiffany Florvil, Cheryl Harris, Emily Houh, Anikó Imre, Ron Jackson, Kristin Kalsem, Angéla Kóczé, Janet Moore, Mathias Möschel, Sami Mustafa, Lena Petrović, Debra Thompson, Evan Torner, Michele Vialet, and Valerie Weinstein.

Sunnie thanks Mária Bogdán and Anna Mirga-Kruszelnicka for conversations about minority representation in art. Her colleagues at the University of Cincinnati selflessly read the many versions of this book's content, including chapters, conference manuscripts, and journal articles. She is indebted in particular to her writing group – Ashley Currier, Gergana Ivanova, Michelle McGowan, Carollete Norwood, Michal Raucher, and Valerie Weinstein – for substantive suggestions as well as for camaraderie and intellectual inspiration. Also important were Jessie Labov and Yana Hashamova, whose input and encouragement have been priceless along this journey. Sunnie acknowledges Catherine Baker and Dušan Bjelić for including her work in their conversations on race and racialization in Southeast Europe.

Felix thanks Rebecca Zietlow and Chris Bryant for the insight that the U.S. legal system, too, underwent conditionality. He is also indebted to the comments, encouragement, and mentorship of Richard Albert, Deepa Badrinarayana, Julianna Beaudoin, Lou Bilionis, Shawn Marie Boyne, Lan Cao, Devon Carbado, Jacob Cogan, Blanche Cook, Oran Doyle, Frank Emmert, Cristina Fasone, Greg Gilchrist, Jill Goldenziel, Joan Heminway, Thaddeus Hoffmeister, Jamila Jefferson-Jones, Donald Kochan, Dimitry Kochenov, Bryan Lammon, David Landau, Betsy Lenhart, Matt Parlow, Cynthia Levine-Rasky, Sheldon Lyke, David Noll, Yaniv Roznai, Jeff Schmitt, Uli Sedelmeier, Sandra Sperino, Dalindyebo Shabalala, Julie Suk, Verna Williams, David Wolitz, and his other colleagues at the University of Cincinnati College of Law. The book benefitted from many workshops, including at Chapman, Dayton, Indiana University–McKinney, Northern Kentucky, Tennessee, and Toledo law schools, as well as the Midwest Law and Society Retreat at the University of Wisconsin–Madison. He thanks Braedon Tabor and Atif Khan for research assistance.

Financial support from the University of Cincinnati was indispensable. Specifically, the Charles Phelps Taft Center, University Research Council, faculty development funds, and summer research stipends provided much-needed resources for research and writing.

Finally, we are grateful to the anonymous reviewers at Cambridge University Press and above all to Matt Gallaway, our wonderful editor.

Portions of Chapter 6 originally appeared in a different form as Sunnie Rucker-Chang, "African-American and Romani Filmic Representation and the 'Posts' of Post-Civil Rights and Post-EU Expansion," 1 *Critical Romani Studies* 132 (2018). Portions of Chapter 2 originally appeared in a different form as Felix B. Chang, "Integration 'All the Way Down': Lessons from Federalism and Civil Rights," 1 *Critical Romani Studies* 62 (2018). Portions of Chapter 4 originally appeared in Felix B. Chang, "Conditionality and Constitutional Change," 1045 *Cornell Law Review Online* 1 (2019). The approach of Chapter 3 was used in Sunnie Rucker-Chang, "Challenging Americanism and Europeanism: African-Americans and Roma in the American South and European Union 'South,'" 16 *Journal of Transatlantic Studies* 181 (2018).

Abbreviations

acquis	*acquis communautaire*
CJEU	Court of Justice of the European Union
COE	Council of Europe
Commission	European Commission
Community	European Community
CRS	Critical Romani Studies
CSEE	Central and Southeast Europe
Decade	Decade of Roma Inclusion 2005–2015
DOJ	U.S. Department of Justice
EC	European Communities/European Community/Treaty Establishing the European Community
ECHR	European Convention for the Protection of Human Rights and Fundamental Freedoms (European Convention on Human Rights)
ECtHR	European Court of Human Rights
EEC	European Economic Community
EEOC	U.S. Employment Opportunity Commission
EU	European Union
EURATOM	European Atomic Energy Community
FCNM	Framework Convention on the Protection of National Minorities
FRA	EU Agency for Fundamental Rights
HEW	U.S. Department of Health, Education, and Welfare
HUD	U.S. Department of Housing and Urban Development
NAACP	National Association for the Advancement of Colored People
NGO	Nongovernmental organization
NORC	National Opinion Research Center
NRIS Framework	EU Framework for National Roma Integration Strategies up to 2020

OSCE	Organization for Security and Co-operation in Europe
PHARE	Poland and Hungary: Assistance for Restructuring their Economies
RED	EU Race Equality Directive of 2000
SCLC	Southern Christian Leadership Conference
SEA	Single European Act
SNCC	Student Nonviolent Coordinating Committee
TEU	Treaty on the European Union
TFEU	Treaty on the Functioning of the European Union
U.S.	United States

Introduction

This book compares the rights and social inclusion of two racialized minority groups: Roma in Central and Southeast Europe (CSEE), and African Americans in the United States (U.S.), primarily in the American South. We couch those attempts loosely in the frameworks of Roma rights and civil rights, though we will focus mainly on Roma rights in post-Communist CSEE (from 1991 until the present) and civil rights during the U.S. Civil Rights movement (roughly 1954–1968). Scholars have made fleeting comparisons between Roma and African Americans for years,[1] and in the last decade the Roma rights–Civil Rights comparison has recurred with increasing frequency.[2] Despite the burgeoning recognition of the broader similarities between Roma and African Americans, including the systems that facilitate their marginalization and the barriers to their representation, no book-length work has sustained these comparisons. *Roma Rights and Civil Rights: A Transatlantic Comparison* seeks to be the first work to do so, through the frames of law and culture.

Certain periods in history have seen more intense development of Roma rights and civil rights than others. We concentrate on two of those periods, the Civil Rights movement in the U.S. and the enlargement of the European Union (EU) into post-Communist CSEE. To provide fuller context, we will

[1] *See, e.g.*, IAN HANCOCK, THE PARIAH SYNDROME (1987); Ian Hancock, *Beyond Poverty, Beyond Europe*, 2 SAIS REV. 181 (2005) (reviewing DENA RINGOLD ET AL., WORLD BANK ROMA IN AN EXPANDING EUROPE: BREAKING THE POVERTY CYCLE (2005)); Belinda Cooper, *"We Have No Martin Luther King": Eastern Europe's Roma Minority*, 20 WORLD POL'Y J. 69, 73 (2001/2002); Mihaela Mudure, *From Gypsies to the African Americans*, 4 J. STUD. OF REL. & IDEOLOGIES 58 (2003).

[2] *See, e.g.*, Margareta Matache & Krista Oehlke, *Taking Stock of European Public Policy: The Impact of Roma Inclusion Strategies, in* REALIZING ROMA RIGHTS 97 (Jacqueline Bhabha et al. eds., 2017); Jack Greenberg, *Report on Roma Education Today: From Slavery to Segregation and Beyond*, 110 COLUM. L. REV. 919 (2010); Martha Minow, Brown v. Board *in the World: How the Global Turn Matters for School Reform, Human Rights, and Legal Knowledge*, 50 SAN DIEGO L. REV. 1 (2013). This comparison has been explored in detail by several conferences at Central European University in Budapest. *See e.g.*, *Inside the Struggle: The U.S. Civil Rights Movement & the European Roma Rights Crisis*, CENTRAL EUROPEAN UNIVERSITY (2015), https://www.ceu.edu/event/2015-12-07/inside-struggle-us-civil-rights-movement-european-Roma-rights-crisis [https://perma.cc/3Z84-3YLE].

also examine their precursors. For precision, we capitalize "Civil Rights" when referring to the movement and use "civil rights" when referring to general civil rights laws, whether connected to the Civil Rights movement or not. "Roma rights" is our umbrella term for the legal and policy protections for Roma, which are sometimes called "Roma integration" or "Roma inclusion." While this book uses those expressions as well, we prefer the term "rights" for several reasons. First, we acknowledge that full equality for these two marginalized groups remains inchoate, despite the burst of activity during Civil Rights and eastern enlargement. Second, we will frequently analyze *governmental* pursuits of equality and their limitations, whereas "rights" more aptly invokes *legal* mechanisms. This approach also highlights the age-old question of whether laws move cultural attitudes or vice versa – a question that we tackle directly in evaluating the successes and failings of Roma rights and civil rights. Finally, we are concerned with how central governments – the supranational institution of the EU and the federal government in the U.S. – both advance rights and foment popular resistance to minority inclusion. We find that the rights framework underscores the center–periphery relations and the federalism questions that are at the heart of Roma rights and civil rights.

In the geographic areas where African Americans and Roma have historically been most numerous – the American South and CSEE – great strides toward equality were made during eras that witnessed the downfall of seemingly unmovable ideologies (i.e., Jim Crow and Communism). During Civil Rights and eastern enlargement, the U.S. and the EU sought to construct a new social order – an endeavor that often presented the American South and European East in contradistinction to the egalitarian and democratic ideals that each polity espoused.[3] In this view, African Americans and Roma were internal Others who had endured subjugation and needed the forceful intervention of the central government to become equal. It was a depiction that the American South and Eastern Europe were familiar with. These two areas can be considered ideological and cultural "Souths," marred by legacies of war, division, and interethnic or interracial problems. The American South, according to the mythology of Civil Rights, was the epicenter of slavery, Black Codes, and Jim Crow, where Reconstruction had failed.[4] Under the European gaze, Eastern Europe has been viewed as liminal and barbaric for centuries.[5] Some CSEE countries have been treated as synonymous with "Balkan" and its historical

[3] *See* Gwendolyn Sasse, *The Politics of EU Conditionality: The Norm of Minority Protection During and Beyond EU Accession*, 15 J. Eur. Pub. Pol'y 842 (2008); Monica Sassatelli, Becoming Europeans: Cultural Identities and Cultural Policies 1 (2009).

[4] *See* Jeanne F. Theoharis, *Introduction*, *in* Freedom North: Black Freedom Struggles Outside the South, 1940–1980, 1 (Jeanne F. Theoharis & Komozi Woodard eds., 2003).

[5] *See* Larry Wolff, Inventing Eastern Europe: The Map of Civilization on the Mind of the Enlightenment 3–9 (1994); Dušan I. Bjelić, *Introduction: Blowing Up the "Bridge," in* Balkan as Metaphor 3–6 (Dušan I. Bjelić & Savić Obrad eds., 2005).

affiliate "Ottoman"; the violent breakup of Yugoslavia seemed to cement the region's essentialization. Cast as Others, the majority populations of the American South and CSEE would come to see minority rights as the incursions of hegemonic, and even hypocritical, outsiders.

And yet, during eastern enlargement and Civil Rights, minority protections became intertwined with the "national" identities that the U.S. and the EU were forging. Formally created with the Maastricht Treaty of 1992, the EU (previously the European Communities) went on to consolidate power and institute a single currency and Union membership. Throughout these transformations, minority protections became incorporated into the European project – that is, the legal and cultural creation of a supranational polity whose member states share certain institutions and "values." As the principal architect of both Roma inclusion and European integration, the EU required CSEE countries that sought to join the Union to devise policies on the social, political, economic, and cultural inclusion of Roma.[6] Initially, Roma inclusion was only a condition imposed upon aspiring members; however, as the EU revamped its constitutional order in the late 1990s and early 2000s, minority protections made their way into the laws and fundamental rights binding existing members.[7] Three tectonic trends therefore coalesced in Europe at this time. The first was the eastward enlargement of the EU into former Communist countries, which nearly doubled both the Union's territory and the number of member states. The second trend was the constitutionalization of the EU, which expanded the Union's competence to prohibit racial discrimination.[8] The third trend was the EU's push to raise living and educational standards and employment opportunities for approximately 10 million Roma, an effort that underwent different incarnations, from accession conditions for candidate countries to laws and policies applicable to all member states.

A similar dynamic unfolded during Civil Rights half a century earlier. Civil Rights saw a convergence of grassroots, legislative, executive, and litigation efforts

6 *See* Presidency Conclusions, Copenhagen European Council (June 21–22, 1993). This pre-accession process was known as "conditionality." *See infra* Chapters 2 & 4.

7 *See* Consolidated Version of the Treaty on European Union, art. 2, 2008 O.J. (C 115) 13 [hereinafter TEU]; Council Directive 2000/43, 2000 O.J. (L 180) 22 (EC).

8 The supranational nature of the EU certainly belies its characterization as a constitutional order, which is typically associated with nation-states, as does the failure of the EU member states to ratify a European Constitution. Nonetheless, in functionalist terms, the EU espouses a constitutionalism that is "shaped by institutional practice rather than some a priori blueprint." TURKULER ISIKSEL, EUROPE'S FUNCTIONAL CONSTITUTION: A THEORY OF CONSTITUTIONALISM BEYOND THE STATE 9 (2016). On the wealth of scholarship on EU constitutionalism, see, e.g., Eric Stein, *Lawyers, Judges, and the Making of a Transnational Constitution*, 75 AM. J. INT'L L. 1 (1981); Daniel Halberstam, *The Bride of Messina: Constitutionalism and Democracy in Europe*, 30 EUR. L. REV. 775 (2005).

to strengthen rights in voting,[9] education,[10] labor,[11] employment,[12] housing,[13] and criminal defense,[14] among other areas.[15] These gains were the result of a vigorous but protracted grassroots fight for equality, which eventually prompted federal civil rights laws that, when challenged as federal overreach, were upheld by federal courts.[16] A momentary confluence of interests brought an otherwise indifferent federal government to the side of African Americans. For the U.S., the motivating interest was the projection of equality as the nation fought the Cold War – a projection that upended the notion of white supremacy, which had so long dominated the construction of national identity.[17] Civil Rights, too, was the product of several seismic changes: the subversion of a centuries-old social order, which had privileged whiteness as a mode of social organization; the expansion of federal powers to make way for civil rights; and the waging of the Cold War, which rallied the nation around a common goal.

CONTEXTUALIZING THE COMPARISON

Contrary to many comparative works,[18] this book undertakes a diachronic comparison. Civil Rights and post-Communist Roma inclusion are half a century (and an ocean) apart. Yet each occurred at a moment that was pivotal to the constitutional development and identity construction of each nation – specifically, a moment where each nation saw fit to accommodate diverse populations. Civil Rights and Roma inclusion implicate center–periphery relations, top-down policy mandates,

9 *E.g.*, the Voting Rights Act of 1965, codified at 42 U.S.C. §§ 10301–10314 (2014); Reynolds v. Sims, 377 U.S. 533 (1964) (legislative districts must be equally apportioned by population).

10 *E.g.*, Brown v. Bd. of Educ. of Topeka, 347 U.S. 483 (1954) (*Brown I*); Sweatt v. Painter, 399 U.S. 629 (1950) (separate law school inadequate); McLaurin v. Oklahoma State Regents, 399 U.S. 637 (1950) (striking the separation of a black student admitted to a white graduate school); Title VI of the Civil Rights Act of 1964, codified at 42 U.S.C. § 2000d et seq. (prohibiting race, color, and national origin discrimination in programs receiving federal financial assistance).

11 *See* Kenneth Quinnell, *King and Meany Brought Civil Rights and Labor Together for a Legacy That Continues Today*, AFL-CIO (Jan. 12, 2018), https://aflcio.org/2018/1/12/king-and-meany-brought-civil-rights-and-labor-together-legacy-continues-today.

12 *E.g.*, Title VII of the Civil Rights Act of 1964, codified at 42 U.S.C. § 2000e et seq. (prohibiting employment discrimination on the basis of sex, race, color, national origin, or religion).

13 *E.g.*, Title VIII of the Civil Rights Act of 1968 (Fair Housing Act), codified at 42 U.S.C. § 3601 et seq.; Jones v. Alfred H. Mayer Co., 392 U.S. 409 (1968) (housing discrimination by private providers banned under existing law).

14 *E.g.*, Gideon v. Wainwright, 372 U.S. 335 (1963) (right to counsel for indigent defendants); Miranda v. Arizona, 384 U.S. 436 (1966) (right to be free from self-incrimination).

15 *E.g.*, Loving v. Virginia, 388 U.S. 1 (1967) (striking down state law prohibiting interracial marriage).

16 *See, e.g.*, Heart of Atlanta Motel Inc. v. United States, 379 U.S. 241 (1964).

17 *See* Derrick Bell, Brown v. Board of Education *and the Interest-Convergence Dilemma*, 93 HARV. L. REV. 518 (1980); MARY L. DUDZIAK, COLD WAR CIVIL RIGHTS (2000).

18 *E.g.*, GEORGE M. FREDRICKSON, WHITE SUPREMACY: A COMPARATIVE STUDY IN AMERICAN AND SOUTH AFRICAN HISTORY (1981).

and the pull, haul, and trade between central and constituent governments[19] – a process that goes by the shorthand of "federalism."[20] More broadly, resistance to civil rights and Roma rights was propelled by similar social, cultural, and political dynamics, such as racialization and white supremacy. Of course, the fact that Roma rights and civil rights have developed in starkly different epochs distinguishes each phenomenon as well. In the fifty years separating Civil Rights and eastern enlargement, colonization and apartheid fell, and an international consensus emerged against state-sanctioned racial exclusion of conationals. For instance, when sued in the European Court of Human Rights for anti-Roma discrimination, CSEE countries have had to resort to nonracial explanations for de facto segregation.[21] This veil of subtlety and respectability has been lifted since the financial crisis, with several CSEE governments adopting xenophobic platforms (a turn not unlike contemporaneous developments in the U.S.). Overall, however, so many structural similarities bind Roma rights and civil rights that their comparative study, even if diachronic, can be profoundly illuminating.

Of course, for the utility of the comparison to emerge, we must account for the distinct temporal, cultural, and institutional features of each comparator. In other words, we must show that comparing Roma inclusion and civil rights is not only novel – it is right.[22] Elsewhere, we have evaluated whether any differences between Roma rights and civil rights render their comparison too "thin" and "ahistorical."[23] We argue that one of the core similarities is that the EU and the U.S. are federalist systems encased in geographies large enough for center–periphery relations to translate meaningfully. As Roma rights and civil rights emerged, they were often enforced by the top rung of the federalist system (i.e., the supranational EU and the U.S. federal government) and against actors at the geographic and cultural peripheries (i.e., CSEE and the American South). Further, Roma and African Americans have experienced centuries of racialized subordination, a process informed by their

19 This metaphor is taken from the seminal voting rights case Johnson v. De Grandy, 512 U.S. 997, 1020 (1994).

20 In the EU, the federalism discourse often unfolds over the concepts of competence and subsidiarity. *See* Consolidated Version of the Treaty on the Functioning of the European Community arts. 2–4, 2012 O.J. (C 326) 47 [hereinafter TFEU]; TEU art. 5; Paul Craig & Gráinne de Búrca, EU Law: Text, Cases, and Materials 78–89, 94–100 (5th ed. 2011); Deborah Cass, *The Word That Saves Maastricht? The Principle of Subsidiarity and the Division of Powers Within the European Community*, 29 Common Market L. Rev. 1107 (1992).

21 *See, e.g.*, D.H. and Others v. Czech Republic, App. No. 57825/00, 47 Eur. H.R. Rep. 59, para. 26 (2007) ("The [Czech] Ministry of Education denied any discrimination and noted a tendency on the part of the parents of Roma children to have a rather negative attitude to school work. It asserted that each placement in a special school was preceded by an assessment of the child's intellectual capacity and that parental consent was a decisive factor.").

22 Rosalind Dixon, *Toward a Realistic Comparative Constitutional Studies?*, 64 Am. J. Comp. L. 193, 199 (2016).

23 Ran Hirschl, Comparative Matters: The Renaissance of Comparative Constitutional Law 152 (2014). *See also* Felix B. Chang, *Roma Integration "All the Way Down": Lessons from Federalism and Civil Rights*, 1 Critical Romani Stud. 62 (2018).

transnational origins – real or perceived – as slaves and migrants. This combination of traits, if thoroughly explored, underscores the utility and rigor of the Roma rights–civil rights comparison.

Racialized difference has long separated Roma and African Americans from majority populations. In part, racialization can be attributed to the distant ancestries of these two groups. African Americans, historically the largest minority in the U.S., descend from slaves taken primarily from West Africa. Similarly, it has been advanced that Roma, Europe's largest minority, are Indic people whose ancestors hailed from Northern India and started migrating westward in the eleventh century, settling by the 1300s in parts of the Byzantine Empire that would become modern-day CSEE.[24] While the India hypothesis remains controversial, it has fostered the perception that Roma lack roots in Europe, a perception that keeps Roma outside the cultural imaginary in CSEE, just as the roots of African Americans has inhibited their full embrace in the American imaginary.[25] The racialization of African Americans and Roma is also influenced by the construction of their visible and cultural difference. For both African Americans and Roma, difference has revolved around a global color line that delineates "white" from "black."[26] For Roma, another aspect of difference is the presumption of their innate nomadism, even though Roma have lived sedentary lives for centuries. A host of additional traits is ascribed to these two groups, including criminality, vagrancy, licentiousness, and idleness. All in all, despite how national identities have ebbed and flowed, and despite the regular misappropriation of their culture, African Americans and Roma cannot avoid being framed as Others.

Racialization therefore reduces these two groups to the "simplicity of essence"[27] while facilitating their subordination. The process of racial formation creates an expedient category that denies any possibility of variation. For example, although some in the field of Romani studies has embraced the notion of Rromanipen – a Romani way of life that connects the Romani peoples to Indian traditions, customs, and beliefs – the groups falling under the endonym of Roma are diverse, and not all of them accept the label. "Roma" is more a political construct than a cultural marker, an identity often wrapped up in a history of exclusion and marginalization.[28] Interestingly, while some activists have shied away from this label, others have recently

[24] *See* IAN HANCOCK, WE ARE THE ROMANI PEOPLE 2–16 (2002).

[25] *See* MIHAI SURDU, THOSE WHO COUNT: EXPERT PRACTICES OF ROMA CLASSIFICATION 77–92 (2016). For a fuller discussion, see *infra* Chapter 1.

[26] *See* W.E. BURGHARDT DU BOIS, THE SOULS OF BLACK FOLK: ESSAYS AND SKETCHES 96 (A.C. McClurg & Co., 8th ed. 1909); Anikó Imre, *Whiteness in Post-Socialist Eastern Europe: The Time of the Gypsies, the End of Race*, *in* POSTCOLONIAL WHITENESS: A CRITICAL READER ON RACE AND EMPIRE 79, 82 (Alfred J. Lopez ed., 2005); MARILYN LAKE & HENRY REYNOLDS, DRAWING THE GLOBAL COLOUR LINE: WHITE MEN'S COUNTRIES AND THE INTERNATIONAL CHALLENGE OF RACIAL EQUALITY (2008).

[27] ROLAND BARTHES, MYTHOLOGIES 129 (1975).

[28] *Compare* Thomas Acton & Ilona Klímová, *The International Romani Union: An East European Answer to West European Questions?*, *in* BETWEEN PAST AND FUTURE: THE ROMA OF CENTRAL AND EASTERN EUROPE 157 (Will Guy ed., 2001), *with* Nicolae Gheorghe & Thomas Acton, *Citizens of the*

pushed to reclaim it,[29] a trend that echoes the shift from "colored" to "Negro" to "black" to "African American," generations earlier in the U.S.[30] In contesting the labels imposed from outside, Roma and African Americans have tried to purge their identities of stereotypes, assumptions, and their pernicious effects. These effects have spanned centuries. Across Europe, Roma have endured both state-sanctioned and vigilante persecution, based on stereotypes of vagrancy, criminality, and foreignness. From roughly the fourteenth to the nineteenth centuries, Roma were enslaved in parts of modern-day Romania.[31] During World War II, they were systematically targeted for extermination in the Holocaust.[32] When CSEE fell under Communism and Socialism, Roma were forcibly settled and, in some instances, forcibly sterilized; in the post-Communist transition, they have suffered extreme social and economic dislocation. All of these episodes transpired on account of the stereotypes associated with their racialized difference.

For many Roma in contemporary CSEE, the reality of marginalization and exclusion persists, despite the flurry of inclusion initiatives. By virtually any metric, Roma remain separated by chasms from their non-Roma compatriots in educational attainment, living standards, health, and employment.[33] While these disparities correlate with the disproportionate effect that the fall of Communism and Socialism wrought upon Romani communities,[34] a myriad of institutions operating at multiple levels (e.g., EU, national, and civil society) have pursued legal and policy reforms that attempt to remove the structural barriers to equality for Roma.[35] These reforms include EU initiatives undertaken in preparation for eastern enlargement and even after accession candidates became member states. Nonetheless, the conundrum remains that daily life for many Roma lags far behind the aspirations of

World and Nowhere: Minority, Ethnic and Human Rights for Roma, *in* BETWEEN PAST AND FUTURE: THE ROMA OF CENTRAL AND EASTERN EUROPE 54 (Will Guy ed., 2001).

29 *See, e.g.*, Anna Mirga-Kruszelnicka, *Romani Studies and Emerging Romani Scholarship*, *in* NOTHING ABOUT US WITHOUT US? ROMA PARTICIPATION IN POLICY MAKING AND KNOWLEDGE PRODUCTION 39 (Kieran O'Reilly & Marek Szilvasi eds., 2015); Ioanida Costache, *Reclaiming Romani-ness: Identity Politics, Universality and Otherness or, Towards a (New) Romani Subjectivity*, 1 CRITICAL ROMANI STUD. 30 (2018).

30 *See* Tom W. Smith, *Changing Racial Labels: From "Colored" to "Negro" to "Black" to "African American,"* 56 PUB. OPINION Q. 496 (1992).

31 VIOREL ACHIM, THE ROMA IN ROMANIAN HISTORY 27, 42–43 (Richard Davies trans., 2004) (1998), *originally published as* ŢIGANII ÎN ISTORIA ROMÂNIERI.

32 HANCOCK, *supra* note 24, at 35–48. *See also* Ágnes Daróczi & János Bársony, *Preface to the English Edition*, *in* PHARRAIJMOS: THE FATE OF THE ROMA DURING THE HOLOCAUST ix, x (János Bársony & Ágnes Daróczi eds., 2008).

33 *See* EUROPEAN COMM'N, THE SITUATION OF ROMA IN AN ENLARGED EUROPEAN UNION (2004).

34 Kálmán Mizsei, *Reconstructing Roma Integration in Central and Eastern Europe: Addressing the Failures of the Last Quarter Century*, *in* REALIZING ROMA RIGHTS 127, 127 (Jacqueline Bhabha et al. eds., 2017).

35 *See, e.g.*, Council Recommendation of 9 December 2013 on Effective Roma Integration Measures in the Member States, 2013 O.J. (C 378) 1; *An EU Framework for National Roma Integration Strategies up to 2020*, COM (2011) 173 final (Apr. 5, 2011); *Frequently Asked Questions*, DECADE OF ROMA INCLUSION 2005–2015, *archived at* http://perma.cc/RJR5-JHRP.

sweeping legal change, so that the last quarter century constitutes the unfulfilled promise of Roma inclusion.

To explicate the incongruity between daily life and legal change, this book looks across the Atlantic, to civil rights. Until recently, much of the scholarship on Roma rights has been descriptive and undertheorized.[36] Civil rights scholarship, by contrast, is extremely robust and has had decades to amass. The fact that civil rights have had to withstand time and backlash has bolstered this scholarship, by forcing it to account for fluctuations in societal attitudes and political commitment. This legacy is all the more salient for Roma rights today; in moving from one crisis to another, Europe has had to confront a xenophobic and populist recalcitrance powerful enough to gut the transformative expansions in minority protections – a trend that U.S. civil rights scholars know all too well.[37]

Similarly, because both Roma and African Americans are burdened by their racialized distance from the dominant constructs of the nation, their experiences, histories, and cultures are excluded from mainstream narratives. Within cultural products, political discourse, and national narratives, the imagination and representation of these two groups is negative and unidimensional. Consequently, our book counterbalances its analyses of laws and legal processes with analyses of cultural formations that challenge the long-held dislocated positions of Roma and African Americas. The complementary perspectives of law and culture provide a more holistic assessment of Roma rights and civil rights.

Our comparisons with civil rights should not be taken as reflexive endorsement of the U.S. model. During Civil Rights, the uneven actions of the federal government not only frustrated African American leaders but also fed into charges of hypocrisy that often solidified resistance to integration.[38] As American scholars, we are also cognizant that our own contemporary setting belies the efficacy and legacy of Civil Rights, from mass incarceration to violence directed at black bodies. Indeed, the post-2016 political climate in the U.S., where xenophobic and jingoist rhetoric has been deployed to rally certain voters, parallels the nationalist zeal in a number of European countries.

Viewing Roma rights solely through the lens of African American experiences during Civil Rights has other shortcomings. Most obviously, the U.S. and EU are vastly different entities, constrained by different sets of competences, comprised of different types of members, and presided over by central governments with different

36 For exceptions, see, e.g., PETER VERMEERSCH, THE ROMANI MOVEMENT: MINORITY POLITICS & ETHNIC MOBILIZATION IN CONTEMPORARY CENTRAL EUROPE (2006); CAROL SILVERMAN, ROMANI ROUTES: CULTURAL POLITICS AND BALKAN MUSIC IN DIASPORA (2012). *Critical Romani Studies*, the newly launched journal of Central European University, is also a notable exception. *See About the Journal*, CRITICAL ROMANI STUDIES, https://crs.ceu.edu/index.php/crs/about (last accessed June 19, 2019).

37 *See, e.g.*, Kimberlé Williams Crenshaw, *Race, Reform, and Retrenchment: Transformation and Legitimation in Antidiscrimination Law*, 101 HARV. L. REV. 1331, 1352–56 (1988).

38 *See* Justin Driver, *Supremacies and the Southern Manifesto*, 92 TEX. L. REV. 1053 (2014).

arsenals of tools to enforce their authority. Since post-Civil War Reconstruction, the U.S. has sought to federalize the protection of racial minorities so as to preempt state and local practices.[39] This is notwithstanding the endorsement of federalism in the Tenth Amendment of the U.S. Constitution, which reserves certain enumerated powers for the federal government, leaving the rest to the states.[40] By contrast, the EU, which hovers between an intergovernmental and supranational organization, is an amalgamation of different sovereign countries, each with its own distinct language, culture, and tradition.[41] At the most basic level, the constituency that the EU manages is more unwieldy and the reserved powers at its disposal more limited.[42]

At the grassroots level, civil society has also played a key role in advancing Roma rights and civil rights. Most prominently, civil society can hold governments accountable by filing cases challenging school segregation, police misconduct, and forced evictions.[43] For Roma in particular, nongovernmental organizations (NGOs) founded and staffed by Roma offer an opportunity for self-representation and empowerment where little exists.[44] Romani leaders have emerged to advocate not only for Roma rights but also for a unifying political consciousness based on an imagined political community of Roma. As with any minority rights movement, minority leadership confers legitimacy and ensures fair representation; yet Romani visibility is particularly important because the Roma rights movement has often lacked Romani decision-makers at the top, so that the agenda for change is externally driven. This stands in stark contrast to Civil Rights, where the primary drivers in civil society were African Americans themselves, heading up organizations such as the National Association for the Advancement of Colored People (NAACP).

The contributions of Romani scholars and non-Roma allies, many of whom consider themselves to be "scholar activists," pushing back against entrenched viewpoints of Roma that merely perpetuate Romani exoticization, have bolstered civil society. On this front, one of the most interesting developments has been the critical turn in the centuries-old field of Romani studies, by way of a movement calling itself Critical Romani Studies (CRS). CRS has been ushered along by the

39 For details, see *infra* Chapters 4 & 5.

40 *See* U.S. Const. amend. X. *See also* Shelby County v. Holder, 570 U.S. 529, 543 (2013).

41 *See* Tanja A. Börzel & Thomas Risse, *Who Is Afraid of a European Federation? How to Constitutionalize a Multi-Level Governance System*, *in* WHAT KIND OF CONSTITUTION FOR WHAT KIND OF POLITY? RESPONSES TO JOSCHKA FISCHER 45, 59 (Christian Joerges et al. eds., 2000).

42 As will be explored in Chapter 2, the balance between intergovernmental and supranational has tipped in recent years to the latter. *See* Alec Stone Sweet & Wayne Sandholtz, *Integration, Supranational Governance, and Institutionalization of the European Polity*, *in* EUROPEAN INTEGRATION AND SUPRANATIONAL GOVERNANCE 1 (Alec Stone Sweet & Wayne Sandholtz eds., 1998); J.H.H. Weiler, *The Transformation of Europe*, 100 YALE L.J. 2403 (1991).

43 *See* MATHIAS MÖSCHEL, LAW, LAWYERS AND RACE: CRITICAL RACE THEORY FROM THE UNITED STATES TO EUROPE (2014); EUROPEAN ROMA RIGHTS CENTRE, STRATEGIC LITIGATION OF RACE DISCRIMINATION IN EUROPE: FROM PRINCIPLES TO PRACTICE (2004).

44 *See* AIDAN MCGARRY, WHO SPEAKS FOR ROMA? POLITICAL REPRESENTATION OF A TRANSNATIONAL MINORITY COMMUNITY (2010).

conferences and publications of Central European University in Budapest. In challenging the ethnographic approach that dominates Romani studies, CRS scholars have directly engaged with race, which had been a taboo subject in Europe for decades.[45] Along the way, they have managed to tie the critical turn in Romani studies to an earlier generation of U.S. scholarship on civil rights and positionality (in particular, intersectionality and critical race theory), as well as other critical frameworks (e.g., postcolonial theory).[46] Here, too, are echoes of prior trends in the U.S. The explosion of scholarly output, often by Romani intellectuals, and the institutionalization of the critical turn, such as through Romani studies departments and academic journals, mirrors the creation of black studies departments in the U.S. in the 1960s and 1970s, when "Negros" became "African Americans" and demanded that their history and culture be integrated into educational curricula.

GOALS AND METHODOLOGIES

This book seeks to enrich the understanding of Roma rights – of its failures and potential for success – by engaging with the scholarship on how similar developments unfolded in the U.S. We chose civil rights for the rich body of secondary literature that scholars have compiled to critically and holistically assess its evolution. In pursuing these goals, we have chosen to undertake the comparison by integrating three perspectives: interest convergence, federalism, and constructs of American and European culture. Because civil rights scholarship is so broad, our methodology itself had to undergo a selection process to whittle down the approaches to those most appropriate for the comparison. We did so by asking three overarching questions:

First, what motivated the relevant actors to push for civil rights and Roma rights, and how are these rights supported? We focus frequently on governmental actors – specifically, the U.S. and EU – and deploy the interest convergence theory to explain why these actors backed minority rights when they did. As one of the most iconic by-products of critical race theory, interest convergence has morphed from a provocative axiom to a well-documented fact. In 1980, Derrick Bell posited that it

45 *See* Maria Bogdan et al., *Introducing the New Journal Critical Romani Studies*, 1 CRIT. ROMANI STUD. 2 (2018); Mathias Möschel, *Color Blindness or Total Blindness? The Absence of Critical Race Theory in Europe*, 9 RUTGERS RACE & L. REV. 57, 73–74 (2007).

46 *See, e.g.*, Angéla Kóczé & Márton Rövid, *Pro-Roma Global Civil Society: Acting for, with or Instead of Roma?*, *in* GLOBAL CIVIL SOCIETY 2012: TEN YEARS OF CRITICAL REFLECTION 110, 120 n.1 (Mary Kaldor & Henrietta L. Moore eds., 2012) (citing Spiak's concept of "epistemic violence"); Angéla Kóczé, *The Limits of Rights-Based Discourse in Romani Women's Activism: The Gender Dimension in Romani Politics*, *in* ROMANI POLITICS IN CONTEMPORARY EUROPE: POVERTY, ETHNIC MOBILIZATION, AND THE NEOLIBERAL ORDER 135, 144 (Nando Sigona & Nidhi Trehan eds., 2009) (citing Kimberlé Williams Crenshaw on intersectionality); Mirga-Kruszelnicka, *supra* note 29, at 42 (citing Patricia Hill Collins's concept of "the outsider within"); Bogdan et al., *supra* note 45, at 6 (welcoming cross-fertilization between Romani studies and critical race studies).

was a convergence of interests among whites and blacks that facilitated *Brown* and school desegregation; for whites, especially political elites in the federal government, the interests were a quest for legitimacy in foreign policy and suppression of black radicalism at home. Since that time, Bell's theory has been vindicated by the work of historians such as Mary Dudziak and Thomas Borstelmann, who documented the connections between domestic Civil Rights policies and Cold War foreign policy.[47]

Interest convergence is simple and accessible, but it is also a clear-eyed approach that eviscerates the dearly held imaginary of civil rights. It specifically challenges schoolbook accounts of civil rights by contending that the majority conveys rights to minorities only when doing so furthers the majority's interests.[48] Applied to the European context, interest convergence upends the conventional version of Roma inclusion, a version which portrays the effort as part of the expansion of EU minority protections. Instead, what emerges from an analysis of the historical setting is that Roma integration grew out of a Western European desire to curtail refugee influxes and contain interethnic conflict within CSEE. Roma had long faced scapegoating and persecution in CSEE, but anti-Roma violence intensified during the transition to the market economy, becoming so unbearable that many Roma began fleeing westward, with some going as far as Canada in the 1990s.[49] Receiving countries in Western Europe and North America responded by tightening immigration and refugee policies, and the CSEE candidates were enlisted to stem the tide by integrating their Roma populations.[50]

To be sure, others have written on the use of CSEE as a buffer for Roma immigration into the EU.[51] What interest convergence adds, however, is a unifying approach that can guide the vindication of this hypothesis.

Second, how did the relevant institutions, processes, and legal systems accommodate or co-opt the fight for minority rights in these two settings? Much of our analysis revolves around the competences and enforcement powers of the U.S. and EU as drivers of minority rights – in essence, issues germane to federalism. In the U.S., the federal government's attempts to redress segregation and discrimination can be situated in a long-standing tug-of-war between

47 Thomas Borstelmann, The Cold War and the Color Line: American Race Relations in the Global Arena (2001); Dudziak, *supra* note 17.

48 *See* Dudziak, *Desegregation as a Cold War Imperative*, 41 Stan. L. Rev. 61, 64 (1988) ("[A]n effort to examine desegregation within the context of Cold War American culture may be more than an interesting addition to a basically well told tale. It may ultimately cause us to recast our interpretations of the factors motivating the critical legal and cultural transformation that *Brown* has come to represent.").

49 *See* Vermeersch, *supra* note 36, at 138–40; Sean Rehaag et al., *No Refuge: Hungarian Romani Refugee Claimants in Canada*, 52 Osgoode Hall L.J. 705 (2015).

50 *See* Antje Wiener & Guido Schwellnus, *Contested Norms in the Process of EU Enlargement: Non-discrimination and Minority Rights*, *in* Law and Governance in an Enlarged European Union 451, 477 (George A. Bermann & Katharina Pistor eds., 2004); Cooper, *supra* note 1, at 73.

51 *See supra* note 50.

federalism and minority rights.[52] Under the vision of federalism that tips the balance of power in favor of states, racial minorities have fared badly; thus, since Reconstruction, actions to protect racial minorities have mostly sprung from the federal government, as opposed to state governments. During Civil Rights, admittedly, federal institutions moved slowly, tempering African American expectations until massive resistance to desegregation provoked legislation. Overall, though, what transpired during Civil Rights was a federal government coming into its own, so to speak, a government becoming comfortable with its power to pass and enforce antidiscrimination laws as it recrafted American "values."[53]

When comparisons are drawn with Roma rights, several threads emerge. First, during eastern enlargement, the EU had the capacity to demand Roma inclusion in the CSEE candidate countries, but not in the existing members. This power emanated from the EU's authority in external relations and was not subject to the parameters of competence in internal affairs.[54] In other words, so long as CSEE countries were candidates for Union accession and not yet Union members, the EU could avoid the thorny federalism questions that hound regulation by central governments. Second, within each federalist union, minority protections during Civil Rights and eastern enlargement began as antidiscrimination law, which worked reasonably well against overt discrimination but proved unable to dismantle the structural barriers to equality. Because African Americans and Roma encounter these barriers at nearly every turn, equality would not be accomplished simply through the "negative" right of antidiscrimination; "positive" rights and a multifaceted system of enforcement would have to step in. Such a system has begun to emerge with newer Roma rights initiatives, such as the EU's Framework for National Roma Integration Strategies up to 2020 (the "NRIS Framework"), which comprise a second generation of solutions to racialized subordination. However, the form of governance pursued by the EU, as well as the relatively feeble remedies wielded by the EU, have ended up weakening the implementation of these second-generation solutions.

Third, how receptive has mainstream society been toward minority inclusion? In the face of enforcement deficits by governmental actors, for instance, was there sufficient momentum from popular demands for inclusion to push through laws, policies, and reforms? Here, Americanism and its analog Europeanism serve as useful counterpoints to provide greater context to the legal transformations. Competing strands of Americanism and Europeanism have shaped majority discourse on African Americans and Roma. One strand embraces liberty, inclusion,

52 *See* Heather K. Gerken, A *New Progressive Federalism*, DEMOCRACY J. 37 (2012).

53 *See, e.g.*, Heart of Atlanta Motel Inc. v. United States, 379 U.S. 241 (1964) (upholding Congress's power under the Commerce Clause to prohibit discrimination in public accommodations).

54 *See* DIMITRY KOCHENOV, EU ENLARGEMENT AND THE FAILURE OF CONDITIONALITY: PRE-ACCESSION CONDITIONALITY IN THE FIELDS OF DEMOCRACY AND THE RULE OF LAW 82 (2007).

and diversity, while the other strand retreats to exclusion, xenophobia, and nativism. Which strand dominates depends upon the prevailing cultural, social, political, and economic situation of the time. Entirely different factors might influence the attitudes of political leaders as opposed to majority populations. Accounting for such attitudes can help gauge the efficacy of minority rights. For example, scholars place great emphasis on school integration as a catalyst for social acceptance of racial equality, arguing that diverse classrooms can foster interracial interactions for children to help dispel stereotypes before they ossify.[55] In the CSEE countries that have desegregated their schools, we see that attitudes toward Roma have *not* changed, however.[56] This may be because in every other segment – for instance, housing and employment – discrimination and de facto segregation persist.

We utilize two means to gauge mainstream social perceptions: films and public opinion polls. Our choice of film might seem unexpected, in that their revelations are refracted by the director, audience, and contemporary setting. For scholars of culture, however, film is an illuminating medium. Film reflects "our deepest fantasies about the nature of social life, both as we live it now, and as we feel in our bones it ought rather to be lived."[57] It has therefore become axiomatic that film reveals a society's most basic values, impulses, fears, and aspirations.[58] We integrate these ideas into our comparisons to illustrate how cinematic representations of Roma and African Americans track their shifting social acceptance. To corroborate the findings from film analysis, we piece together European public opinion polls (Eurobarometer and social Eurobarometers) to map the evolution of the larger society's perceptions of Roma. Eurobarometer surveys are public opinion polls regularly conducted by the European Commission across EU member states.[59] These surveys suggest that in CSEE intransigence toward Roma and their meaningful inclusion into society is widespread and deeply held.[60]

For all their cultural and temporal differences, our two comparators resemble one another in the way racial differences are formed and then harden. To use Charles Mills's terminology, a "racial contract" maintains social hierarchies by "racing"

55 *See, e.g.*, National Academy of Education, Race-Conscious Policies for Assigning Students to Schools: Social Science Research and the Supreme Court Cases (Robert L. Linn & Kevin G. Welner eds., 2007).

56 *See* European Comm'n, Special Eurobarometer 393: Discrimination in the EU in 2012, 113 (2012), http://ec.europa.eu/commfrontoffice/publicopinion/archives/ebs/ebs_393_en.pdf (over half of respondents in Slovakia and the Czech Republic believe their citizens would feel uncomfortable if their children had Romani schoolmates). In fact, most respondents in Hungary, Slovakia, and the Czech Republic rate their country's efforts at Roma integration as ineffective. *Id.* at 108. Incidentally, these three countries were the subject of infringement proceedings brought by the European Commission for violating EU law by segregating Romani schoolchildren.

57 Fredric Jameson, *Reification and Utopia in Mass Culture*, 1 Social Text 130, 147 (1979).

58 Stuart Hall, *Encoding/Decoding*, *in* Media and Cultural Studies: Key Works 163, 169 (Meenakshi Gigi Durham & Douglas M. Kellener eds., 2006) (1980).

59 *See* European Comm'n, 35 Years of Eurobarometer: European Integration as Seen by the Public Opinion in the Member States of the European Union 1973–2008 (2008).

60 For analysis, see *infra* Chapter 3.

difference.[61] Race has permeated the world but derives from European roots; it reigns over the U.S. as much as in Europe. Racial hierarchies are also enshrined in the notion of whiteness – and a Europe and European heritage rooted in whiteness – as a marker of privilege for those at the top of the social order.

The first two questions above are guided by approaches from law and legal studies – specifically, interest convergence and federalism. The third question is guided by approaches from cultural studies – specifically, nationalism and subsets such as Americanism and Europeanism. We view this combination of methodologies as complementary because neither law nor cultural studies alone can fully explicate civil rights or Roma rights. For instance, interest convergence goes only so far in explaining *Brown*; historically, international disapproval has not been sufficient in itself to change American practices.[62] Further, the cold, hard assumptions about human behavior that underpin interest convergence begin to unravel when individuals act against their rational self-interests (e.g., whites who were willing to sacrifice their social status because segregation was morally repugnant). Similarly, examining the efficacy or legitimacy of desegregation laws solely from the perspective of federalism tells us nothing about whether the majority supported the laws. Finally, restricting the study of minority rights solely to their reception by the broader society overlooks how majority opinion might change – or be swept aside by legal transformations.

SCOPE

As with any study of a group as diverse as the Roma in a setting as complex as CSEE, several caveats must be laid bare before the remainder of the book proceeds. First, we use the term "Roma" as a convenient catchall without intending to imply uniformity across this broad group. The diversity of European Roma is well known. In some countries, members of this minority group self-identify by other names (e.g., "Travellers and Gypsies" in the UK, "Sinti" in Germany, and "Egyptians," "Ashkali," and "Kalle" elsewhere). In other countries, the ostensible Roma often do not even refer to themselves as "Roma." We realize as well that "African Americans" may encompass immigrants racialized as black but not necessarily descended from slaves. Yet for the purposes of this work, a transatlantic comparison that begins with slavery in the U.S. and extends to Reconstruction and Civil Rights, we are concerned precisely with those descendants of slaves racialized as black.

We also focus on Roma rights within CSEE. The alternative referent, Eastern Europe, is convenient yet imprecise, for it represents a large group of countries whose links have less to do with geography than with a shared legacy of Socialism and Communism. Especially as the shadow of Communism recedes, those countries might more precisely be referred to in smaller blocs, as "Central Europe" and

[61] Charles W. Mills, The Racial Contract 41 (1997).

[62] Justin Driver, *Rethinking the Interest-Convergence Thesis*, 105 Nw. U. L. Rev. 149, 170 (2011).

"Southeast Europe." Some are EU members while others are not, and even within each bloc the countries might be separated by very different histories and political realities. Therefore, this book looks primarily at Central (i.e., Czech Republic, Hungary, and Slovakia) and Southeast (i.e., Bosnia, Bulgaria, Croatia, Kosovo, Macedonia, Montenegro, Romania, and Serbia) Europe.[63] Our focus on CSEE is not intended to sidestep Western Europe's exclusion of its own Roma populations. Recent deportations by France and demolition of housing blocks in Italy populated primarily by Roma do not just show that the marginalization of Roma is pan-European; such actions also taint the EU's inclusion initiatives with the specter of hypocrisy.[64] But because we are interested in center–periphery relations, we will tend to evaluate Roma rights in CSEE and civil rights in the American South.

We should also spell out what we mean by "Europe" and the associated concepts of "Europeanization," "European integration," and "European Union." Europe is, of course, the continent bounded by the Arctic Ocean to the north, the Mediterranean to the south, and the Atlantic to the west; it stretches as far eastward as Ukraine and, depending on perspectives, might also encompass Turkey and Russia. In determining the metes and bounds, we quickly discern that "Europe" is a geographic construct, since no natural border separates Europe from the rest of Eurasia. This geographic construct springs from a geographical and cultural imaginary of Europe, as a territory whose peoples share similar values and characteristics.[65] The notion of Europeanization is particularly relevant to that construction of European identity. In this book, we adopt the definition of Europeanization as the construction of a civic and cultural Europe based on European norms such as equality for minority groups, the unity of member states, and liberal democratic principles.[66] Europeanization is not to be confused with EU integration, which we associate with the more institutionally driven and process-oriented political, legal, and economic normalization of EU member states and candidates for membership. Finally, in speaking of the "EU," we intend to include its antecedents such as the European Communities. In subsequent Chapters, where context requires, we will distinguish between those entities.

63 We realize that our use of "CSEE" contrasts with "CEEC," which is prevalent in political science and other disciplines. However, from the perspective of Slavic studies, Central and Southeast Europe is more culturally and geographically fitting. Further, we do not focus on East European countries such as Poland, where Romani populations are not as large and Roma integration was not emphasized as much during pre-accession.

64 *See* Editorial, *Fundamental Rights and EU Membership: Do as I Say, Not as I Do!*, 499 COMMON MKT. L. REV. 481, 487 (2012).

65 GERARD DELANTY, INVENTING EUROPE (1995).

66 *See* SASSATELLI, *supra* note 3, at 1. *Cf.* Frank Schimmelfennig & Ulrich Sedelmeier, *Introduction: Conceptualizing the Europeanization of Central and Eastern Europe*, *in* THE EUROPEANIZATION OF CENTRAL AND EASTERN EUROPE 1, 7 (Frank Schimmelfennig & Ulrich Sedelmeier eds., 2005) ("We define 'Europeanization' as a process in which states adopt EU rules."). In a broader sense, though, Schimmelfennig and Sedelmeier, too, seem to refer to norms rather than rules when they speak of Europeanization.

Within the parameters of these caveats, the remainder of the book proceeds as follows:

Chapters 1 and 2 delve into the historical parallels between civil rights and Roma rights, as well as between African Americans and Roma and also between the U.S. and the EU. The objectives are to emphasize affinities in the plights of African Americans and Roma, especially (i) the patterns of exclusion and neglect that characterize the majority of the histories of the two groups and, nonetheless, (ii) the historical transformations in the U.S. and the EU that enabled gains in rights for these two groups. World War II serves as the point of demarcation between these two Chapters. Across Europe, as many as 1.5 million Roma died during the Holocaust, a period known in Romani as *Porrajmos* (the Devouring). During World War II, African Americans also fought valiantly as soldiers abroad and worked in the war industry at home; this service would prime the country for the Civil Rights movement. Chapter 1 therefore treats the historical comparisons up to World War II, while Chapter 2 considers the aftermath, including Communism and Socialism in CSEE, the decades of EU integration, and the post-Communist eastern enlargement, as well as Civil Rights itself.

In Chapter 3, we explore the dominant constructions of "European" and "American" to underscore the long-standing positioning of African Americans and Roma as outsiders. Given their systemic marginalization, we highlight how similar practices of exclusion and entrenched imaginings of difference have produced similar results for the two groups – especially in the American South and CSEE, where African Americans and Roma are most numerous. In these spaces where interactions between minorities and majorities are pervasive, the persistence of interracial antagonisms can be attributed to cultural and economic rivalries. Beyond tracking the means of exclusion, we also mine information from public opinion polls to uncover how such exclusion manifests in society, particularly as African Americans and Roma make social, economic, and legal advancements.

Chapter 4 compares how conditionality advanced minority rights within the constitutional frameworks of the EU and the U.S. More specifically, this Chapter argues that the EU's eastern enlargement illuminates a little-known dynamic of post-Civil War Reconstruction in the U.S.: the influence of the Reconstruction Act of 1867 upon the Fifteenth Amendment. The Reconstruction Act imposed conditions upon the readmission of former Confederate states that were out of step with laws governing the states already within the Union. Southern states had to uphold the suffrage rights of freedmen, even though Northern states denied African Americans the vote at almost every opportunity – a disparity that spurred the passage of the Fifteenth Amendment prohibiting the denial of voting rights on account of race. Chapter 4 frames this disparity as a feature of conditionality, the process of negotiation over conditions for membership. Although conditionality is more closely associated with the eastern enlargement of the EU, another federalist system that demanded more of candidates than of existing members in the area of Roma integration, it is a novel perspective from which to assess racial equality during Reconstruction, the era that laid the groundwork for Civil Rights.

Chapter 5 continues the civil rights–Roma rights comparison after CSEE acceded to the EU and the American South was readmitted into the U.S., concentrating in particular on Civil Rights and post-accession. During these two periods, minority rights were enshrined more prominently in the constitutional order as the top rung of both federalist systems consolidated power. In the U.S., an expansive reading of the Fourteenth Amendment anchored desegregation cases in federal courts, and an expansive reading of federal powers under the Commerce Clause allowed Congress to passed sweeping legislation that outlawed discrimination. The development of antidiscrimination law followed a pattern that had been laid out during Reconstruction, under which the federal government conferred enforcement authority upon itself by defining certain rights as federally guaranteed. The EU would chart a similar path in prohibiting racial and ethnic discrimination by giving itself the competence to combat discrimination under the Amsterdam Treaty of 1997 and then passing the broad Race Equality Directive of 2000 to exercise that competence. Antidiscrimination laws in the U.S. and the EU constitute a first generation of minority rights, but they were beset by several vulnerabilities, such as structural barriers as well as fluctuations in federalism jurisprudence. However, the EU has recently experimented with a multifaceted approach to overcome the structural barriers to Roma inclusion; emblematic of this approach is the NRIS Framework, which follows the open-ended solutions of new governance. In implementation, though, the NRIS Framework has proven to be hollow because of deficits in enforcement, political will, and benchmarks for success.

Finally, Chapter 6 turns to film to track the social perceptions of Roma in CSEE since 2004. The depiction of Roma in film has a long and rich history throughout CSEE countries, and here we analyze these filmic productions as a means of offering the outsider a view into Roma society. We examine films that resort to stereotypes as well as films that feature more nuanced images, to arrive at a composite that moves beyond flat characterizations of Roma as criminal, performer, or leech. Similarly, this Chapter sifts through both outsider and insider portrayals to extrapolate the differences – or, as some argue, lack thereof. As a means of comparison, Chapter 6 also analyzes the representation of African Americans in American films, particularly the blaxploitation films of the 1970s that emerged in the immediate aftermath of the post-Civil Rights period. Those films provided a filmic critique of the civil rights period but, in their overwhelming defining feature of blackness, normalized African Americans on screen. This Chapter argues that the blaxploitation films of the 1970s provided a context for the cultural integration of African Americans in the U.S. as a movement from otherization to mainstream, ending with ostensible acceptance of black culture as simply American culture. We offer this example to question whether it is possible that new developments in the representation of Roma could create conditions for a shift in majority perceptions of Roma in a way similar to what happened following blaxploitation.

We end with a Conclusion that summarizes the major themes of the book, highlighting where comparisons between Roma and African Americans resonate most powerfully and where the comparisons are most problematic. The Conclusion also hazards a prediction for Roma rights over the next few years, in contradistinction to U.S. civil rights. As a legal construct, Roma rights has not been underway in CSEE long enough to inspire transformative societal change. The enforcement of integration mandates is too inconsistent and half-hearted to overcome the deeply entrenched social antipathy toward Roma. As a political construct, Romani identity tends to be ascribed by international organizations and Roma elites; this identity is not strong enough to bind the disparate minority groups that stand to benefit from rallying around it. These realities perpetually frustrate efforts to improve the situation of the majority of Roma. Civil Rights, by contrast, benefitted from an almost diametric set of realities. The Cold War, decolonization, and the antiapartheid movement lasted for decades, thereby maintaining constant pressure on the U.S. government. Over time, government action and case law swayed public opinion regarding African Americans.

The passage of half a century gives us the benefit of a longer arc with which to assess civil rights. Today, we can see that while African Americans have made tremendous inroads into American culture and society, there has also been a reactionary groundswell against the legal advances of the Civil Rights era. This groundswell would culminate in sophisticated efforts to utilize the "race-neutral" aspiration of civil rights to dismantle its legacy. In CSEE, detractors of Roma rights need not wage these legal battles. In our view, Roma rights has not managed to change social attitudes enough for a reactionary movement to be necessary, hence the persistence of deep-seated discrimination against Roma. It is with this cultural and social intransigence that we begin our study, with an eye toward unpacking and illuminating the structural, legal, and cultural mechanisms that maintain these positions. It is our goal that, through our book and its systematic examination of the interplay of law and culture, we may shed light on the utility of this comparison.

1

Historical Comparisons: From Slavery to World War II

To properly contextualize Roma rights and explore the parallels with civil rights, we must first trace the history of Romani peoples in CSEE, a history that stretches back over a millennium. Scholars have studied the origins of the Roma as well as their paths into CSEE for centuries. For nearly as long, this scholarship has objectified, exoticized, and marginalized its very subjects – in short, replicating society's exclusion of the Roma. To highlight and avoid these perils, we begin this Chapter by surveying how Romani studies as a field has evolved to a juncture that now facilitates broader structural comparisons with other minority groups.

Since the nineteenth century, scholarship on European Roma has been dominated by the ethnographic approach of "Gypsiology," or Gypsy lore, which is preoccupied with Roma culture, folklore, and origins.[1] This approach rests on a proposition, often attributed to the German historian Heinrich Mortiz Gottlieb Grellmann (1753–1804), that the itinerant groups scattered across Europe, frequently (and pejoratively) called Gypsies, constitute an ethnic group bound by a common language and land of origin, India.[2] Under the spell of this thesis, successive generations of Gypsiologists attempted to uncover the paths that the first Roma had traveled into Europe, using historical and linguistic evidence to prove or disprove the links to India.[3] Along the way, they classified Roma into intricate categories based on culture, dialect, and geography. Rather than seeing that all the variations challenged a unifying ethnic categorization of "Gypsy," Gypsiologists bemoaned the imminent extinction of the "true Gypsy," an archetype that hewed close to the central features of the ethnicity.[4]

1 David Mayall, Gypsy Identities 1500–2000: From Egipcyans and Moon-men to the Ethnic Romany 23–26 (2004).

2 *See* Heinrich Mortiz Gottlieb Grellmann, Die Zigeuner. Ein Historischer Versuch über die Lebensart und Verfassung (English ed., 1807) (1783).

3 *See, e.g.*, Augustus Pott, Die Zigeuner in Europa und Asien (Heynemann Verlag 1844); John Sampson, *On the Origin and Early Migration of the Gypsies*, 2 J. Gypsy Lore Soc. 156 (1923); Ralph Turner, *On the Position of Romani in Indo-Aryan*, 5 J. Gypsy Lore Soc. 145 (1927); Angus Fraser, The Gypsies (1992).

4 Wim Willems, *Ethnicity as a Death-Trap: The History of Gypsy Studies*, *in* Gypsies and Other Itinerant Groups: A Socio-historical Approach 17, 25–26 (Leo Lucassen et al. eds., 1998).

Grellmann and other foundational figures of Gypsy lore have been discredited for their associations with evangelism, eugenics, and criminology, all of which at some point tried to tie Roma to vagrancy as a basis for their criminalization or assimilation.[5] While contemporary scholars in this tradition have abandoned its problematic aspects, the ethnographic approach still endures today, and it still draws censure for its obsession with the exotic origins of Roma, their distinctive cultural identity, and their reification into labyrinthine categories.[6] Although the approaches are new, the mindset is redolent of the nineteenth-century folklorists: it treats Romani people as an object of inquiry, to be studied by fieldwork.[7] Ethnographies of Roma, both old and modern, are therefore replete with accounts of scholars living among Roma, as if to observe them in some natural setting. These works often present the scholar as a mediator between two worlds, Roma and *gadje* (non-Roma).

Many Romani studies scholars are not Roma themselves; thus, their representations of Roma become contested. Scholarly representations can be labeled inaccurate or inauthentic. Worse, they can reinforce the separateness of Roma from the dominant society. By fetishizing the true roots of the Roma, however distant (in time and geography), as well as the distinct and impenetrable culture of the Roma, these ethnographies perpetuate the notion that Roma cannot become part of mainstream society.[8] Concomitantly, by concentrating on the most distinctive features of the Roma, these studies create a caricature of the "true Gypsy" as an amalgam of exaggerated features.[9] Roma who do not conform to these depictions – in other words, most Roma – can be either dismissed as assimilated Gypsies or ignored altogether by scholars. In this way, the full complexity of Romani experiences, including the forces that exclude them from mainstream society and the similarities that they share with other populations, is rarely explored.[10]

In the last few decades, a countervailing trend has emerged to challenge the entrenched narratives of Gypsiology. It was propelled by different forces but has recently begun to coalesce under the umbrella of "critical approaches to Romani studies." We trace critical approaches back to three interrelated developments. First, after World War II, the field of Romani studies began to align with trends in the

5 MAYALL *supra* note 1, at 25, 32, 33, 94.

6 *See* MIHAI SURDU, THOSE WHO COUNT: EXPERT PRACTICES OF ROMA CLASSIFICATION 77–92 (2016).

7 *Id.* at 22–24.

8 *See id.* at 16–17 (arguing that preoccupation with the Roma/non-Roma distinction "normalizes," in Foucault's parlance, the Romani predicament). Scholars are not the only ones vulnerable to these impulses; artists, general-interest authors, and well-meaning architects of inclusion policy have all succumbed to normalizing stereotypes of the Roma.

9 ANGUS BANCROFT, ROMA AND GYPSY-TRAVELLERS IN EUROPE: MODERNITY, RACE, SPACE AND EXCLUSION 159–60 (2005). This line of criticism descends from Edward Said, Benedict Anderson, and Eric Hobsbawm, who have written on Orientalism, imagined communities, and nationalism.

10 In fact, the complexity and dynamism of Roma society manifest in a curious fact: many contemporary Roma do not care about their Indic roots; the academic obsession with these roots therefore reveals that the definition of "Roma" is pushed by outsiders.

social sciences that explored the repression and stigmatization of certain groups by the dominant society and the state. Scholars saw that Roma were bound not necessarily by ethnicity but by a cycle of social and economic marginalization and exclusion. These scholars included Thomas Acton, Zoltan Barany, Nicolae Gheorghe, Ian Hancock, and Jean-Pierre Liégeois, all of whom searched for larger, structural explanations for the persistence of "anti-Gypsyism."[11]

Second, Roma organizations formed after World War II to advocate for reparations for the Nazi genocide, a cause that eventually morphed into Romani nationalism.[12] For example, the Comité International Tsigane (previously the Communauté Mondiale Gitane), founded in Paris in the 1960s, worked to establish a Gypsy homeland, secure reparations, and offer coordination to other Roma rights groups that were springing up across Europe.[13] In the following decades, such groups developed in influence and sophistication. Their efforts centered around the creation of a common identity in furtherance of a shared political cause: where outsiders previously classified Roma into ornate taxonomies, now Romani leaders sought to emphasize the experiences borne by all Roma (and thereby minimize differences); where governments previously stigmatized and persecuted Roma, now Romani leaders sought to strengthen the community's defenses by unifying its disparate peoples.[14]

Finally, the postwar period also coincided with attempts to find common cause among subjugated peoples worldwide. Civil Rights in the United States and decolonization across the Third World clearly influenced one another. Decolonization forced African Americans to reassess their status, and Civil Rights in turn inspired other movements such as anti-apartheid in South Africa. Within Romani studies and Romani rights movements, the focus on structural causes of anti-Roma persecution both linked the modern Roma with their ancestors and tied Roma to other marginalized groups.[15] Thus, Roma rights became more compelling because the

11 *See, e.g.*, Romani Culture and Gypsy Identity (Thomas Acton & Gary Mundy eds., 1997); Gypsy Politics and Traveller Identity (Thomas Acton ed., 1997); Zoltan Barany, The East European Gypsies: Regime Change, Marginality, and Ethnopolitics (2002); Ian Hancock, The Pariah Syndrome: An Account of Gypsy Slavery and Persecution (1987); Jean-Pierre Liégeois, Gypsies and Travellers: Socio-cultural Data (1987); Nicolae Gheorghe, *The Social Construction of Romani Identity*, *in* Gypsy Politics and Traveller Identity (Thomas Acton ed., 1997). A unidimensional focus on marginalization, too, has its detractors. *See, e.g.*, Willems, *supra* note 4.

12 Mayall *supra* note 1, at 204; Liégeois, *supra* note 11, at 170.

13 Mayall *supra* note 1, at 204.

14 *Id.* at 207–08 (classifying these developments as Romani nationalism and construction of ethnic identity). *See also* Nicolae Gheorghe & Thomas Acton, *Citizens of the World and Nowhere: Minority, Ethnic and Human Rights for Roma*, *in* Between Past and Future: The Roma of Central and Eastern Europe 54 (Will Guy ed., 2001); Thomas Acton & Ilona Klímová, *The International Romani Union: An East European Answer to West European Questions?*, *in* Between Past and Future: The Roma of Central and Eastern Europe 157 (Will Guy ed., 2001).

15 *See* Mayall *supra* note 1, at 235, criticizing Thomas Acton for extending the term "genocide" to episodes of anti-Roma persecution between 1520 and 1600 in Europe.

movement fought against a system of oppression that had endured for centuries and was coterminous with other rights movements.

Innovative as these forbears of Critical Romani Studies were, they seldom confronted the issue of race – specifically, the racialization of the Roma. After World War II, with the continent rebuilding from the fallout of eugenics and pseudoscientific racial theories, European scholars were understandably hesitant to touch race.[16] This was despite the fact that Roma were persecuted in the same manner as Europe's racialized Jewish populations during the Holocaust. In the U.S., however, racial formation theory was gaining traction as a paradigm for dissecting the persistence of racial hierarchies. Closely identified with the sociologists Omi and Winant, racial formation theory holds that race is a sociohistorical process influenced not by biology but by societal struggle.[17] It supplanted the biological and cultural determinism that had pervaded racial theories since the nineteenth century. Today, a new generation of scholars has infused Romani studies with racialization and other paradigms.[18] Many of these scholars are Roma, and they are less interested in classifications and cultural practices than in the endurance of persecution, even in the face of reforms such as the European Union's Roma integration efforts. Some among them would even argue that marginalization and exclusion persist because of these efforts – because anti-Gypsyism inheres in laws and society itself.[19]

We see ourselves as continuing the critical approaches discourse by extending the comparisons between Roma rights and civil rights. To do so, we must first explore the forces that have excluded both African Americans and Roma. Racialization is central to that exercise: race is inseparable from the African American experience and central to the construction of American identity and the positioning of African Americans in contradistinction to that identity. Yet race is not a uniquely American institution.[20] Race can also explain the plight of the Roma, for all their heterogeneity.[21] With due regard to

16 There is reluctance in Europe to employ the term "race," which is redolent of eugenics. Race, ethnicity, and nation are frequently conflated, particularly in the former Eastern bloc, where minorities were often referred to as "nations" or "nationalities." *See* Mathias Möschel, *Color Blindness or Total Blindness? The Absence of Critical Race Theory in Europe*, 9 Rutgers Race & L. Rev. 57, 73–74 (2007); *Towards a European Critical Race Theory*, 34 Ethnic & Racial Stud. 1648 (2011); Peter Vermeersch, The Romani Movement: Minority Politics & Ethnic Mobilization in Contemporary Central Europe 16 (2006). *See also* Pierre Bourdieu & Loïc Wacquant, *On the Cunning of Imperialist Reason*, 16 Theory Culture Soc'y 41 (1999) (arguing that class is a more appropriate framework than race in the European context).

17 Michael Omi & Howard Winant, Racial Formation in the United States (3d ed. 2014).

18 *See, e.g.*, Miglena S. Todorova, *Race and Women of Color in Socialist/Postsocialist Transnational Feminisms in Central and Southeastern Europe*, 16 Meridians: Feminism, Race, Transnationalism 114 (2018); Nidhi Trehan & Angéla Kóczé, *Racism, (Neo-)colonialism and Social Justice: The Struggle for the Soul of the Romani Movement in Post-socialist Europe*, *in* Racism Postcolonialism Europe 50 (Graham Huggan & Ian Law eds., 2009); Mathias Möschel, Law, Lawyers and Race: Critical Race Theory from the United States to Europe (2014).

19 *See* Mathias Möschel, The Relevance of Critical Race Theory to Europe (2011).

20 *See* Fatima El-Tayeb, European Others: Queering Ethnicity in Postnational Europe xix (2011).

21 Möschel, *supra* note 18.

the origins and distinctness of African Americans and Roma, this Chapter surveys the historical parallels that have kept both groups at bay through the centuries.

RACIALIZATION OF CONSTRUCTED DIFFERENCE

By now, the origins of African Americans and Roma have been voluminously documented. From the earliest days of the American colonies to the nineteenth century, a brutal trade took enslaved peoples from the West African coast to the Americas, typically by way of Brazil and the Caribbean.[22] Upon arrival in America, the slaves were sold and bought, individually or in lots, frequently through a succession of brokers. Many slaves ended up working on plantations in the American South. Yet slavery and its footprint extended far beyond the South: slavery was the icon that defined the U.S., the engine that drove its growth. Slavery produced "the cotton that fed Rhode Island's mills," "the wealth that filled New York's banks," and "the markets that inspired Massachusetts manufacturers."[23] Indispensable to the new republic's prosperity, slavery made the American economy.

The roots of the Roma have been harder to substantiate, but scholars generally assert that they are an Indic people.[24] According to this narrative, in the eleventh century ancestors of the Roma started migrating westward from northern India.[25] Over the next two centuries, some groups would settle in territories that became modern-day CSEE, where they took up work as artisans, craftsmen, and tinkerers.[26] Regardless of its truthfulness, the foreignness of Roma is a migration narrative that, in European contexts, cast them as outsiders, as "European Others."[27] Although scholars have criticized this linkage of Roma to the Indian subcontinent, it has endured nonetheless, producing some interesting cultural connections between Romani groups and India.[28]

Apart from the migration narrative, the Otherness of Roma has been bolstered by the legacy of slavery in parts of CSEE. Some Roma were enslaved in the Wallachian

22 This gruesome journey has come to be known as the Middle Passage. For further discussion, see HERBERT S. KLEIN, THE ATLANTIC SLAVE TRADE 132–61 (2010).

23 Sven Beckert & Seth Rockman, *Introduction*, *in* SLAVERY'S CAPITALISM: A NEW HISTORY OF AMERICAN ECONOMIC DEVELOPMENT 1, 26 (Sven Beckert & Seth Rockman eds., 2016).

24 On the controversy surrounding the origins of the Roma, see IAN HANCOCK, WE ARE THE ROMANI PEOPLE 2–6 (2002).

25 *See id.* at 6–14. The eastward spread of Islam through conquests of the Ghaznavid Empire likely prompted this exodus. Ancestors of the Roma may have been part of the militias that fought the Ghaznavids, whether as soldiers or noncombatants who tended to the camps. Subsequently, these populations would continue westward as the Seljuqs advanced.

26 *See id.* at 14–16; DENA RINGOLD ET AL., WORLD BANK, ROMA IN AN EXPANDING EUROPE: BREAKING THE POVERTY CYCLE 6–7 (2005).

27 *See* EL-TAYEB, *supra* note 20, at xxvii.

28 *See, e.g.*, MAYALL, *supra* note 1; SURDU, *supra* note 6, at 37 (discussing the emergence of an "Indian corner" in schools with significant numbers Romani pupils in Central and Eastern Europe after 1990).

and Moldavian principalities and also Transylvania, areas that correspond to modern-day Romania.[29] The reasons for Roma slavery are disputed. The institution has been attributed to the Tatars, who ruled the area in the mid-thirteenth century and enslaved their enemies, as well as to landowners (*boyars*) who relied on forced labor where feudalism was the organizing principle of society and the economy.[30] Whatever its genesis, slavery was condoned by the state, which divided slaves (*robili* in Romanian) into various categories and enacted laws governing every aspect of their lives, from taxation and marriage to punishment and emancipation.[31] Slaves worked in a number of occupations, but Roma *robili* tended to be skilled artisans such as blacksmiths.[32] While slavery was localized within portions of CSEE, the institution has exercised an outsized influence over modern perceptions of Roma. In particular, some influential studies have correlated the legacy of slavery with contemporary marginalization.[33]

These early roots and narratives formed the basis for the racialization of African Americans and Roma. Racialization, or racial formation, is "the sociohistorical process by which racial categories are created, inhabited, transformed, and destroyed."[34] On the basis of skin color, African Americans have long been racialized as blacks, in contradistinction to whites, who constitute the dominant race. As an early observer of the color line, W.E.B. Du Bois noted that "black" and "white" are social constructs premised on perceived phenotypic differences between African Americans and whites.[35] Racial categories cohere with hegemonic power and social hierarchies.[36] In fact, colorism often stands as a measure of individuals' distance from the power center – and therefore whiteness. Whiteness embodies dominance so well that the phenomenon has taken on the character of property.[37] The further one slips from whiteness (i.e., the darker one's classification), the lower one's social standing.

Race in America attempts to fit all members of society into a hierarchy, but the fluidity of the color line challenges the orderliness of the racial project. After one or two generations, a slave's light-skinned descendants, produced from sexual violence by her master, could pass as white. In fact, passing becomes an indelible part of

29 Viorel Achim, The Roma in Romanian History 27, 42–43 (Richard Davies trans., 2004) (1998), *originally published as* Ţiganii în istoria Românieri.

30 *Compare id.* at 27–28, *with* Hancock, *supra* note 24, at 17–18. *See also* Nicolae Gheorghe, *Origins of Roma Slavery in the Romanian Principalities*, 7 Roma 12 (1983).

31 Slaves were categorized by their owners and also by occupation. *See* Achim, *supra* note 29, at 88; Hancock, *supra* note 24, at 19.

32 Achim, *supra* note 29, at 45–47.

33 *See, e.g.*, Ringold et al., *supra* note 26, at 6. *See also* Surdu, *supra* note 6, at 188 (detailing citations of World Bank studies of Romani poverty, disease, exclusion, and isolation).

34 Omi & Winant, *supra* note 17, at 55.

35 *See* W.E. Burghardt Du Bois, The Souls of Black Folk: Essays and Sketches 96 (A.C. McClurg & Co. 8th ed. 1909).

36 Charles W. Mills, The Racial Contract (1997).

37 Cheryl I. Harris, *Whiteness as Property*, 106 Harv. L. Rev. 1709 (1993).

American history, with blacks living entire lives as whites and enjoying all the attendant privileges.[38] Similarly, some Roma attest to "coming out" to others about their Romani heritage, which would otherwise have remained hidden. For those who can pass, forsaking blackness or Romani heritage becomes a life choice of privilege over burden.[39] Beyond passing, the arbitrariness of racial divides has been laid bare in other ways. For centuries, U.S. citizenship through naturalization was restricted to "white persons." An explosion in immigration in the late nineteenth and early twentieth centuries forced courts to classify applicants from Mexico, the Middle East, the Caucasus, and East, South, and Southeast Asia as either white or nonwhite, which courts did haphazardly.[40] Yet, however haphazardly the racial system operates, its taxonomies are enforced by law. The state was often both the creator and enforcer of racial categories – categories that were as imprecise as they were artificial, but maintained with utmost rigidity.

The racial formation of the Roma has unfolded along similar lines, that is, with the dominant majority and the state exploiting, augmenting, and inventing Romani differences (and therefore distance) and then translating those differences into law. While the difference of African Americans is primarily gauged by the color line, the difference of Roma is marked in part by a color line, but equally importantly by their cultural traits and purported proclivities – chiefly nomadism and associated qualities such as vagrancy and idleness, all of which supposedly distinguished Roma from majority populations. Roma have been characterized as peripatetic since their earliest history. Doubtless this association stems in part from the theory of how Roma made their way into Europe, through successive waves of migration.[41] After arriving in Europe, groups of Roma carried on nomadic and seminomadic lifestyles,[42] as itinerant craftsmen, musicians, farmhands, and, for a small minority, thieves and marauders.[43] Often the migration patterns were shaped by external forces. Episodes of state-sanctioned violence and vigilante persecution drove Roma out of and into certain territories, as did their emancipation in the 1800s in Wallachia, Moldavia, and Transylvania, which lifted restrictions on movement.

For the dominant society, nomadism became synonymous with Romani identity, thereby eclipsing the reality that large populations had settled into sedentary lives as

38 There is a rich body of literature and scholarship on "passing" by light-skinned African Americans. *See, e.g.*, ALLYSON HOBBS, A CHOSEN EXILE: A HISTORY OF RACIAL PASSING IN AMERICAN LIFE (2014); JAMES WELDON JOHNSON, THE AUTOBIOGRAPHY OF AN EX-COLORED MAN (1912).

39 *See* Kata Horváth, *"Passing": Rebeka and the Gay Pride: On the Discursive Boundaries and Possibilities of Skin Colour, in* MULTI-DISCIPLINARY APPROACHES TO ROMANY STUDIES 123 (Michael Stewart & Márton Rövid eds., 2010).

40 IAN HANEY LOPEZ, WHITE BY LAW: THE LEGAL CONSTRUCTION OF RACE 3–7 (2d ed. 2006).

41 After sojourning in CSEE, groups of Roma then moved westward in waves. *See* FRASER, *supra* note 3, at 226–38.

42 *See, e.g.*, ACHIM, *supra* note 29, at 51 ("During the Middle Ages, on the Romanian territory, the Gypsies had their own habitat and social organization, which differed from those of the Romanian population. The most distinctive feature was the nomadism of the Gypsies.").

43 *See id.* at 47; MAYALL *supra* note 1, at 67–68.

early as the medieval period. During slavery and its immediate aftermath in the Romanian principalities, for example, the iconic Roma was an itinerant metalsmith, considered to be "the most authentic of all the Gypsies."[44] This popular perception captivated writers, artists, and Gypsiologists, but the image of the wandering Gypsy was not merely romantic and innocuous. In 1787, Grellmann defined Gypsies as a people with Indian origins, marked by nomadism, distinct physiognomy (e.g., dark brown or olive-colored skin), and a set of undesirable traits – idleness, deceit, childishness, and licentiousness.[45] These traits, of course, ran counter to the virtues of mainstream society. Grellmann's succinct formulation captures all the prejudices that went into the racialization of the Roma, whose difference from the majority was delineated by nomadism and reinforced by the combination of a color line and certain immutable characteristics.[46] Now, in addition to nomadism, Roma were perceived to be swarthy and prone to vagrancy, thievery, and trickery.

Racial formation is a multidimensional process. The second-class status of African Americans was etched into the color line, but also reinforced by a litany of traits, habits, and cultural practices that were framed as diametric to those of whites. Over the centuries, African Americans have been depicted as docile (as opposed to vivacious), predatory (as opposed to safe), impulsive (as opposed to disciplined), lazy (as opposed to industrious), buffoonish (as opposed to serious), and savage (as opposed to sentient), to name just a few tropes. For both Roma and African Americans, the weight given to certain traits would change with the times; some eras were marked by the predominance of particular archetypes, such as the childishness of African Americans before the Civil War, as opposed to their supposed villainy afterward. Whatever the variations, all the markers of difference – from skin color to the immutable characteristics foisted upon both groups – were mutually reinforcing and ensured the confinement of both peoples to the lower rungs of the social hierarchies.

EXCLUSION UNDER LAW

Since their earliest days in the U.S. and Europe, African Americans and Roma have contended with a racialized exclusion woven into the social fabric. The clearest illustration of this similarity, from a comparative perspective, is the lifting of both groups out of slavery, even though, again, the institution affected only some Roma in some parts of modern-day CSEE. Racialization persisted after the emancipation of these groups, that is, after changes in legal status from slaves to freemen. After emancipation, the dominant society would invent novel mechanisms to preserve the socioeconomic hierarchies. Here, the law played no small part by reorienting the

44 ACHIM, *supra* note 29, at 89.
45 MAYALL *supra* note 1, at 153 (citing Grellmann, *supra* note 2, at ix–xiii).
46 *See id.* at 68–69.

chasms separating the majority and the racialized Other around new markers of difference.

In the U.S., the legal status of slaves changed through a quick succession of transformative constitutional amendments after the Civil War. Collectively known as the Reconstruction Amendments, the Thirteenth, Fourteenth, and Fifteenth Amendments abolished slavery, recognized equal protection under the law, and granted all citizens (implicitly, African Americans) the right to vote. The Reconstruction Amendments were preceded by President Lincoln's Emancipation Proclamation in 1863, which freed slaves in states that were in rebellion against the Union, and followed by several pieces of federal legislation designed to enforce the amendments. Because the Constitution itself had endorsed slavery, the Reconstruction Amendments were necessary to override that framework. Thus, after the Civil War, the Constitution would evolve from a document primarily concerned with federalism and property rights to a legal framework animated by racial equality.[47] The balance of power between states and the federal government, too, would change, for the constitutional amendments and civil rights acts of Reconstruction enshrined the supremacy of the Union and vested racial equality in national citizenship.[48]

In implementation, however, these advancements, premised on federal power, were limited. Although scholars continue to debate the progressiveness of the Reconstruction era, the gains to African Americans were short-lived, even at their zenith. Each achievement was matched by setback and terror.[49] Granted, the U.S. Bureau of Refugees, Freedmen, and Abandoned Lands fed, educated, and nursed millions of ex-slaves, but it was dismantled in 1872, seven years after its creation. True, the presence of federal troops in the South emboldened African Americans to sue for rights conferred by law, but federal troops steadily left the South in the late 1860s under President Andrew Johnson.[50] Where law blocked the ability of white Southerners to assert supremacy, they resorted to violence. The Ku Klux Klan and kindred groups killed thousands of African Americans, both indiscriminately and as part of targeted campaigns to suppress voting and political expression. The federal response was feeble, but in 1870 Congress passed the Enforcement Act to uphold African American suffrage under the Fifteenth Amendment, and the next year President Ulysses S. Grant dispatched federal troops to South Carolina to protect black residents. Yet federal troops completed their retreat when Rutherford B. Hayes took office as a result of the Compromise of 1877, which formally ended

47 Eric Foner, *The Strange Career of the Reconstruction Amendments*, 108 YALE L.J. 2003, 2006 (1999).

48 *See* Guy-Uriel E. Charles & Luis Fuentes-Rohwer, *Race, Federalism, and Voting Rights*, 2015 U. CHI L. F. 113 (arguing that the Civil War and the Reconstruction Amendments altered the federalism calculus).

49 *See* CAROL ANDERSON, WHITE RAGE: THE UNSPOKEN TRUTH OF OUR RACIAL DIVIDE 12–14 (2016) (chronicling reactionary white rage to black advancements).

50 DOUGLAS R. EGERTON, THE WARS OF RECONSTRUCTION: THE BRIEF, VIOLENT HISTORY OF AMERICA'S MOST PROGRESSIVE ERA 16, 18 (2014).

Reconstruction. In the end, Reconstruction lasted only a few years, "violently overthrown by men who had fought for slavery during the Civil War and continued that battle as guerrilla partisans."[51] It was not until the state managed to safeguard the lives of African Americans that Civil Rights could step in to fulfill the tattered legacy of Reconstruction.[52]

In CSEE, the emancipation of Romani slaves began in the western part of the region with Hapsburg Emperor Joseph II, who abolished slavery in 1783.[53] Abolition moved slowly eastward, eventually reaching Wallachia and Moldavia, where slavery was most widespread. As in the U.S., abolitionists would agitate, organize, and proselytize for decades before emancipation was fully realized.[54] In the 1830s, a generation of intellectuals who had studied in Western Europe returned to Wallachia and Moldavia with the intention of unifying the principalities into a Romanian state – while also inculcating public opinion against slavery.[55] In 1837, Grigore Alexandru Ghica, a prominent boyar and eventually prince of Moldavia, freed Romani slaves on his estate. The Wallachian Church followed suit in 1837. A liberal uprising in Wallachia in 1848 ushered in a short-lived government that embraced emancipation, but this trend was reversed after the Ottoman and Russian empires moved in to quell the rebellion. Moldavia and Wallachia advanced emancipation legislation in 1855, prompted by Ghica. It took until 1864 (coincidentally, within a year of Lincoln's Emancipation Proclamation) for a unified Romania under Mihail Kogălniceanu to recognize the legal freedom of Romani slaves.

Abolitionist trends in the American South and CSEE share some similarities. In both places, abolitionists had to agitate for decades to lay the groundwork for legal emancipation. Similarly, in the U.S. and Romania, abolition was tied to national unification. Finally, in the agrarian economies of the American South and the Romanian principalities, lawmakers had to balance the tension between abolitionists who favored immediate emancipation and landowners who favored gradualism.[56] Yet the movements to free African American and Romani slaves depart in the pace at which emancipation unfolded for each group. CSEE was divided into many discrete and sovereign states; naturally, then, abolition transpired in fits and starts. Slavery ended first in the western territories of the Austro-Hungarian Empire, but the institution persisted in the south and east, where boyars were more powerful. This pattern corresponded to economic development as well. Economies that were more feudal relied more heavily on Roma labor, so the landed estates held onto slavery more firmly.[57] By contrast, more industrialized economies had less need

51 *Id.* at 19.

52 Megan Ming Francis, Civil Rights and the Making of the Modern American State (2014).

53 Barany, *supra* note 11, at 128. In Hapsburg-controlled Moldavia, however, implementation of the order was weak due to opposition from landowners. *Id.*

54 *See* Foner, *supra* note 47, at 2004–05.

55 Achim, *supra* note 29, at 97–99.

56 *See* Barany, *supra* note 11, at 87.

57 Hancock, *supra* note 24, at 24.

for a Roma workforce and therefore suffered less in granting them freedom. Thus, in Hungary, Slovakia, Austrian-controlled Bukovina, and Hapsburg-controlled Transylvania, Roma either were not enslaved or were set free far earlier.[58] Here, Roma also tended to adopt sedentary lifestyles earlier, though they were often consigned to the countryside or economically depressed outskirts of cities. Yet in the Wallachia and Moldavia principalities, Roma toiled for centuries as slaves. Even further to the east, large parts of the region fell under the Ottoman Empire, a melting pot of peoples and faiths. The Ottomans pursued comparatively lax policies that taxed Roma heavily but did not enslave them, so they enjoyed some autonomy within the multiethnic *millet* system, whereby religious communities were accorded self-governance in exchange for payment of taxes.[59]

The heterogeneity in the legal status of the Roma was inevitable, given how many states cut across CSEE. One central authority did not reign over the territory in the mold of the U.S. federal government, nor could one central authority abolish slavery with a sweeping, uniform measure. Therefore, while all the dominant societies excluded Roma, there was variation in how that exclusion was translated into law. Where there was a history of slavery, the effect of emancipation on the status of the Roma was uneven; life for many Roma did not improve appreciably after emancipation. Where Roma had enjoyed more autonomy, such as under the Ottoman Empire, they still found themselves, at a minimum, marginalized by the state's classification systems.[60]

The plights of Roma fell into four broad and interrelated molds. First, Roma were stigmatized as an itinerant people, a fallacy that produced severe policies. The Ottoman Empire, for example, grouped Roma with nomadic or seminomadic groups such as Turkomans, Kurds, and Vlachs.[61] Because the empire assessed taxes on the basis of a group's classification, Roma sometimes had to pay higher taxes due to a perception that they had sought to avoid taxes elsewhere.[62] Certain cities in the Ottoman territories of Southeast Europe also segregated their Romani populations, banishing them unless they had demonstrable skills.[63] In the Austro-Hungarian Empire, Roma were shunted into ramshackle settlements, frequently on the outskirts of towns, as part of mass sedentarization campaigns.[64] This typified the policies of states whose economies had little room for Roma labor. During the reign of Maria Theresa (1740–1780), for example, the Hapsburgs eschewed mass

58 *See* Barany, *supra* note 11, at 88–89; Achim, *supra* note 29, at 128.

59 *See* Barany, *supra* note 11, at 84–86, 91–92. Recent scholarship has questioned the millet paradigm, as well as the place of the Roma within it. *See* Faika Celik, Approaching Gypsies (Roma) in Early Modern Ottoman Balkans: Challenges and Prospects, Presentation at the Critical Approaches to Romani Studies Conference, May 25–26, 2017, Central European University, Budapest (unpublished manuscript) (on file with authors).

60 *See* Celik, *supra* note 59.

61 *Id.*

62 Eyal Ginio, *Neither Muslims nor Zimmis: The Gypsies (Roma) in the Ottoman State*, 14 Romani Stud. 117 (2004).

63 *Id.* at 134.

64 For a detailed demographic breakdown, see Achim, *supra* note 29, at 132–37.

deportation for assimilation by prohibiting marriage between Roma, restricting their free movement, and removing children from families and placing them in state schools and foster homes.[65] The stigma of itinerancy also meant that Roma were targeted by vagrancy laws, which aimed to criminalize the ostensibly Romani way of life. Over time, vagrancy laws worked hand in hand with sedentarization policies to round up Roma, making them more vulnerable to pogroms. Second, in the region's more primitive economies, freed slaves faced the threat of re-enslavement. Because emancipation left a gaping void, Romanian boyars would find ways to bring Roma back into slavery or its functional equivalent, such as indentured servitude. And because emancipation was not accompanied by land distribution, impoverished Roma sometimes sold themselves back into slavery for survival.[66] Third, where freed Roma competed with non-Roma peasants, they faced violence and intimidation from vigilantes displaced by economic modernization. This history aligns with the ethnic competition model, which posits that majority populations persecute minorities when resources are scarce.[67] Finally, in areas either contiguous with or part of the Ottoman Empire (primarily the Balkans), Roma were often accused of being Turkish spies.[68] A constructed seditiousness therefore plagued the dominant society's conception of them. All in all, these patterns bolstered the Roma's perceived foreignness, even though they had resided in these territories for centuries and contributed to their cultures and economies.

Of course, fragmentation and a glacial pace of change also characterized the experiences of African Americans in the postbellum South. Some localities were simply more progressive than others, but living in the North or a nonslave state was no guarantee of safety. In CSEE, decolonization (i.e., the emergence of independent states out of the Austro-Hungarian and Ottoman empires) also did not meaningfully transform the position of Roma. Home rule in the constituent polities was too powerful, and officials could rest on local laws or customs to defend the old ways of life. Thus, localities managed to retain the social hierarchies through segregation and replicated slavery through sharecropping, industrial servitude, and excessively punitive laws.[69] For both African Americans and Roma, emancipation was insufficient by itself to ensure liberty and equality.

A common thread that runs through the postemancipation period for both African Americans and Roma was the attribution of criminality to the newly freed peoples. Previously, African Americans had been infantilized to justify the slave master's guiding hand; after emancipation, they became criminal, menacing, and wanton –

65 Fraser, *supra* note 3, at 157–59. Note, however, that Fraser and Barany differ on whether the Hapsburg economy required Romani labor (*see id.* at 157–58) or had outgrown it (*see* Barany, *supra* note 11, at 88–89, 92).

66 David M. Crowe, A History of the Gypsies of Eastern Europe and Russia 121–22 (1996).

67 *See, e.g.*, Susan Olzak, The Dynamics of Ethnic Competition and Conflict (1992).

68 Ringold et al., *supra* note 26, at 57–58.

69 *See* Douglas A. Blackmon, Slavery by Another Name: The Re-Enslavement of Black Americans from the Civil War to World War II (1992).

portrayals that endure today. This metamorphosis had juridical roots: the Thirteenth Amendment abolished slavery and involuntary servitude "except as a punishment for crime whereof the party shall have been duly convicted." If one could be convicted, one could be kept servile. Criminalization became the basis for re-enslavement, abetted by a legal system that convicted falsely and sentenced excessively – a system that placed auction houses adjacent to courthouses so as to sell convicts back into slavery.[70] Criminalization of Roma, whether after emancipation or decolonization, revolved around their perceived nomadism. For many states, Roma policy meant sedentarization policy, a conflation that persisted even during the Socialist and Communist period after World War II. Romani populations were subjected to registration requirements, tax incentives, and forcible settlement, often as part of antivagrancy campaigns.[71] Implementation of these policies varied, though, since it required faithful execution by local authorities. In the face of economic realities, local authorities resisted imperial mandates. For instance, landed estates in the Romanian principalities and Hapsburg Empire retained Roma as craftsmen or farmhands under some degree of indentured servitude, in violation of the crown's abolition of slavery and conscription of Roma into military service. Given both the expansive lands that monarchs ruled over and the fluctuations in their power, local officials enjoyed wide latitude in complying with legal changes.

As the U.S. and Europe entered the twentieth century, criminalization pursued African Americans and Roma at every step. The small victories of Reconstruction were swept away by the economic crises of the 1890s, when Jim Crow laws started to outlaw any transgression of the racial hierarchy.[72] African Americans were barred from whites-only schools, restaurants, hotels, and public accommodations; prohibited from having sex and producing children with whites; and subjected to voting restrictions. State and local authorities not only failed to uphold racial equality, they subverted the Reconstruction Amendments altogether through Jim Crow laws. Segregation was hardly unique to the South. Sundown towns – municipalities that excluded racial minorities through ordinances and violence – dotted the North and West.[73] The "separate but equal" doctrine, which formed the pillar of segregation and was validated by the Supreme Court in *Plessy v. Ferguson* in 1896, was closely associated with the South but in fact permeated the entirety of the nation. From

70 On the location of auction sites at or near courthouses, see MAURIE D. MCINNIS, SLAVES WAITING FOR SALE: ABOLITIONIST ART AND THE AMERICAN SLAVE TRADE 81, 118 (2011).

71 ACHIM, *supra* note 29, at 130–37.

72 This is the central thesis of Woodward's *Strange Career of Jim Crow*, which argued that Jim Crow laws were hardly inevitable and arose after a period of experimentation with integration. *See* C. VANN WOODWARD, THE STRANGE CAREER OF JIM CROW (1955). Subsequent scholars have pushed at the margins of Woodward's thesis, arguing that de jure segregation had in fact existed prior to the 1890s and that where it was not upheld by law, segregation persisted by custom. *See, e.g.*, Howard N. Rabinowitz, *More Than the Woodward Thesis: Assessing the Strange Career of Jim Crow*, 75 J. AM. HIST. 842, 846–47 (1988).

73 *See* JAMES LOEWEN, SUNDOWN TOWNS: A HIDDEN DIMENSION OF AMERICAN RACISM (2005).

Reconstruction until Civil Rights, segregationist and exclusionary laws preserved the antebellum order.

Meanwhile, in CSEE, the end of the nineteenth century was a time of intense political upheaval. With the 1878 Treaty of Berlin, the Ottomans had lost Bulgaria, Montenegro, Romania, and Serbia. Thirty years later, with the end of World War I, the Austro-Hungarian Empire, too, would dissolve. From its ruins, the Czechoslovak Republic, the First Hungarian Republic, the Republic of Poland, and the Kingdom of Serbs, Croats, and Slovenes emerged. These new states typically began as republics or constitutional monarchies but then devolved into dictatorships during the interwar period. Just as often, their borders were redrawn, leaving large minority populations whose allegiances lay with kin states across the border. Roma sometimes played pivotal roles in the upheavals; for instance, Roma served as soldiers in Bulgaria's wars of independence from the Ottomans.[74] But their primary advancements came with the burgeoning of organized Romani advocacy. In Bulgaria, Romania, Serbia, and Macedonia, Roma formed social organizations, published community newspapers, and participated in local elections.[75] Unfortunately, socioeconomic marginalization continued unabated. As the economies of CSEE modernized, the Roma fared poorly. In the industrialized cities, unskilled Romani workers were usually the first to lose employment. In rural areas, Roma and non-Roma tended to coexist, but a spate of agricultural crises left Roma at the mercy of angry farmers. Governments, for their part, tended to ignore the Roma, since officials were more concerned with the large minority populations that had ties to kin states. Except for the occasional sedentarization campaign, states seldom directed their policies at the Roma.

For all the diversity of the region, the rise of the Nazis and their satellite states had a unifying effect on Roma policy. Persecution of the Roma would culminate in the *Porrajmos*, or the Devouring, when as many as 1.5 million Roma – over half the Romani population in Europe – were killed in the Holocaust.[76] The *Porrajmos* is the darkest chapter of Romani history and, simultaneously, the most singularly unifying experience for European Roma. The *Porrajmos* affected European Roma regardless of their ethnic, geographic, and linguistic differences. Because of the centrality of the *Porrajmos*, World War II stands as an important milestone in the political formation of the European Romani nation.

From a comparative perspective, the World War II era is noteworthy because it marks the first instance in which American and European minority policies influenced one another, rather than merely developing side by side. Further, the

74 Crowe, *supra* note 66, at 9.

75 Barany, *supra* note 11, at 101–03.

76 Hancock, *supra* note 24, at 35–48. For a summary of the literature on quantifying the numbers of victims, see Barany, *supra* note 11, at 107–10. For a discussion of the problematic nature of the term *Porrajmos*, see Ágnes Daróczi & János Bársony, *Preface to the English Edition*, *in* Pharrajimos: The Fate of the Roma During the Holocaust x (János Bársony & Ágnes Daróczi eds., 2008).

aftermath of the war effectively cleaved Europe in half. The eastern half, where most Roma lived, would undergo a radical shift in minority policies under Communism.

Even before World War I, German scholars and jurists had been fascinated by American race laws, including not only antimiscegenation Jim Crow laws but also American immigration and naturalization laws. Shortly after the Nazis came to power in 1933, Germany adopted the infamous Nuremburg Law for the Protection of German Blood and Honor, commonly known as the Nuremburg Laws, in the mold of these American race laws.[77] The Nuremburg Laws prohibited racial mixing between Jews and Aryans and relegated Jews to second-class citizenship.[78] While the Nuremburg Laws did not mention Roma and Sinti (German Roma), these laws were invoked to deport Roma and Sinti to internment camps in occupied Austria.[79] Other measures paved the way to the mass extermination of these groups. They include anti-Gypsy holdovers from the Weimar Republic – laws that required registration, prohibited vagrancy, and conscripted Roma into labor camps. Contemporaneously with the Nuremburg Laws, the Nazis also sterilized and imprisoned Roma and established a research unit, directed by the psychiatrist Robert Ritter, to study, categorize, and experiment on Roma. Ritter's work profoundly influenced SS commander Heinrich Himmler, the architect of the "Final Solution for the Gypsy Question." The "Final Solution" articulated a path for the systematic killing of Roma and Sinti, facilitating their eventual deportation to the Auschwitz-Birkenau concentration camp.[80]

The killing of Roma unfolded in different ways. Tens of thousands of Roma were executed outside any formal campaign.[81] Because Roma were scattered across Europe and concentrated in CSEE, most of the continent's Roma perished in the Nazi satellite states of Eastern Europe – states that had emerged from the breakup of

77 James Q. Whitman, Hitler's American Model: The United States and the Making of Nazi Race Law (Princeton 2017). This is an iconoclastic book. For the voluminous literature arguing the contrary position – that, for all the coincidences, Jim Crow laws did not influence the Nazi race laws – as well as Whitman's dialogue with it, *see id.* at 3–5.

78 *Id.* at 19.

79 United States Holocaust Memorial Museum, *Sinti and Roma: Victims of the Nazi Era, archived at* https://perma.cc/2D9N-H777.

80 For all of its purported grounding in science, the Nazi's racialization of the Roma conflated science with tautology and sociology. A quote from Himmler's circular is illustrative:

> Experience gained in combatting the Gypsy nuisance, and knowledge derived from race-biological research, have shown that the proper method of attacking the Gypsy problem seems to be to treat it as a matter of race. Experience shows that part-Gypsies play the greatest role in Gypsy criminality. On the other hand, it has been shown that efforts to make the Gypsies settle have been unsuccessful, especially in the case of pure Gypsies, on account of their strong compulsion to wander. It has therefore become necessary to distinguish between pure and part-Gypsies in the final solution of the Gypsy question. *Id.* at 5.

81 Anton Weiss-Wendt, *Introduction*, *in* The Nazi Genocide of the Roma: Reassessment and Commemoration 1, 1 (Anton Weiss-Wendt ed., 2013); János Bársony, *20th Century Roma History and the Pharrajimos*, *in* Pharrajimos: The Fate of the Roma During the Holocaust 23, 27 (János Bársony & Ágnes Daróczi eds., 2008).

the region's two great empires, the Ottoman Empire and the Austro-Hungarian Empire, and then devolved into autocracies aligned with the Third Reich. Even prior to this alignment, eugenics movements in Bulgaria, Estonia, Hungary, Poland, Romania, and the Kingdom of Yugoslavia created fertile ground for separating those who belonged to a nation from those who did not.[82] Eugenics provided the justification for national and local moves to situate Roma outside the nation, fomenting anti-Romani sentiment through pseudoscience. Importantly, these movements reveal that notions of race and the mobilization of whiteness were not exclusively Nazi phenomena, or externally imposed. The grip of the Nazis was not always secure across CSEE. There was a great deal of autonomy and variety in the way Nazi satellite states persecuted Roma.[83] In the Independent State of Croatia (1941–1945), the fascist Ustaša government murdered its Roma without prompting by the Nazis. The Ustašas enacted racial laws modeled on the Nuremburg Laws to single out "Jews" and "Gypsies," eventually sending 16,000 to 40,000 Roma to the notorious Jasenovac concentration camp, where they died quickly and violently.[84] Another regime in CSEE to have initiated the systematic killing of Roma was Romania under the dictator Ion Antonescu, where over 20,000 Roma were deported to Transnistria – part of Nazi-occupied Ukraine under the administration of Romania – to "purify" the country.[85] With virtually no public outcry,[86] Roma toiled in labor camps; over half of the inmates either succumbed to disease or were executed.[87] In Hungary, sterilization, internment, and forced labor preceded the fiercest onslaught against Roma, which transpired after German occupation in 1944.[88] Roma were then imprisoned in ghettoes and concentration camps, pressed into labor, and massacred.[89]

ROMA AND THE NARRATIVES OF THE NATION

The World War II era constitutes the height of Romani exclusion from the dominant narratives of the nation. Hand in hand with the racialization of their perceived differences from the majority, Roma were invoked as an illustration of the need for ethnic purification. This antagonism between Roma and the nation transcends

82 *See* Todorova, *supra* note 18, at 120 (citing MARIUS TURDA & PAUL J. WEINDLING, BLOOD AND HOMELAND: EUGENICS AND RACIAL NATIONALISM IN CENTRAL AND SOUTHEAST EUROPE (2007)).

83 Weiss-Wendt, *supra* note 81, at 2–3.

84 Alexander Korb, *Ustaša Mass Violence Against Gypsies in Croatia*, 1941–1942, *in* THE NAZI GENOCIDE OF THE ROMA: REASSESSMENT AND COMMEMORATION 72, 79, 89 (Anton Weiss-Wendt ed., 2013).

85 Vladimir Solonari, *Ethnic Cleansing or "Crime Prevention"? Deportation of Romanian Roma*, *in* THE NAZI GENOCIDE OF THE ROMA: REASSESSMENT AND COMMEMORATION 96, 96–97, 113–14 (Anton Weiss-Wendt ed., 2013). *See also* RADU IOANID, THE HOLOCAUST IN ROMANIA: THE DESTRUCTION OF JEWS AND GYPSIES UNDER THE ANTONESCU REGIME, 1940–1944 (2000).

86 Solonari, *supra* note 85, at 111–12.

87 ACHIM, *supra* note 29, at 178.

88 BARANY, *supra* note 11, at 32–34.

89 *Id.* at 34–42.

regimes. In CSEE, as new states formed, coalesced, and dissolved throughout history, Roma were portrayed as outsiders; consequently, discourses of the nation occurred without – or, more often, in opposition to – the Roma. In the U.S., African Americans have managed to dictate some counternarratives about the meaning of "America," staking a claim to the national ideals of freedom and equality. Nonetheless, the dominant strain of Americanism, the fundamental cultural ideology of the U.S., equates America with white.[90] The construction of national identities in America and Europe has therefore excluded African Americans and Roma, with the differences being more in degree rather than in substance.

Distant origins, constructed or actual, and migration narratives have worked in tandem to cast Romani populations as outsiders, despite their centuries-long history in Europe. This outsider status is reinforced by a litany of racially ascribed deficiencies, each of which implicates an opposite trait that then defines the nation. Roma are vagrants while the majority is rooted, idle while the majority is industrious, deceitful while the majority is honest, and licentious while the majority is temperate. When the state criminalizes traits associated with Roma, it justifies the purging of Romani populations. From a cultural standpoint, when differences between Roma and the majority harden, those differences can exclude Roma from the ideological formation of the nation, whereby a dominant majority envisions itself as comprising one collective people (a "nation") sharing linguistic, geographic, historical, and ethnic affinities as well as territory.[91] According to ethno-symbolist paradigms, nation formation derives from the cultural elements of symbol, myth, memory, value, ritual, and tradition.[92] For most of Europe's history, each of these pillars of the nation evolved without contemplation of the Roma; worse, when a nation actively assessed the place of the Roma in society, the nation's symbols were often refashioned in antipathy to the Roma. In this way, most nations' dominant ethnicities have come to see themselves as definitively not Roma and also un-Roma.

Interestingly, distant origins have not had the same effect on African Americans. The American imaginary brims with migration stories, of immigrants who triumphed over obstacles to achieve the American dream.[93] In that retelling, which was historically the essence of the definition of America, untold waves of immigrants have assimilated into the nation, from the Irish to the Italians and others who have

90 *See* Robert Shalhope, *Anticipating Americanism: An Individual Perspective on Republicanism in the Early Republic*, *in* AMERICANISM: NEW PERSPECTIVES ON THE HISTORY OF AN IDEAL 53, 67 (Michael Kazin & Joseph A. McCartin eds., 2006). Some would say Americanism is the country's "civic religion." Michael Kazin & Joseph A. McCartin, *Introduction*, *in* AMERICANISM: NEW PERSPECTIVES ON THE HISTORY OF AN IDEAL 1, 9 (Michael Kazin & Joseph A. McCartin eds., 2006).

91 *See* ANTHONY D. SMITH, MYTHS AND MEMORIES OF THE NATION 13 (1999); BENEDICT ANDERSON, IMAGINED COMMUNITIES (1983).

92 ANTHONY D. SMITH, ETHNO-SYMBOLISM AND NATIONALISM: A CULTURAL APPROACH 18 (2009).

93 *See, e.g.*, Woodrow Wilson, *Americanism and the Foreign Reborn*, *in* THE AMERICAN STUDIES ANTHOLOGY 127 (Richard P. Horwitz ed., 2001) (1915).

successfully been able to become "white," primarily because of their physical features.[94] Within this framework, these immigrants needed only to assimilate by adopting aspects of American culture – in particular, language. Because race is such a powerful force in America, there are limited possibilities for people who cannot be coded as white, which is reinforced by other differences projected onto them to minimize the prospect of assimilation. This type of assimilation has eluded African Americans.

America's cultural ideologies are rooted as deeply in the construct of whiteness[95] as in core values and other markers: the republic, liberty, and free enterprise.[96] According to the dominant strain of Americanism, the nation's heritage lies in the ideals defended by the founding fathers – white colonists who settled the land in the seventeenth and eighteenth centuries, often fleeing religious persecution.[97] This formulation leaves no room for multitudes of others, such as indigenous peoples and African Americans.

Is there a Europeanism that stands as a counterpart to Americanism? Today, Europeanism does exist, as a cultural construction of Europe around antiquity, civilization, and Enlightenment thought.[98] As with Americanism, the dominant variation of Europeanism identifies Europe with racial (white) and religious (Christian) markers.[99] Europe and the U.S. are now viewed as the primary components of the West.[100] When they do depart, they often serve as foils of one another, alternate realities that each could have pursued had it charted a different path.[101] Until recently, however, it could not be argued that Europe is a "nation." From its earliest history and arguably until today, Europe has been constantly feuding with itself, militarily, politically, and culturally. For Romani peoples, however, time has had little effect on their exclusion and marginalization: Roma were kept out of the dominant nation during medieval times, when they were enslaved; during the Enlightenment, when science-based racism corroborated their inferiority; during the nineteenth century, when fledgling nation-states maintained age-old anti-Gypsyism policies; and during the early twentieth century, when persecution culminated in the Holocaust. Not surprisingly, exclusion persists today. One of the most

94 *See, e.g.*, NOEL IGNATIEV, HOW THE IRISH BECAME WHITE (1995); DAVID R. ROEDIGER, WORKING TOWARD WHITENESS: HOW AMERICA'S IMMIGRANTS BECAME WHITE (2005). However, these trends were not consistent; there were periods in U.S. history when Italians were not considered white because of their skin color.

95 *See, e.g.*, Frances L. Ansley, *Stirring the Ashes: Race, Class and the Future of Civil Rights Scholarship*, 74 CORNELL L. REV. 993, 1024 n.129 (1989); Harris, *supra* note 37.

96 Shalhope, *supra* note 90, at 67.

97 *See id.*

98 CHIARA BOTTICI & BENOIT CHALLAND, IMAGINING EUROPE: MYTH, MEMORY, AND IDENTITY (2013).

99 *See id.* at 28–29.

100 JOHN MCCORMICK, EUROPEANISM 12 (2010).

101 *See* Jürgen Habermas & Jacques Derrida, *February 15, or What Binds Europeans Together: A Plea for a Common Foreign Policy, Beginning in the Core of Europe*, 10 CONSTELLATIONS 291 (2006).

interesting contemporary turns, however, is the depiction of Roma as the "blacks of Europe," a trend that Chapter 6 will explore.[102]

To be sure, other varieties of Americanism and Europeanism exist, varieties that celebrate diversity and extend the protections of liberal values to racial minorities. In the struggle for dominance among these strains, one subset of the nation (whiteness) is pitted against another (liberal values). At that point, state intervention can tip the balance. As the next Chapter explores, the U.S. federal government's projection of unity and diversity during the Cold War helped to counter the recalcitrant defense of segregation by many Southern states. In Europe, this dynamic has taken on additional dimensions. At various times in its history, CSEE was home to empires not traditionally considered European: the Byzantine and Ottoman empires. Nonetheless, when CSEE candidates sought to join the European Union after the Cold War, they adopted West European claims to antiquity and the Enlightenment. Consequently, CSEE also embraced hierarchies that excluded racial, ethnic, and religious minorities such as Muslims, Greek Orthodox, Turks, and Roma.

The strains of Americanism and Europeanism are further complicated by their intersections with populism, for another hierarchy cuts through Americanism and Europeanism. Subgroups of majority populations that do not conform to the paragons of liberal values are also consigned to the periphery. For the U.S., this is the South, in particular the Deep South, which has sometimes fetishized whiteness in a way that forced the nation to confront the sincerity of its values. At times, as in the Civil War and the Cold War, these extreme displays of allegiance to whiteness have been inconvenient.[103] In Europe, the imagined cultural division is between East and West, a distinction that would be reinforced during and after the Cold War. Southeast Europe is also tainted by the bloody civil wars of Yugoslav succession, with the word "Balkan" often conjuring images of barbarity and liminality.[104] Finally, Eastern Europe is hobbled by its ties to the defunct hegemonies of Communism and empire.

102 *See, e.g.*, Mihaela Mudure, *Blackening Gypsy Slavery: The Romanian Case*, *in* BLACKENING EUROPE: THE AFRICAN AMERICAN PRESENCE 263 (Heike Raphael-Hernandez ed. 2004); Alaina Lemon, *What Are They Writing About Us Blacks? Roma and "Race" in Russia*, 33 ANTHROPOLOGY OF E. EUR. REV. 34 (1995); Oscar Prieto-Flores, *Does the Canonical Theory of Assimilation Explain the Roma Case? Some Evidence from Central and Eastern Europe*, 32 ETHNIC & RACIAL STUD. 1387 (2009); Khachig Tölölyan, *Rethinking Diaspora(s): Stateless Power in the Transnational Moment*, 5 DIASPORA: J. TRANSNAT'L STUD. 3 (1996). *See also* HANCOCK, *supra* note 11.

103 *See* Mary L. Dudziak, *Desegregation as a Cold War Imperative*, 41 STAN. L. REV. 61, 62–63 (1988) ("At a time when the U.S. hoped to reshape the postwar world in its own image, the international attention given to racial segregation was troublesome and embarrassing. . . . U.S. government officials realized that their ability to sell democracy to the Third World was seriously hampered by continuing racial injustice at home.").

104 *See, e.g.*, LARRY WOLFF, INVENTING EASTERN EUROPE: THE MAP OF CIVILIZATION ON THE MIND OF THE ENLIGHTENMENT 3–9 (1994); Dušan I. Bjelić, *Introduction: Blowing Up the "Bridge," in* BALKAN AS METAPHOR 1, 3–6 (Dušan I. Bjelić, I. & Savić Obrad eds., 2005).

2

Historical Comparisons: From the Cold War to Eastern Enlargement

The paths of Roma and African Americans diverged sharply after World War II, when Europe was cleaved in half by the victors of the war. Western Europe allied itself with the U.S., embracing capitalism and democracy, while Eastern Europe – including CSEE, where the majority of the continent's Roma lived – adopted Socialism and Communism.[1] For both Roma and African Americans, the postwar years ushered in unparalleled gains, though under very different paradigms.

In the U.S., grassroots agitation culminated in the Civil Rights movement, a vigorous but protracted fight for equality that eventually prompted transformative federal civil rights legislation. In CSEE, post–World War II advances for Roma unfolded on an altogether different plane. Amid the governments' bids to provide universal employment, schooling, housing, and health care, Roma, who had been the most marginalized segment of society, often benefitted from social and economic reforms. Overall, however, Socialist and Communist policies that directly targeted Roma were variegated, inconsistent, and often incoherent. The different countries dealt with their Romani populations in a variety of ways; even within a country, policies could swing from indifference to benign paternalism to forced assimilation.[2] If any general theme can be extrapolated from this period, it is that many Roma made great strides in the material dimensions of their lives, such as employment and education, but all Roma had to suppress their ethnic and racial identities. Further, government practices during this time (e.g., shunting Romani workers into unskilled employment and Romani students into special schools) left most Roma socioeconomically precarious during the tectonic shifts of the post-Communist transition. Thus, while many Roma made advances during Socialism and Communism, they still lagged behind majority populations. The next period of

[1] Some countries, such as Yugoslavia and Czechoslovakia, defined themselves as Socialist, while others, such as Bulgaria and Romania, embraced more faithfully the Soviet Union's variant of Communism. For precision, we will refer to both camps as "Socialist and Communist."

[2] On the tangled legacy of Communism for the CSEE Roma, see Elena Marushiakova & Vesselin Popov, *European Policies for Social Inclusion of Roma: Catch 22?*, 3 Social Inclusion 19, 21 (2015).

major gains in CSEE, of course, was the slew of social inclusion initiatives,[3] legislation,[4] and legal cases[5] starting in the mid-1990s as the European Union (EU) moved into the post-Communist space.

This book primarily compares civil rights with Roma rights. It is for the most part a diachronic comparison: while the U.S. underwent the Civil Rights movement, CSEE was contending with Socialism and Communism. Civil Rights and Roma rights are apt comparators because of the affinities between the U.S. and the EU in governance, center–periphery relations, and federal or quasi-federal expansion. In some respects, then, Communism might seem like an aberration. Communism drove a wedge into the heart of Europe, dividing it between East and West.[6] In the half century that CSEE formed part of the Eastern bloc, the region undertook a very different path than the rest of Europe, which began to coalesce around shared governance, open markets, and common visions of human rights. Hence, CSEE had to commit to radical transitions after Communism to enter the EU.

Yet Communism is central to an understanding of the contemporary setting for Roma in CSEE. Communism might have rendered Roma vulnerable to the market liberalization and reactionary xenophobia of post-Communism, but this period also educated a generation of Romani activists and whetted their desire for political and ethnic expression. East European Communism also prompted the first kernels of European integration in Western Europe, which would eventually transform first into the European Coal and Steel Community (1952), then the European Economic Community (1957), and then the European Union (1993).[7] Finally, Communism is even important for its effect on the U.S. Civil Rights movement. As Derrick Bell posited and historians have corroborated, the federal government grudgingly embraced civil rights to project unity to the world as it fought the Cold War.[8] This was particularly important in newly decolonized Africa and Southeast Asia, where

3 *E.g.*, *An EU Framework for National Roma Integration Strategies up to 2020*, COM (2011) 173 final (Apr. 5, 2011).

4 *E.g.*, Council Directive 2000/43, 2000 O.J. (L 180) 22 (EC).

5 *E.g.*, D.H. and Others v. Czech Republic, App. No. 57825/00, 47 Eur. H.R. Rep. 59 (2007); Chance for Children Found. v. Town of Hajdúhadház, Legfelsöbb Bíróság, Pvf. IV.20.936/2008/4 (Hungarian Supreme Court 2008); ERRC v. Bulgarian Ministry of Education and Science (Sofia District Court 2007); Sampanis v. Greece, App. No. 32526/05, Eur. Ct. H.R. (2008); Oršuš and Others v. Croatia, App. No. 15766/03, 52 Eur. H.R. Rep. 7 (2010); Stoica v. Romania, No. 42722/02 (Third Section 2008).

6 This division within Europe – or the perception of this division – has existed for centuries. *See, e.g.*, Rebecca West, Black Lamb and Grey Falcon (1941). *See also* Larry Wolff, Inventing Eastern Europe: The Map of Civilization on the Mind of the Enlightenment 3–9 (1994); Dušan I. Bjelić, *Introduction: Blowing Up the "Bridge," in* Balkan as Metaphor 1, 3–6 (Dušan I. Bjelić, I. & Savić Obrad eds., 2005); Maria Todorova, Imagining the Balkans (1997).

7 Peter van Ham, The EC, Eastern Europe and European Unity: Discord, Collaboration and Integration Since 1947, 19, 31–33 (1993).

8 Derrick Bell, *Brown v. Board of Education and the Interest-Convergence Dilemma*, 93 Harv. L. Rev. 518 (1980); Mary L. Dudziak, Cold War Civil Rights (2000); Thomas Borstelmann, The Cold War and the Color Line: American Race Relations in the Global Arena (2001).

the U.S. was countering Soviet influence. Desegregation, in other words, was a foreign policy imperative as much as it was a domestic movement.

To continue laying the groundwork for this book's primary comparison, we begin with an exploration of how Roma fared during Socialism and Communism in CSEE. The panoramic sweep of history is crucial to a proper analysis of the contemporary Roma rights movement. While studies of Roma rights frequently begin with post-Communist EU-driven Roma inclusion (and bemoan its failings), those policies are not without precedent. The legacies of Socialism and Communism can not only explain the position of Roma in CSEE but also illuminate why certain initiatives fail while others succeed.

The history of the EU is just as important. This includes the political and institutional evolution of EU precursors, the values these entities espoused, the competences they claimed, and the powers they wielded: all would eventually shape EU Roma policy. To that end, this Chapter briefly traces the arc of European integration, focusing on events most salient to Roma rights.

In the end, what animates this Chapter is a simple question, carried over from the historical survey of Chapter 1: Why did America and Europe – or, more precisely, the U.S. and the EU – embrace civil rights and Roma rights? More pointedly, given the long-standing exclusion and marginalization of both minority groups, why did the very same political structures that had oppressed both groups for so long suddenly enact policies to bring them into mainstream society?

For these questions, American scholarship on civil rights provides an apt starting point. In 1980, Derrick Bell argued that desegregation was spurred by a convergence of interests among whites and blacks, especially the U.S. government's interests in containing Communism abroad and black radicalism at home.[9] Since that time, interest convergence has progressed from a provocative axiom to well-documented fact. Bell's theory has been vindicated by historians such as Mary Dudziak and Thomas Borstelmann, who documented the ties between Civil Rights and the Cold War.[10] In applying the theory to Roma rights in post-Communist CSEE, we have to examine two sets of convergences. The first is the convergence of Romani interests and the interests of national governments. Because the EU was a driver of Roma inclusion, we also have to look at a second set of interest convergences: interests of the EU and national governments.

This Chapter therefore compares civil rights with Roma rights in the early post-Communist years as well, when Europe was barreling toward integration under the EU. The Chapter trains its focus on the motivations behind the federal and supranational governments' endorsement of the Rights movements.

[9] *See* Bell, *supra* note 8.

[10] *See* Dudziak, *supra* note 8; Borstelmann, *supra* note 8.

Admittedly, the interest convergence hypothesis cannot fully explain Civil Rights or Roma rights. Interest convergence was formulated primarily to explicate the 1954 U.S. Supreme Court decision *Brown v. Board of Education*. Bell postulated that the Court sided with African Americans to enable the federal government to pursue its foreign policy goals. However, vociferous as was international condemnation of segregation, historically international sentiments have not been sufficient to change American practices.[11] Further, even before *Brown*, African Americans had been winning battles against segregation in Southern localities, and American presidents had desegregated the armed forces and banned discrimination in the defense sector.[12] Thus, American historians have argued that Civil Rights began not in the 1950s or 1960s but much earlier – during World War II or even with the antilynching campaigns of the 1920s.[13]

For our purposes, interest convergence operates as a starting point to explore the impetus of post-Communist Roma rights. The theory not only interrogates the entrenched narratives of rights movements, it also brings a host of associated viewpoints that broaden our perspectives on Roma rights. The conclusion of this Chapter attempts to do just that. It reexamines Socialism and Communism as a formative period for the Roma rights movement and ends by pondering whether one particular lesson from the scholarship on *Brown* might illuminate the Roma rights setting, specifically, that the massive resistance to school desegregation "shocked the conscience" of the nation and its lawmakers into passing civil rights laws elsewhere.[14]

SOCIALISM AND COMMUNISM

Like the rest of society, Roma experienced extraordinary transformations under Socialism and Communism. In the Eastern bloc, governments exalted the working classes but suppressed ethnic, social, and cultural affinities.[15] Consequently, they tended to deal with Roma tangentially rather than head-on, through economic reforms designed to upend the long-standing economic order for the entire society. Having languished on the lowest rungs of the prior economies, Roma benefitted by default from these reforms. One particularly important advance was that they gained employment at greater levels than ever before or since.[16] While Socialism and Communism channeled Roma into unskilled work such as low-level construction,

11 Justin Driver, *Rethinking the Interest-Convergence Thesis*, 105 Nw. U. L. Rev. 149, 170 (2011).

12 Michael J. Klarman, *How* Brown *Changed Race Relations: The Backlash Thesis*, 81 J. Am. Hist. 81, 89 (1994).

13 *See* Megan Ming Francis, Civil Rights and the Making of Modern American State (2014).

14 Michael J. Klarman, *Unfinished Business: Racial Equality in American History*, 93 Va. L. Rev. in Brief 249, 253 (2008); Klarman, *supra* note 12, at 81–82, 87.

15 *See* Peter Vermeersch, The Romani Movement: Minority Politics and Ethnic Mobilization in Contemporary Central Europe 49 (2006).

16 *See, e.g.*, Iulius Rostas et al., *Interview with Rumyan Russinov from Bulgaria, in* Ten Years After: A History of Roma School Desegregation in Central and Eastern Europe 131, 132 (Iulius Rostas ed., 2012) [hereinafter Ten Years After]; Viorel Achim, The Roma in Romanian History 190–91

street sweeping, and seasonal farm work, the mass employment of such a historically marginalized group was a notable achievement.[17] Another accomplishment was the integration of Romani students into the education system. Because schooling was compulsory, teachers and administrators actively pushed Romani children to attend schools – another departure from the past.[18] Segregation did exist in some settings (e.g., funneling Romani students into vocational schools, schools for disabled children, and predominantly Romani schools built in Romani residential districts),[19] yet the sheer scale of Romani students being incorporated into the education system for the first time enabled the state to confront pervasive problems such as illiteracy.[20]

During Socialism and Communism, ethnic identity took a back seat to socio-economic class. Accordingly, ethnic and racial problems – or problems that inhered in particular ethnic or racial groups – were often not addressed as such. If poverty correlated closely with an ethnic group, many governments tackled this correlation indirectly, through general poverty alleviation policies rather than policies targeted at the particular ethnic group.[21] One exception to this general rule was any population classified as a "nation" or "people" (i.e., the pan-Slavic *narod*), meaning a people with roots in a particular land. Minorities with kin states (e.g., Hungarians in Romania, Romanians in Hungary, and Germans in Romania and the Czech Republic) automatically fell under the nationalities model, as did minorities bound to another land that was not necessarily a kin state (e.g., Ruthenians, or Rusyns, who came from the Baltic states).[22] Thus classified, "nations" typically enjoyed political and economic representation. The Roma, who were not seen as having ties to any territory, did not fit the nationalities mold but were instead categorized as a "nation" or "small people" (e.g., the Yugoslav *nacije*) or, worse, were not designated as a distinct ethnic group.[23] Consequently, national constitutions did not identify Roma as a national

(Richard Davies trans., 2004) (1998); ZOLTAN BARANY, THE EAST EUROPEAN GYPSIES: REGIME CHANGE, MARGINALITY, AND ETHNOPOLITICS 139 (2002).

17 BARANY, *supra* note 16, at 138–39; ACHIM, *supra* note 16, at 192–93.

18 BARANY, *supra* note 16, at 132; Iulius Rostas et al., *Interview with Costel Bercus from Romania, in* TEN YEARS AFTER, *supra* note 16, at 267, 268

19 *See, e.g.*, Iulius Rostas et al., *Interview with Ivan Vesely from the Czech Republic, in* TEN YEARS AFTER, *supra* note 16, at 165, 165; Gwendolyn Albert, *Education Policies in the Czech Republic, in* TEN YEARS AFTER, *supra* note 16, at 179, 188–89; Krassimir Kanev, *The Politics and Reality of Romani School Desegregation in Bulgaria, in* TEN YEARS AFTER, *supra* note 16, at 145, 146–47.

20 BARANY, *supra* note 16, at 132–33; Albert, *supra* note 19, at 187.

21 Vis-à-vis Roma policy, Marushiakova and Popov categorize this as the "mainstream approach." *See* Marushiakova & Popov, *supra* note 2, at 21.

22 *Narod* and its derivative *narodnost* are pan-Slavic. *Compare, e.g.*, BENJAMIN PINKUS, THE JEWS OF THE SOVIET UNION: THE HISTORY OF A NATIONAL MINORITY 212 (1988) (classification of the Jewish peoples in the Soviet hierarchy), *with* Tone R. Bringa, *Nationality Categories, National Identification and Identity Formation in "Multinational" Bosnia*, 11 ANTHROPOLOGY E. EUR. REV. 80, 87 (1993) (classifications in Bosnia and Yugoslavia).

23 *See, e.g.*, Albert, *supra* note 19, at 188; ACHIM, *supra* note 16, at 190 (Romania).

minority,[24] and state institutions did not commit resources to advocating for them.[25] For most CSEE states, it took until the post-Communist transition for Roma to be mentioned alongside other ethnicities in national constitutions and, consequently, to be granted constitutional rights.[26] Given the long-standing ties of Roma to the land, their omission from national constitutions was a glaring oversight.

Hence, the great irony of Socialism and Communism is not that Roma made great strides during this period and lost ground during the post-Communist transition,[27] but that they made such great strides despite the general neglect by Socialist and Communist regimes.[28] For the majority of their five decades in power, these regimes ignored Roma,[29] displaying a remarkable capacity to "conjure away" the most problematic aspects of this neglect.[30] Rather than acknowledge their sizeable Romani populations on census forms, Czechoslovakia forced its Roma to self-identify as one of the recognized nationalities, while Romania absorbed its Roma into the catchall of "other nationalities."[31] Rather than confront the legacy of centuries of anti-Roma exclusion and marginalization that Socialism had inherited, Yugoslavia denied that Roma were plagued by housing shortages, insisting instead that poverty and homelessness simply did not exist in the country.[32].

This is not to say that Roma were never the subject of targeted campaigns. States periodically adopted policies to deal with the "Gypsy problem."[33] According to the few scholars who have painstakingly examined the treatment of Roma under Socialism and Communism, state policies generally fell into a few patterns that varied by degree of specificity and coercion. Elena Marushiakova and Vesselin Popov, for example, divide states into two camps: those that tried to resolve the Romani predicament through facially neutral socioeconomic reforms (Albania, East German, the Soviet Union, and Yugoslavia) and those that devised programs tailored to Roma (Bulgaria, Czechoslovakia, Hungary, and Romania).[34] By contrast, Zoltan Barany groups Romani policies by extent of intrusiveness, including

24 *See, e.g.*, Barany, *supra* note 16, at 115 (Czechoslovakia and Romania).

25 *See id.* at 114; Achim, *supra* note 16, at 190.

26 *See* Barany, *supra* note 16, at 115. *See also* Iulius Rostas et al., *Interview with Viktória Mohácsi from Hungary*, *in* Ten Years After, *supra* note 16, at 197, 199; Albert, *supra* note 19, at 189.

27 *See, e.g.*, Kálmán Mizsei, *Reconstructing Roma Integration in Central and Eastern Europe: Addressing the Failures of the Last Quarter Century*, *in* Realizing Roma Rights 127, 127 (Jacqueline Bhabha et al. eds., 2017).

28 *See* Achim, *supra* note 16, at 190.

29 *Id.*; Barany, *supra* note 16, at 114.

30 Achim, *supra* note 16, at 190.

31 Barany, *supra* note 16, at 115.

32 *See* Zlata Vuksanović-Macura & Vladimir Macura, Stanovanje i Naselja Roma u Jugoistočnoj Evropi: Prokaz Stanja i Napretka u Srbiji (2006).

33 Barany, *supra* note 16, at 113.

34 Marushiakova & Popov, *supra* note 2, at 21.

"consistent coercion" (Bulgaria and Czechoslovakia), "erratic coercion" (Poland and Romania), "decreasing pressures" (Hungary), and "constructive interference" (Yugoslavia).[35] Notable variations in Romani policy therefore distinguished the nations from one another. Even within a state, the approaches could shift from indifference to obsession.[36]

However catalogued, all policies targeting Roma sought to assimilate them. Despite their clear break from the past in most respects, Socialism and Communism pursued assimilationist policies that recycled the same pernicious tropes of prior epochs. Roma were identified principally with vagrancy, peddling, criminality, illiteracy, and squalor. Thus, some states, including Romania, resettled Roma by demolishing their neighborhoods and pushing them into tenements.[37] Resettlement campaigns sometimes came from a desire to root out nomadism and other times were part of a societywide postwar campaign to build housing for the masses. Either way, Roma suffered greatly from the razing of their traditional, close-knit communities. Elsewhere, states tried to outlaw or regulate out of existence trades associated with Roma, such as metalsmithing and begging, directing Roma instead to factory work and construction.[38] These campaigns, too, were motivated by a desire to break the attachment of Roma to traditional trades and crafts. Flaws, loopholes, and unintended consequences afflicted these heavy-handed measures. As a result of housing reforms, Roma were scattered across new neighborhoods and lost their ties to traditional communities.[39] Over the long term, many Roma tried to replicate traditional living by recongregating in makeshift Romani-only settlements farther from cities and towns, exacerbating their marginalization. As a result of employment reforms, Roma were dispossessed of their trades and livelihoods, paid poorly for the unskilled work that they took on, and concentrated on the lowest rungs of the command economy.[40] Majority populations filled the ensuing vacancies, effectively purging trades such as metalsmithing of Roma. Meanwhile, some states resurrected the most offensive practices of imperial and Nazi eras. Czechoslovakia forced Romani women to submit to sterilization,[41] while Bulgaria forced Romani populations to adopt Bulgarian names.[42]

Overall, the record of Socialism and Communism is mixed for Roma. On the one hand, living standards increased dramatically for many Roma due to housing,

35 Barany, *supra* note 16, at 117–23.

36 Achim, *supra* note 16.

37 *Id.* at 196.

38 Barany, *supra* note 16, at 138.

39 Achim, *supra* note 16, *Id.* at 192.

40 *Id.* at 193–95.

41 Center for Reproductive Rights, Body and Soul: Forced Sterilization and Other Assaults on Roma Reproductive Freedom 42 (2003).

42 Bucking scholarly consensus, Mary Neuberger notes that Roma in Bulgaria were also forced to take on Turkish names. *See* Mary Neuburger, The Orient Within: Muslim Minorities and the Negotiation of Nationhood in Modern Bulgaria 154 n.49 (2004).

employment, and other reforms. Integration into the educational system also made it more likely that a cadre of Romani intellectuals would be produced. These intellectuals would emerge as leaders and advocates during the post-Communist transition. Socialism and Communism also primed the flourishing of Romani identity and organization after 1989 by simultaneously denying Roma this expression during Communism and permitting state-sanctioned organizations to form. For all their flaws, these organizations paved the way for others more representative of Romani peoples subsequently to form. Finally, Communism allowed some Roma to exploit the flaws of the command economy as entrepreneurs.[43]

On the other hand, Socialism and Communism also rendered Roma vulnerable to the post-1989 transition. By consolidating Roma in the bloated and inefficient sectors of unskilled labor, states unwittingly put them on the front line for layoffs when privatization came. By driving Roma to resettle in the countryside, states amplified their exclusion and marginalization. And by creating a two-track education system, where Roma were placed in Romani-language schools, majority-Roma schools, or special schools reserved for children with mental and physical disabilities, the state minimized their chances of upward mobility. After the transition, school administrators would double down on the practice of steering Romani students toward special schools whose graduates are only allowed to enter technical secondary schools, thereby foreclosing many employment opportunities.[44]

Whether facially neutral or tailored to Roma, Socialist and Communist policies that benefitted Roma were not in place long enough to truly undo centuries of harm. The benefits were not far-reaching or systematic enough, and the stratagems were wholly dependent on the state. Thus, when the state receded as the focal point of society, Roma were bereft of their most powerful patron. Worse, an impression had been created that Roma were the primary beneficiaries of Communist reforms, which set the stage for resentment when majority populations themselves were unmoored after the fall of Communism.

EUROPEAN INTEGRATION

While Central and Eastern Europe lived under Socialism and Communism, Western Europe was experimenting with transnational political and economic integration. After World War II, six countries – Belgium, France, Germany, Italy, Luxembourg, and the Netherlands – founded the European Coal and Steel Community (ECSC), which centralized the production of coal and steel and created a common market for these products. The ECSC was the first supranational European authority to have the power to bind its members, which were sovereign

43 *See* ISABEL FONSECA, BURY ME STANDING 153 (1995).

44 *See* D.H. and Others v. Czech Republic, App. No. 57825/00, 47 Eur. H.R. Rep. 59, para. 25 (2007).

states.[45] The ECSC was an also an important mechanism to prevent war among European states, as they collectively controlled and shared the markets for coal and steel – products necessary for war. This impetus led to the creation of two other international organizations, the European Economic Community (EEC) and the European Atomic Energy Community (EURATOM), under the 1957 Treaty of Rome. Collectively known as the "European Communities" (EC), the ECSC, EEC, and EURATOM worked to establish a common economic market by progressively removing tariffs and trade barriers, harmonizing monetary policies, and facilitating the free movement of capital, goods, and workers.[46]

From then on, European integration would "deepen" by centralizing the EC's power, while also "widening" or expanding membership to other countries. Thus, in 1965, the Merger Treaty, or Brussels Treaty, combined the commissions and councils of all three communities into the Commission and Council of the EEC. Meanwhile, the EC expanded its membership over several rounds of enlargement to other countries: Denmark, Ireland, and the United Kingdom in 1973 (the first enlargement), Greece in 1981 (the second enlargement), Portugal and Spain in 1986 (the third enlargement), and Austria, Finland, and Sweden in 1995 (the fourth enlargement). Between the accession of Greece and the accessions of Portugal and Spain, often collectively called the "Mediterranean" or "Southern" enlargements, the EC adopted the Single European Act (SEA) in 1985. Among other reforms, the SEA enhanced the legislative power of the European Parliament, propelled the EC toward a single internal market, and added new competences to the EC.[47] In other words, the SEA allowed the EC to take on greater political powers, in addition to its economic powers.

The SEA and the Mediterranean enlargements reflect how the EC's intensifying push for integration in the 1980s collided with its intensifying heterogeneity. Greece, Portugal, and Spain were all fledgling democracies with less industrialized economies when they negotiated for accession to the EC. Given the premium that the EC placed on democracy and market economies for candidacy, the pre-accession process for these newcomers was protracted.[48] Portugal and Spain faced the challenge of having to meet the requirements of bilateral accession

45 Paul Craig & Gráinne de Búrca, EU Law: Text, Cases, and Materials 5 (5th ed. 2011). The ECSC was "the first significant step towards European integration going beyond intergovernmentalism," *id.*, the theory from political science that states, pursuing their own interests, drive the integration process, *id.* at 2–3. Intergovernmentalism is closely associated with realism, which posits that international institutions will have limited powers, due to the balance of power among sovereign states. *See* Francesca Bignami, *Creating European Rights: National Values and Supranational Interests*, 11 Colum. J. Eur. L. 241, 254–55 (2005).

46 Craig & de Búrca, *supra* note 45, at 6.

47 Craig & de Búrca, *supra* note 45, at 11–12.

48 Dimitry Kochenov, EU Enlargement and the Failure of Conditionality: Pre-accession Conditionality in the Fields of Democracy and the Rule of Law 30–31 (2007). *See also* Christopher Preston, Enlargement and Integration in the European Union 46–55, 62–63, 69–73 (1997).

treaties, which governed the terms of their accession and imposed specific demands for economic liberalization. At the same time, Portugal and Spain had to conform to the demands of the SEA just as quickly as existing EC members did.[49] To soften the impact and facilitate economic cohesion, the SEA allowed the EC to offer sizeable financial support to the newcomers in the form of Structural Funds.[50]

Up to this point, the EC had managed to avoid the politics of minority policies, and certainly Roma inclusion. Instead, the early mover on minority rights was the Council of Europe (COE), a larger and looser international organization headquartered in Strasbourg that aims to promote democracy, human rights, and the rule of law.[51] In 1969, the Parliamentary Assembly of the COE adopted Recommendation 563, which encouraged member states to stop discrimination against "Gypsies and other travellers" and create national bodies advocating for them.[52] For the most part, however, European organizations engaged with minority rights through international human rights law. Consequently, minority rights were framed more as individual rights – since human rights inhere in a person by virtue of being human – than collective rights.[53] Here, the COE's most prominent achievement was the passage in 1950 of the European Convention on Human Rights (ECHR), which established the European Court of Human Rights. Predictably, incorporation of the ECHR into EC law was rejected by a veto from France in 1954, perhaps out of fidelity to the concept of republicanism.

Despite the primacy that the EC placed on economic integration, the European Court of Justice (CJEU), the Community's highest court, recognized early on that human rights occupied a central place in the European legal order. In 1969, the CJEU acknowledged that EC law protected fundamental rights.[54] Subsequently, the Court affirmed that fundamental rights are enshrined in the general principles of Community law.[55] Significantly, the development of the CJEU's human rights jurisprudence coincided with the Court's "bold moves" to uphold the supremacy of Community law in the face of conflict with national

49 Santiago Delgado Fernández et al., *Portugal and Spain in the Process of European Integration, in* Iberian Elites and the EU: Perceptions Towards the European Integration Process in Political and Socioeconomic Elites in Portugal and Spain 38, 44 (Miguel Jerez-Mir et al. eds., 2015); Preston, *supra* note 48, at 140–41.

50 *See* Eleni Panagiotarea, Greece in the Euro: Economic Delinquency or System Failure? 44 (2013).

51 On the relationship between the EU and the COE, see Tony Joris & Jan Vendenberghe, *The Council of Europe and the European Union: Natural Partners or Uneasy Bedfellows?*, 15 Colum. J. Eur. L. 1 (2008/2009).

52 Jean-Pierre Liégeois, The Council of Europe and Roma: 40 Years of Action 33–34 (2012).

53 Tove Molloy, National Minority Rights in Europe 5 (2005). One exception to the contrary is the Framework Convention on the Protection of National Minorities (FCNM), adopted by the COE in 1995.

54 Case 29/69, Stauder v. City of Ulm, 1969 E.C.R. 419.

55 Case 11/70, Internationale Handelsgesellschaft, 970 E.C.R. 1125; Case 4/73, Nold v. Commission, 1974 E.C.R. 491.

law.[56] These moves included the seminal 1963 case *Van Gend en Loos*,[57] which established the doctrine of direct effect – that Community law (including not only the treaties but also regulations and directives) is directly binding on, and can be enforced directly within, the member states – as well as the 1964 case *Costa v. ENEL*,[58] which established the doctrine that Community law enjoys supremacy over national law. The CJEU's fundamental rights jurisprudence assured member states that Community law would remain faithful to the human rights principles in their national constitutions, so as not to be trampled on by supremacy and direct effects. Through these developments, the EC began to look more and more like a constitutional system, a "vertically integrated legal regime conferring judicially enforceable rights and obligations on all legal persons and entities, public and private, within EC territory."[59]

European integration reached its next milestone with the Maastricht Treaty in 1992, which established the Treaty on the European Union (TEU). It was the TEU that created the European Union. By the TEU's design, the EU comprised three "pillars": one dealing with economic, social, and environmental matters (the Communities); another dealing with foreign policy and military matters; and a third dealing with justice, crime, asylum, and immigration matters.[60] The TEU also instituted a single currency, expanded Community competences, and introduced the principle of subsidiarity, which delineated Community and national powers.[61] Finally, for our purposes, the TEU established the notion of EU citizenship and etched human rights into a treaty obligation binding on member states.[62] In doing so, the Maastricht Treaty implied that EU citizens were bound by more than the economic interests of their nations: citizens shared a culture, which paved the way for inserting pluralism and respect for minority protections as European values.

For the next twelve years, the EU would attempt to draft a European constitution through additional treaties and intergovernmental conferences, only some of which were successful. In 1997, the Amsterdam Treaty amended the TEU to proclaim that the Union was founded on the principles of liberty, democracy, respect for human

56 J.H.H. Weiler, *The Transformation of Europe*, 100 YALE L.J. 2403, 2417 (1991). *See also* J.H.H. Weiler, *Eurocracy and Distrust: Some Questions Concerning the Role of the European Court of Justice in the Protection of Fundamental Human Rights Within the Legal Order of the European Communities*, 61 WASH. L. REV. 1103 (1986).

57 Case 26/62, Van Gend en Loos v. Nederlandse Administratie der Belastingen, 1963 E.C.R. 1.

58 Case 6/64, Flaminio Costa v. ENEL, 1964 E.C.R. 585.

59 Alec Stone Sweet, *Constitutional Dialogues in the European Community*, *in* THE EUROPEAN COURT AND NATIONAL COURTS – DOCTRINE AND JURISPRUDENCE: LEGAL CHANGE IN ITS SOCIAL CONTEXT 305 (Anne-Marie Slaughter et al. eds., 1998).

60 CRAIG & DE BÚRCA, *supra* note 45, at 13–15.

61 *Id.* at 14–15.

62 *See* Treaty on European Union (Maastricht text), July 29, 1992, art. F, 1992 O.J. C 191/1, 5 ("The Union shall respect fundamental rights, as guaranteed by the European Convention for the Protection of Human Rights and Fundamental Freedoms signed in Rome on 4 November 1950 and as they result from the constitutional traditions common to the Member States, as general principles of Community law.").

rights and fundamental freedoms, and the rule of law;[63] that respect for these principles was a condition for EU membership;[64] and that if a member were to be found in serious and persistent breach of those principles its treaty rights could be suspended.[65] Overall, however, the reforms of the Amsterdam Treaty were modest: they failed to tackle the institutional and legitimacy issues that needed to be resolved before the next round of enlargement. To that end, the Nice Treaty of 2001 adopted some governance reforms and, more ambitiously, the Laeken Declaration on the Future of the EU in 2001 set the stage for drafting an EU constitution. Yet the product of that effort, the Constitutional Treaty of 2004, would never be fully ratified after its rejection by popular referenda in France and the Netherlands.[66]

Nonetheless, all the successful treaties would form the backbone of primary EU law, supplemented by regulations, directives, court decisions, and soft law that the Union had amassed and was continuing to develop. All of these sources – some tens of thousands of pages of legal documents – comprised the guiding principles of the EU, commonly known as the *acquis communautaire* (the "acquis").[67]

From 1992 to 2004, as the EU prepared for enlargement into post-Communist Central and Eastern Europe, the acquis entered a period of frenetic expansion following the activity surrounding the attempt at an EU constitution. The sheer scale of expansion was unprecedented. No prior incarnation of the EU had been widened this far, and certainly not while the Union was careening toward integration at this pace. Even the Mediterranean enlargement does not fully compare. By its fifth enlargement, the EU had amassed a body of law in the acquis that dwarfed what had been in place prior to the second and third enlargements, which allowed the EU to be more exacting with the eastern enlargement than the EC had been with the southern enlargement.[68]

The scope of the acquis can be difficult to pin down.[69] At the very least, it encompasses the core principles of Community law.[70] This naturally includes economic and financial laws promoting integration, as well as democracy, the rule of law, and human rights. Regarding minority protections, however, the acquis is murkier.[71] One element of minority protection is the principle of equality and nondiscrimination, a cornerstone of human rights that is well

63 Treaty on European Union, November 10, 1997, art. 6, 1997 O.J. (C 340) 145.

64 *Id.* art. 49.

65 *Id.* art. 7.

66 For a summary, see Craig & de Búrca, *supra* note 45, at 13–24.

67 Kochenov, *supra* note 48, at 43.

68 *Id.* at 298.

69 *Id.* at 43.

70 *See id.* at 41–42. *See generally* Christine Delcourt, *The* Acquis Communautaire: *Has the Concept Had Its Day?*, 38 Common Mkt. L. Rev. 329 (2001).

71 *See* Bruno de Witte, *Politics Versus Law in the EU's Approach to Ethnic Minorities*, *in* Europe Unbound: Enlarging and Reshaping the Boundaries of the European Union 137 (Jan Zielonka ed., 2002).

defined internationally and within the EU, and therefore incorporated into the acquis.[72] In this camp, for instance, is the EU's Race Equality Directive of 2000, which prohibits discrimination on the basis of racial or ethnic origin and was passed when the Union adopted "United in Diversity" as its motto.[73] Because EU directives enjoy supremacy and have direct effects, the Race Equality Directive is automatically transposed into the national laws of EU members and prevails in the event of conflict.[74]

Yet the Race Equality Directive is a prohibition on discrimination, or a negative discrimination right.[75] Another element of minority protection is positive state action, that is, positive discrimination or special protections. These are less clearly defined and may fall outside the scope of the acquis.[76] The closest iteration of special protections for minorities comes not from the EU but from the COE. In 1995, the COE passed the Framework Convention on the Protection of National Minorities (FCNM),[77] which set high-level goals for achieving equality for national minorities in law, cultural expression, language rights, and education while also fostering intercultural communication between minority and majority groups.[78] The FCNM supplemented, and was also made a part of, the accession process during the fifth enlargement. Ratification of the FCNM was a precondition for EU membership despite a lack of universal ratification by West European members.[79]

Ill-defined as minority protections were under the rubric of the acquis, the EU was free to demand more robust minority protections from accession candidates than existing members. This incongruence stems from the greater authority that the EU possesses in external relations than in internal affairs.[80] During the fifth enlargement, for instance, the EU imposed on accession candidates a set of

72 *See* Antje Wiener & Guido Schwellnus, *Contested Norms in the Process of EU Enlargement: Non-discrimination and Minority Rights, in* Law and Governance in an Enlarged European Union 451, 457–59 (George A. Bermann & Katharina Pistor eds., 2004).

73 Council Directive 2000/43/EC.

74 *See* Craig & de Búrca, *supra* note 45, at 191–94.

75 Wiener & Schwellnus, *supra* note 72, at 461.

76 *See id.* at 458–60.

77 Currently, the FCNM applies to thirty-nine ratifying states. *FCNM Factsheet,* Council of Europe, http://www.coe.int/en/web/minorities/fcnm-factsheet (last accessed Apr. 16, 2019).

78 The FCNM covers all national minorities, not just Roma. Notably, "national minorities" is not defined in the FCNM. *See FCNM Factsheet, supra* note 77. Article 3(2) provides that national minorities "may exercise the rights and enjoy the freedoms flowing from the principles enshrined in the present framework Convention individually as well as in community with others." In its interpretation of Article 3(2), however, the COE restricts this "collective dimension" to the right to use a minority language. *See* Council of Europe, *Framework Convention for the Protection of National Minorities and Explanatory Report*, para. 31 (1995) ("no collective rights of national minorities are envisaged").

79 Most notably, France. *See State Parties to the Framework Convention for the Protection of National Minorities,* Council of Europe, https://www.coe.int/en/web/minorities/etats-partie (last accessed Apr. 16, 2019).

80 Kochenov, *supra* note 48, at 82.

conditions called the "Copenhagen criteria."[81] Overall, this pre-accession process of negotiation and monitoring was known as "conditionality," that is, conditioning accession on the fulfillment of certain goals.

The Copenhagen criteria included a set of political conditions that required the "stability of institutions guaranteeing democracy, the rule of law, human rights and *respect for and protection of minorities*,"[82] which became the fulcrum of Roma inclusion. Like other political conditions, minority protections were covered in the accession partnerships, treaties that spelled out the priority areas for each candidate country.[83] The accession partnerships were supplemented by annual reports compiled by the European Commission (the "Commission") on each candidate country's progress toward accession goals; these reports constitute the EU's compliance mechanism for the Copenhagen criteria.[84] Here, Roma inclusion, or, more accurately, its inadequacy, was featured prominently.

CONVERGENCES OF INTERESTS IN CIVIL RIGHTS AND ROMA RIGHTS

We now come to the comparison at the heart of this book: civil rights and Roma rights, or, more specifically, the post-Socialist and post-Communist EU initiatives for Roma inclusion. Given the history of racialized exclusion of African Americans and Roma, why did the U.S. and the EU buy into civil rights and Roma rights? Answering this question can generate insights into the limitations of both movements.

On the impetus behind civil rights and Roma rights, we can begin with Derrick Bell's interest-convergence hypothesis, an iconic but controversial product of critical race theory. Clear-eyed and accessible, interest convergence holds that the dominant majority does not sign onto the fight for minority rights unless doing so furthers the majority's interests, that is, unless the interests of majority and minority converge.[85] Yet interest convergence also eviscerates dearly held myths.[86] It challenges schoolbook accounts of civil rights by contending that milestones such as *Brown v. Board of Education* arose from the self-interests of whites, especially political elites waging the

81 *See* Presidency Conclusions, Copenhagen European Council (June 21–22, 1993) [hereinafter Copenhagen European Council].

82 *Id.* at 13 (emphasis added). *See also Accession Criteria (Copenhagen Criteria)*, Eur-Lex, http://eur-lex.europa.eu/summary/glossary/accession_criteria_copenhague.html (last accessed Mar. 7, 2018).

83 European Comm'n, *Accession Partnership*, http://ec.europa.eu/enlargement/policy/glossary/terms/accession-partnership_en.htm (last accessed Mar. 7, 2018).

84 *See* European Comm'n, *European Neighbourhood Policy and Enlargement Negotiations*, https://ec.europa.eu/neighbourhood-enlargement/countries/package_en (search under "Previous Documents") (last accessed Mar. 7, 2018).

85 *See* Bell, *supra* note 8.

86 *See* Driver, *supra* note 11, at 157 (noting that, despite its flaws, "the theory nevertheless serves as a valuable corrective to the narrative of unambiguous triumph that plagues a disconcertingly large portion of scholarship regarding racial considerations in constitutional law").

Cold War.[87] In analyzing *Brown*, Bell therefore looks beyond the confines of the Fourteenth Amendment, from which the antidiscrimination principle emanates; because a century of segregated education had been legitimized by the Supreme Court under the separate but equal doctrine, the Court's about-face must have been rooted in exogenous interests rather than law.[88] In Bell's account, the interests behind *Brown* were fighting Communism, mollifying African Americans, and catalyzing the industrialization of the agrarian South.[89]

Applied to Roma inclusion, interest convergence upends the conventional narrative of the Copenhagen criteria's minority protections as part of a march toward democratic principles and fundamental human rights.[90] In fact, the historical setting of conditionality belies this gloss. During the mid-1990s, the EU's preparations for enlargement into CSEE coincided with the violent breakup of the Socialist Federal Republic of Yugoslavia. The ensuing wars in Europe's backyard and the outward flow of refugees raised both the profile and stakes of ethnic conflict. Consequently, the EU called on the post-Socialist and post-Communist accession candidates, all of which had sizeable minority populations, to improve their minority policies.

Corroboration of the Yugoslavia hypothesis of minority rights – that the Balkan wars shaped Europe's approach to minority rights – can be found in legal instruments of the time. In 1993, during the adoption of the FCNM, the COE worked on a protocol to the ECHR that detailed the protection of minorities. The ensuing Recommendation 1201 would have recognized affirmative collective rights of national minorities, going further than the FCNM in sanctioning positive discrimination.[91] Yet the recommendation was rejected. Fears of secession effectively confined the struggle for minority rights to negative discrimination and language rights, even though the understanding of the structural challenges faced by minorities had become more sophisticated in the fifty years since the adoption of the first human rights instruments.

CSEE's Roma, however, were in no danger of seceding. In the early and mid-1990s, Roma were not subjects of concern for the EU or the COE,[92] which were preoccupied with violent interethnic conflicts that had the potential to overrun borders or catalyze

87 *See* Bell, *supra* note 8, at 524 ("[*Brown*] helped to provide immediate credibility to America's struggle with Communist countries to win the hearts and minds of emerging third world peoples."); Mary L. Dudziak, *Desegregation as a Cold War Imperative*, 41 STAN. L. REV. 61, 64 (1988); BORSTELMANN, *supra* note 8, at 7.

88 Bell, *supra* note 8, at 523–24.

89 *Id.* at 524–25.

90 *See* Copenhagen European Council, *supra* note 81.

91 *See* Eur. Parl. Ass., *Additional Protocol on the Rights of Minorities to the European Convention on Human Rights*, 22d Sess., Doc. No. 6742, para. 25 (1993) ("Nothing in this protocol may be construed as limiting or restricting an individual right of persons belonging to a national minority or a collective right of a national minority embodied in the legislation of the contracting state or in an international agreement to which that state is a party.").

92 *See* VERMEERSCH, *supra* note 15, at 196.

secession.[93] Anti-Roma discrimination simply did not fit that model. The Commission's first set of monitoring reports, which came out in 1998, did not devote much space to the Roma issue.[94] The next year, however, the Commission pivoted to address major influxes of Roma refugees into Western Europe and Canada. The treatment of Roma by both CSEE governments and disaffected citizens had escalated to unbearable levels. Incidents such as the burning of Roma homes by vigilantes in Romania in 1993 were becoming more common, often with state complicity.[95] More brazenly, in 1999, the Czech city of Ústí nad Labem began construction of a wall around buildings inhabited primarily by Roma.[96] The move to wall off Roma neighborhoods has been replicated in Slovakia and Romania, despite its association with the Berlin Wall.[97] As persecution intensified in the late 1990s, Roma began fleeing to Western Europe and North America.[98]

Alarm over Roma refugee influxes spilled over into the accession process. One by one, the Commission's monitoring reports began to take note of the exodus.[99] As Western Europe and Canada tightened immigration policies, the CSEE candidate countries were enlisted to stem the tide by integrating their Roma populations in order to address the root causes of their westward flight.[100] CSEE therefore became a buffer. In one controversial example, British officials stationed at Prague's airport

93 Peter Vermeersch & Melanie H. Ram, *The Roma*, *in* Minority Rights in Central and Eastern Europe 61, 68 (Bernd Rechel ed., 2009).

94 This is not to say that the plight of Roma was wholly ignored. *See, e.g.*, European Comm'n, *Hungary: Accession Partnership* (1997); European Comm'n, Regular Report from the Commission on Slovakia's Progress toward Accession (1998). Ironically, in Slovakia's monitoring report, the Commission even noted that ill-treatment of Roma in Slovakia justified the decisions of British authorities to grant refugee status to Slovakian Roma applicants.

95 *See* Doug Merlino, *Roma v. Romania*, Legal Aff., Mar./Apr. 2006. During the incident, two Roma were beaten to death, allegedly under the watch of the local police commander and his officers. It took four years for the prosecutor to file charges, another year for the local court to deliver criminal convictions, and one more year for the Romanian Supreme Court to acquit two of the defendants and reduce the charges for the remaining three.

96 *See* Vermeersch, *supra* note 15, at 140–42.

97 *See, e.g.*, Dan Bifelsky, *Walls, Real and Imagined, Surround Roma*, N.Y. Times, Apr. 2, 2010.

98 Vermeersch, *supra* note 15, at 138–40. *See also* Sean Rehaag et al., *No Refuge: Hungarian Romani Refugee Claimants in Canada*, 52 Osgoode Hall L.J. 705 (2015).

99 *See*, e.g., European Comm'n, Regular Report from the Commission on Slovakia's Progress toward Accession 17 (1999) (citing the rejection by Finland of Romani migrants from Slovakia); European Comm'n, Regular Report on Slovakia's Progress toward Accession 21 (2000) ("The outflow of Slovaks of Roma origin to a number of EU countries has continued and outflows to the Czech Republic have equally been detected. This has resulted in the imposition of visa requirements in certain cases."). *See also* European Comm'n, The Situation of Roma in an Enlarged European Union 15 (2004) ("[an] impetus for addressing the situation of Roma in Central and Eastern Europe was the flight of Roma to Western Europe to claim asylum from persecution").

100 *See* Belinda Cooper, *"We Have No Martin Luther King": Eastern Europe's Roma Minority*, 20 World Pol'y J. 69, 73 (2001/2002). *See also* Wiener & Schwellnus, *supra* note 72, at 32 (characterizing the shift of European minority policy from focusing on national minorities with kin states to Roma as part of the EU's "security agenda").

no less were reportedly turning away Roma who had bought airline tickets to the UK.[101]

Thus, a momentary confluence of interests brought otherwise indifferent elites to the Roma's side. For the EU, it was the fear that if candidate countries were admitted without improving the lives of their most vulnerable minorities, then a vast underclass would enjoy free movement and take advantage of "benefit tourism" across Europe under the Schengen regime.[102] The motivation of CSEE governments to integrate their Roma lay in joining the EU. And so, these governments could adopt the political conditions of membership, and even ratify the FCNM, while holding off meaningful implementation of the very same conditions. These interests were aligned only briefly, during accession negotiations; as soon as the candidates became members, the force of conditionality dissipated.

Due to the fragility of aligned interests, Roma inclusion suffers from charges of hypocrisy. The high-minded language of political conditionality almost invites this. Slovakia, for example, deflected criticism over anti-Roma discrimination by pointing out that the EU members themselves had not all ratified the FCNM.[103] Indeed, the minority policies of Western Europe signaled to candidate countries that the EU could be flexible about its political conditions.[104]

The charge of hypocrisy is not unique to the EU. Across the Atlantic and half a century earlier, the same charge was leveled at the U.S. during the Cold War, by both its nemeses abroad and detractors at home.[105] The year after the Supreme Court handed down the second *Brown v. Board of Education* decision (*Brown II*), an alliance of Southern representatives and senators drafted a response that would be introduced in 1956 as the Declaration of Constitutional Principles.[106] The drafters of the Southern Manifesto, as it came to be known, delighted in noting that the "separate but equal" doctrine of *Plessy v. Ferguson* originated not in the South but in the North.[107] For its part, the federal government sat mostly on the sidelines throughout the 1950s, passing civil rights legislation in the 1960s only after massive,

101 *British Officials Continue Policy of Stopping Roma at Czech Airport; Czech Roma and ERRC Sue U. K. Government*, European Roma Rights Centre (Nov. 7, 2001), http://www.errc.org/article/british-officials-continue-policy-of-stopping-roma-at-czech-airport%3B-czech-roma-and-errc-sue-uk-government/1289 [https://perma.cc/YHL2-3UUM].

102 *See Schengen Area*, European Comm'n (2018), http://ec.europa.eu/home-affairs/what-we-do/policies/borders-and-visas/schengen_en (last accessed Apr. 17, 2019).

103 *See* Vermeersch, *supra* note 15, at 199.

104 Gwendolyn Sasse, *The Politics of EU Conditionality: The Norm of Minority Protection During and Beyond EU Accession*, 15 J. Eur. Pub. Pol'y 842 (2008). More recent examples include France's deportation of Roma "back" to Romania and Bulgaria.

105 For an example of a critique of American racism in Soviet films, see Circus [Цирк] (Mosfilm Studios 1936).

106 Brown v. Bd. of Educ. of Topeka, 349 U.S. 294 (1955); 102 Cong. Rec. 4459–61 (1956) (statement of Sen. Walter George). *See also* Justin Driver, *Supremacies and the Southern Manifesto*, 92 Tex. L. Rev. 1053 (2014).

107 *See* Driver, *supra* note 106, at 1064.

violent resistance to school integration had shocked Northern lawmakers into action.[108]

One limitation of interest convergence is that the framework can quickly descend into a hunt for hypocrisy, which erodes the framework's usefulness. Interest convergence may simply view human nature too cynically; sometimes noble values do animate decision-making.[109] At the very least, mixed motives may have compelled white elites to embrace civil rights. Some of those motives may even have been altruistic, but their predominance over naked self-interest is impossible to quantify. Interest convergence also fails to credit the struggles of activists, protestors, and civil society.

A related quandary that plagues interest convergence is the extent to which civil rights were spurred by anti-Communist concerns as opposed to domestic pressures, which is also impossible to ascertain.[110] If, consequently, scholars have overplayed the importance of external factors such as the Cold War to the Civil Rights movement, then the buffer hypothesis also cannot fully capture the EU's motivations for Roma inclusion or fully explain the EU's failures in realizing inclusion. As subsequent Chapters explain, the EU attempted to inculcate "European" values of democracy and fundamental rights throughout the course of post-Communist integration. Minority protections were not solely a utilitarian calculus to keep migrants at bay; they espoused broader aspirations built into conditionality, aspirations of an idealized Europe.[111] For all its ethereal aspirations, conditionality did score victories. As a result of the accession process, some countries managed to incorporate aspects of the EU political conditions into national law and culture.[112]

108 Michael J. Klarman, From Jim Crow to Civil Rights: The Supreme Court and the Struggle for Racial Equality 324–25 (2004); Derrick Bell, Silent Covenants: *Brown v. Board of Education* and the Unfulfilled Hopes for Racial Reform 7 (2004). More recently, scholars have tackled the thorny entanglement with slavery of the North's most prized educational institutions. *See, e.g.*, Craig Steven Wilder, Ebony and Ivy Race, Slavery and the Troubled History of America's Universities (2013); Gillian B. White, *How Money from Slave Trading Helped Start Columbia University*, Atlantic, Jan. 25, 2017.

109 *See* Driver, *supra* note 11, at 169. One retort to interest convergence is that individuals are not always rational utility maximizers – they can sacrifice their own interests for the good of the group. The response is that members of a group might sacrifice their material well-being in exchange for the elevation of social stature when the intragroup bonds are reinforced. This literature is particularly well developed in the back-and-forth between the Chicago economist Gary Becker and his critics. *See, e.g.*, Gary S. Becker, The Economics of Discrimination (2d ed. 1971); Richard H. McAdams, *The Origin, Development, and Regulation of Norms*, 96 Mich. L. Rev. 338 (1997); Daria Roithmayr, *Racial Cartels*, 16 Mich. J. Race & L. 45 (2010).

110 *See* Curtis A. Bradley, *Foreign Affairs and Domestic Reform*, 87 Va. L. Rev. 1475, 1476 (2001).

111 *See* Sasse, *supra* note 104; Monica Sassatelli, Becoming Europeans: Cultural Identities and Cultural Policies 1 (2009).

112 Ulrich Sedelmeier, *After Conditionality: Post-Accession Compliance with EU Law in East Central Europe*, 15 J. Eur. Pub. Pol'y 806 (2008); Judith G. Kelley, Ethnic Politics in Europe. The Power of Norms and Incentives (2004).

COROLLARIES OF INTEREST CONVERGENCE

Interest convergence can only be a starting point for our comparative analysis. The hypothesis is beset by empirical uncertainties over the degree to which self-interest and external concerns drove policy, as well as the efficacy of conditionality if the convergence of EU, national, and Romani interests was ephemeral. Further, there are questions about the duration of interest convergence, for conditionality can linger after EU accession. For instance, despite gaining membership in the sixth and seventh rounds of enlargement, Bulgaria, Croatia, and Romania have yet to formally enter the Schengen area because they have not met all the benchmarks.[113] In some respects, the pressures of conditionality, and therefore the convergences of interest, have not fully dissipated.

Beyond these empirical questions, interest convergence can inspire further conversations that enhance our understanding of Roma rights. One implication of interest convergence is the power of civil society to drive minority rights. After all, there must be some group for political elites to converge with. If civil society is strong, then it can act as a bulwark against minority rights retrenchment. It was a grassroots push in the U.S. that spurred civil rights legislation. Analyzing civil rights exclusively from the standpoints of legislation and litigation only feeds into the "great man" narrative of history, which views the movement as a product of visionary lawmakers and courageous lawyers.[114] Contrary to this top-down narrative, grassroots participation was pivotal not only in the advocacy and local enforcement of desegregation cases, but also in the orchestration of reactionary violence that shocked the popular conscience into action.[115]

For both civil rights and Roma inclusion, civil society often came to embody the priorities of minority populations, regardless of whether they truly reflected local preferences.[116] Yet the coalescence of Romani civil society faces formidable obstacles. The fracturing of the Romani community due to weak ethnic identity, infighting, and poor leadership is compounded by throngs of NGOs claiming to represent Roma interests.[117] Hundreds of Roma rights NGOs are scattered across CSEE; many of them merely entrench a narrow group of elites who specialize in procuring EU

113 Jon Stone, *EU President Invites Bulgaria and Romania to Join Borderless Schengen Area "Immediately,"* INDEPENDENT (Sept. 13, 2017), http://www.independent.co.uk/news/world/europe/eu-brexit-bulgaria-romania-schengen-area-immigration-passportless-jean-claude-juncker-president-a7944196.html.

114 Tomiko Brown-Nagin, *The Impact of Lawyer-Client Disengagement on the NAACP's Campaign to Implement* Brown v. Board of Education *in Atlanta, in* FROM THE GRASSROOTS TO THE SUPREME COURT: *BROWN V. BOARD OF EDUCATION* AND AMERICAN DEMOCRACY 227, 227 (Peter F. Lau ed., 2004).

115 Samuel Issacharoff & Pamela S. Karlan, *Groups, Politics, and the Equal Protection Clause*, 58 U. MIAMI L. REV. 35, 37–38 (2003).

116 TOMIKO NAGIN-BROWN, COURAGE TO DISSENT: ATLANTA AND THE LONG HISTORY OF THE CIVIL RIGHTS MOVEMENT 7–10 (2011); AIDAN MCGARRY, WHO SPEAKS FOR ROMA?: POLITICAL REPRESENTATION OF A TRANSNATIONAL MINORITY COMMUNITY 122–27 (2010).

117 MCGARRY, *supra* note 116, at 104.

grants.[118] While this challenge of authenticity for civil society is not unique, Roma are a transnational group; their advocacy groups must traverse national borders to concentrate political power while staying true to local concerns.

Another question inspired by interest convergence is how far back we should go to unearth the roots of the Roma rights movement. In the literature on civil rights, *Brown* initially elicited strong commentary over its sweeping rhetoric and, afterward, its effectiveness. Most prominently, Herbert Wechsler, a progressive voice, dismantled each of the legal arguments mustered by the *Brown* Court.[119] Wechsler's criticisms eventually moved Derrick Bell to formulate the interest convergence hypothesis, which then prompted historians to assess how transformative *Brown* really was. Constitutional change can be meaningless without a corresponding shift in societal attitudes. Further, if constitutional change is defined narrowly around landmark Supreme Court decisions, we might overlook the obscure episodes that had incrementally changed the law and societal expectations beforehand and that had made those decisions possible.[120] To counter the academic fixation with *Brown*, Michael Klarman assembled historical studies of small local triumphs in the South prior to *Brown*, while also revealing how little *Brown* mattered in the South through the 1950s.[121] The crux of this analysis is that civil rights started earlier, perhaps with the "democratic ideology of World War II."[122] Some historians have even argued that prior to *Brown*, the South had been changing from within, in large part through the struggles of African American Southerners.[123] Others would trace those roots further back, to the NAACP's antilynching crusade in the early twentieth century, which strengthened federal oversight of state criminal proceedings and elevated litigation over public opinion and political lobbying as the chief stratagem for advancing rights.[124]

A similar overhaul of Roma rights scholarship is due, to look beyond the EU-centric paradigm. While the remainder of this book focuses on Roma rights after the 1990s, we pause here to reevaluate the legacies of Communism and proto-European integration. For all of their misguided and uneven policies, Socialism and Communism sowed the seeds of the contemporary Roma rights movement. In some countries, assimilationist policies fomented an urban-rural divide, but

118 Martón Rövid & Angela Kóczé, *Pro-Roma Global Civil Society: Acting for, with or Instead of Roma?*, *in* GLOBAL CIVIL SOCIETY 2012: TEN YEARS OF CRITICAL REFLECTION 110 (Mary Kaldor et al. eds., 2012).

119 Herbert Wechsler, *Toward Neutral Principles of Constitutional Law*, 73 HARV. L. REV. 1 (1959).

120 *See* Eric Foner, *The Strange Career of the Reconstruction Amendments*, 108 YALE L.J. 2003, 2004 (1999).

121 Klarman, *supra* note 12, at 84–86, 89.

122 *Id.* at 88.

123 *See* DAVID R. GOLDFIELD, BLACK, WHITE, AND SOUTHERN: RACE RELATIONS AND SOUTHERN CULTURE 1940 TO THE PRESENT (1990).

124 *See* FRANCIS, *supra* note 13, at 8–10.

among urban Romani communities, which were more thoroughly integrated, a small middle class and intelligentsia burgeoned.[125] As part of this group, a generation of intellectuals like Nicolae Gheorghe, Ágnes Daróczi, and Rajko Đurić eventually became high-profile Romani activists.[126] They would be tremendously influential after Communism as conduits between Romani communities and international organizations.[127]

Another contribution of Socialism and Communism was the growth of Romani civic organizations during this period. Romani organizations ranged from informal cultural associations to officially recognized groups, varying in degree of autonomy extended by the state.[128] Most groups were closely controlled, but in Yugoslavia, where Roma faced less pressure to assimilate, the Federation of Yugoslav Gypsies exercised greater independence.[129] Working with the International Romani Union, the Yugoslav government even organized an international conference on Romani language and history in 1986.[130] Generally, though, because of their close association with the state, Romani organizations were often seen as mechanisms of state control, yet they provided a model by which Roma could organize after the fall of Socialism and Communism.[131] These groups also inadvertently facilitated the rise of the contemporary Romani elite. In Hungary during the 1980s, insurgent Romani activists feuded with loyalists; while the latter were promoted within party-led institutions, the former took the helm of the Roma rights movement after Communism.[132] This splintering of Romani figures into "radicals" and "opportunists" echoes the broader fracturing of Romani society during Socialism and Communism, when urban dwellers pulled away from villagers. Nonetheless, because of opportunities

[125] *See* Renata Weinerová, *From East to West: The Roma Migration from Slovakia*, *in* Social Networks in Movement: Time, Interaction and Interethnic Spaces in Central Eastern Europe 191, 197, 208 n.6 (Davide Torsello & Melinda Pappová eds., 2003); Nicolae Gheorghe & Andrzej Mirga, *The Roma in the Twenty-First Century: A Policy Paper* (Project on Ethnic Relations Policy Paper, 1997), http://www.per-usa.org/1997–2007/21st_c.htm [https://perma.cc/8GP9-5Y85]; Rostas et al., *Interview with Costel Bercus*, *supra* note 18, at 269.

[126] For biographies, see *Romani Elders*, http://www.theromanielders.org (last accessed Mar. 6, 2018).

[127] *See* Mihai Surdu, Those Who Count: Expert Practices of Roma Classification 171 (2016) (tracing Gheorghe's influence). For an account of Gheorghe's work in his own words, as well as his strong views on Romani identity, see Nicolae Gheorghe, *The Social Construction of Romani Identity*, *in* Gypsy Politics and Traveller Identity 153 (Thomas Acton ed., 1997).

[128] *See* Barany, *supra* note 16, at 145–48; Zoltan Barany, *Ethnic Mobilization and the State: The Roma in Eastern Europe*, 21 Ethnic & Racial Stud. 308, 314–15 (1998). In-depth analysis of Romani organizations during Socialism and Communism is lacking. Perhaps the most thorough study is a recent one examining how the All-Russian Gypsy Union and other groups employed Soviet ideology to influence the Soviet Union's conceptions of Roma within society. *See* Brigid O'Keeffe, New Soviet Gypsies: Nationality, Performance, and Selfhood in the Early Soviet Union (2013).

[129] Barany, *supra* note 16, at 147–48.

[130] *Id.* at 148; Ljubomir Bratić, *Romske organizacije i aktivisti sa područja bivše Jugoslavije*, Interview with Romani Activist from Vienna, MigraZine (2012) [https://perma.cc/P7GF-FRF6].

[131] On the continuity between civil society during and after Communism in Hungary, see Vermeersch, *supra* note 15, at 62–63. Vermeersch notes, however, that there is little evidence of such continuity in Slovakia or the Czech Republic.

[132] *Id.* at 61–63.

presented during Socialism and Communism for the nascent Romani middle class, this period is remembered with fondness by many veterans of the Roma rights movement.

The final implication of interest convergence is whether the EU's forays into Roma inclusion spurred backlashes in CSEE that shocked the conscience of technocrats in Brussels to push for Roma rights more aggressively. In civil rights scholarship, the backlash thesis holds that *Brown* inflamed Southern intransigence over integration, but the extremism of the South's "massive resistance" in turn forced the federal government to pass transformative civil rights laws a decade later.[133] The violence of white Southerners "seared the national conscience," so to speak, paving the way for the Civil Rights Act of 1964 and the Voting Rights Act of 1965.[134] A chronology of Roma rights could be selected to fit this mold: the Copenhagen criteria were followed by rampant anti-Roma discrimination in CSEE, which eventually led the European Commission to initiate proceedings against three CSEE countries – the Czech Republic (2014),[135] Slovakia (2015),[136] and Hungary (2016)[137] – for violating EU law by diverting Romani students to special schools.

This narrative hinges on several assumptions. First, the laws pushing for Roma inclusion should be out of step with popular sentiment. Law must lead, rather than follow, the dominant culture. Second, there should be sympathetic elites in Brussels and Western Europe who are willing to usher in transformative legislation to protect Roma in CSEE. Yet the record suggests that West European leaders often associate the Roma problem with Eastern Europe, where they hope it will remain contained. Antipathy and racism toward Roma are so entrenched across Europe that it can be hard to find evidence that persecution or discrimination shocks the conscience. Third, if the backlash thesis is to hold for Roma rights, then the EU should pursue more comprehensive minority protections than what conditionality provided. As we shall see, given disparities in the EU's competence, or authority, toward members versus accession candidates, EU minority protections will be inherently weaker once a country enters the Union. Of course, this does not prevent Roma rights from springing up

133 Klarman, *supra* note 12, at 82; KLARMAN, *supra* note 109, at 164.

134 Issacharoff & Karlan, *supra* note 115, at 38. The term "sear the conscience" comes from Justice Franfurter's dissent in the redistricting decision *Baker v. Carr. See* 369 U.S. 186, 270 (1962) (Frankfurter, J., dissenting).

135 *EU Action Against Czech Republic for Discrimination in Schools Is a Victory for Rights, Justice, and Roma*, AMNESTY INT'L (Sept. 25, 2014), https://www.amnesty.org/en/latest/news/2014/09/eu-action-against-czech-republic-discrimination-schools-victory-rights-justice-and-roma/ [https://perma.cc/26Z7-8P5P].

136 *European Commission Targets Slovakia over Roma School Discrimination*, OPEN SOC'Y (Apr. 29, 2015), https://www.opensocietyfoundations.org/press-releases/european-commission-targets-slovakia-over-roma-school-discrimination [https://perma.cc/H4HK-EPPF]; European Comm'n, Answer Given by Ms. Jourová on Behalf of the Commission to the European Parliament, June 19, 2015.

137 *Commission Probe Must Spell the End of Romani Segregation in Hungarian Schools*, EUROPEAN ROMA RIGHTS CENTRE (May 26, 2016), http://www.errc.org/article/eu-commission-probe-must-spell-the-end-of-romani-segregation-in-hungarian-schools/4485 [https://perma.cc/N66H-5MBZ].

elsewhere, such as in civil society, member states themselves, other international organizations, or even the EU if it deepens its competences. Fourth, each of the above junctures – conditionality, anti-Roma backlash, and firm EU response – should be bound by causation, or at least close correlation. Causation is difficult to verify. Correlation is inhibited by a pervasive anti-Roma persecution that transcends time and place, as well as by episodes of progress that defy simple explanations.

These messy findings are not necessarily a failing. They suggest instead that interest convergence and its associated perspectives must be paired with other frameworks for a complete exploration of Roma rights. In other words, interest convergence can account for why minority rights sometimes become a priority for political elites, but the theory is limited in explaining why some efforts fail while others succeed. Pressing ahead, the remainder of the book grapples with several of the questions outlined above. Our transatlantic comparison turns next to the socio-cultural roots of resistance and then to the legal tools that the U.S. possessed, and which the EU lacks, to drive home equality over local and regional objections.

3

Resistance and the Nation

One theme common to both Roma rights and civil rights is the role played by anti-integrationists and ethnonationalists, who argue that the nation and one particular ethnicity or race should be synonymous. These contingents within the majority populations oppose the two rights movements in order to maintain the status quo. During the Civil Rights movement, this camp insisted on preserving the "Southern way of life," a racial stasis where "whites exercised power and blacks acquiesced."[1] In CSEE, anti-integrationists and ethnonationalists have defended old social and political hierarchies to protect their privileged position – a position that, in the U.S. and Europe alike, is coded with the idea that whiteness is an integral element of the nation.[2] In this worldview, blackness is the antithesis of whiteness. Where whiteness is a nation's organizing principle, blackness becomes the embodiment of minority populations (e.g., Roma and African Americans), who are purged from the constructed coherence of the nation.[3]

In this Chapter, we explore not only how resistance to integration and inclusion maintained the distance of Roma and African Americans from the majority, but also how it forms the basis for the construction of the nation. While we focus primarily on the American South and the EU "South," or more precisely CSEE and the Union's non-Schengen eastern periphery,[4] we do not mean to imply that the same constructed hierarchies did not exist in the American North or Western and Northern Europe. Across the U.S. and the EU, resistance enlists various power mechanisms, both formal and informal, to defend the organizing principles of the national imaginary while pushing minority populations outside its brim. As one such organizing principle, whiteness – as well as its counterpart, blackness – plays a prominent

1 *See* Jason Sokol, There Goes My Everything 6 (1997).
2 *Id.*
3 Floya Anthias & Nira Yuval-Davis, Racialized Boundaries: Race, Nation, Gender, Colour, and Class and the Anti-Racist Struggle 9 (2005).
4 *See* Sunnie Rucker-Chang, *Challenging Americanism and Europeanism: African-Americans and Roma in the American South and European Union "South,"* 16 J. Transatlantic Stud. 181 (2018).

role, reining in any expansion of the national imaginary and any advances, actual or perceived, for minority groups.

A useful framework for understanding resistance, as well as the endurance of whiteness and blackness, is conflict theory,[5] which distills rivalry between majority and minority populations into competition for scarce resources. In interethnic competition, the majority fights for cultural primacy, while minorities push for cultural acceptance and inclusion.[6] Arjun Appadurai provides a similarly useful framework in *The Fear of Small Numbers*, where he extends Michael Ignatieff's discussion of the Freudian concept of "narcissism of small differences" to majority–minority relations. This idea explains how communities that reside in close quarters and share similar features (in this case, socioeconomic and cultural features) strive to emphasize their distinctiveness, thereby heightening the differences between community groups.[7] Because they have to work so hard to differentiate themselves, differences must be constructed, frequently through hostility, and competition for primacy becomes particularly fierce.[8] Appadurai notes that while a majority needs minorities to construct and maintain its dominance, the very existence of minorities (or "small numbers") precipitates insecurity over the possibility that the majority could one day slip into a numerical minority, with the attendant powerlessness, and a minority today could assume the majority.[9] Both conflict theory and the concept of small numbers explicate the tensions between minorities and majorities as well as how some groups control the mechanisms of power. In tandem, these two theories reveal the role of race and racialization in attempted differentiation; further, they highlight the arbitrariness and constructed nature of race and nation.

These dynamics played out with the resistance of Southern whites to civil rights and also help explain fiercely held resistance to Romani communities in CSEE. More specifically, the frameworks of whiteness, conflict theory, and small numbers explicate the almost primordial persistence of East and West binaries in Europe, which are supported by images, media representations, and policies. Echoing Foucault, we argue that the critical gaze from Europe's West to its East in turn motivates an internal gaze in CSEE societies from the majority to Romani communities to stress Romani differences and lack of belonging in furtherance of

5 *See* Marcel Coenders et al., *Majority Populations' Attitudes Towards Migrants and Minorities* 9–10 (Report for the European Monitoring Centre on Racism and Xenophobia Ref. No. 2003/04/01, 2001), https://fra.europa.eu/sites/default/files/fra_uploads/148-Report-1.pdf (last accessed Oct. 10, 2019).

6 For more on conflict theory, also known as competition theory, see David Cunningham, Klansville, U.S.A.: The Rise and Fall of the Civil Rights-Era Ku Klux Klan94–95 (2012) (discussing how the Klan flourished in communities with scarce resources and minimal outlets for white economic and cultural expression in what at the time were considered the politically moderate states of North Carolina and Florida).

7 One example relevant to CSEE is Serbs and Croats, who share common histories and languages, among other things, resulting in the need to highlight differences and hence the descend into war.

8 Arjun Appadurai, Fear of Small Numbers 82 (2006).

9 *See id.* at 1.

a "normalizing judgement," whereby sameness is championed and difference is defined by distance or "gaps" from the norm.[10] Though part of the cultural matrix of CSEE for centuries, Roma are pinned to an imagined migration that casts them outside the nation; they are an out-group rather than participants in the nation. Of course, multiculturalism runs deep in the history of CSEE societies, so the sense of uniqueness and individuality held by CSEE states is false; yet this sense perpetuates the vaunting of one group over another through the labels "minority" and "majority." Thus, where a majority exhibits tolerance toward diversity or conviviality – "ideal multiculturalism," to use Paul Gilroy's term[11] – there is reason to suspect that tolerance will be temporary.

This Chapter begins by framing resistance through the lenses of nationalism and racialization. It then moves to evidence of resistance in the U.S. and the EU, to set up the quandary that legal advancement will occur without complementing cultural shifts. As evidence, we use public opinion polls from the early period of Civil Rights and its immediate aftermath, as well as European surveys such as European Social Surveys, Standard Eurobarometers, and Eurobarometer special reports on discrimination. Eurobarometers are public opinion polls that the European Commission conducts primarily in EU countries (both member states and countries at varying points of accession) to assess the pulse of European society. They have been conducted regularly since 1973 and provide insight into respondents' needs, fears, and desires.[12] The European Social Survey, administered since 2001, is a biannual survey to gauge Europeans' attitudes and behaviors.[13] The reports from 2002 to 2005 analyzed in this Chapter date to the culmination of the fifth enlargement and reveal how, over a decade after the end of Communism, Europe continued to be bifurcated into East and West. This schism has a long history, in which Eastern culture and political practices were viewed as incompatible with Western lifestyles and values such as freedom and democracy. The reports from 2012 to 2015 follow critical periods in contemporary EU history – notably, the financial crisis and ensuing austerity and the migrant crisis and the rise of right-wing populist xenophobia. The westward movement of East Europeans, Roma in particular, and Western Europe's reluctance to incorporate them challenge the very diversity and inclusion embraced by the European project, especially at a time when the Union itself was espousing what was deemed to be progressive political and cultural values.[14]

10 Michele Fouccault, Discipline and Punish 203–204 (2012).

11 *See* Paul Gilroy, Postcolonial Melancholia 8 (2005).

12 *See* European Comm'n, 35 Years of Eurobarometer: European Integration as Seen by the Public Opinion in the Member States of the European Union 1973–2008, at 1 (2008).

13 *See Frequently Asked Questions*, European Soc. Survey, https://www.europeansocialsurvey.org/about/faq.html (last accessed Apr. 20, 2019).

14 Many view the signing of the Maastricht Treaty as the beginning of a cultural union in the EU because the Union moved beyond simply economic terms and began forging deeper connections, especially political and cultural, among the European countries. For a deeper discussion, see Monica Sassatelli, Becoming Europeans: Cultural Identity and Cultural Policies (2009).

Because the more recent opinion polls analyzed in this Chapter were conducted after Civil Rights and the EU's Roma inclusion initiatives were underway, they show the limits of a top-down approach to minority inclusion and integration pursued by the federal or quasi-federal government. Sometimes the majority's stigmas toward minority groups are held too fiercely to be overturned by government efforts, and minority inclusion fails to meaningfully expand the construct of the nation.

HISTORICAL CONTEXT

The early years of transition from Communism to capitalism in the 1990s and early 2000s proved challenging for much of CSEE. Jobs, savings, and the social safety net crumbled as markets collapsed, and for the former Yugoslavia in particular, the brutality of its breakup dispelled any illusion that modern Europe had moved beyond war.[15] As the CSEE states emerged from Communism, however, they sought to claim, or reclaim, a European heritage believed to have been eclipsed by Soviet occupation and influence; in the case of the Yugoslav successor states, it was overreach by a hegemonic Serbia that had obscured national identity.[16] Within months of Soviet disentanglement from the political affairs of Eastern Europe in 1988, the Berlin Wall fell in 1989, and nearly all of the Eastern bloc countries claimed independence in quick succession, precipitating the dissolution of the Warsaw Pact by 1991.[17]

Despite variations in the timing and nature of independence, each state set out to define itself by connecting its present to its past through the traditional markers of a nation's cohesion: shared linguistic, geographic, historical, ethnic, and territorial features.[18] Religion, too, played a major role in the reconstruction of

15 The Yugoslav wars are important because two current EU members were once part of Yugoslavia. For an in-depth discussion of the significance of the Yugoslav wars to the EU project, see CATHERINE BAKER, THE YUGOSLAV WARS OF THE 1990S (2015); APPADURAI, *supra* note 8. For more on the economic significance of the Yugoslav wars, see ROBERT LAMPE, YUGOSLAVIA AS HISTORY: TWICE THERE WAS A COUNTRY (2000).

16 In a speech to the Polish Sejm and Senate in Warsaw, Václav Havel spells out how Western-thinking Central European nations can reclaim a "European heritage" after decades of Soviet control. *See* Václav Havel, *The Future of Central Europe*, Speech to the Polish Sejm and Senate (Jan. 21, 1990), https://www.nybooks.com/articles/1990/03/29/the-future-of-central-europe/. For a useful framework for studying the Yugoslav relationship with Croatia as internal colonization, illustrating the unequal distribution of power and resources in Yugoslavia, see N.L. Karlovic, *Internal Colonialism in a Marxist Society: The Case of Croatia*, 5 ETHNIC & RAC. STUD. 276 (1982).

17 For more on the fall of the Berlin Wall and its aftermath, see Robert Snyder & Timothy J. White, *The Fall of the Berlin Wall: The Counterrevolution in Soviet Foreign Policy and the End of Communism, in* AFTER THE BERLIN WALL GERMANY AND BEYOND 127 (Katharina Gerstenberger & Jana Evans Braziel eds., 2011). Macedonia, Croatia, and Slovenia declared independence in 1991 and Bosnia Herzegovina in 1992. Montenegro was the last former Yugoslav state to declare independence, in 2006, after seceding from the State Union of Serbia and Montenegro.

18 There were some notable exceptions to this formula for independence, especially Romania and Yugoslavia, but even these countries eventually went through similar processes to declare

identity.[19] It became a trait that illustrated proximity to the West – nations with a Catholic majority claimed to belong to a Central European heritage, and therefore had an affinity with the West, which simultaneously distanced them from Orthodox Russia with its Soviet legacy of colonization and atheism.[20] In the Balkans, specifically the former Yugoslavia, religion was the cudgel that differentiated peoples who had shared a common history. Here, religion identified the members of in- and out-groups, while also insinuating proximity to or distance from the West. Notwithstanding its multiconfessional past, where Catholicism, Orthodoxy, and Islam intermingled, the Balkans fell victim to the "narcissism of small differences," with culturally and historically similar nations striving to differentiate themselves from one another.[21]

Competing national and religious metanarratives in Yugoslavia provided a means for groups to further splinter and assert the primacy of each nation, in order not to deviate from what was conventionally accepted or advanced as typical for the nation. The EU motto of "united in diversity," adopted in 2000, had not fully taken hold; rather, groups found ways to distinguish themselves and underscore their uniqueness, as the Yugoslav case illustrates. Quite the contrary, diversity in the East was looked upon with suspicion, much as it was in the West, despite the arguments of intellectuals that the turn of the century heralded new potential for diversity. Against the backdrop of this reality, pronouncements by governments and NGOs in support of diversity rang hollow.[22]

When CSEE accession candidates had to confront the long-standing marginalization of Romani communities through reforms and democratic liberalization campaigns, it was coupled with obvious irony. Politicians and governments were forced to address the very issue that they had chosen to ignore or suppress for generations. In Communist Romania and Bulgaria, for example, Roma had to assimilate and subsume their ethnic identity into the majority population.[23] Indeed, increased attention to Romani marginalization faced myriad resistance,

independence. In the case of Yugoslavia, each nation's identity was deeply connected to its religious affiliation, particularly in the countries where dialects of the same language are spoken (e.g., Serbia, Croatia, Macedonia, and Bosnia-Herzegovina). For more on the connections between religion and the nation, see ANTHONY SMITH, MYTHS AND MEMORIES OF THE NATION (1999).

19 In the Czech Republic, however, religion ultimately became inconsequential because the majority of its citizens declared themselves to be atheist.

20 *See* Havel, *supra* note 16.

21 MICHAEL IGNATIEFF, THE WARRIOR'S HONOR: ETHNIC WAR AND THE MODERN CONSCIENCE (1998).

22 *See* JACQUES DERRIDA, THE OTHER HEADING: REFLECTIONS ON TODAY'S EUROPE (1992); Jürgen Habermas, *Why Europe Needs a Constitution*, NEW LEFT REV. (Sept./Oct. 2001), https://newleftreview.org/issues/II11/articles/jurgen-habermas-why-europe-needs-a-constitution.

23 *See* MIHAI SURDU, THOSE WHO COUNT: EXPERT PRACTICES OF ROMA CLASSIFICATION (2017). This has significant implications for census-taking. Under Communist regimes, Roma had been encouraged to assimilate and consider themselves as members of the majority ethnic group. *Id.* at 15–16. As a counterpoint to forced assimilation, however, Yugoslavia was an outlier, having officially recognized Roma as a *nacija* (national minority) since 1971, a status that most countries in the region would only bestow at the insistence of outside actors.

such as virulent anti-Roma sentiment (Hungary, Kosovo, Poland, Romania), explicitly anti-Roma political parties (Bulgaria, Hungary, Slovakia), arson directed toward Roma-majority communities (Hungary), and the erecting of so-called Roma walls (Bulgaria, the Czech Republic, Romania, Slovakia).[24] These reactions come as no surprise, given the clash between forceful mandates from Brussels and the lack of interest and political will from national governments, politicians, and the majority populations in ensuring Romani equality. Integration threatened the status quo and was met with recalcitrance, which then positioned majority populations in CSEE as white European Union "Southerners," similar to white American Southerners who saw their social supremacy slip following the landmark *Brown* decision and forced desegregation.[25]

The American nation was arguably founded on the displacement of indigenous populations, and its economic prosperity was secured through slave labor, which concentrated wealth in the hands of privileged white landowners and their descendants.[26] Unsurprisingly, with slavery and displacement forming the bedrock of America and American culture, the fundamental principles of the American nation revolve around the primacy of whiteness and Anglo-Saxon heritage. These principles would serve as the benchmarks for belonging and acceptance for centuries. The centrality of whiteness in the dominant culture was such that immigrants embraced whiteness in order to belong.[27] Central to the definition of American whiteness were Anglo-Saxon Europeans. Immigrants from Southern and Eastern Europe were viewed not as fully European but, rather, peripherally European;[28] even they had to assimilate in order to be accepted, as Woodrow Wilson insinuated in a 1915 speech on Americanism explaining the necessity of assimilation for immigrants.[29] Of course, the ability to assimilate and eventually achieve whiteness was never an option for most racialized groups in the U.S., particularly African Americans, given the staunchness of the majority's racism.[30] The blackness imposed upon African Americans inhibited them from attaining a fully American identity.

24 Such Roma walls also exist in France and Italy. For civil society campaigns against these walls, see *Wall-Free Europe*, ERGO Network, http://ergonetwork.org/our-work/campaigning/wall-free-europe/ (last accessed Apr. 21, 2019).

25 *See* Sokol, *supra* note 1.

26 On the enslavement of American Indians in particular, see Andrés Reséndez, The Other Slavery: The Uncovered Story of Indian Enslavement in America (2016). On the connection between the rise of American economic power and slavery, see Edward E. Baptist, The Half Has Never Been Told: Slavery and the Making of American Capitalism (2012).

27 *See* Noel Ignatiev, How the Irish Became White (1995); David Roediger, Working Toward Whiteness: How America's Immigrants Became White (2006).

28 Groups considered peripherally European include Slavs, Germans, Greeks, and other non-Anglo Saxons.

29 *See* Woodrow Wilson, *Americanism and the Foreign Reborn*, *in* The American Studies Anthology 127 (Richard P. Horwitz ed., 2001) (1915).

30 There are some notable exceptions to this rule, including Syrians and Mexicans. For more on this subject, see Ian Haney Lopez, White by Law: The Legal Construction of Race (2d ed. 2006). *See also* Anthias & Yuval-Davis, *supra* note 3.

Arguably, Americans and Europeans each comprise a nation, with the U.S. and Europe as their associated territories, and ethno-symbolist nationalist frameworks tie both nations to "cultural elements of symbol, myth, memory, value, ritual and tradition."[31] Ethnicity is also an important factor in the ethno-symbolist framework; ethnicity is inherently linked to the nation, which, in turn, is intrinsically linked to race.[32] It is important to note, however, that a nation is not always restricted to a single version.[33] In fact, in the U.S. and Europe there are competing notions of the nation: a liberal one that accepts a diverse and inclusive identity, and one that is limited and confined. These differences can track political positions and leanings, but frequently they are aspirational, as the dominant national narratives remain mired in singular discourses. Chief among them in Europe and the U.S. is whiteness. These dominant narratives in the U.S. and Europe maintain that the nation is a closed system of belonging, which leaves minimal space for the meaningful inclusion of minorities in frameworks and discourses about it.[34] These closed systems create fertile ground for the emergence and maintenance of nationalism, affecting both America and Europe.

Nationalism defines, or seeks to define, who has the potential to constitute the nation. The very nature of nationalism is exclusionary, as it underscores who belongs in the nation and who must remain outside of it. The themes of nationalism – "autonomy, or freedom from outside interference; unity, or social solidarity fraternity, and sorority; identity or distinctiveness; authenticity, or a sense of belonging, memory or attachment to 'their' historical territory; the idea of a homeland; dignity or prestige according to 'inner worth,' continuity of community; and destiny or exceptionalism," as Anthony Smith writes – help to illustrate how exclusive features of the nation do not provide a space for deviation or nuance.[35] African Americans and Roma are working against these closed systems, and against an undercurrent of exclusionary specificity, to urge for an expansion of the narrative of the nation.

Given the rigid definitions of "nation," in relation to both broad constructs of Europe and individual nations in Europe, Roma as a transnational community necessarily exist outside understandings of the nation. This is particularly relevant in European contexts, where the notion of being a minority is connected to an individual's belonging to another nation, associated with a particular territory, hence

[31] Anthony Smith, Ethno-symbolism and Nationalism: A Cultural Approach 25 (2009).

[32] For a more pointed discussion on the intersection of race and nation, see Etienne Balibar, *Racism and Nationalism*, *in* Race, Nation, Class: Ambiguous Identities 37 (Etienne Balibar & Immanuel Wallerstein eds., 1991); Anthias & Yuval-Davis, *supra* note 3.

[33] *See* Smith, *supra* note 31; Anthias & Yuval-Davis, *supra* note 3.

[34] *See* Paul Gilroy, There Ain't No Black in the Union Jack (1987); Stuart Hall, Representation: Cultural Representations and Signifying Practice (1997); Charles W. Mills, The Racial Contract (1997); Anthias & Yuval-Davis, *supra* note 3.

[35] While we are aware of the tradition of viewing Europe and America as affected by patriotism rather than nationalism, we employ the arguments of Smith, *supra* note 31, and Michael Billig, Banal Nationalism (1995), to acknowledge that, irrespective of nomenclature, the processes of nationalism and patriotism are similar, if not identical.

the stress on connections between minority language and self-determination rights, and protections enshrined through reciprocity agreements with kin states. The majority do not view Roma as geographically, ethnically, or linguistically tied to the lands in which they live. Rather, they are viewed as outsiders owing to the accepted idea that Roma migrated to Europe from India and their perceived visible difference, even if that is not always the case. Their connection to "minority" is tenuous, and in some CSEE countries Roma became a national minority only after EU accession. Moreover, as we wrote about in the previous Chapter, during Communism many Romani communities were treated poorly and disregarded. Roma were viewed as outside the nation and became convenient scapegoats for crime and various other deficiencies in those transition societies and economies. In fact, following the fall of Communism, Roma refugees from the Czech Republic, Hungary, and Slovakia left the newly independent nations for Western Europe. Many even went as far as Canada to seek asylum and refuge from harsh treatment in their home countries.[36]

When the EU set the improvement of material and social conditions of the Roma as a requirement for EU accession (see Chapter 4), Romani communities became yet another obstacle to the construction of a homogeneous image of the nation, indicating limited possibilities of being normalized as European. Despite the EU's focus on the inclusion of Romani communities in CSEE states, supporting Romani causes in those countries has been an effective way for political leaders to lose votes. Rather, politicians who espouse anti-EU views and decry multiculturalism have become increasingly popular. Without external support, Romani communities cannot garner broad political representation.[37] Thus, the question of Romani inclusion remains simultaneously a local and European issue, as Romani communities are not viewed as having the power to give their social situation the recognition it deserves.

By contrast, the mistreatment and systematic marginalization of African Americans during the 1950s and 1960s did become an international issue, particularly in the Communist East and capitalist West.[38] The plight of the suffering "Negro" became a rallying cry to galvanize Communist resistance to the West. The racist white Western capitalist became a common caricature in animation and political propaganda. One well-known Soviet example was *Mister Twister* (1963), based on the 1933 poem by Samuel Marshak.[39] In the cultural imaginary of the

[36] *See* ROMA MIGRATION TO AND FROM CANADA: THE CZECH, HUNGARIAN, AND SLOVAK CASE (Zsuzsanna Vidra ed., 2013); Sean Rehaag et al., *No Refuge: Hungarian Romani Refugee Claimants in Canada*, 52 OSGOODE HALL L.J. 705 (2015).

[37] Attila Szep, *Some Aspects of Roma Migration from Slovakia*, *in* SOCIAL NETWORKS IN MOVEMENT: TIME, INTERACTION AND INTERETHNIC SPACES IN CENTRAL EASTERN EUROPE 185 (Davide Torsello & Melinda Pappová eds., 2007).

[38] *See* MARY L. DUDZIAK, COLD WAR CIVIL RIGHTS (2000); THOMAS BORSTELMANN, THE COLD WAR AND THE COLOR LINE: AMERICAN RACE RELATIONS IN THE GLOBAL ARENA (2001).

[39] MISTER TWISTER (Soyuzmultfilm 1963) was a short Communist-era cartoon about a rich white American who came to the Soviet Union on business and was frustrated and angered to find so many service people and hotel guests of color staying in the same hotel as him. Even in going from

Soviet Union, Soviet tolerance functioned as an antipode to the racist Jim Crow reality of the West, and the U.S. in particular. Therefore, politicians in the U.S. could not ignore the Civil Rights movement. To do so would have been akin to abdicating the role of the U.S. in claiming the victory of Western capitalism over Eastern Communism and losing the Cold War.[40] Thus, various branches of the U.S. government set changes in motion to promote African American integration and provide equal access to schooling, employment, and housing. However, the more African Americans advanced legally, the more intense was white resistance to black liberation, illustrating the incongruence between laws and society.[41] What follows are some examples of resistance in both CSEE and the U.S. after the fifth enlargement and during Civil Rights.

FORMS OF RESISTANCE IN THE U.S.

In the U.S. context, the 1954 landmark Supreme Court *Brown v. Board of Education* ruling provides a compelling point of departure in the study of the Civil Rights movement. Even prior to the ruling mandating the desegregation of schools, however, movements for equal rights were well entrenched. To understand some of the early pushes for equality, it is necessary to look to the African American soldiers who fought during World War II and their reaction to their treatment upon returning home from the European battlefields. These soldiers fought and died for their country abroad, but returned home to Jim Crow laws in the South and Jim Crow mentalities in the North, legal and systematic oppression and exclusion. These soldiers returned home to worse treatment than what they had received in foreign countries, which they chose to challenge rather than accept.

Interest convergence also provides a compelling rationale for the advancement of civil rights. From this point of view, we learn that because the Soviet Union touted itself as a society lacking racism and welcoming people of color, the U.S. moved to deinstitutionalize racism to prove its moral superiority.[42] *Brown* paved the way for the legal, social, and cultural inclusion of African Americans as it institutionalized desegregation, which on the surface was a major victory for civil rights activists and those impacted by those changes. The contradictions of the *Brown* ruling, however, proved key to understanding the incongruent developments that followed, as the aftermath of *Brown* highlights the challenge of mediating change only through laws without parallel social and cultural inclusion strategies. *Brown* was a launching pad for educational and civil rights for African Americans, and the legal advances that

hotel to hotel, Mr. Twister was unable to find the type of whites-only space he was accustomed to and, when confronted with accepting the diversity of the Soviet Union, he chose to return to the U.S. rather than stay in spaces with so many black, brown, and Asian people, illustrating the deep racism held by Americans in opposition to the profound tolerance of the Soviet Union.

40 DUDZIAK, *supra* note 38.

41 CAROL ANDERSON, WHITE RAGE: THE UNSPOKEN TRUTH OF OUR RACIAL DIVIDE 12 (2016).

42 Dudizak, *supra* note 38.

followed were nothing short of revolutionary. However, as Klarman notes, the ruling was most effective at solidifying white resistance to African American integration,[43] illustrating the relative weakness of laws or top-down legal processes in the face of widespread resistance to change and competition for scarce resources.[44] This competition was as much cultural as it was economic, however, for the advancement of African Americans threatened to minimize the primacy of the majority and its culture.

For many American whites in the 1950s and 1960s, the potential integration of blacks into white educational, social, and political spaces was viewed as an affront, as it could challenge their privileged position in American society and alter the zero-sum game of defining the nation. Hostility toward blacks, especially in the Southern states, increased as the white majority population, representing all social classes from poor to wealthy, believed that it was going to lose its privileged position in society with African American advancement.[45] Violence, both organized and spontaneous, became a commonplace form of resistance to racial interaction. Even more nefarious and restrictive, institutional barriers were put in place with the goal of reversing black advancement, a sociopolitical structural phenomenon that Carol Anderson terms "white rage," which works to suppress "blackness that refuses subjugation."[46]

During Civil Rights, white rage manifested in political organizations and political parties pandering to disgruntled white citizens to express their anger and frustrations with *Brown*. Southern whites believed these top-down actions from the federal government were an affront to the entrenched patriarchy and racial order. This "federal tyranny" enacted by the U.S. government led them to believe that their culture and way of life were under attack.[47] In Arkansas towns, for example, whites saw themselves as victims and "associated defiance with manhood," such that choosing not to react to desegregation was akin to emasculation.[48] Thus, in challenging the ruling, those who actively resisted integration were simultaneously maintaining the social order, the patriarchy, and the racial order that conflated "American" with whiteness. Organized resistance in Arkansas, Georgia, and Texas, for example, came from citizen's councils and similar organizations that tasked themselves with protecting the racial order of the Deep South and working to overturn *Brown*.[49] By the second anniversary of the *Brown* ruling, there were at least

43 *See* Michael J. Klarman, *How* Brown *Changed Race Relations: The Backlash Thesis*, 81 J. AM. HIST. 81 (1994).

44 *See* CUNNINGHAM, *supra* note 6, at 94–95.

45 *See* MASSIVE RESISTANCE: SOUTHERN OPPRESSION TO THE SECOND RECONSTRUCTION (Clive Webb ed., 2005).

46 ANDERSON, *supra* note 41, at 12.

47 Michael J. Klarman, *Why Massive Resistance?*, *in* MASSIVE RESISTANCE: SOUTHERN OPPRESSION TO THE SECOND RECONSTRUCTION 21 (Clive Webb ed., 2005).

48 Karen S. Anderson, *Massive Resistance, Violence, and Southern Social Relations: The Little Rock, Arkansas, School Segregation Crisis, 1954–1960*, *in* MASSIVE RESISTANCE: SOUTHERN OPPRESSION TO THE SECOND RECONSTRUCTION 203, 206 (Clive Webb ed., 2005).

49 ANDERSON, *supra* note 41, at 91.

90 of these groups, with 250,000 to 300,000 members from all walks of life, whose goal was to maintain racial stasis in the South.[50] Political leaders like Strom Thurmond and George Wallace, and organizations such as the far-right American Independent Party, gave voice to white supremacy and consoled the populations that deemed legal changes out of sync with historical and cultural norms in the region, much like the abolition of slavery had done a century earlier. In more moderate regions, such as North Carolina and Florida, there was no outlet for those frustrated and angered by school desegregation and eventual advancement of African Americans, which proved even more problematic.[51] Without outlets for these feelings, violence ensued.[52] It was in these seemingly politically moderate spaces that the Ku Klux Klan hate group proved most successful, as it provided group solace in working through the anxiety present in those disaffected by the *Brown* ruling and subsequent push for black equality.[53]

Minority exclusion with the goal of bolstering the nation is an old form of resistance with a long history, including white resistance to school integration during the Civil Rights era. The methods of antiminority parties and citizens are familiar, as they share means of resistance used in attempts to dehumanize and dislocate African American populations in the lead up to and following the Civil Rights movement. While there was movement toward the inclusion of African Americans in some localities,[54] once the Supreme Court decided *Brown*, Southern whites and politicians acting on their behalf definitively rejected African American integration, opting instead to support their "Southern way of life" and the idea of the nation as white.[55] The *Brown* decision forced the hands of Southern whites who were uninterested in losing their privileged position in the South, and so they reacted violently to top-down changes that they felt were foisted on them. Local culture was unprepared for and uninterested in federal laws as the instrument of change. As such, the changes predictably caused a backlash from those who felt themselves to be on the losing side as the progress of civil rights marched on. Their rage was directed at black bodies and at the government they felt had betrayed them.

RESISTANCE AND THE CONSTRUCTION OF NATIONAL IDENTITY AND "EUROPEANNESS" IN CSEE

Resistance to Roma inclusion in CSEE is based similarly on racialized hierarchies and attempts to preserve, or at least project, an image of ethnic and racial

50 Neil McMillen, The Citizens' Council: Organized Resistance to the Second Reconstruction, 1954–64, at 11 (1994).

51 *See* Cunningham, *supra* note 6.

52 For more on extremism amid a dearth of expression in a European context, see Cynthia Miller-Idriss, Blood and Culture: Youth, Right-Wing Extremism, and National Belonging in Contemporary Germany (2009).

53 *See* Cunningham, *supra* note 6.

54 *See* Klarman, *How* Brown *Changed Race Relations*, *supra* note 43, at 84–86, 89.

55 *See id.* at 82–83.

homogeneity undergirded by whiteness.[56] The resistance to the EU's pre-accession focus on minority protections, and specifically Roma integration, was equally broad in scope. In fact, as Chapter 2 notes, in many ways ostracism and segregation of Roma was simply a legacy of the Socialist period, when Roma were forced for generations to assimilate: professionally, by way of the erosion of traditional Romani trades and occupations; socially, by way of disavowing an association with their communities; and even ethnically and culturally, by encouraged and forced assimilation and sedentarization campaigns such as those in Bulgaria, Czechoslovakia, and Romania.

The harmonization of CSEE politics, economies, and even cultures with European norms also mandated that these states integrate their Romani populations. Because this push was dictated from the outside, it worked against the desired self-definition that these recently independent states were seeking to forge. Because the focus of these states seeking EU membership was staunchly situated in European belonging, the inclusion of Roma necessarily existed outside those boundaries and posed a threat to a coherently constructed idea of the nation, its people, and its ideas. Violence against Roma increased, precipitating mass outward flight from nearly all of the countries considered in this book. School segregation was rampant throughout these countries, and in Slovenia many Roma were among the estimated 19,000 to 25,000 individuals who became "erased" following the Ten-Day War after Slovenia declared independence from Yugoslavia. Individuals not of Slovenian heritage were compelled to declare permanent residency within six months following independence. Those who did not were denied citizenship rights; their documents were destroyed and their identities negated. They became stateless, and without legal status it was as if they did not exist at all. A significant number of Roma were affected by these harsh policies. For the purposes of this law, Roma in Slovenia were divided into two categories: "autochthonous," or Roma families who had resided in the country for at least 100 years, and "nonautochthonous," or Roma who migrated to Slovenia from other Yugoslav republics, primarily in the 1970s.[57] The majority of Roma who were "erased" were nonautochthonous, but those considered autochthonous were also erased as a result of living in informal Romani settlements.[58] As a result of becoming erased, these already marginalized groups had no citizenship and therefore no employment. Without employment,

[56] Anikó Imre, *Whiteness in Post-Socialist Eastern Europe: The Time of the Gypsies, the End of Race*, *in* POSTCOLONIAL WHITENESS: A CRITICAL READER ON RACE AND EMPIRE 79 (Alfred J. Lopez ed., 2005).

[57] Erased people who were former Yugoslavs who had been given six months to apply for citizenship in September 1999, utilizing the same avenues as any other foreigner. However, many Roma and other non-Slovenian nationals missed the short deadline, causing significant numbers of Slovene citizens to lose their citizenship rights and become erased. *See Slovenia's "Erased People*," DEUTSCHE WELLE (Nov. 27, 2004), https://www.dw.com/en/slovenias-erased-people/a-1408564.

[58] *See* Jelka Zorn, *Ethnic Citizenship in the Slovenian State*, 9 CITIZENSHIP STUD. 135 (2005); Julia Sardelic, *Romani Minorities and Uneven Citizenship Access in the Post-Yugoslav Space*, 14 ETHNOPOL. 159 (2015).

they had no income. Without income they could not secure documents necessary to apply for citizenship, and without documents they were trapped.[59] The process of erasing people in Slovenia illustrates a severe action against those deemed undesirable.

Periods of economic crisis heighten challenges to the understanding of the nation, expanding the categories of internal Others to recalibrate in-groups and out-groups, or internal and external Others, in the competition for scarce resources. These challenges came to the fore during the financial crisis of 2008, even as the EU pushed for greater political and cultural harmonization. The financial crisis strained the underpinnings of European cultures and ultimately challenged what had been purportedly informed by enlightened democratic principles, including, in a contemporary setting, multiculturalism and equality for minority populations. These goals were knocked off course, and a sizable number of Europeans were motivated instead by Euroscepticism, nativism, even jingoism, and racist violence, all of which threatened to raze the very foundations of citizenship and cultural belonging. These new tensions recharged the debates surrounding the nation, despite a postmodern and almost global consensus around transnationalism. This departure from multicultural values and the ensuing revitalization of the nation and its primacy disproportionately affected marginalized and racialized minority populations, who were viewed as distant from the nation and from the ideological assumptions and assertions conflating race and the nation that dominant groups sought to protect.

As the rebirth of the nation in the years following the financial crisis illustrates, segments of majority populations were deliberately moving to protect the uniqueness and solitary definition of nation, consequentially rejecting spaces for inclusion and multiculturalism that had been the cultural and national norm, replacing them with protectionist and exclusionary practices. Roma, in particular, had minimal representation and could rely on few organizations and outlets to move the system beyond the status quo. This predicament has worsened following the global financial crisis of 2008, which triggered an increase in anti-Roma policies, persecution, and culturally coded racist language across CSEE. The assertion of cultural differences and incongruences between majority and minority cultures has become linked to an ideation of unaccepted and unacknowledged communal diversity that can be eschewed in order to bolster the national narrative of self. In periods of financial insecurity, these assertions of the primacy and individual nature of the nation can become extreme.

In Bulgaria, for example, there were anti-Roma protests in 2011, 2015, 2016, and 2017.[60] In one protest, members of the far-right Attack Party (Ataka) donned shirts

59 Tanja Perić, *Insufficient: Governmental Programmes for Roma in Slovenia*, European Roma Rights Centre, http://www.errc.org/cikk.php?cikk=1717 (last accessed Apr. 21, 2019) [https://perma.cc/T9LY-KFVF].

60 *See Bulgarian Nationalists Stage Anti-Roma Rally*, Al Jazeera (Oct. 1, 2011), https://www.aljazeera.com/news/europe/2011/10/2011101173254692117.html [https://perma.cc/2A4L-Z2QX]; Maria Chereseva, *Clashes at Anti-Roma Rally in Radnevo, Bulgaria*, BalkanInsight (May 5, 2016), https://balkaninsight.com/2016/

that read, "I do not want to live in a 'Gypsy' country."[61] Additionally, in the fall of 2017, Bulgarian deputy prime minister Valeriy Simeonov, who was also chairman of the National Council for Collaboration on Issues Related to the Integration of Minorities, was found guilty in a local court of spewing hate speech against Roma by publicly proclaiming that the entire Romani population of Bulgaria essentially consisted of criminals, usurpers, and inhuman.[62] While Simeonov's conviction was a local legal victory, he nevertheless remained in power, illustrating that racism and hate speech directed at Roma are legally unacceptable but forgivable nonetheless, even in the EU.

Another example comes from Romania, where in 2010 Silviu Prigoană, a member of the Chamber of Deputies (the lower house of the parliament), proposed that the ethnonym *Roma* be changed to *Tsigan* so that people would not confuse Roma with Romanians.[63] The Romanian president at the time, Traian Băsescu, suggested that adopting the term "Roma" in the 1990s was a big mistake because many Europeans were confused by the words "Roma" and "Romania": "They wonder if it is an ethnicity or a nation of 22 million citizens."[64] The message was clear in this recent EU member state: there was no place for "Roma" to be considered or conflated with "Romanian," and those with power would work to distance the two terms, and consequentially the people, legally and politically. The irony of this position was that only one year later, in 2011, Roma in Romania were directed to select the "correct" identity (i.e., "Roma") on census forms to ensure that the Romanian government could receive EU funds for their minority Roma population.[65] The government was seeking to benefit from the very ethnic category that it had attempted to erase.

These examples from Bulgaria and Romania exemplify how various political parties cast Roma as outsideers. What holds constant for other CSEE countries is that many political parties harbor anti-Romani sentiment, and as Eurobarometer surveys reveal, the majority of citizens view Roma as outsiders. All of this sentiment directed at Romani populations was energized by the goal of projecting a uniform nation. Governments and majority populations alike pursued a goal to edge closer to their perception of Europeanness, an identity that was attainable

05/05/ethnic-tensions-provoke-violent-clashes-in-bulgarian-town-radnevo-05–05-2016/ [https://perma.cc/X8LQ-FX3E]; Dienne Dickens, *Bulgaria: Anti-Roma Protests Continue After Alleged Romani Attacks on Teenagers*, Romea (July 4, 2017), http://www.romea.cz/en/features-and-commentary/reportage/bulgaria-anti-roma-protests-continue-after-alleged-romani-attacks-on-teenagers [https://perma.cc/5SDJ-R48E].

61 Alexander Andreev, *Right-Wing Populist Appointed Integration Minister in Bulgaria*, Deutsche Welle (June 1, 2017), http://www.dw.com/en/right-wing-populist-appointed-integration-minister-in-bulgaria/a-39086764.

62 Bulgarian Helsinki Committee, *Bulgarian Deputy PM Guilty of Anti-Roma Hate Speech*, Liberties (Oct. 30, 2017), https://www.liberties.eu/en/news/valeri-simeonov-case-hate-speech/13328.

63 *See* Rupert Wolfe Murray, *Romania's Government Moves to Rename the Roma*, Time (Dec. 8, 2010), http://content.time.com/time/world/article/0,8599,2035862,00.html.

64 *Id.*

65 Surdu *supra* note 23, at 137.

only by removing connections to blackness and aligning the countries and its people with the same whiteness scaffolding the majority identity of Europe as a whole.

The possible conflation of "Romanian" and "Roma" could have consigned Romania to marginality akin to blackness in Europe and subjected the Romanian majority to the same maltreatment Roma have experienced throughout history. The 2010 push for universal frames of "Romanian" came at a time of increased pressure on Romani communities in Europe. This was only three years after Romania and Bulgaria acceded to the EU in the sixth enlargement, and only six years after the Union had expanded into post-Communist CSEE in the fifth enlargement. Coincidentally, 2010 also marked the destruction of Roma communities in France and Italy, deemed "illegal settlements" by the authorities, and their forced deportation from France and Italy to Romania and Bulgaria.[66] To conflate Romania and Roma identities would challenge the already tenuous relationship that Romania, and by extension East European countries, had with the EU and European belonging.

The broader context of these deportations was increased resentment in Western Europe toward East Europeans who were exercising their rights as new EU citizens and inhabitants of the Schengen area to travel, live, and work in the EU. Given the deeply entrenched notion of East European distance from the idea of "Europe," there was a great deal of skepticism among long-standing EU members regarding any contributions that East Europeans could make. For leaders in the EU, East Europeans were burdened by perceptions that they were overly reliant on the state because of the legacy of Communism and that EU membership would enable them to take advantage of favorable economies and generous welfare states in Western Europe, also known as "benefit tourism." Those accused of taking advantage of this system were affected by a phenomenon that was initially dubbed the "Polish plumber problem" and reflected generations of East–West European bifurcation as a result of decades of division between capitalism and Socialism or Communism. This history rendered those on the other side of the Iron Curtain peripherally European at best, and even after undergoing years of pre-accession and accession to achieve Union membership, East Europeans were viewed as usurpers abusing the prosperity of the West – taking jobs, opportunities, and welfare from their rightful beneficiaries in prosperous Western countries, particularly the United Kingdom. This Polish plumber "problem" relied on deeply entrenched stereotypes and imaginings of migrant workers and East European backwardness. Despite the reunification of Europe, these nations were not rectified or properly incorporated within the imaginary of "Europe." With the further eastern expansion of the EU in 2007, the

66 As compensation for deportation, Roma received 300 euros per adult and 100 euros per child. Kristi Severance, *France's Expulsion of Roma Migrants: A Test Case for Europe*, MIGRATION POLICY INST. (Oct. 21, 2010), https://www.migrationpolicy.org/article/frances-expulsion-roma-migrants-test-case-europe.

sentiment that Polish people were coming to Western Europe to take jobs evolved to encompass people from those new EU member states, and though it never acquired an accompanying alliterative phrase, the sentiment was the same: East Europeans from EU nations were not welcome in the West, particularly those from Romania and Bulgaria, the then newest EU members. Whereas Poles were viewed as taking work from other more deserving citizens, Bulgarians and Romanians, who hail from countries known for large Romani populations, were viewed as violating the neoliberal order: they would introduce even more people into affluent EU nations, people who not only had little or nothing to contribute to the economy but would simply take and live on the dole, much to the chagrin of their Western hosts.[67]

This division represents a comingling of approaches of the West toward former Eastern bloc countries – for instance, a neocolonial gaze as well as a form of normative judgment that imagines the East as incompatible with the West and out of sync with EU values. In addition, suspicion toward Roma in Europe, which persists in both East and West, makes Roma symbolic in their alterity, both as a result of their projected, inassimilable East European difference and their perceived rootlessness, which render them incapable of realizing Europeanness.[68] Given that these stereotypes of Roma persist, CSEE nations eager to project their European credentials directed their desire for a homogenous nation toward their local Romani communities, whom states excluded, suppressed, or forcibly assimilated. These projections are linked to similar, if not parallel, imaginings of Romani communities as outsiders, vagrants, and thieves – features that cannot mesh with the imagined face of the European nation. This distancing of Romani communities reflects a desire to dictate national and cultural norms under the mantle of the majority culture, all in the name of projecting and mediating Europeanness.

In this regard, Europe is making East European nations (even new EU members) acutely aware of their outsider status, challenging their Europeanness despite the hard work these nations have undertaken to come into Europe's fold. For these nations, what is perhaps most important in sloughing off the legacy of Communism is the right to culturally define themselves as European without qualifiers. The deportations of Roma from Western nations to Romania and Bulgaria illustrated the conflation of East European nations with the Roma; these deportations represent a failure to achieve Europeanness because the new EU members had not successfully projected a hegemonic cultural narrative with whiteness at its core.

The movement against diversity has intensified in light of the so-called migrant crisis that began in 2015. In Hungary, a major transit point, media portrayals have conflated Roma with migrants, implicitly justifying the evisceration of protection for refugees as a means of countering de-Europeanization, while lumping Roma into an

[67] For an in-depth discussion on the concept and uses of the "Polish plumber," see Kalypso Nicolaïdis, *Trusting the Poles? Constructing Europe Through Mutual Recognition*, 14 J. EUR. PUB. POL'Y 682 (2007).

[68] *See* FATIMA ALI, EUROPEAN OTHERS: QUEERING ETHNICITY IN POST-NATIONAL EUROPE xvii (2011).

undifferentiated mass that is defiling the normative (white) Hungarian body politic.[69] Conflating refugees ("migrants" in local parlance) and Roma made it possible to collectively categorize Romani Hungarian citizens alongside refugees so that they become "detached from the Hungarian nation and relegated to the category of disposable alien."[70] Oddly, Hungarian Roma in this situation were deemed a problem that only the Hungarians could deal with – a burden and responsibility that should not need to be passed to other European countries. This presents a strange contradiction, for in making this connection, the Hungarian government positioned Hungary's Romani communities as simultaneously foreign but also native, illustrating that it alone understood how to deal with the internal Other, which is known, as opposed to the unknowable external Other. Though seemingly odd, this Hungarian characterization of "our" Roma presupposes that there are also "their" Roma from elsewhere. This sentiment is similar to the Slovenian distinction between autochthonous and nonautochthonous. What these two examples illustrate is that, at least in these cases, Roma are recognized as constituting part of the population, but not part of the nation.

Events and political parties in Hungary and Bulgaria parallel the backlash in Romania. The political parties Jobbik in Hungary and Ataka in Bulgaria are openly anti-Roma in their actions and political stances. The Fidesz (Alliance) Party in Hungary, headed by Victor Orban, first came to the national stage in 2010 when it won the election with an overwhelming majority. The tactics of Fidesz as they relate to Hungarian Roma are more subtle, however, as they actively seek support from the Roma community while carrying out political platforms that work directly in opposition to their professed antiracist stance.[71] Ataka, in Bulgaria, by great contrast, takes a hard-line stance against globalism and decries the EU as unfair in its application of the laws, highlighting a double standard for the West and East, where the East is unfairly impacted by EU laws and mandates.[72] Ataka is part of a three-member coalition, United Patriots, which also includes the National Front for the Salvation of Bulgaria and the Bulgarian National Movement. In the March 2017 election, following the formation of their coalition a month earlier, the group of three won 27 seats out of 240 total seats in the Parliament, highlighting its broad support.[73]

[69] Angéla Kóczé & Márton Rövid, *Roma and the Politics of Double Discourse in Contemporary Europe*, 24 IDENTITIES 684 (2017).

[70] *Id.* at 689.

[71] For an example of how this functions, see *Jaroka: Roma Immigration Is "Positive" for Countries*, BBC (Feb. 20, 2014), https://www.bbc.com/news/av/world-europe-26273052/jaroka-roma-immigration-is-positive-for-countries. The woman interviewed is the sole Romani member of the European Parliament and represents Fidesz, the very party whose policies actively distance Roma from the national narrative and cast them as outsiders in Hungary.

[72] Kristen Ghodsee, *Left Wing, Right Wing, Everything: Xenophobia, Neo-totalitarianism and Populist Politics in Bulgaria*, 55 PROBS. POST-COMMUNISM 26 (2008).

[73] *See Bulgaria: Narodno sabranie (National Assembly)*, INTER-PARLIAMENTARY UNION, http://archive.ipu.org/parline/reports/2045_E.htm (last accessed Apr. 21, 2019) [https://perma.cc/SE3D-HAAJ].

All of these far-right political parties offer a vessel for citizens to express their anxieties and fears about the racialized Others in their countries. This phenomenon corresponds to the attempts of political parties and anti-integration affinity groups in the U.S. during Civil Rights to silence the voices and render moot the progress of those marginalized in society. Recalling conflict theory and Klarman's discussion on the emergence of the Klan, these far-right political parties have become quite successful in former Communist and Socialist states that once vaunted their tolerance and inclusivity toward their minority groups.[74] Like Southern whites in the middle of the twentieth century who feared losing their primacy in society, which in turn insinuated an emerging disconnect between the convergence of race and the nation, East European supporters of far-right groups found solace in political parties and politicians who promised to maintain the status quo or even improve material conditions for the majority. The ethnonationalists promote what they argue is fundamental to the nation: racialized homogeneity, a singular narrative of history connecting the majority to the land, and the inalienable right of the majority to take what they deem to have been stolen from them by minorities. Also related is the comingling of the far right and religion, which explains why religion proved so significant after the fall of Communism. The seemingly unusual coalition of anti-migrant and Christian right-wing political parties has parallels in the U.S. civil rights and Romani rights movements, and highlights the comfortable coexistence of the hateful and the righteous, a trend that corresponds with Eurobarometer findings highlighted below.

WHY RESISTANCE?

Minorities disrupt static notions of the nation and make manifest the anxiety of incompleteness that majorities fear.[75] Such difference from the majority renders these groups outside the dominant narratives of the ideological formations of the nation, in which individuals view themselves as part of a collective or a nation based on constructed ties – linguistic, geographic, historical, ethnic, and possible shared territory, among others.[76] Maintained distances of populous minorities from the majority underscore how the majority envisions the nation as devoid of difference. Roma and African Americans challenge this imagined homogeneous image of the nation and remind the majority that the positions of minorities and majorities are not so distant that majorities cannot become minorities, and minorities majorities, with the passage of time.[77] They heighten the uncertainty of the national body and

74 One exception to this would be in Bulgaria, where Muslim minorities were forced to Bulgarize themselves or face harsh punishment.

75 Appadurai, *supra* note 8.

76 BENEDICT ANDERSON, IMAGINED COMMUNITIES: REFLECTIONS ON THE ORIGIN AND SPREAD OF NATIONALISM (1983); SMITH, *supra* note 18.

77 *See* Appadurai, *supra* note 8.

call into question and render doubtful a clear consensus on "who exactly are among the 'we' and who are among the 'they.'"[78] The fear that there will be demographic shifts, also known as census fears (perpetuated frequently through a correlation between recipients of state aid and minority groups), subvert notions of stable national and ethnic categories. These uncertainties surface through a surplus of rage and various forms of resistance, many of which are violent.

Consider in this context the constant movements to encourage reproduction to restore the nation, which frequently surface in CSEE countries, where there are regular news stories and reports on unbalanced reproduction, whereby minority birth rates greatly exceed the majority's.[79] This unbalanced reproduction, perceived or actual, challenges the notion of the national body, rendering insecure the imagined self. Similar discussions in the U.S. around population increases in minority communities are also articulated in zero-sum terms as well, whereby an increase in the minority population is framed as a challenge to the preservation of the nation, its norms, and its goals. This is particularly salient in discussions of racialized populations who are framed as external Others. In framing minorities as harmful to the national body, it becomes necessary to distance them from the dominant discourses of the imagined national self, hence the need to de-Europeanize or de-Americanize them.

In moving to distance minorities from the narrative of the nation, members of the majority population maintain their dominant, even sole, position of primacy in society and dictate the terms of the nation, its politics, and even the image of its people. Race is always imposed from the outside, as are the burdens that accompany it. Those who choose to resist the inclusion of racialized populations advance the idea that minorities have no place in their society, signifying also that there will be no attempt at including them.

Forms of resistance, on the part of both citizens and politicians, correspond to a broad mistrust and disregard of migrants and minorities in general and a widespread mistrust of difference, multiculturalism, and diversity in large portions of the population. Early explorations of levels of tolerance of the European citizenry toward difference and diversity came through a series of questions focused on exposing the differences in opinions about diverse groups in Europe. The European Union Agency for Fundamental Rights (FRA), a decentralized EU organization, is responsible for a number of reports evaluating the situation of minorities in Europe, including the report *Majorities' Attitudes Towards Minorities in Western and Eastern European Societies*, which compiled findings from the 2002–2003 European Social Survey.[80] These findings came just prior to the

78 *See id.* at 11.

79 For a general discussion on the uses of censuses in the Balkans, see Gëzim Visoka & Elvin Gjevori, *Census Politics and Ethnicity in the Western Balkans*, 29 E. EUR. POL. 479 (2013).

80 *See* Marcel Coenders et al., *Majorities' Attitudes Towards Minorities in Western and Eastern European Societies: Results from the European Social Survey 2002–2003* (Report for the European

2004 eastward expansion of the European Union, a pivotal period in the history of the EU politically and geographically, as well as in the bourgeoning cultural Europe. The report uncovered "resistance to immigrants [prevails] among approximately half of the general public."[81]

According to the 2002–2003 European Social Survey, approximately 33 percent of respondents overall felt resistance to asylum seekers and around 20 percent avoided social interaction with minorities and migrants in their country. The survey also revealed a belief in the limits of multiculturalism. Negative views toward minorities were held by self-employed individuals and those among the lowest socioeconomic levels, as well as those living outside urban settings.[82] Religious adherence correlated with resistance to ethnic diversity, as did cultural practices and political preferences. Some less surprising correlations include the impact of in-migration, which predictably has a negative effect on views toward minorities, as the stranger can never truly be welcomed or understood.[83] Furthermore, the introduction of a stranger causes members of a particular nation to push back against even a potential change in who the nation is or what the imagined nation could look like. Evidence of this widespread resistance to inclusion of migrants surfaced during the migrant crisis, when European countries in both the East and West had relatively uniform negative reactions to the large influx of refugees. Parallels can be found in the period prior to Civil Rights, when negative views of African Americans held constant across the nation, not just in the South. In fact, prior to the great migration of African Americans from the South to the North, they were such an insignificant percentage of the population in Northern cities that they were seen as outsiders, and when they arrived they became migrants, also complicating the position of the majority.

According to *Majorities' Attitudes towards Minorities in Western and Eastern European Societies*, which summarized findings from Standard Eurobarometers in 1997, 2000, and 2003, unfavorable views of migrants and minorities were pervasive among rural populations and those with lower educational attainment.[84] The inverse was also true: those with higher educational levels held more favorable views toward diverse populations, a trend that is consistent among the findings of European surveys as well as American surveys focused on majority opinions toward minorities in the period leading up to Civil Rights.

The European surveys broke the results into respondents from Eastern and Western Europe. However, as these views were fairly consistent in both East and West European countries, the comparison between the halves of Europe was unnecessary. Unfortunately, these surveys ask fairly general questions and cannot

Monitoring Centre on Racism and Xenophobia No. 4, 2005), https://fra.europa.eu/sites/default/files/fra_uploads/151-Report-4.pdf.

81 *Id.* at v.

82 *Id.* at 23.

83 Jacques Derrida, Of Hospitality (2000).

84 *See* Coenders et al., *supra* note 80, at v–vi.

offer much specificity regarding the question of Roma and majority attitudes toward them. These early survey questions did not specifically address any particular minority group; rather, the position of Roma and other ethnic and racial minorities in the EU appear in polls only after the financial crisis, a time that corresponds with an increased focus on the position of Romani communities in Europe.

To gauge European sentiment toward minority groups and others perceived as different, we look to EU public opinion polls, especially the Eurobarometer. Each Eurobarometer includes the opinions of around 1,000 citizens per country and reflects the movement of opinion as well as the changing face of EU citizenry over the years. The Eurobarometers focusing on discrimination are of primary concern here, not only because of the focus of the content but also because of the time frame in which they emerged. The first one appeared in 2006 in the lead up to the 2007 European Year of Equal Opportunities for All and coincided with the accession of Romania and Bulgaria, which have significant Romani populations. The need to conduct a survey focused on equal opportunity at this time immediately recalls Western mistrust of the East and the presumed inability of East European countries to conform to Western cultural, legal, and political standards. As such, this report seemed poised to underscore officially the differences between East and West in relation to their minority populations and perpetuate the unequal ill-treatment of minorities in the East in comparison to countries in Western Europe. Interesting to note is how these reports focus for the first time on European attitudes toward minority groups in the EU. This exploration begins with a general examination of categories, including gender, disability, religion, ethnicity (with no specific mention of groups), and Roma – an outlier in what were general categories in the broad survey.

The 2006 Eurobarometer on Discrimination includes average responses from people in the then twenty-five EU member states. It excludes Romania and Bulgaria from the overall findings but accounts for opinions in the two countries collectively. This report correlates well with others, such as the American surveys referenced below, according to which people with higher educational attainment have more diverse groups of friends. These surveys presume that people who have connections to those different than them possess the empathy necessary to perceive and understand the mechanisms of discrimination – a contested idea at best. The Eurobarometer on Discrimination includes five types of diversity: religious, ethnic, disability, queer, and Roma. The discussion of Roma in this 2006 survey appears to be tied directly to the incoming member states with significant Roma populations, as this issue was absent in previous Eurobarometer reports, as was language on equal and civil rights. The report recognizes an increase in discrimination in the last five years, but a sampling of questions indicates trends in opinions reflecting a desired increase of diversity in the workplace with regard to age (72 percent in favor versus 22 percent opposing), gender (77 percent in favor versus 18 percent opposing), and diversity (74 percent in favor versus 19 percent opposing), but a near even split for those desiring an increase in people of different ethnic origins (44 percent for and 48 percent against).[85] This question illustrates a contradiction between people's opinions on theoretical points of view and the impact on an individual, also observed in public opinion polls in the U.S. during Civil Rights, some of which we analyze below, in relation to racial diversity. This phenomenon, known as response bias, reflects people's tendency to answer survey questions in a way that is contradictory to their actual beliefs in order to be polite or to save face. In other words, when the question of diversity is theoretical, there is a recognition of challenges and the need for change, but when the question of diversity references the real world, for instance inclusion of racial minorities, the personal proximity of those minorities to the respondent mediates the respondent's reaction, giving us results such as the ones above. This question specifically addresses the desirability of increasing the number of members of parliament from different ethnic origins but indirectly tackles the possibility of minorities to represent the nation, a notion that the survey responses to this question reveal as undesirable for the majority.

The 2009 Eurobarometer on Discrimination, like the one that preceded it, also assumes that individuals with diverse groups of friends and acquaintances are likely to perceive discrimination more acutely than those with homogenous groups of friends. This proves to be an important data point, as it becomes the assumed position for the reports on discrimination that follow. It is taken for granted that such people will be more attuned to disparities in equality and pay greater attention to diversity issues. Advancing an agenda to promote diverse interactions among European citizens becomes a motivating factor for EU initiatives and directives. Subsequent Eurobarometers on Discrimination, however, illustrate that even though more respondents indicate they have diverse friends, the numbers of those with Romani friends or those who have positive attitudes toward Roma are stagnant, particularly in regions with small or presumably assimilated Romani communities.[86] Given the conflation of Roma with East European populations and the negative associations with both groups, this assumption that diversifying connections will produce greater tolerance and acceptance of Roma communities remains questionable because attitudes toward Romani communities remain virtually stagnant.

These survey results indicate a growing acceptance and tolerance of other minority groups. The surveys specifically categorize minorities by way of race and ethnicity, such as black and Asian. Sexual orientation also appears as a category,

85 European Comm'n, Special Eurobarometer: Discrimination in the European Union 11 (2006), http://ec.europa.eu/commfrontoffice/publicopinion/archives/ebs/ebs_263_en.pdf. The specific questions excerpted for these points respond to the following question: "Would you like to see more: Women in management positions in the workplace; Disabled people in the workplace; People aged over 50 in companies; Female MPs; MPs of a different ethnic origin than the rest of the population?"

86 *See, e.g.*, European Comm'n, Special Eurobarometer 437: Discrimination in the EU in 2015, 7 (2015), https://data.europa.eu/euodp/en/data/dataset/S2077_83_4_437_ENG; European Comm'n, Special Eurobarometer 393: Discrimination in the EU in 2012, 111 (2012).

presumably to address feelings toward the LGBTQ communities. The specificity included in this report is refreshing because it recognizes diversity in Europe, but it fails in its reliance on the old metrics of "black" and "Asian" without any critical analysis of these terms. Moreover, the 2009 Eurobarometer on Discrimination does not account for intersectional belonging and the complications that arise in public opinions when people are confronted with individuals self-identifying as more than one minority. Thus, the methodology allows for broader exploration of views in EU countries but relies on artificially constructed categories to reach those conclusions, serving a similar function to the census in that it treats racial and ethnic categories as if they are real and fixed.[87]

The negative perceptions of Roma communities confirmed by the 2009 survey surfaced again in the 2012 Eurobarometer on Discrimination, which found a general mistrust and general disregard for Romani people – an attitude that factored even into the majority's opposition to having their children attend school with Romani children. The CSEE countries with large Romani populations (Hungary, the Czech Republic, and Slovakia) again had some of the most unfavorable results on this question, which should come as no surprise given the visceral reaction against Roma in those countries. In Hungary, 46 percent of respondents reported that their citizens would be totally uncomfortable with their children having Roma classmates; in Slovakia the number was 58 percent, and in the Czech Republic it was 52 percent. The result in Romania was more positive, with only 22 percent responding so unfavorably (a significant percentage nonetheless). With the exception of the Czech Republic, all of the respondents in these countries were in favor of better policies for Roma integration. However, their opinions about actually being instrumental in impacting that integration contradict those findings. The survey noted that the responses "indirectly . . . capture respondents' own feelings towards the Roma."[88]

Interestingly, American public opinion polls just prior to and following the Civil Rights period similarly illustrate the challenge of connecting cultural will and laws. Resistance has frequently proven to be as strong as, if not stronger than, laws, and laws in their own right are frequently not powerful enough to move the pulse of a society or sentiment of a particular population, which is also demonstrated in the European case by way of the incongruence between pre-accession conditions and citizenry sentiment toward Roma. Incongruence in the American setting was noted by sociologist Mildred Schwartz, who analyzed public opinion polls prior to and during Civil Rights, in response first to school integration and then to other markers of African American inclusion. Conducted by the National Opinion Research Center (NORC), Roper, and Gallup, these polls gauged the opinions of the majority in both the North and South and their sentiment regarding key indicators of civil rights: housing, education, and employment. From the results, Schwartz gleaned

[87] For more on the use of census data to reify constructed categories, see SURDU, *supra* note 23.

[88] EUROPEAN COMM'N, SPECIAL EUROBAROMETER 393, *supra* note 86, at 13.

that the goals of the government and citizenry were frequently out of sync.[89] Irrespective of laws and legislation, much of this distance was predicated on a continued belief that African Americans were not simply legally unequal, but also inferior to the majority population in biology and intellect. These polls further demonstrated that a majority of Americans believed African Americans were uneducable. This position is reflected in a 1942 poll in which only 42 percent of white respondents believed that African Americans were as intelligent as them. Fortunately, that number increased to 72 percent by 1956, two years following the *Brown* decision. Even with the increase in belief that African Americans could be educated and should attend the same schools as whites, a majority of whites in the South were still reluctant to send their children to schools where African Americans constituted the majority in the classroom, a finding that resonates with the 2007 Eurobarometer referenced above. Similarly, there was a general reluctance to live alongside African Americans, a trend that actually increased in the 1960s with the Civil Rights movement.[90]

Consider in this context the NORC trend question, asked in 1942, 1956, and four times between 1963 and 1965: "If a Negro with just as much income and education as you had moved into your block, would it make any difference to you?" To this question, 35 percent answered affirmatively in 1963. In 1967, that number rose to 67 percent. Gallup posed a similar question: "If colored people came to live next door, would you move?" In 1958 and 1963, 55 percent said they would move; in 1965, the number rose to 65 percent. This increase in percentages suggests that whites, particularly in the South, espoused a normative idea that African Americans should be entitled to the same benefits of citizenship as whites, but when the impact became personal, opinions diverged, and the majority was unwilling to grant the same rights to the minority, a trend that Schwartz highlights, resonating with the idea that the advance of African Americans would precipitate a loss for the white majority. American legal changes upended the social order that had existed for generations.

In expressing their aversion to inclusion that would have a direct impact on their lives, those whites feared that the privilege they held as a majority was tenuous and fluid. Moreover, the possibility of having African Americans living next to them in their own neighborhoods "suggests the possibilities of contact that immediately results in an increase in social intimacy as a result of proximity."[91] This was irrespective of the fact that many respondents indicated they believed that blacks and whites should have the same access to education on the whole. The divergent,

[89] *See* Mildred A. Schwartz, *Trends in White Attitudes toward Negros* 1 (Report for the National Opinion Research Center No. 119, 1967), http://www.norc.org/PDFs/publications/NORCRpt_119.pdf.

[90] *Id.* at 61. *See also* MICHAEL J. KLARMAN, BROWN V. BOARD OF EDUCATION AND THE CIVIL RIGHTS MOVEMENT 192 (2007) ("Polls taken after *Brown* revealed that 15–25 percent of southern whites favored violence, if necessary, to resist school desegregation.").

[91] Schwartz, *supra* note 89, at 58.

even contradictory, poll responses illustrate a cognitive dissonance between ideas about what one should say and the actuality of fiercely held beliefs, a trend that closely resembles the findings of the Eurobarometer survey reports.

In the 2015 Eurobarometer on Discrimination, for example, 63 percent of respondents indicated that they have friends of different ethnic origins from their own, an 8 percent increase from the 2006 survey. However, only 18 percent of those respondents had a friend of Romani heritage. This number was the same as in 2012, whereas the number of individuals with friends of different ethnicity, who were already in the majority in 2012, increased by 3 percent. In the 2015 survey, 94 percent of respondents said they would be at ease working with whites, 83 percent would be comfortable working with blacks or Asians, and 63 percent would be comfortable working with someone who was Roma. Similarly, only 45 percent of people surveyed for this report said that they would be comfortable with their son or daughter being romantically involved with someone who was Roma, compared to 92 percent for whites and 64 percent for Asians and blacks.

These figures illustrate that the concerted efforts of European governments to project an image of inclusivity and diversity have proven successful for some groups, blacks and Asians in this case. However, the top-down efforts to dispel deeply held pejorative associations and racist stereotypes about Roma have been ineffective, as Roma consistently receive low percentages of acceptance rates among fellow Europeans. This result challenges us to consider how, or even if, laws and society interact to produce a desired result of inclusivity and diversity, because, despite more than a decade of European directives and initiatives to promote and cultivate "Europe" and "Europeanness," these opinion polls show how little public opinion has moved away from staunchly held anti-Roma positions. These results further advance the inability and reluctance of nations to include their minorities and reinforce the distance that Roma have in relation to other minorities, who, perhaps because of their indisputable connections to a kin nation, present to the majority as European minorities as opposed to the Roma, whose murky origins render them inveterate outsiders. The position of Roma is further complicated by their connection to Eastern Europe, which proves problematic in the construction of Europeanness. This distance inevitably raises the question of whether Roma can be considered European and under what terms. Instead of offering any resolution to the question of European diversity and Roma belonging, these polls highlight the resistance that surfaces in reaction to the Roma through political alignment and limited cultural and nation formation.

The limited constructs of the nation are also reflected in the American case, where we can observe how general acceptance of African Americans in both the North and the South decreased after the Civil Rights movement with government intervention and school desegregation. The U.S. government, like the European Union, took a heavy-handed approach in mandating equality without any consideration for the cultural implications of such a radical move. Instead of an expanded notion of America and Americanism, resistance ensued, as would happen in Europe decades later. Government challenges to political, cultural, and social norms set in motion the possibility of an expanded notion of the nation that took root with some, but bypassed the majority, giving birth to limited progress and possibilities for those unable to assimilate or "become white."[92] Given the disconnect between words and action, resistance rather than acceptance continues to dominate the discourse on minorities in both Europe and the U.S., pushing minorities, especially Roma and African Americans, to the sidelines to bear the brunt of resistance.

92 *See* IGNATIEV, *supra* note 27.

4

Minority Protections and Conditionality

For all the contested meanings of Europeanness, the EU projected a singular vision of Europe in its preparations for the fifth enlargement, which culminated in 2004. During that process, which began in the early 1990s, the EU imposed on the mostly Eastern and mostly post-Communist accession candidates a set of preconditions that included respect for and protection of minorities.[1] In other words, to join the Union, candidate countries had to espouse the pluralistic values of the European nation. This marked the first time that the EU injected minority protections into the conditionality process, that is, the articulation of, negotiation over, and compliance with specific criteria for EU membership.[2] Conditionality quickly became the EU's primary mechanism for spurring Roma integration in CSEE candidate countries, drawing widespread commentary and eclipsing other forms of advocacy for Roma rights.[3]

Soon, however, the limits of conditionality became apparent. Despite the flurry of monitoring reports by the Commission and initiatives by accession candidates, living conditions for most Roma in CSEE countries remained stagnant. A popular comparison emerged that contrasted the EU's conditionality-driven Roma integration mandate with the U.S. government's civil rights legislation half a century earlier. Obliquely, and sometimes even directly, this comparison implied that the EU was hamstrung by limited competences while the U.S. thrived because of its robust equal-protection jurisprudence.[4] This hagiography of Civil Rights also

1 *See* Presidency Conclusions, Copenhagen European Council (June 21–22, 1993).

2 On the history behind the unprecedented move to incorporate minority protections, see Bruno de Witte, *Politics Versus Law in the EU's Approach to Ethnic Minorities*, *in* EUROPE UNBOUND: ENLARGING AND RESHAPING THE BOUNDARIES OF THE EUROPEAN UNION 137, 137 (Jan Zielonka ed., 2002).

3 *See, e.g.*, EUROPEAN COMM'N, THE SITUATION OF ROMA IN AN ENLARGED EUROPEAN UNION (2004); Gwendolyn Sasse, *EU Conditionality and Minority Rights: Translating the Copenhagen Criterion into Policy* (European Union Institute Working Paper RSCAS No. 2005/16, 2005); Peter Vermeersch, *EU Enlargement and Minority Rights Policies in Central Europe: Explaining Policy Shifts in the Czech Republic, Hungary and Poland*, 14 J. ON ETHNOPOL. & MINORITY ISSUES IN EUR. 114 (2015).

4 *See, e.g.*, James A. Goldston, *The Unfulfilled Promise of Educational Opportunity in the United States and Europe: From* Brown v. Board *to* D.H. *and Beyond*, *in* REALIZING ROMA RIGHTS 163 (Jacqueline Bhabha et al. eds., 2017).

dovetails with the views of some progressive scholars of American federalism, who tout legislation such as the Voting Rights Act of 1965 as an effective federal check on state and local behavior.[5] As the U.S. Supreme Court cabins federal powers in the contemporary era, these progressive scholars bemoan the Court's inability to see that the federalism debate over minority protections should have ended long ago.[6]

But there is another way to both tell the Roma rights story and draw parallels to the American context. It begins by reorienting the U.S.–EU comparison to an earlier period than Civil Rights. For the relationship between Roma inclusion and EU conditionality, a better American parallel is post-Civil War Reconstruction (roughly 1863 to 1877), when racial equality became a precondition for statehood.[7] Reconstruction was a formative time for the U.S., when notions of citizenship, civil rights, federalism, and national ideals and national identity all coalesced. Reconstruction laid the groundwork for Civil Rights by realigning the balance of power between federal and state governments so as to enable civil rights legislation. However, Reconstruction also failed so spectacularly that a "Second Reconstruction," as the Civil Rights movement is sometimes known, was needed to give full effect to the meaning of freedom.[8]

As the country grappled with these tectonic legal shifts, it also had to project a vision of itself – of American ideals and aspirations – to territories that sought to join the Union. During Reconstruction two Western territories gained statehood, and the Southern states that had lost the Civil War were readmitted. The U.S. foisted conditions on these candidates for statehood and readmission that supposedly reflected its values. More to the point, the Union imposed minority protections that ranged from ratification of the Fourteenth Amendment to guarantees of African American suffrage. These conditions were often more demanding than what the federal government required of existing (primarily Northern) states. For instance, while Southern states had to guarantee African American suffrage, Northern states declined to extend the vote to African Americans at almost every opportunity.[9] Overall, however, the nation was attaining a new level of federally guaranteed minority rights, including passage of the Thirteenth, Fourteenth, and Fifteenth Amendments (commonly called the "Reconstruction Amendments") as well as enforcement legislation. Thus, while Reconstruction would take our U.S.–EU comparison farther apart temporally, it presents a better comparator than Civil

[5] *See* Heather K. Gerken, *A New Progressive Federalism*, DEMOCRACY J., No. 24, Spring 2012, at 37.

[6] *See* Guy-Uriel E. Charles & Luis Fuentes-Rohwer, *Race, Federalism, and Voting Rights*, 2015 U. CHI. L. F. 113.

[7] These starting and ending points are taken from Professor Foner. *See* ERIC FONER, RECONSTRUCTION: AMERICA'S UNFINISHED REVOLUTION, 1863–1877, xxvii (1988) (explaining the use of the Emancipation Proclamation and the withdrawal of federal troops from the South as the bookends for Reconstruction).

[8] Howard N. Rabinowitz, *More Than the Woodward Thesis: Assessing the Strange Career of Jim Crow*, 75 J. AM. HIST. 842, 852 (1988).

[9] *See* FONER, *supra* note 7, at 222–24.

Rights for the Roma integration mandates of conditionality – a comparator where America's version of conditionality coincided with the nation's evolution from an "incipient" to a "mature" federalism.[10]

At times, the conditions of statehood and readmission elevated the racial equality standards for all states. The U.S. appeared to pass the Fifteenth Amendment, for example, which guarantees the vote to all male citizens, to put to rest the uneven imposition of suffrage.[11] Comparison to Reconstruction therefore shows how the internal and external competences of a federal government can influence one another, illuminating whether bold demands on candidates can lift up the standards for member states in the future.

There are bleaker lessons from Reconstruction. This "most progressive" of American eras disappointed African Americans in several ways.[12] Within the government, the drivers of equality during this period, most prominently the Radical Republicans in Congress, relied on legal reforms, frequently through the Constitution, to the detriment of almost all other avenues.[13] This tendency to overconstitutionalize reform without steady enforcement or popular support is bound to disappoint when political will recedes and the old ways resurface. Additionally, it was always impossible to keep the federal government's attention trained on the plight of newly freed African Americans; eventually a barrage of distractions, from internal divisions among Republicans to intransigence within the former Confederacy to an economic collapse, sapped the impetus from Reconstruction. This has particular resonance for the EU, which, at the time of the writing of this book, seems to be bouncing from crisis to crisis almost monthly, if not daily, in ways that undermine its authority and even its existence.

This Chapter focuses primarily on the conditionality–Reconstruction comparison. The analysis of conditionality extends the thread from prior Chapters on the hypocrisy that plagues minority rights in the U.S. and the EU. At times, the disparity between how applicants and incumbents are treated spurs each union to raise the bar for incumbents (thereby lifting the floor); at other times, this disparity weakens the ambitious mandates placed on the applicants (thereby lowering the ceiling). In the American example, the interplay between federalism and equality during Reconstruction sets up the

[10] Mark Tushnet, *Conclusion*, *in* COMPARATIVE CONSTITUTIONAL FEDERALISM: EUROPE AND AMERICA, 139, 139–42 (Mark Tushnet ed., 1990). *See also* Larry Catá Backer, *The Extra-National State: American Confederate Federalism and the European Union*, 7 COLUM. J. EUR. L. 173, 179 (2001) ("In 1865, the United States finally settled the question of federalism . . . . This settlement was accomplished violently . . . .").

[11] *See* ALEXANDER KEYSSAR, THE RIGHT TO VOTE: THE CONTESTED HISTORY OF DEMOCRACY IN THE UNITED STATES, 74–75 (2000).

[12] *See* DOUGLAS R. EGERTON, THE WARS OF RECONSTRUCTION: THE BRIEF, VIOLENT HISTORY OF AMERICA'S MOST PROGRESSIVE ERA (2014).

[13] WILLIAM GILLETTE, RETREAT FROM RECONSTRUCTION: 1869–1879, 364–65 (1979).

constitutional framework for the Civil Rights movement, and that interplay continues to ebb and flow today. Of course, tracing the evolution of certain themes, such as equality and federalism, from Reconstruction to Civil Rights has the luxury of a longer timeline with America's project of racial equality.

The conditionality comparison is equally illuminating for Reconstruction. While some scholars have explored the conditions imposed on statehood and the influence of the Northwest Ordinance on the Thirteenth and Fourteenth Amendments,[14] none have ever framed this relationship between the U.S. government's internal and external governance as *conditionality*, that concept associated with EU enlargement that has come to embody the challenge of sustaining reforms once an applicant becomes a full-fledged member.[15] The conditionality framework is particularly apt for the South during Reconstruction, when the former Confederate states had to accept certain stipulations of racial equality to be readmitted into the Union – stipulations that often went beyond the bare-bones protections within the Union. We believe that our comparison of conditionalities is a major contribution to the literature on Reconstruction. Hence, this Chapter lingers on the U.S. more than the other chapters so as to draw out the signifiers of conditionality in Reconstruction.

In making its comparisons, this Chapter also evaluates how constructs of the nation are embedded in the conditions of accession and statehood. These conditions balance the ideals that each nation aspired to and the compromises that were struck out of expediency. Because these conditions forcefully propelled minority rights, they could be unpopular with prospective and existing members. Thus, conditionality in the U.S. and EU contexts echoes one of this book's central questions: How crucial are popular mores to societal change? In the absence of popular support, can societal change be successfully imposed by a federal or quasi-federal government? Further, minority protections under conditionality were more progressive than, and therefore out of step with, U.S. and EU laws governing existing members. Ironically, this progressiveness threatens to

14 E.g., Eric Biber, *The Price of Admission: Causes, Effects, and Patterns of Conditions Imposed on States Entering the Union*, 46 AM. J. LEGAL HIST. 119 (2004); George Rutherglen, *State Action, Private Action, and the Thirteenth Amendment*, 94 VA. L. REV. 1367, 1372 (2008); Matthew J. Hegreness, *An Organic Theory of the Fourteenth Amendment: The Northwest Ordinance as the Source of Rights, Privileges, and Immunities*, 120 YALE L.J. 1820, 1840–45 (2011). The Northwest Ordinance governed the Northwest Territory before it was divided and admitted as separate states. It had a powerful effect on two of the three Reconstruction Amendments, which governed existing states.

15 Professor Ackerman has noted the dearth of legal scholarship on the influence of the Reconstruction Act of 1867 on the Fourteenth Amendment, though he has not framed this dynamic as the influence of external conditions on internal governance. *See* BRUCE ACKERMAN, 2 WE THE PEOPLE: TRANSFORMATIONS 190 (1998) ("The debate surrounding [the Reconstruction Act of 1867] might be of antiquarian interest, but it is not part of the canon that provides the legislative history of the Fourteenth Amendment.").

undercut the long-term efficacy of conditionality, since candidates can backslide on their commitments after becoming members.

CONDITIONALITY DURING EASTERN ENLARGEMENT AND AMERICAN RECONSTRUCTION

Like any other club, a federalist system can require conditions for membership.[16] The EU imposed terms for accession in each round of negotiations to bring in a prospective member. The framework for accession lies in Article 49 TEU, a short provision that, prior to the fifth enlargement, began: "Any European State which respects the principles set out in Article 6(1) may apply to become a member of the Union."[17] Article 49 provided scant guidance for a process this complex; thus, a tome of treaty provisions, judicial decisions, bilateral agreements, and monitoring reports fleshed out not only the procedure for accession but also the meaning of Article 6 TEU. The Lisbon Treaty then changed Article 49's criterion to any "European State which respects the *values referred to in Article 2 and is committed to promoting them*" (emphasis added). Because the understanding of the fundamental rights referenced in Article 2, as well as the corpus of the *acquis communautaire*, which candidates must incorporate into domestic law, is constantly changing, no two rounds of accession are ever the same.[18]

During the fifth enlargement, candidate countries faced the most voluminous acquis, the most robust set of fundamental rights, and yet the most unyielding conditions that the EU had ever devised.[19] As a precondition for accession negotiations – that is, before they could even begin accession talks – candidates had to abide by a set of conditions devised by the European Council during a 1993 meeting in Copenhagen.[20] These conditions encompassed economic criteria (e.g., functioning market economies), legal criteria (e.g., the ability to implement the acquis), and the political criteria of "guaranteeing democracy, the rule of law, human rights and *respect for and protection of minorities*."[21] While political criteria had appeared in prior rounds of enlargement, the insertion of minority protections in the fifth

[16] Karen E. Smith, *The Evolution and Application of EU Membership Conditionality*, *in* The Enlargement of the European Union 105, 106 (Marise Cremona ed., 2003).

[17] Treaty on European Union, art. 49 (ex art. O), November 10, 1997 O.J. (C 340) 145 (Amsterdam Treaty amendments). *Cf.* Treaty on European Union, art. 49, 2008 O.J. (C 115) 13 (Lisbon Treaty amendments).

[18] Dimitry Kochenov, EU Enlargement and the Failure of Conditionality: Pre-accession Conditionality in the Fields of Democracy and the Rule of Law 11 (2007).

[19] By the fifth enlargement, a robust body of law had built up around the acquis and Article 6. Nonetheless, CSEE candidates had to comply strictly with pre-accession conditions, despite the distance that the candidates had to traverse from Communism to democracy and the market economy, and no derogation could be permitted. *See* Smith, *supra* note 16, at 112.

[20] Marc Maresceau, *Pre-accession*, *in* The Enlargement of the European Union 9, 18–19 (Marise Cremona ed., 2003).

[21] *See* Presidency Conclusions, *supra* note 1 (emphasis added).

enlargement was entirely new.[22] Moreover, minority protections were incongruous with the fundamental rights recognized by EU law. EU law made no provision for minority protections, even though EU courts had amassed a rich jurisprudence in human rights.[23]

Because application for membership in any club is beset by power dynamics,[24] the CSEE candidates had little choice but to acquiesce, even if the accession criteria were more exacting than the rules binding current members. Invoking respect for and protection of minorities, the Commission censured CSEE candidates repeatedly for failing to integrate Romani communities,[25] even threatening at one point to hold up the accession of Slovakia.[26] For Roma rights, the eastern enlargements of 2004, 2007, and 2013 have been especially consequential: these rounds marked the first time that the EU was willing to use accession conditions to pressure states on Roma policies.

Within the Union, however, the EU did not hold its existing members to the same level of scrutiny. Members with sizeable Romani populations or thorny minority issues did not draw comparable condemnation for treating their minorities badly. Well before the fifth enlargement, the CJEU had steadily expanded the protections of human rights under European Community law, an expansion endorsed in the Maastricht Treaty's formulation of "fundamental rights."[27] Yet even into the fifth enlargement, minority rights lagged, having never matched the ascension of human rights and fundamental rights under EU law.[28] Aggrieved minority groups in the member states therefore had to articulate their claims under other frameworks such as human rights. In the end, of course, the power disparity between the EU and CSEE accession candidates required those candidates to accept minority

22 Maresceau, *supra* note 20, at 13. Respect for minority rights was not required of Austria, Finland, and Sweden, who were in fact the first post-Communist accession candidates but who sailed through the accession process to join the Union in 1995.

23 de Witte, *supra* note 2, at 137.

24 Smith, *supra* note 16, at 106.

25 *See, e.g.*, European Comm'n, Regular Report from the Commission on Slovakia's Progress Towards Accession 12 (1998) [hereinafter European Commission, 1998 Slovakia Progress Report]; Regular Report from the Commission on Slovakia's Progress Towards Accession 16–17 (1999); Regular Report from the Commission on Bulgaria's Progress Towards Accession 21–22, 25–26 (2003); Croatia 2010 Progress Report 13, 15 (2010).

26 *See* Peter Vermeersch, *Ethnic Mobilisation and the Political Conditionality of European Union Accession: The Case of the Roma in Slovakia*, 28 J. Ethnic & Migration Stud. 83, 87–88 (2002). *See also* European Comm'n, *supra* note 3, at 13 (noting that the European Parliament considered, before rejecting, a proposal to monitor Slovakia *after* accession because of human rights concerns with respect to its Romani community).

27 For a succinct summary of this development, see Elizabeth F. Defeis, *Human Rights, the European Union, and the Treaty Route: From Maastricht to Lisbon*, 35 Fordham Int'l L.J. 1207 (2012). For the significance of the term "fundamental rights," see Turkuler Isiksel, Europe's Functional Constitution: A Theory of Constitutionalism Beyond the State 100 (2016).

28 *See* Antje Wiener & Guido Schwellnus, *Contested Norms in the Process of EU Enlargement: Non-discrimination and Minority Rights*, *in* Law and Governance in an Enlarged European Union 451 (George A. Bermann & Katharina Pistor eds., 2004).

protections under the Copenhagen criteria, however out of step they may have been with the EU's own fundamental rights rubric.

The U.S., too, imposed requirements on candidates for statehood whenever a new state was inducted.[29] For racial equality, the most important developments came not during admission of any territory as a state, but during the *readmission* of former Confederate states to the Union after the Civil War. This started in 1865, when the U.S. was in the midst of a radical transformation. The country had just concluded a war over secession and slavery, and the Union emerged with newfound supremacy. The U.S. government could not only punish secession and outlaw slavery, but also legislate and regulate in more areas than ever before, areas that had been thought to be wholly within the authority of the states. The balance of power between the federal government and the states had tipped unequivocally toward the former.

From the Civil War onward, laws upholding racial equality would come primarily from the federal government.[30] These measures proliferated during Reconstruction, the postwar period when the former Confederate states of the South were rebuilt and brought back into the *United* States. To be sure, not all lawmakers during Reconstruction believed that the former Confederate states had truly left the Union; some lawmakers, as well as scholars ever since, argued that the Southern states merely succumbed to usurpers who had thrown off legal, loyal governments.[31] Thus, the conditions imposed during Reconstruction were less about the readmission of Southern states or the terms of their surrender than the seating of their congressional representatives. This debate over the extent of secession certainly has implications for weighty questions such as the legality of the Reconstruction Amendments, which might have been ratified by hastily formed, if not illegitimate, Southern state governments.[32] The nature of secession also touches on the typology of the South's conditions, whether they were for (re)admission into the Union or for the (re)seating of the congressional representatives of existing states. For our purposes, however, these debates are overly technical. The conditions were typical of criteria imposed on outsiders seeking to join a union: they were more onerous than laws governing existing members, and they reflected the aspirations of the union for its idealized self. In other words, we do not need an airtight correlation between EU accession and Southern readmission to draw broader conclusions from

29 Biber, *supra* note 14, at 129.

30 *See, e.g.*, HEATHER COX RICHARDSON, WEST FROM APPOMATTOX: THE RECONSTRUCTION OF AMERICA AFTER THE CIVIL WAR 3 (2007) (the Thirteenth Amendment "was the first amendment in the history of the American Constitution that increased, rather than limited, the power of the national government"). *See also* ERIC FONER, THE SECOND FOUNDING: HOW THE CIVIL WAR AND RECONSTRUCTION REMADE THE CONSTITUTION 8 (2019).

31 *See* ACKERMAN, *supra* note 15, at 113. *See also* John Harrison, *The Lawfulness of the Reconstruction Amendments*, 68 U. CHI. L. REV. 375, 391–93 (2001) (summarizing the positions of Andrew Johnson and Samuel Shellabarger). For a contrary position, that the South had most certainly seceded and been vanquished or demoted to territorial status, see ACKERMAN, *supra* note 15, at 113–13; Harrison, 390–91 (summarizing the positions of Thaddeus Stevens and Charles Sumner).

32 *See* Harrison, *supra* note 31.

the comparison. Further, as discussed below, conditions for statehood were imposed on other territories that sought, as outsiders, to join the Union during Reconstruction, specifically Nebraska and Nevada, for which the broader trends (incongruity with existing states, expressions of national ideals) held.

Two of the landmarks of racial equality from Reconstruction were the Thirteenth Amendment (passed in 1864 and 1865), which abolished slavery,[33] and the Fourteenth Amendment (passed in 1866), which, among other things, affirmed birthright citizenship and guaranteed equal protection under the law.[34] It is difficult to overstate their momentousness. The Thirteenth Amendment upended an institution – slavery – that the nation had been founded on, that had conscripted the labor to fuel the nation's economic growth, and that had inspired a bloody civil war. The Fourteenth Amendment's Equal Protection Clause would go on to anchor both the desegregation decisions of the Civil Rights era and the birth of contemporary fundamental rights such as privacy.[35] Federal advocacy of racial equality was not limited to constitutional amendments. During Reconstruction, Congress also passed the Civil Rights Act of 1866, which defined citizenship and attendant equal protection rights;[36] three separate Reconstruction Acts, which divided the South into districts administered by the U.S. military and imposed conditions on the readmission of states formerly in rebellion;[37] the Enforcement Act 1871, which allowed the President to use force to suppress the Ku Klux Klan;[38] and the Civil Rights Act of 1875, which ensured equal treatment in public accommodations.[39]

For approximately five years during Reconstruction, roughly 1865 to 1870, much of the above legislation framed the Union's conditions for the readmission of Southern states and the seating of their representatives. The Reconstruction Act of 1867, for instance, required that Southern states ratify the Fourteenth Amendment.[40] Further, the seating of each Southern state's representatives was governed by

33 U.S. CONST. amend. XIII, § 1 ("Neither slavery nor involuntary servitude, except as a punishment for crime whereof the party shall have been duly convicted, shall exist within the United States, or any place subject to their jurisdiction.").

34 U.S. CONST. amend. XIV, § 1 ("All persons born or naturalized in the United States, and subject to the jurisdiction thereof, are citizens of the United States and of the state wherein they reside. No state shall make or enforce any law which shall abridge the privileges or immunities of citizens of the United States; nor shall any state deprive any person of life, liberty, or property, without due process of law; nor deny to any person within its jurisdiction the equal protection of the laws."). On birthright citizenship, see also MARTHA S. JONES, BIRTHRIGHT CITIZENS: A HISTORY OF RACE AND RIGHTS IN ANTEBELLUM AMERICA (2018).

35 *See, e.g.*, Brown v. Bd. of Educ. of Topeka, 347 U.S. 483 (1954); Griswold v. Connecticut, 381 U.S. 479 (1965); Eisenstadt v. Baird, 405 U.S. 438 (1972); Roe v. Wade, 410 U.S. 113 (1973); Lawrence v. Texas, 539 U.S. 558 (2003); Obergefell v. Hodges, 135 S. Ct. 2584 (2015).

36 Civil Rights Act of 1866, ch. 31, 14 Stat. 27–30 (1866).

37 First Reconstruction Act, ch. 153, 14 Stat. 428 (1867).

38 Act of Apr. 20, 1871, ch. 22, 17 Stat. 13 (1871).

39 18 Stat. 335 (repealed in the Civil Rights Cases, 109 U.S. 3 (1883)).

40 ACKERMAN, *supra* note 15, at 199–201. For more on the Reconstruction Act of 1867, see MICHAEL LES BENEDICT, A COMPROMISE OF PRINCIPLE: CONGRESSIONAL REPUBLICANS AND RECONSTRUCTION, 1863–1869, 223–43 (1974).

a separate act of Congress; these acts provided for varying degrees of protection of African American suffrage.[41] All of these terms comprised the conditionality of Southern readmission.

When the conditionalities of EU accession and American Reconstruction are compared, several patterns emerge. The first is a theme that runs throughout this book: during these two periods, it was the top rung of the federalist system – the EU and the U.S. government – that ushered in the reforms of minority rights and racial equality. The 1990s and early 2000s saw the EU growing more comfortable with fundamental rights. As the EU codified the CJEU's human rights jurisprudence in the Maastricht Treaty, the supranational body also took the opportunity to clarify the doctrines of direct effects and subsidiarity to reflect (and temper) its consolidation of power.[42] In the U.S., Reconstruction marks the most significant turning point in the nation's federal–state relations, especially in the sphere of racial equality. The succession of constitutional amendments and federal civil rights legislation was buttressed, albeit sporadically, by enforcement measures such as the dispatching of federal troops to quell racial violence in the South and the creation of the Freedman's Bureau to administer the postemancipation transition. Tellingly, during and after Reconstruction, African Americans would refashion their strategies for advancement by appealing to federal powers rather than laws of friendlier Northern states.[43] After these pivotal constitutional moments of 1865 and 1992, however much the U.S. and the EU regressed periodically on minority rights, federal–state and supranational–state relations would never be the same.

These innovations were consistent with a strategy from EU constitutionalization and Radical Republican lawmaking: that of conferring jurisdiction and enforcement authority on the federal or supranational entity by defining certain actions against minority groups as infractions of federal or supranational law. The EU accomplished this through the Amsterdam Treaty of 1997, which gave the Union the competence to fight racial and ethnic discrimination, and the Race Equality Directive of 2000, which created an infrastructure to push for racial equality.[44] Radical Republicans fought for equality by conferring U.S. citizenship on all persons born or naturalized in the U.S. and guaranteeing the privileges and immunities of U.S. citizens, including equal protection under the law.[45] This conception of federal citizenship was articulated in the Civil Rights Act of 1866, which attempted to fulfill the promise of the Thirteenth Amendment by overruling *Dred*

41 Biber, *supra* note 14, at 143–44.

42 *See* Deborah Cass, *The Word That Saves Maastricht? The Principle of Subsidiarity and the Division of Powers Within the European Community*, 29 Common Mkt. L. Rev. 1107 (1992); Federico Fabbrini, *The Principle of Subsidiarity*, *in* Oxford Principles of European Union Law, vol. 1, 221 (Robert Schütze & Takis Tridimas eds., 2018); Robert Schütze, *Direct Effects and Indirect Effects*, *in* Oxford Principles of European Union Law, vol. 1, 265 (Robert Schütze & Takis Tridimas eds., 2018).

43 *See* Earl M. Maltz, Civil Rights, the Constitution, and Congress, 1863–1869 (1990).

44 For more, see *infra* Chapter 5.

45 For more, see Ackerman, *supra* note 15, at 164.

Scott and declaring persons born in the U.S. (including freed slaves) to be citizens.[46] For its part, the notion of EU citizenship, which was introduced in the Maastricht Treaty, has not developed to anchor as full a panoply of rights as U.S. citizenship, though, for Roma, a salient right is freedom of movement and residence within EU member states.[47] However, the CJEU has stated that Article 20 TFEU "precludes national measures which have the effect of depriving" EU citizens of "the genuine enjoyment of the substance of" their citizenship rights,[48] which commentators have taken to possibly include human rights violations.[49]

As they admitted new members while crafting the notion of federal and supranational citizenship, the U.S. and the EU proffered certain visions of the nation. This is the second pattern to emerge from our comparison. During Reconstruction, that vision appeared to put forth racial equality as a core national value.[50] Southern states had to ratify the Fourteenth Amendment, uphold African American suffrage, and abstain from infringing on the educational and political rights of African Americans, among other requirements.[51] The fact that two Western territories attained statehood during this period – Nevada in 1864 and Nebraska in 1867 – under similar conditions of banning slavery and, in Nebraska's case, repealing a ban on the denial of African American voting rights, suggests that the Union's ideological commitment to racial equality had little to do with the South.[52] Yet that gloss is wrong: the Union's conditions of racial equality were closely tied to punishing the South and preserving the Republican majority in Congress.[53] The same dynamics pervaded the EU's eastern enlargement. One of the criteria to emerge from the Article 49 TEU application process was "Europeanness" – that is, applicants had to demonstrate adherence to European sociocultural values.[54] Consistent with prior rounds of enlargement, these values encompassed democracy, the rule of law, and human

46 *Id.* at 170. *See also* Dredd Scott v. Sandford, 60 U.S. (19 How.) 393 (1857).

47 *See* TFEU arts. 20–21. For more on the comparison between U.S. and EU citizenship rights, see Francesca Strumia, *Individual Rights, Interstate Equality, State Autonomy: European Horizontal Citizenship and Its (Lonely) Playground from a Trans-Atlantic Perspective, in* EU CITIZENSHIP AND FEDERALISM: THE ROLE OF RIGHTS 615 (Dimitry Kochenov ed., 2017).

48 Case C-34/09, Ruiz Zambrano v. ONEM, 2011 E.C.R. I-01177, para. 42.

49 *See* Johanna Croon-Gestefeld, *Reverse* Solange*: Union Citizenship as a Detour on the Route to European Rights Protection Against National Infringements, in* EU CITIZENSHIP AND FEDERALISM: THE ROLE OF RIGHTS 665, 668 (Dimitry Kochenov ed., 2017).

50 *See* FONER, *supra* note 7, at 278–79.

51 Biber, *supra* note 14, at 143–50.

52 *See id.* at 141–43.

53 Conditionality had bootstrapped ratification of the Fourteenth Amendment (whose Section 2 threatened to reduce the proportion of voters in a state by the proportion of disenfranchised voters and whose Section 3 barred rebels from political office) onto the readmission process. *See also* ACKERMAN, *supra* note 15, at 181 (Republicans saw political fealty to the Union as more important than racial homogeneity); Biber, *supra* note 14, at 143 (Nebraska balked at the suffrage requirement because the state had been loyal to the Union, unlike the South).

54 *See* KOCHENOV, *supra* note 18, at 22 (listing (i) statehood, (ii) Europeanness, (iii) adherence to ex Art. 6(1) TEU, and (iv) COE membership as Art. 49 TEU requirements); *id.* at 27–28, 30–33 (analyzing the sociocultural dimensions of Europeanness).

rights. However, breaking new ground, the Copenhagen criteria featured minority protections.[55] In this way, the CSEE candidates of the fifth enlargement became a fun house mirror, augmenting the most idealized version of Europeanness – a version that not even existing members could satisfy.[56]

The third pattern emerging from the Reconstruction comparison is that the conditions required of aspiring members were far more rigorous than the constraints placed on existing members. This incongruity is related to the first pattern: the consolidation of power at the federal/supranational level gave each union the wherewithal to foist bold demands on aspiring members. So, too, did winning a war. The Civil War vindicated American federal supremacy, while the Cold War vindicated the liberal democracies of Western Europe.[57] These victories allowed the U.S. and the EU to press statehood and accession candidates harder than they could the current members. The Copenhagen criteria mandated "respect for and protection of minorities" even though no comparable obligation existed in the EU's treaties or case law. Hence, the EU required minority rights of the East that were being flouted in the West. This disjunction became most prominent in 2010, during France's expulsion of Romani populations "back" to Bulgaria and Romania, two states that had recently joined the Union.

Hypocrisy was manifest in the conditions for the readmission of the Southern states and the seating of their representatives in Congress. The Reconstruction Act of 1867, for example, began by reciting that "no legal State governments or adequate protection for life or property now exists in the rebel States of Virginia, North Carolina, South Carolina, Georgia, Mississippi, Alabama, Louisiana, Florida, Texas, and Arkansas."[58] It then divided the "rebel States" into five military districts, where commanders could deploy a military force to "suppress insurrection, disorder, and violence."[59] Rancor toward the Confederacy permeated the Act, which reaffirmed the disenfranchisement of Confederate soldiers and required senators and representatives to take a loyalty oath to the Union – punitive measures that had been circulating in

55 *See id.* at 33.

56 Recall that, at this point, ex Article 6 TEU did not yet include minority protections as a fundamental value. Thus, it appears that the expressions of national identity inherent in the conditions for accession and statehood depended on the applicants themselves. For Greece, Spain, and Portugal, the EU projected values of democracy and rule of law; for CSEE, the EU added respect for and protection of minorities. For the former Confederacy, Nevada, and Nebraska, the Union projected racial equality; for Utah and the Western states, the Union projected whiteness, Christianity, and tradition.

57 Of course, the Civil War and the Cold War are vastly different. The Civil War was a bloody war that divided families. Vanquished Confederates were, in some respects, truly conquered peoples who might have accepted any conditions for surrender imposed by the victorious North. On the interplay between the "grasp of war" theory and constitutional change, see Ackerman, *supra* note 15, at 115–16; Michael Les Benedict, *Moments of Change: Transformations in American Constitutionalism*, 108 Yale L.J. 2011, 2027–28 (1999).

58 Ch. 153, 14 Stat. 428 (1867).

59 *Id.* §§ 1–3.

congressional bills for years.[60] The denial of suffrage to participants in rebellion stood in stark contrast to the expansion of voting rights for African American men.[61] This stipulation of African American suffrage would become more explicit in the Acts passed by Congress to seat the representatives of Southern states. These Acts barred some states from excluding African Americans from public office and abridging their education rights.[62] Finally, the Reconstruction Act of 1867 mandated ratification of the Fourteenth Amendment, passed by Congress the prior year.[63] Clearly, none of these stipulations applied to the Northern states.

If the disparate treatment of Romani and other communities in Western and Eastern Europe highlighted the unevenness of conditionality in the EU, suffrage was where the divisions between conditions for readmission and the governance of existing states – or between the South and the North in the U.S. – were starkest. While the Reconstruction Act and the various readmission Acts required the South to grant suffrage to African Americans, the North refused to abide by the same.[64] This disparity endured until ratification in 1870 of the Fifteenth Amendment, which prohibits the denial or abridgment – by virtue of race, color, or prior servitude – of the right of citizens to vote.

Fourth, the comparison of conditionalities teaches that charges of hypocrisy may eventually prompt harmonization of internal and external governance, specifically by raising the standards of minority protection in the federalist system. In the U.S., the clearest example is the expansion of voting rights. African American suffrage had long been a point of contention in Congress, where Radical Republicans sparred with conservative Republicans over how to give full effect to the liberty of emancipated slaves.[65] Radicals saw the ballot as a natural extension of abolition, without which freedom was meaningless.[66]

60 *See, e.g.*, *id.* § 5. Disenfranchisement was also provided in Section 2 of the Fourteenth Amendment. *See also* FONER, *supra* note 7, at 253–58; BENEDICT, *supra* note 40, at 214–16.

61 *See* Ch. 153, 14 Stat. 428, § 5, which provided that delegates to conventions to draft state constitutions be elected "by the male citizens of said State, twenty-one years old and upward, of whatever race, color, or previous condition . . . except such as may be disfranchised for participation in the rebellion or for felony at common law" and that "such constitution[s] shall provide that the elective franchise shall be enjoyed by all such persons as have the qualifications herein stated for electors of delegates."

62 Biber, *supra* note 14, at 143–44.

63 Congressional passage does not end the amendment process; under Article V of the Constitution, an amendment passed by Congress must then be ratified by three fourths of the states. For the Article V quandaries presented by the Thirteenth and Fourteenth Amendments, see ACKERMAN, *supra* note 15, at 110–19.

64 *See id.* at 106–07. *See also* GILLETTE, *supra* note 13, at 366 ("when enfranchisement of the southern Negro became a necessity in order to maintain Republican hegemony in the nation, in Congress, and in the South, a double standard prevailed: enfranchisement was required of the powerless South, but not of the unwilling North—a situation that lasted for three years").

65 *See* GILLETTE, *supra* note 13, at 371 ("whereas the radicals tended to make substantive compromises too seldom or too late, the moderates were apt to make them too often and too soon").

66 *See* Benedict, *supra* note 57, at 2024.

Some conservatives and moderates opposed African American suffrage altogether, while others endorsed suffrage in principle but eschewed federal regulation as the means to protect it, believing instead that federalism conveyed this prerogative to the states.[67] Yet Congress did manage to pass, and to override Andrew Johnson's veto against, the Reconstruction Act of 1867, which defended the right of African Americans in Southern states to vote.[68] For the next three years, the South had to submit to federal baselines for elections, even though Northern states were free to disenfranchise African Americans. All the while, pressure mounted for a federal solution to take care of the disparity once and for all, a solution that, as Radicals and moderates converged, took the form of a constitutional amendment.[69] It took some time and much political wrangling for this effort to take off, but eventually Congress passed the Fifteenth Amendment to guarantee universal suffrage. The requisite number of states ratified the Amendment in 1879.

This pattern is not without precedent. The Northwest Ordinance,[70] which governed the Northwest Territory before it was divided and admitted as the states of Indiana, Illinois, Michigan, Minnesota, Ohio, and Wisconsin, guaranteed residents certain privileges and immunities such as religious freedom, habeas corpus, encouragement of education, and free navigation of the waterways.[71] Many of these guarantees served as a template for Congress when it expanded the civil rights of U.S. citizens during Reconstruction.[72] In fact, the language of the Thirteenth Amendment was taken directly from part of the Ordinance, which read: "There shall be neither slavery nor involuntary servitude in the said territory, otherwise than in the punishment of crimes, whereof the party shall have been duly convicted."[73] Of course, the utility of the Ordinance as a comparator for EU conditionality is limited, since it went into effect when the authority of the federal government rested on much shakier foundations – when the federal government could hardly constrain the states and racial equality was not even a fleeting concern.

As for the EU, the double standards between internal and external governance ultimately propelled the adoption of a Union-wide Charter of Fundamental Rights.

67 Maltz, *supra* note 43, at 36–37. *See also* Benedict, *supra* note 40, at 330–35.

68 Historians do not uniformly view the Reconstruction Act of 1867 as revolutionary or expansive. *See, e.g.*, Michael Les Benedict, *The Rout of Radicalism: Republicans and the Elections of 1867*, 18 Civ. War Hist. 334, 335–36 (1972).

69 *See* Foner, *supra* note 30, at 97–99; Gillette, *supra* note 13, at 17–19.

70 Act of July 13, 1787, reenacted by Act of Aug. 7, 1789, ch. 8, 1 Stat. 50, 51 [hereinafter Northwest Ordinance].

71 Hegreness, *supra* note 14, at 1840–45. *See also* Northwest Ordinance, arts. I–IV.

72 Hegreness, *supra* note 14, at 1873–78.

73 Northwest Ordinance, art. VI. *See also* Rutherglen, *supra* note 14, at 1372. Debates over the degree to which the Ordinance prohibited slavery are key to a proper understanding of the Thirteenth Amendment. The Ordinance did not completely abolish slavery and lacked adequate enforcement, which makes the improvements in the language of the Amendment all the more significant. *See* Rutherglen, 1373–74.

In the early 1990s, minority rights in what at the time were the European Community's eastern neighbors became a pressing concern for Community members after the Soviet Union and the Eastern bloc dissolved. The successors of former Yugoslavia had to espouse minority protections to be recognized as independent states by Community members who had themselves not previously done the same.[74] In 1993, minority protections were added to the political conditions for accession.[75] The regular monitoring reports of the European Commission analyzed the progress of CSEE candidates in minority rights, and particularly Roma integration; so, too, did each of the accession partnerships. There were legal justifications for the differences between the fifth enlargement and prior ones, as well as between internal and external minority policies. Because the acquis was constantly growing, subsequent accession candidates would invariably have to adopt more EU and Community laws than earlier candidates. And because accession negotiations were conducted with nonmembers, the negotiations would not be restricted by the competences governing EU relations with member states.[76] Further, the accession process was supplemented by bilateral agreements such as accession partnerships.[77] Yet these justifications were not entirely convincing. In the fourth enlargement of 1995, for instance, Austria, Finland, and Sweden sailed through negotiations more easily than Greece, Portugal, and Spain in the prior enlargements and certainly more easily than the ten countries that joined in the fifth enlargement.

Commentators observed that minority protections were more onerous under preaccession documents than under EU treaties.[78] Additionally, commentators feared that the discrepancy would lead accession candidates to abandon their commitments once they became members.[79] One episode did more than anything else to catalyze reform of this discrepancy: Austria's election of Jörg Haider's far-right Freedom Party to a governing coalition in 1999.[80] Here was a bout of xenophobia in an existing member state that challenged the EU's projection of itself as a defender of minority protections. In response to the Haider affair, the Union broke off diplomatic relations with Austria and imposed half-hearted sanctions.[81]

74 de Witte, *supra* note 2, at 142.

75 *Id.*; Kochenov, *supra* note 18, at 33. While the other political conditions, such as the rule of law, had existed in some form in prior rounds of enlargement, this condition was new altogether.

76 *See* Kochenov, *supra* note 18, at 82.

77 *See* Maresceau, *supra* note 20, at 31–32.

78 *See, e.g.*, Editorial, *Fundamental Rights and EU Membership: Do as I Say, Not as I Do!*, 499 Common Mkt. L. Rev. 481, 487 (2012) (noting that, even though the EU was strengthening fundamental rights, any action of an accession candidate could run afoul of fundamental rights protections, while a member infringes the same only when acting within EU law).

79 *See, e.g.*, Ulrich Sedelmeier, *After Conditionality: Post-Accession Compliance with EU Law in East Central Europe* 15 J. Eur. Pub. Pol'y 806 (2008); Gwendolyn Sasse, *The Politics of EU Conditionality: The Norm of Minority Protection During and Beyond EU Accession*, 15 J. Eur. Pub. Pol'y 842 (2008).

80 *See* Michael Merlingen et al., *The Right and the Righteous? European Norms, Domestic Politics and the Sanctions Against Austria*, 39 J. Common Mkt. Stud. 59 (2001).

81 *See* Gráinne de Búrca, *Beyond the Charter: How Enlargement Has Enlarged the Human Rights Policy of the European Union*, 27 Fordham Int'l L.J. 679, 697–98 (2004).

Of more lasting effect, however, were reforms to the EU's constitutional order. The EU commissioned a report on the Austrian impasse that recommended three major changes that were ultimately adopted: a change to Article 7 TEU to suspend certain rights if a member engaged in a "serious and persistent" breach of fundamental rights; the creation of a new human rights agency; and incorporation of a "bill of rights" in the EU treaties.[82] The Charter of Fundamental Rights was drafted as a response to the third charge. Though the Charter does not expressly address minority rights, it was given effect by the Lisbon Treaty, which added "rights of persons belonging to minorities" to the EU's list of founding values.[83] Finally, it seemed, the time had come to shore up minority protections in EU law.

THE DILUTION OF CONDITIONALITY

The themes linking the conditionalities of accession and statehood – federalism, double standards, and conditionality's "lifting" effect on domestic law – provide some parameters for the Reconstruction–accession comparison. The comparison suggests that when a federalist system imposes staunch minority protections on prospective members, comparable protections in the system's member states can improve over time. Yet the harmonization of conditionality and internal governance is not so straightforward, if it happens at all. Sometimes the laws governing existing members weigh conditionality down; at other times, internal and external laws meet somewhere in the middle. Because one major determinant of how these laws converge is the government, with all its distractions and idiosyncrasies, the mutual influences of conditionality and internal governance are unpredictable.

During American Reconstruction and the fifth EU enlargement, both unions quickly squandered their advantages over aspiring members. Each did so in its own way: the EU misspent the better part of the 1990s through inconsistency and ambiguity, while infighting sapped the momentum of Reconstruction despite the tailwind of victory after the Civil War. In 1993, the European Council presented accession candidates with a nebulous mandate of minority protection, which the Commission enforced unevenly. Romani exclusion and marginalization were not the initial focus of political conditionality, so it took time for the EU to clarify exactly how Roma integration fitted into "respect for and protection of minorities," that open-ended aspiration. By the time the EU signed accession partnerships with the CSEE applicants in 1998, Roma integration had become more prominent.[84] Nonetheless, the Commission remained protean in how it monitored the

82 *See id.* at 697–99.

83 *See* TEU art. 2.

84 *See, e.g.*, Czech Republic: Accession Partnership, 98/C 202/02 (1998) (Roma integration identified as a political criterion of medium-term priority, singling out monitoring of anti-Romani discrimination, especially through the citizenship law).

candidates' progress. In its 1998 report on Slovakia, for example, the Commission noted that Roma suffered discrimination, harassment, and lack of police protection; the report then lauded the government for approving a "Plan for Solving Romany Problems," before concluding without further analysis that the program had been criticized for lack of funding and commitment.[85] Similarly, in 1999 the Commission remarked that Roma in the Czech Republic continued to suffer discrimination, prejudice, and lack of police and judicial protection; meanwhile, the government had adopted some helpful policies and laws, but those measures, too, were underfunded, understaffed, and ineffective.[86] Apart from making general observations on the status quo and pointing out the shortcomings of the candidates' meager efforts, the Commission had no clear formulation of what integration looked like – no guidelines to aspire to and no benchmarks to measure progress.[87]

If the Commission was inconsistent in its approach, it could at least lead the way on conditionality. The Commission is at once the executor that oversees implementation of the Copenhagen criteria and the lawmaker that establishes the ancillary procedures to supplement Article 49 TEU.[88] In the U.S., by contrast, executive and legislative functions are more clearly delineated.[89] During Reconstruction, stark divisions split the Presidency, and frequently Congress itself. At the outset, whether control of Reconstruction was vested in the executive or legislative branch was unsettled.[90] When the Civil War raged, President Lincoln had the authority to dictate the direction of the war, and he repeatedly pursued rapprochement with the Confederacy. Under the cloak of war powers, Lincoln devised a "Ten Percent Plan" in 1863, which would have readmitted any Confederate state if 10 percent of its population had pledged allegiance to the Union and acceptance of abolition.[91] Radical Republicans in Congress thought Lincoln was too generous. They countered with a plan of their own, the 1864 Wade–Davis Bill, which conditioned readmission on a majority within each state taking an "ironclad oath."[92] Neither approach succeeded, and the rift endured. Shortly after Andrew Johnson assumed the Presidency, he became a co-conspirator of the recalcitrant South, extending leniency at every turn and eventually campaigning as the

85 European Comm'n, 1998 Slovakia Progress Report, *supra* note 25, at 12.

86 European Comm'n, Regular Report from the Commission on Czech Republic's Progress Towards Accession 16–17 (1999);

87 *See* Peter Vermeersch, The Romani Movement: Minority Politics & Ethnic Mobilization in Contemporary Central Europe 198–99 (2006); James Hughes & Gwendolyn Sasse, *Monitoring the Monitors: EU Enlargement Conditionality and Minority Protection in the CEECs*, 4 J. on Ethnopol. & Minority Issues in Eur. 1 (2003).

88 *See* Paul Craig & Gráinne de Búrca, EU Law: Text, Cases, and Materials 36–39 (5th ed. 2011).

89 *See id.* at 31 ("The EU does not therefore conform to any rigid separation-of-powers principle of the sort that has shaped certain domestic political systems.").

90 Proponents of congressional primacy cited the Guarantee Clause. *See* Harrison, *supra* note 31, at 388.

91 Foner, *supra* note 7, at 35–36; Harrison, *supra* note 31, at 385–87.

92 *See* Benedict, *supra* note 40, at 70–83.

bulwark against Radical Reconstruction.[93] Betrayed, the progressive faction of the Republican Party assumed control over Reconstruction, shepherding virtually all of the legislation identified with the era, often over Johnson's vetoes.

As the threat of war receded, it was Congress that rightfully controlled the procedure for admission.[94] In theory, one major constraint on congressional authority was the equal-footing doctrine, which prohibited Congress from imposing statehood conditions on an unequal footing with existing states;[95] in practice, however, case law and power dynamics have allowed Congress the freedom to disregard this doctrine.[96] This does not mean that Congress was unified in its approach to Reconstruction, because deep schisms also cut across the legislative body. Because Radicals and Democrats were bitter antagonists, conservative Republicans played an outsized role in legislation. To cajole conservatives into breaking impasses, Radicals had to compromise, and so the Reconstruction Amendments almost had to be narrowly construed.[97] This means that the Thirteenth Amendment might have done no more than simply abolish slavery, without granting any additional rights;[98] that the Fourteenth Amendment, as originally conceived, might have endorsed only a few basic liberties, rather than broadly prohibiting racial discrimination outright;[99] and that the Fifteenth Amendment might have required only the racially neutral application of voting laws, regardless of disparate impacts.[100] The shortcomings of each amendment necessitated a subsequent amendment – and eventually the Civil Rights movement. Thus, laws on racial equality *within* the Union never matched the vigor of demands placed on territories *outside* the Union. Even if the Thirteenth Amendment was modeled on language from the Northwest Ordinance that appeared to be a "resounding declaration of liberty,"[101] the horse trade around the Amendment reduced it to a thin compromise.[102] On the question of whether slavery was abolished, the answer was clearly yes; on all other questions, such as whether other rights flowed from abolition and whether the federal government even possessed the authority to grant such rights, the answer was a resounding

93 *See* Heather Cox Richardson, The Death of Reconstruction: Race, Labor, and Politics in the Post-Civil War North, 1865–1901, 16–17 (2001); Foner, *supra* note 7, at 182–97.

94 *See* U.S. Const. art. IV, § 3, cl. 1 ("New states may be admitted by the Congress into this union . . . . The Congress shall have power to dispose of and make all needful rules and regulations respecting the territory or other property belonging to the United States . . . ."). Congress has exhibited variation in how it admits states. *See* Biber, *supra* note 14, at 125–29.

95 *See* Coyle v. Smith, 221 U.S. 559 (1911); Pollard's Lessee v. Hagan, 44 U.S. 212 (1845).

96 *See* Biber, *supra* note 14, at 175–84.

97 *See* Benedict, *supra* note 40, at 222, 325–35.

98 Maltz, *supra* note 43, at 27–28. *But see* Foner, *supra* note 30, at 40–43.

99 Maltz, *supra* note 43, at 96. *But see* Foner, *supra* note 30, at 71–78.

100 Maltz, *supra* note 43, at 156. *But see* Foner, *supra* note 30, at 109.

101 Hegreness, *supra* note 14, at 1824.

102 The Northwest Ordinance might not have been that progressive. *See* Rutherglen, *supra* note 14, at 1373–74 (Northwest Ordinance may have tolerated slavery in the territories).

maybe.[103] And even if the Reconstruction Act provided a model for upholding suffrage, by spelling out the voting restrictions that would be prohibited and the voting expansions that would be encouraged, when time came for the template to be extended to the entire Union, Congress settled on the Fifteenth Amendment, whose final language was watered down from the initial proposals.[104] The Fifteenth Amendment would foment the ire of women suffragists, tolerate Chinese voting prohibitions in the West, and confer on states the freedom to regulate the "privilege" of voting as they saw fit.[105] The poll taxes, literacy tests, and other voting restrictions that sprang up would endure for nearly a century until the federal government definitively intervened again with the Voting Rights Act of 1965.

Crucially, it must be acknowledged that neither scholarship nor case law takes a uniformly conservative, restrictive view of the constitutional and legislative accomplishments of Reconstruction. For example, despite the brevity of its two sections, the Thirteenth Amendment has been interpreted as abolishing not only slavery itself but also the "badges and incidents" of that institution.[106] And because slavery is a "bundle of disabilities, bound together by conventions,"[107] its badges and incidents may include hate speech,[108] racial profiling,[109] environmental racism,[110] and reproductive rights,[111] all arguably barred by the Thirteenth Amendment.[112] Recent work has even lauded the Grant administration, which presided over the readmission of the last ex-Confederate states and the bulk of Reconstruction.[113] The valor, skill, and dedication of African American troops during the war helped convince Grant that racial equality was worth supporting; after the war, he oversaw the South's division into military districts under the Reconstruction Act of 1867.[114] As President, Grant

103 Maltz, *supra* note 43, at 27–28.

104 Foner, *supra* note 7, at 446 (the language was "more remarkable for what it does not than for what it does contain") (quoting the historian and chronicler of Reconstruction Henry Adams).

105 *See id.* at 447–49.

106 *See* Civil Rights Cases, 109 U.S. 3 (1883); Jones v. Alfred H. Mayer Co., 392 U.S. 409 (1968).

107 Darrell A.H. Miller, *The Thirteenth Amendment and the Regulation of Custom*, 112 Colum. L. Rev. 1811, 1848 (2012).

108 *See* Akhil Reed Amar, *The Case of the Missing Amendments:* R.A.V. v. City of St. Paul, 106 Harv. L. Rev. 124 (1992).

109 William M. Carter, Jr., A *Thirteenth Amendment Framework for Combating Racial Profiling*, 39 Harv. C.R.–C.L. L. Rev. 17 (2004).

110 Marco Masoni, *The Green Badge of Slavery*, 2 Geo. J. on Fighting Poverty 97 (1994).

111 Pamela D. Bridgewater, *Reproductive Freedom as Civil Freedom: The Thirteenth Amendment's Role in the Struggle for Reproductive Rights*, 3 J. Gender Race & Just. 401 (2000).

112 For a fuller catalogue of examples, see William M. Carter, Jr., *Race, Rights, and the Thirteenth Amendment: Defining the Badges and Incidents of Slavery*, 40 U.C. Davis L. Rev. 1311, 1316 n.13 (2007). For other accounts of this expansive view, see, e.g., Alexander Tsesis, The Thirteenth Amendment and American Freedom: A Legal History (2004); Rebecca Zietlow, The Forgotten Emancipator: James Mitchell Ashley and the Ideological Origins of Reconstruction (2018).

113 *See, e.g.*, Ronald C. White, American Ulysses: A Life of Ulysses S. Grant (2016); Ron Chernow, Grant (2017).

114 Richardson, *supra* note 93, at 10.

deployed federal troops to protect African Americans and enforce their voting rights. Bolstering those efforts, Congress passed the Enforcement Act of 1870 and the Ku Klux Klan Act of 1871 to combat white terrorism. In keeping with the era's theme, these laws federalized certain crimes against African American citizens and created a federal apparatus – the U.S. Department of Justice – to oversee prosecution of these crimes.[115]

Whether Reconstruction's accomplishments were modest or extraordinary is, for our comparative endeavor, somewhat immaterial. It suffices that the Union imposed conditions on the South's readmission that were stricter than the Union's laws of internal governance. The Reconstruction Act of 1867 and each state's readmission act illustrated this disparity clearly, and the additional conditions that were sometimes heaped on the newly readmitted states, as well as the occasional presence of federal troops, suggest that the South was not entirely on an equal footing with the North during Reconstruction.[116] Nor were new EU members from CSEE on an equal footing with older members in Western and Northern Europe. Despite attaining accession in the sixth enlargement in 2007, Bulgaria and Romania could not join the Schengen area of visa-free travel in the EU.[117] One of the principal reasons was the fear of influxes of Romani migrants,[118] echoing similar concerns during the fifth enlargement.[119]

The conditionalities of the U.S. and EU also resembled each other in how the lofty aspirations of external standards fell prey to dissension, sabotage, and lack of conviction. For instance, the Charter of Fundamental Rights, which the EU championed in part as redress for the incongruence of conditionality, was slow to take effect and rather unsatisfactory when it did. The drafters managed to complete the Charter quickly, within a year of the Haider affair.[120] Yet, because its status was

115 To head the Department, Grant appointed Amos Akerman as attorney general, who in his short tenure enforced these laws vigorously. *See* FONER, *supra* note 7, at 457–58; William S. McFeely, *Amos T. Akerman: The Lawyer and Racial Justice*, *in* REGION, RACE, AND RECONSTRUCTION: ESSAYS IN HONOR OF C. VANN WOODWARD 395 (J. Morgan Kousser & James M. McPherson eds., 1982). For more on the enforcement Acts, see Robert J. Kaczorowski, *Federal Enforcement of Civil Rights During the First Reconstruction*, 23 FORDHAM URB. L.J. 155 (1995); Kermit L. Hall, *Political Power and Constitutional Legitimacy: The South Carolina Ku Klux Klan Trials, 1871–1872*, 33 EMORY L.J. 921 (1984).

116 *See* FONER, *supra* note 7, at 452–53 (detailing the additional conditions pertaining to voting, education, and political rights for African Americans in Virginia, Mississippi, and Texas even after these states approved their Reconstruction constitutions).

117 The latest development, at the time of the writing of this book, is that the European Parliament expressed support for Bulgaria and Romania's entry into the Schengen zone. Ana Maria Luca, *MEPs Vote for Romania and Bulgaria to Join Schengen*, BALKANINSIGHT (Dec. 11, 2018), https://balkaninsight.com/2018/12/11/meps-vote-for-romania-and-bulgaria-to-join-schengen-12-11-2018/. However, accession to the Schengen zone requires the approval of the members of the EU Council; it is thus a more multilateral process than accession to the EU itself.

118 Tony Todd, *France Opposes Border-Free Travel for Romania, Bulgaria*, FRANCE24 (Sept. 30, 2013), https://www.france24.com/en/20130930-france-against-romania-bulgaria-schengen-roma-europe-immigration.

119 *See supra* Chapter 2.

120 *See* CRAIG & DE BÚRCA, *supra* note 88, at 393.

intertwined with the Union's contemporaneous project of adopting a Constitutional Treaty, the Treaty's inability to secure ratification cast the status of the Charter into doubt for nearly a decade.[121] The Charter only entered into force with the Lisbon Treaty in 2009. Even then, the Charter was tangentially integrated into the EU's constitutional order, declared to be on a parity with the treaties rather than being incorporated directly into them.[122] Even then, the Charter did not address minority rights.[123] Moreover, the notable change that the Lisbon Treaty made to the TEU's catalog of fundamental values was not matched by a significant change to the EU's minority protections. When the Lisbon Treaty changed Article 6 TEU to Article 2, the provision was restated to begin: "The Union is founded on the values of respect for human dignity, freedom, democracy, equality, the rule of law and respect for human rights, *including the rights of persons belonging to minorities*."[124] Yet the Article's use of "persons" suggests that minority rights are still embedded in a human rights framework, which predicates these rights on the rights held by individuals rather than collective or group rights.[125] As the next Chapter details further, few minority protections under EU law or enforcement accompanied this constitutional tweak.

These results in the EU and the U.S. are to be expected, with conditionality pursued only half-heartedly and the bar for minority rights inside the unions only half-raised. After all, the coalitions that adopted these reforms were disparate, and the convergences of interests that held them together were narrow and temporary. Minority protections under conditionality were spurred by the EU's desire to stabilize its eastern front and, later, to stem the flow of Romani refugees into Western Europe and Canada. Once the candidate countries joined, they would be subject to the same Treaty and other acquis obligations as other members; hence, even if Western Europe wanted to contain refugee movement, the ability to do so was more limited.[126] The Union improved minority protections somewhat through the Lisbon Treaty (which was signed, incidentally, when Bulgaria and Romania, countries with large Romani populations, joined). Yet the gap between those reforms and conditionality remained.[127] In the U.S., the

[121] *See id.*

[122] *Id.*

[123] *Id.* at 395 (noting that, despite the Charter's innovative provisions, it did not feature minority protections). It still remained the case that only member actions under EU law could run afoul of the Charter, not all actions. *See* Ulrike Barten, *Minority Rights in the European Union After Lisbon*, 33 Nordic J. Hum. Rts. 1, 4 (2011).

[124] TEU art. 2 (emphasis added).

[125] *See* Barten, *supra* note 123, at 5–6.

[126] EU citizens enjoy freedom of movement and residence within the Union. TFEU arts. 20–21. *But see supra* note 117 and accompanying text (accession to the Schengen zone for Bulgaria and Romania stalled by EU members).

[127] When fundamental rights protections under the Charter and Article 2 TEU are compared side by side with the Commission's vision of fundamental rights protections under the acquis for accession candidates, the demands upon candidates still dwarfs the restrictions upon members. *See* Editorial, *supra* note 78, at 487.

conditions imposed on the reconstructed South derived from several interests: punishing the Confederacy,[128] securing Republican votes,[129] limiting the movement of African Americans into the North,[130] and guaranteeing rights for emancipated slaves.[131] These concerns were thought to have been resolved by the Fourteenth Amendment, which barred Confederates from political office and threatened to shrink congressional representation in the event of voter suppression,[132] and the various Reconstruction Acts, which conditioned readmission on ratification of the Fourteenth Amendment and set standards for the treatment of African Americans.[133] To further shore up loyal Republican votes, Congress passed the Fifteenth Amendment, expanding suffrage to African Americans.[134] By then, the hypocrisy of civil rights was becoming moot: over half of the former Confederate states had been admitted by 1869, and the rest would soon follow. Civil rights could never command Republican attention for long; it alienated white voters and split the Republican coalition.[135] A fractious and tired Republican Party heralded the passage of the Fifteenth Amendment as a panacea that was to solve the race problem at last.[136]

The story of conditionality in the EU and U.S. is not completely dark. In the EU, conditionality-based minority rights followed a trajectory of gradual improvement. While the EU did not apply the Copenhagen criteria with the utmost clarity, other groups acted in the interstices to nudge European states toward Roma inclusion. The Council of Europe, a much larger and looser association that aims to foster human rights and European values, passed the Framework Convention on the Protection of National Minorities in 1995.[137] It set goals for achieving equality for national minorities in law, cultural expression, language rights, and education.[138] Ratification of the FCNM was a precondition for EU membership despite, embarrassingly, a lack of universal ratification by the accession candidates' West European counterparts.[139] More significantly, after the fifth enlargement, many European governments signed onto

128 Foner, *supra* note 7, at 254; Benedict, *supra* note 40, at 216–18, 227.

129 Biber, *supra* note 14, at 146.

130 Gillette, *supra* note 13, at 372.

131 Foner, *supra* note 7, at 256–59.

132 *See* U.S. Const. amend. XIV, §§ 2, 3. *See also* Foner, *supra* note 7, at 253–54.

133 *See* Biber, *supra* note 14, at 143–50.

134 *See* Richardson, *supra* note 93, at 42; Gillette, *supra* note 13, at 17–19. *But see* Benedict, *supra* note 40, at 325–26 (countering Gillette's view).

135 *See* Benedict, *supra* note 68.

136 *See* Benedict, *supra* note 40, at 335–36.

137 The COE is often called a "sister organization" to the EU. On the relationship between the EU and the COE, see Tony Joris & Jan Vendenberghe, *The Council of Europe and the European Union: Natural Partners or Uneasy Bedfellows?*, 15 Colum. J. Eur. L. 1 (2008/2009).

138 The FCNM covers all national minorities, not just the Roma. Notably, "national minorities" is not defined in the FCNM. *See Factsheet on the Framework Convention for the Protection of National Minorities*, Council of Europe, http://www.coe.int/en/web/minorities/fcnm-factsheet (last accessed Oct. 24, 2019).

139 Most notably, France. Coincidentally, France also stonewalled adoption of the ECHR, due to its rejection of the associated Defence Community Treaty in 1954. Craig & de Búrca, *supra* note 88, at 362.

commitments as part of the Decade of Roma Inclusion 2005–2015 (the "Decade"). The Decade consisted of pledges and initiatives by participating governments to end anti-Roma discrimination and close the gaps between Roma and the rest of society.[140] Initiated by two powerful NGOs, the Open Society Institute and the World Bank, the Decade tackled Roma inclusion in four key areas: education, employment, health, and housing.[141] Its methodical approach helped to sharpen the EU's framing of integration as a four-part approach.[142] Finally, a host of civil society organizations advocated for Roma in a variety of dimensions.[143] Over time, then, the EU did manage to give shape to the goal of Roma integration, an evolution that occurred in tandem with pressure from other organizations.[144]

There were bright spots, too, in Reconstruction's progression toward racial equality. While this book focuses on government initiatives, those should not obscure the centrality of civil society and private efforts. Indeed, government initiatives usually came as a response to grassroots compulsion. African Americans were frequently the prime movers of the period, forcing the government's hand in emancipation by virtue of their bravery during the Civil War, after which they had to fight again to "stake a claim to equal citizenship."[145] White Unionists in state government and Southern whites were also important partners in a racially egalitarian Reconstruction.[146] Finally, when Grant won the Presidency, congressional Republicans could lean on an ally in the executive;

140 *Frequently Asked Questions*, Decade of Roma Inclusion 2005–2015, *archived at* http://perma.cc/RJR5-JHRP. The member states were Albania, Bosnia and Herzegovina, Bulgaria, Croatia, the Czech Republic, Hungary, Macedonia, Montenegro, Romania, Serbia, Slovakia and Spain. Slovenia and the United States have observer status. *Id.*

141 *See* Peter Vermeersch & Melanie H. Ram, *The Roma, in* Minority Rights in Central and Eastern Europe 61, 66 (Bernd Rechel ed., 2009). The roots of the Decade lie in a 2003 conference on the Roma in Europe, when it became clear that the Copenhagen criteria would exert no lasting pressure. Dena Ringold et al., World Bank, Roma in an Expanding Europe: Breaking the Poverty Cycle vii, 184–85 (2005). *See also* World Bank, *Conference Briefing Note: "Roma in an Expanding Europe: Challenges for the Future"* (2003), http://documents.worldbank.org/curated/en/872391468749375351/pdf/26415.pdf.

142 Henceforth, many of the Commission's progress reports – particularly for Bulgaria, Croatia, and Romania, which joined the EU after the fifth enlargement – would frequently examine Romani well-being in those four dimensions, or mention the Decade itself. *See, e.g.*, European Comm'n, Bulgaria: 2005 Comprehensive Monitoring Report 15–16 (2005). Interestingly, this four-part approach echoes the four areas of action in CSEE during Communism and Socialism. *See* Elena Marushiakova & Vesselin Popov, *European Policies for Social Inclusion of Roma: Catch 22?*, 3 Soc. Inclusion 19, 21 (2015).

143 *See* Angéla Kóczé & Márton Rövid, *Pro-Roma Global Civil Society: Acting for, with or Instead of Roma?, in* Global Civil Society 2012: Ten Years of Critical Reflection 110 (Mary Kaldor & Henrietta Moore eds., 2012).

144 Between the fifth and the sixth enlargements, the Union pivoted from integration as political imperative to inclusion as economic necessity; by Croatia's accession, the Union had become more systematic in its insistence on Roma inclusion, despite the fact that Croatia's Romani population was rather small.

145 This revelation was one of the innovations in Foner's work on Reconstruction. *See* Foner, *supra* note 7, at xxv.

146 *See id.* at 17–18.

when the two branches acted in unison, they ushered in a spate of civil rights laws and saw to their enforcement.[147]

In totality, the period of conditionality during Reconstruction was brief, from roughly 1863, when the Emancipation Proclamation liberated slaves in the South (but not the North), to 1870 or so, when the ex-Confederate states were readmitted to the Union and their representatives seated in Congress. Some would argue that these states never really left the Union despite their proclamations of secession, so the conditions for readmission applied only to congressional representation and did not constitute external governance.[148] Conditionality as part of the EU's eastern enlargement, by contrast, stretched over a lengthier period, when the supremacy of EU powers was less vulnerable. Eastern enlargement still has a way to go, with other Yugoslav successor states and Turkey currently engaged in *pre*-pre-accession talks. Reconstruction, on the other hand, had a finite end, since there were only so many ex-Confederate states that could be readmitted, and toward the end the stragglers sensed that the Union could only insist on so much. Whereas the precision and rigor of the EU's accession criteria have increased over time, both the demands imposed on the South and the political will to see them through began to recede by the 1870s.[149] Enforcement measures, such as the dispatching of federal troops to quell racial violence in South Carolina in 1871, were the scant exceptions rather than the rule – exceptions prompted by extreme violence in the South.[150] The federal civil rights and enforcement legislation enacted through 1875 were seldom invoked and, in some instances, quickly struck down by the Supreme Court for overreach.[151] Thus, conditionality did not have the opportunity to mature as meaningful policy during Reconstruction. The scholarly literature regarding the effect of conditionality on domestic policy in CSEE might be mixed, but there is at least some evidence that minority protections demanded under the Copenhagen criteria made their way into domestic law or international precedent.[152] During Reconstruction, progress on racial equality was neither genuine nor lasting without federal oversight.[153] Military rule, the most severe cudgel for enforcing readmission conditions, ended formally by 1877, if not well beforehand.[154] In the ensuing void, the South would

147 *See supra* notes 113–15 and accompanying text.

148 *See* Harrison, *supra* note 31, at 391–93.

149 *See* Foner, *supra* note 7, at 524–53.

150 *See* Hall, *supra* note 115.

151 *E.g.*, Slaughterhouse Cases, 83 U.S. (16 Wall.) 36 (1873); U.S. v. Cruikshank, 92 U.S. 542 (1876); Civil Rights Cases, 109 U.S. 3 (1883). *See also* Egerton, *supra* note 12, at 298–99.

152 *See, e.g.*, Sedelmeier, *supra* note 79; Judith G. Kelley, Ethnic Politics in Europe. The Power of Norms and Incentives (2004).

153 *See* Foner, *supra* note 7, at 459 ("National power had achieved what most Southern governments had been unable, and Southern white public opinion unwilling, to accomplish: acquiescence in the rule of law. Yet the need for outside intervention was a humiliating confession of weakness for the Reconstruction regimes.").

154 *Id.* at 582–87. *See also* Vincent P. DeSantis, *Rutherford B. Hayes and the Removal of the Troops and the End of Reconstruction*, *in* Region, Race, and Reconstruction: Essays in Honor of C. Vann Woodward 417, 417 (J. Morgan Kousser & James M. McPherson eds., 1982).

flout the Fifteenth Amendment, the most obvious product of conditionality, for the next ninety years. Perhaps it is too much to have expected lasting success from the conditionality of Reconstruction: the wounds of Civil War were too raw, the liberation of slaves too recent, and the distance too far to traverse from the antebellum vision of federalism to full enforcement of civil rights.

Evaluated from the perspective of institutional enforcers, conditionality led to unexpected results. The U.S. had federal troops at its disposal, while the EU could only punish transgressions by withholding or threatening to withhold Union membership, technical assistance, and funds through programs such as PHARE (Poland and Hungary: Assistance for Restructuring their Economies).[155] The fact that CSEE adopted the acquis and internalized its norms more readily than the American South accepted federal laws and norms signals a willingness on the part of CSEE to join the EU and espouse its vision of Europe. The CSEE accession candidates were often led by dissidents from the Communist era who were keen to join the EU "club" and adopt all the liberal values it represented, while the Southern states were merely vanquished rebels. Truly, EU accession candidates were supplicants and the ex-Confederate states only malcontents. This willingness on the part of applicants could overcome even dysfunction in the central government to usher in something as unpopular as minority rights.

Newly emboldened courts also played unexpected roles. The U.S. asked much of federal courts during Reconstruction, expanding their power to remove cases from state courts so that citizens could have a fair hearing on national rights. Yet federal courts were loath to usurp jurisdiction from state courts, and in the epoch's most prominent cases the Supreme Court intervened on behalf of white plaintiffs bucking Reconstruction.[156] By contrast, during the pre-accession of CSEE candidates EU courts did not get involved in minority rights. Instead, cases originated from the European Court of Human Rights (ECtHR), a COE organ. The most notable was *D.H. v. Czech Republic*, filed in 2000, where the ECtHR's Grand Chamber found that the Czech education system had discriminated against Roma schoolchildren by diverting them to "special schools" for remedial students or students with disabilities.[157] While the Court relied more on the COE's Convention for the Protection of Human Rights and Fundamental Freedoms than anything else, it noted that the COE's human rights monitoring body did "draw inspiration" from the EU's Race Equality Directive.[158] The substantive laws of the EU and COE were beginning to influence one another, if not converge – a trend that would extend to

[155] On PHARE and other pre-accession financial instruments, see Maresceau, *supra* note 20, at 35–36.

[156] *See, e.g., ex parte* Milligan, 71 U.S. (4 Wall.) 2 (1866); *Slaughterhouse Cases*, 83 U.S. *See also* FONER, *supra* note 7, at 529–30. *But see ex parte* McCardle, 74 U.S. (7 Wall) 506 (1868) (Supreme Court assenting to congressional removal of the Court's jurisdiction in habeas cases); Jesse Choper & John Yoo, *Wartime Process: A Dialogue on Congressional Power to Remove Issues from the Federal Courts*, 95 CALIF. L. REV. 1243, 1254–55 (2007).

[157] *See* D.H. and Others v. Czech Republic, App. No. 57825/00, 47 Eur. H.R. Rep. 59, para. 26 (2007).

[158] *See id.* at paras. 60, 61 (discussing Council Directive 2000/43/EC).

the institutions of the CJEU and ECtHR after the accession of Bulgaria and Romania.[159]

If conditionality can succeed on applicants' enthusiasm, then it can fail on their recalcitrance. As explored in Chapter 3, antipathy toward Roma in CSEE is deeply entrenched, manifesting in law and culture. During Reconstruction, racial equality faced resistance from white Southerners, though the difference was in degree. In response to the gains of African Americans, whites joined the Klan and other white supremacy groups, terrorizing African Americans and occasionally their Republican allies.[160] The scale of murder, rape, violence, and terror is difficult to estimate, since these groups often operated under the cloak of anonymity, but the brutality is easy to convey.[161] The Klan drew supporters among whites from all walks of life;[162] thus, the breadth of Klan activity both confirms and defies ethnic competition theory, which holds that competition between similarly situated, but ethnically distinct, labor groups foments inter-ethnic tension.[163] Over time, states with rather progressive governments ironically saw the rise of the fiercest Klan structures. Today, historians attribute the failure of Reconstruction largely to the violence inflicted by white Southerners on their neighbors.[164] Violence, terror, and exclusion perpetrated against Romani neighbors also plagued CSEE countries when they were accession candidates. Police and vigilantes alike killed Roma and burned their homes, while cities built walls around Romani neighborhoods, in addition to all the other ways that Roma were excluded from participation and representation in society. Persecution was severe enough to cause Roma to flee to Western Europe and North America seeking asylum.[165] Yet, until the recent crises engulfing Europe, anti-Romanyism generally did not translate into organized campaigns or platforms of major political parties.[166] In the American South, persecution of African Americans was the way of life under the prior social order; when Reconstruction threatened to upend that order, whites resorted to fraud, sabotage, violence, and downright insurrection to restore it.

159 *See infra* Chapter 6.

160 While these groups had existed prior to Reconstruction, it is the era's progress on equality that caused their ranks to swell. FONER, *supra* note 7, at 425.

161 *See, e.g.*, EGERTON, *supra* note 12, at 294–95 (Klansmen castrating, mangling, and lynching African American and Republican activists).

162 FONER, *supra* note 7, at 432–33.

163 *See* DAVID CUNNINGHAM, KLANSVILLE, U.S.A.: THE RISE AND FALL OF THE CIVIL RIGHTS-ERA KU KLUX KLAN 8–10 (2013) (discussing the ethnic competition model).

164 *See* EGERTON, *supra* note 12, at 19 ("Reconstruction did not fail; in regions where it collapsed it was violently overthrown by men who had fought for slavery during the Civil War and continued that battle as guerrilla partisans over the next decade.").

165 For how Canada has handled these claims, see Sean Rehaag et al., *No Refuge: Hungarian Romani Refugee Claimants in Canada*, 52 OSGOODE HALL L.J. 705 (2015).

166 One exception is Vladimir Mečiar, the prime minister of Slovakia in the 1990s, who routinely denigrated Roma. *See* Matthew Rhodes, *Slovakia after Mečiar*, 48 PROB. POST-COMMUNISM 3 (2001).

By itself, the majoritarian impulse to attack minority rights does not necessarily doom progress on equality. It is against the backdrop of disorganized and lackluster federal (or, in the EU's case, supranational) leadership that local resistance prevails. The determination of member-state governments plays an important role as well. Here, the distinction between CSEE and the American South was not in degree but in kind. In 1865, of the states that had seceded, only a handful were established under the governance of loyal Unionists or Lincoln's Ten Percent Plan; the remainder had governors appointed by President Johnson.[167] None of the state governments reflected popular will, if "popular" is measured by the desires of *all* citizens in the state.[168] In CSEE, national governments were cut from an entirely different cloth. They legitimately represented their citizens, some political leaders having braved incarceration under Communism. These leaders did speak for the populace, reflect liberal democratic values, and, even if Romani rights were unpopular, side philosophically with human rights. They would stand in stark contrast to the governors and lawmakers who succeeded the initial batch of Unionists backed by Lincoln and Johnson. Many of these successors had fought for the Confederacy. Where CSEE nations in the 1990s were led by artists and dissidents, Southern states in the 1870s and onward were led by Confederates, Democrats, and segregationists.

For its part, the U.S. government confused reconstruction with reconciliation too frequently.[169] It would take a century and new, external threats for the federal government to move past the specter of reconciliation and demand minority protections with the same vigor exhibited by the EU toward CSEE states.

167 Harrison, *supra* note 31, at 394–96.

168 Some would even contest the legitimacy of these governments, not to mention the constitutional amendments they ratified. *See* Harrison, *supra* note 31.

169 Michael Perman, Reunion without Compromise: The South and Reconstruction 1856–1868, 7 (1973).

5

Minority Protections and Internal Governance

In the century after Reconstruction in the U.S., Jim Crow laws installed a caste system that tenaciously separated whites and "coloreds"; poll taxes, literacy tests, fraud, and intimidation suppressed the black vote; and peonage, chain gangs, and convict leasing conscripted African Americans and poor whites into hard labor. For Roma in Europe, the EU's eastern enlargement failed to create genuine protections at the local and national levels. School administrators shunted Romani children into facilities for students with disabilities; municipal governments built walls around Romani communities; and national governments rounded up and deported their Romani populations. Above all, these societies could inflict extreme violence on African Americans and Roma at any time. Lynching, rape, and violence terrorized African Americans, who after the Thirteenth Amendment no longer fetched value as chattel.[1] Romani villages were burned, sometimes with the complicity of political parties and local government, and often with impunity.[2]

Far from delivering equality or even physical security, the legal protections that had come with the federal and supranational consolidation of power proved ephemeral. Both minority groups faced obstacles that were simply too steep and enduring to overcome in a few decades. The legacies of slavery, violence, exclusion, and racialized difference were, in a word, structural. Thus, when the U.S. and EU tried again to integrate the two groups, the governments needed to contend with

[1] *See, e.g.*, Equal Justice Initiative, Lynching in America: Confronting the Legacy of Racial Terror (3d ed. 2017); Ida B. Wells, Southern Horrors: Lynch Law in All Its Phases (1892); Patricia Hill Collins, *The Tie That Binds: Race, Gender and US Violence*, 21 Ethnic & Racial Stud. 917 (2010); David Garland, *Penal Excess and Surplus Meaning: Public Torture Lynchings in Twentieth-Century America*, 39 Law & Soc'y Rev. 793 (2005).

[2] *See, e.g.*, *Attacks Against Roma in Bulgaria: September 2011–July 2012*, European Roma Rights Ctr. (July 31, 2012), http://www.errc.org/uploads/upload_en/file/attacks-list-in-bulgaria.pdf; François-Xavier Bagnoud Center for Health and Human Rights et al., *Accelerating Patterns of Anti-Roma Violence in Hungary* (Feb. 2014), https://cdn2.sph.harvard.edu/wp-content/uploads/sites/114/2017/12/FXB-Hungary-Report_Released-February-3–2014.pdf; *"We Ask for Justice": Europe's Failure to Protect Roma from Racist Violence*, Amnesty Int'l (Apr. 8, 2014), https://www.amnesty.org/en/documents/eur01/007/2014/en/; Moldovan and Others v. Romania, App. No. 41138/98 & 64320/01, Eur. Ct. H.R. (2005).

the shortcomings of Reconstruction and eastern enlargement, that is, the inability of conditionality to produce lasting change.

This Chapter compares racial equality and minority protections principally during the U.S. Civil Rights movement and following the EU's eastern enlargement after the candidates for statehood and accession became members. In contrast to Chapter 4, the comparison here revolves around minority protections as internal governance within the federalist union, rather than as conditions imposed on aspiring members. Much of the literature on these eras presumes that federal competences had been settled years earlier and that both unions had already amassed the authority to require minority protections of existing members, as well as the power to enforce those mandates.[3] Because there was now sustained external pressure to bolster minority protections (e.g., from the Cold War and Roma refugee movement), this literature often frames failures to integrate as failures of enforcement or, more precisely, faltering political will and weak institutional design.[4] These criticisms are certainly valid. However, the federal authority to integrate was not entirely clear during Civil Rights or after eastern enlargement. In the U.S., the seemingly bold pronouncements in the Reconstruction Amendments were the product of hard-fought compromises. Hobbled by compromise, the Amendments were an unstable bedrock for reform, and federal cases read them narrowly at first.[5] In the EU, the Lisbon Treaty expanded the fundamental values espoused in the Treaty on the European Union to include "the rights of persons belonging to minorities," but this lofty aspiration was not accompanied by any enhanced competence to legislate minority protections – other than preexisting antidiscrimination powers dating back to the 1997 Amsterdam Treaty.[6] The Lisbon Treaty also elevated the EU's bill of rights framework (i.e., the Charter of Fundamental Rights) to the standing of EU treaties.[7] Yet, while the Charter features some minority protections,[8] those protections cannot exceed the scope of the EU treaties.[9] These limitations on authority made it more likely that the U.S. and EU would be tentative rather than sweeping in their implementation of equality and integration.

3 *E.g.*, COSTANZA HERMANIN & EEFJE DE KROON, OPEN SOC. FOUND., THE RACE EQUALITY DIRECTIVE: A SHADOW REPORT (2013); Guy-Uriel E. Charles & Luis Fuentes-Rohwer, *Race, Federalism, and Voting Rights*, 2015 U. CHI. L. F. 113.

4 *See, e.g.*, HERMANIN & DE KROON, *supra* note 3.

5 *See, e.g.*, Slaughterhouse Cases, 83 U.S. (16 Wall.) 36 (1873); U.S. v. Cruikshank, 92 U.S. 542 (1876); Civil Rights Cases, 109 U.S. 3 (1883); Plessy v. Ferguson, 163 U.S. 537 (1896).

6 Treaty on European Union, art. 2, 2008 O.J. (C 115) 13 [hereinafter TEU]; Consolidated Version of the Treaty Establishing the European Community, arts. 12 & 13, 2002 O.J. (C 325) 33 [hereinafter EC]. *See also* Gabriel N. Toggenburg, *The Lisbon Treaty: A Rich Cocktail Served in an Only Half-Full Glass*, 5 EUROPÄISCHES J. FÜR MINDERHEITENFRAGEN 78, 85 (2012).

7 TEU art. 6(1); Charter of Fundamental Rights of the European Union, art. 21, 2000 O.J. (C 364) 1 [hereinafter Charter].

8 *See* Charter arts. 21 (prohibiting discrimination on the bases of ethnicity, language, or religion) and 22 (affirming that the EU respects cultural, religious, and linguistic diversity).

9 Tawhida Ahmed, *The Treaty of Lisbon and Beyond: The Evolution of EU Minority Protection?*, 38 EUR. L. REV. 30, 45–47 (2013).

Other problems stood in the way. African Americans and Roma faced deeply entrenched structural obstacles that could not be razed by incremental and technocratic reforms of law. Sweeping as they were, civil rights statutes became increasingly mired in procedure, while failing to tackle structural barriers to equality.[10] Later, across the Atlantic, the EU fared better at acknowledging the exclusion and marginalization of Roma, adopting the four-part approach of the Decade.[11] However, the polity's ambitious agenda was hampered by its inability to ensure true inclusion beyond a handful of nonbinding mandates.

In enforcement, the U.S. and the EU took slightly different tacks. Sometimes, congressional paralysis forced the President to become the first mover by executive action; at other times, Congress passed sweeping legislation, but administrative agencies frustrated progress by focusing on procedural minutiae. In the EU, on the other hand, the European Commission has tended to act sparingly, late, and ineffectively on Roma inclusion. Where possible, it has pushed primary responsibility for inclusion down to the member states.[12] For both comparators, courts also played important roles in ushering in rights and protections, though here, too, differences in the federalist design have yielded divergent approaches. In the U.S., federal courts constituted an important situs of wrangling over the scope of federal power, as well as a parallel track to enforce integration (i.e., by litigation). In Europe, while the Court of Justice of the European Union has produced some notable case law on minority rights,[13] the majority of Roma rights cases have been brought in the European Court of Human Rights, a Council of Europe institution.[14]

There was, of course, evolution in the enforcement of civil rights and minority protections. During certain spurts, the central governments expanded the bureaucracy attending to civil rights laws (e.g., the Office of Civil Rights in the U.S. Department of Justice and the Agency for Fundamental Rights in the EU) and utilized courts and constitutional authority more forcefully (e.g., infringement

10 Stephen C. Halpern, On the Limits of the Law: The Ironic Legacy of Title VI of the 1964 Civil Rights Act 132–33, 137 (1995).

11 *See* European Comm'n, *National Roma Integration Strategies: A First Step in the Implementation of the EU Framework*, Communication to the European Parl., the Council, the European Econ. and Soc. Comm. and the Comm. of the Regions 4 (2012).

12 *See id.* at 2.

13 *See* CHEZ Razpredelenie Bulgaria AD v. Komisia za zashtita ot diskriminatsia, and Anelia Nikolava, and Darzhavna Komisia za energiyno i vodno regulirane, Case C-83/14, 2015 O.J. C 311/8 [hereinafter *CHEZ*] (Bulgarian power company's practice of placing electricity meters higher in Romani neighborhoods than in majority neighborhoods violates the RED); Criminal Proceedings against Bickel and Franz, C-274/96, 1998 E.C.R. I-7637 (protection of national minorities may constitute a legitimate aim of member states).

14 *See, e.g.*, D.H. and Others v. Czech Republic, App. No. 57825/00, 47 Eur. H.R. Rep. 59 (2007) [hereinafter *D.H.*] (also often referred to as "*D.H. II*" to denote the Grand Chamber opinion); Oršuš and Others v. Croatia, App. No. 15766/03, 52 Eur. H.R. Rep. 7 (2010); Sampanis v. Greece, App. No. 32526/05, Eur. Ct. H.R. (2008). On the approaches of the ECtHR versus the CJEU toward human rights, see Sionaidh Douglas-Scott, *A Tale of Two Courts: Luxembourg, Strasbourg and the Growing European Union Human Rights* Acquis, 43 Common Mkt. L. Rev. 629 (2006).

proceedings against CSEE states). This does not mean, however, that change was always on the side of racialized minorities. Progress could become mired in periods of retrenchment, as during a Nixon administration that redirected the Justice Department's priorities,[15] or financial and then refugee crises in Europe that forced the EU and member states to cope with right-wing populism.[16] Even during sympathetic administrations, there were setbacks. Agencies might generate a flurry of activity, giving the appearance of activism and support, but no real gains would flow from their efforts.[17]

It did not help that, along the way, other developments distracted or diverted the governments' attention. Over time, both rights movements took on an increasingly neoliberal turn, rooted in choice and individual responsibility. School integration gave way to voucher programs and religious and charter schools, handing parents private alternatives to racially mixed public schools. In the U.S., an expansive vision of equal protection devolved into a restrictive reading whereby state actors could not use racial preferences even to redress discrimination.[18] In the EU, Roma inclusion was increasingly pitched as a way to foster economic growth, which obscured other concerns.[19] Further, just when Roma inclusion was gaining momentum, Europe was beset by a spate of crises.

So, to move the dial on racial equality and minority protections, government efforts can be only part of the solution. Civil society must enter the fray. Part of this Chapter therefore compares the efforts of grassroots advocacy in the U.S. and EU. Looking ahead, this Chapter also anticipates a discussion on shifting mainstream attitudes toward African Americans and Roma, to be covered in Chapter 6. Societal attitudes are integral to any law-based movement for rights or equality. Lack of popular acceptance can gut the political impetus of legal reforms; conversely, lack of political impetus can be mitigated by society's acceptance of equality and minority protections.

Finally, it should be noted that, while this Chapter focuses mainly on the Civil Rights movement (roughly 1954 to 1968) as the U.S. comparator, bounded by *Brown v. Board of Education* (1954) at one end and the trio of civil rights legislation at the

15 *See* HALPERN, *supra* note 10, at 85–91.

16 *See* ANDREA L.P. PIRRO, THE POPULIST RADICAL RIGHT IN CENTRAL AND EASTERN EUROPE: IDEOLOGY, IMPACT, AND ELECTORAL PERFORMANCE (2015).

17 *See, e.g.*, Angéla Kóczé, *Political Empowerment or Political Incarceration of Romani? The Hungarian Version of the Politics of Dispossession*, *in* THE HUNGARIAN PATIENT: SOCIAL OPPOSITION TO AN ILLIBERAL DEMOCRACY 91, 95 (Péter Krasztev & John Van Til eds., 2015) (poor record of the social-liberal government of Hungary's prime minister Gyula Horn on Roma inclusion); HALPERN, *supra* note 10, at 187–89 (Office of Civil Rights during President Carter's DOJ more concerned with procedural regularity and managerial efficiency than substantive reform).

18 *Compare* Regents of the Univ. of Cal. v. Bakke, 438 U.S. 265 (1978), *with* City of Richmond v. J.A. Croson Co., 488 U.S. 469 (1989). For a succinct summary, see Gabriel J. Chin, *Volume Introduction*, *in* AFFIRMATIVE ACTION AND THE CONSTITUTION: VOLUME 3, JUDICIAL REACTION TO AFFIRMATIVE ACTION, 1989–1997 1 (Gabriel J. Chin ed., 1998).

19 *See* Morag Goodwin & Roosmarijn Buijs, *Making Good European Citizens of the Roma: A Closer Look at the EU Framework for National Roma Integration Strategies*, 14 GERMAN L.J. 2041 (2013).

other,[20] the Chapter also aims to trace the evolution of civil rights, as well as parallel developments in Roma rights, from desegregation to more structurally minded measures to achieve equality. Naturally, then, discussions will delve into the post–Civil Rights era, showing that civil rights and Roma rights did not always chart a trajectory of uninhibited success. At the other end, Civil Rights and Roma rights were preceded by other crucial developments. For Roma rights in CSEE, Communism had improved living standards, educated a generation of intellectuals, and introduced society to integration, and international Romani organizations laid the groundwork for contemporary Roma rights NGOs.[21] Prior to Civil Rights, World War II had instilled in the U.S. a sense of national purpose that helped to overcome racial divides. Looking even farther back, the legal advances of Civil Rights were enabled by the NAACP's antilynching campaign,[22] the movement to incorporate the Bill of Rights against the states,[23] and the interwar revolution in criminal procedure.[24] Hence, while this Chapter revolves around Civil Rights and eastern enlargement, it will at times take up the precursors and postscripts of both comparators.

EARLY PROTECTIONS: DESEGREGATION AND NONDISCRIMINATION

Some of the early advances in equality for the EU and the U.S. came in the form of desegregation and antidiscrimination laws. Both comparators framed nondiscrimination as a right of citizenship within the union, thereby vesting themselves with the authority to combat racial or ethnic discrimination against individuals. Federal antidiscrimination powers in the U.S. emanated from the Equal Protection Clause of the Fourteenth Amendment, which conferred national citizenship on "[a]ll persons born or naturalized in the United States, and subject to the jurisdiction thereof"[25] and conscripted the federal government into local battles over citizens' rights.[26] In the EU, antidiscrimination competences developed from workplace sex equality laws that were expanded over time to cover race, ethnicity, religion, belief,

[20] Civil Rights Act of 1964, Pub. L. No. 88-352, 78 Stat. 241 (codified as amended in scattered sections of 42 U.S.C.); Voting Rights Act of 1975, 42 U.S.C. §§ 1973–1973aa-6 (transferred to 52 U.S.C. §§ 10301–10314); Civil Rights Act of 1968, Title VIII (Fair Housing Act), 42 U.S.C. §§ 3601–3619.

[21] *See* Thomas Acton & Ilona Klímová, *The International Romani Union: An East European Answer to West European Questions?*, *in* Between Past and Future: The Roma of Central and Eastern Europe 157 (Will Guy ed., 2001).

[22] Megan Ming Francis, Civil Rights and the Making of the Modern American State (2014).

[23] Michael Kent Curtis, No State Shall Abridge: The Fourteenth Amendment and the Bill of Rights (1986); Akhil Reed Amar, The Bill of Rights: Creation and Reconstruction (1998).

[24] Michael J. Klarman, *The Racial Origins of Modern Criminal Procedure*, 99 Mich. L. Rev. 48 (2000).

[25] U.S. Const. amend. XIV, § 1.

[26] *See* Eric Foner, Reconstruction: America's Unfinished Revolution, 1863–1877, 258–59, 529–31 (1988) (discussing, among other things, the *Slaughterhouse Cases*, 83 U.S. (16 Wall.) 36 (1873), and *U.S. v. Cruikshank*, 92 U.S. 542 (1876)).

disability, age, and sexual orientation.[27] As the EU consolidated power and clarified its competences, these nondiscrimination rights began to appear alongside articulations of EU citizenship. The 2007 Lisbon Treaty, for example, affirms nondiscrimination and citizenship rights in the same section.[28]

Tying racial equality to federal and supranational citizenship provided the foundation for the central governments to legislate against and regulate discrimination. Despite its inscription in the constitutional order, this power had not always been on a sure footing. Nearly a century after Reconstruction, segregation remained legal[29] and federal Acts implementing the Fourteenth Amendment were struck down as overreach for banning discrimination by private actors.[30] It took explicit overruling by the Supreme Court and subsequent federal legislation in a very different era (Civil Rights) with urgent external threats (the Cold War) to blot out these stains.[31] The EU, too, tethered antidiscrimination rights to citizenship, but these concepts did not evolve in tandem. As a union devoted to an integrated and liberalized market, the EU aimed first to eliminate disparities between men and women. Since women were the largest minority in the workforce, these measures were more efficient at creating workplace equality than protections for racial minorities. Through the Rome Treaty (1957), former Article 119 EEC (now Article 141 EC) introduced the principle of equal pay between men and women for equal work, prohibiting not only workplace discrimination but also discriminatory legislation.[32] Yet the article was not timely implemented, so gender equality had to be ushered along by a slew of directives and CJEU decisions.[33] It was forty years later, with the 1997 Amsterdam Treaty, that the EU formally gained the competence to combat

[27] Paul Craig & Gráinne de Búrca, EU Law: Text, Cases, and Materials 855–56 (5th ed. 2011). *See also* EC arts. 12 (prohibiting discrimination on the grounds of nationality) and 13(1) (conferring on the European Council the power to combat sex, racial, ethnic, religious, disability, age, and sexual orientation discrimination); Consolidated Version of the Treaty on the Functioning of the European Community art. 19, 2012 O.J. (C 326) 47 [hereinafter TFEU]; Council Directive 2000/43, 2000 O.J. (L 180) 22 (EC) [hereinafter RED]; Council Directive 2000/78, 2000 O.J. (L 303) 16 (EC).

[28] *See* Treaty of Lisbon Amending the Treaty on the European Union and the Treaty Establishing the European Communities, Part Two ("Non-Discrimination and Citizenship of the Union"), 2007 O.J. (C 306) 1. On the mixed results of the Lisbon Treaty in minority protections, see Ahmed, *supra* note 9; Toggenburg, *supra* note 6.

[29] *See* Plessy v. Ferguson, 163 U.S. 537 (1896).

[30] *See* Civil Rights Cases, 109 U.S. 3 (1883) (striking down the Civil Rights Act of 1875).

[31] *E.g.*, Brown v. Bd. of Educ. of Topeka, 347 U.S. 483 (1954); Civil Rights Act of 1964; Voting Rights Act of 1975; Fair Housing Act.

[32] *See* Case 43/75, Gabrielle Defrenne v. Société Anonyme Belge de Navigation Aérienne Sabena, 1976 E.C.R. 455, paras. 21–22.

[33] *See, e.g.*, Council Directive 75/117, 1975 O.J. (L 45) 19 (EEC) (equal pay for men and women, or "First Equal Pay Directive"); Council Directive 76/207, 1976 O.J. (L 39) 40 (EEC) (equal treatment between men and women in employment); Council Directive 79/7, 1979 O.J. (L 6) 24 (EEC) (equal treatment of men and women in statutory social security schemes); Case C-167/97, Regina v. Sec'y of State for Emp't, *ex parte* Seymour-Smith and Perez, 1999 E.C.R. I-666; Enderby v. Frenchay Health Auth. and Sec'y of State for Health, Case C-127/92, 1993 E.C.R. I-5535; Jenkins v. Kingsgate (Clothing Prods.) Ltd., Case 96/80, 1981 E.C.R. 912.

discrimination based on race or ethnic origin – under a renumbered Article 13(1) EC. Thus, rather than "reasoning from race," as gender and pregnancy discrimination laws did in the U.S.,[34] racial discrimination laws in the EU appear to have reasoned from gender.[35]

When the U.S. and the EU finally worked up the resolve to fight segregation and racial discrimination, federal and supranational antidiscrimination competences spurred a patchwork of legislation, court decisions, and other initiatives. The most emphatic development in the EU was the Race Equality Directive of 2000 (the "RED"), which became the backbone of the Union's antidiscrimination edifice.[36] The RED prohibits racial and ethnic discrimination across many segments of society and the economy. Adopted in response to the Haider affair in Austria and one year after the Amsterdam Treaty became effective, the Directive opens with a set of grandiose recitals that pledge, among other things, to combat racism and xenophobia, reform the rules giving effect to equality, and anticipate "an ever closer union among the peoples of Europe."[37] Beyond legal accomplishments such as revamping and broadening the definition of and recourses for discrimination, the RED prompted the creation of national equality bodies and raised the profile of civil society organizations.[38] Similar changes percolated down to the national level: as an EU law with direct effects, the RED required member states to pass implementing legislation that was no less ambitious than what the Directive itself set out to do.[39]

The RED produced two significant victories for Roma: (1) infringement proceedings brought by the Commission against the Czech Republic (2014), Slovakia (2015), and Hungary (2016) for disproportionately placing Romani students in classes and schools for disabled children; and (2) a pair of cases before the CJEU against a Bulgarian power company for the discriminatory installation of electricity meters (2013 and 2015). The infringement proceedings were the Commission's response to the failure of strategic litigation to integrate Romani students into mainstream

34 *See* Serena Mayeri, Reasoning from Race: Feminism, Law, and the Civil Rights Revolution (2014).

35 *See* Katerina Linos, *Path Dependence in Discrimination Law: Employment Cases in the United States and the European Union*, 35 Yale J. Int'l L. 115 (2010). To get to questions of race, European scholars often started from theoretical perspectives of gender studies. *See, e.g.*, Floya Anthias & Nira Yuval-Davis, Racialized Boundaries: Race, Nation, Gender, Colour and Class and the Anti-Racist Struggle (2005).

36 *See* European Union Agency for Fundamental Rights, The Racial Equality Directive: Application and Challenges 9 (2012) [hereinafter FRA, Race Equality Directive]; *Introducing FRA: The EU Agency for Fundamental Rights*, European Union Agency for Fundamental Rights (May 2014), https://fra.europa.eu/en/publication/2014/introducing-fra-eu-agency-fundamental-rights. *But see* Andrew Williams, EU Human Rights Policies: A Study in Irony 86 (2004) ("By adopting directives rather than regulations the Commission again fell foul of treating the Member States with undeserved deference in a matter [racial discrimination] that is supposed to be core to the Community's human rights policies.").

37 *See* RED recitals.

38 *See* FRA, Race Equality Directive, *supra* note 36, at 9.

39 *See id.*; Robert Schütze, *Direct Effects and Indirect Effects*, *in* Oxford Principles of European Union Law, vol. 1 (Robert Schütze & Takis Tridimas eds., 2018).

schools.[40] Between 2014 and 2016, the Commission initiated proceedings against the Czech Republic,[41] Slovakia,[42] and Hungary[43] for violating EU law by disproportionately directing Romani students to special schools. Authority for infringement proceedings derives from Article 258 TFEU, which provides for a two-year preliminary investigation period, after which a case can be referred to the CJEU, potentially resulting in damages against the offending state.[44] These cases rested on the RED, and EU antidiscrimination law more broadly, and evidence was compiled through the increasingly rigorous and quantitative gauges of Roma inclusion.[45] While detractors criticize Article 258 generally both for its weakness as an enforcement mechanism and for the Commission's biased selection of cases,[46] the launch of these proceedings – contemporaneously with the two CJEU cases – signaled that the EU was finally taking CSEE states to task under EU law for anti-Roma discrimination.

In the CJEU cases, Bulgarian power companies had installed electricity meters in Romani neighborhoods much higher from the ground than normal (six or seven meters, compared to less than two meters elsewhere), so that customers could not verify their electricity usage.[47] This triggered two lawsuits against the companies for violating the national law that implemented the RED. Both cases were referred to the CJEU, but only one saw the plaintiff prevail.

In the successful case, *CHEZ Razpredelenie Bulgaria AD v. Komisia za zashtita ot diskriminatsia, Anelia Nikolova* (*CHEZ*), the plaintiff herself was not Roma, but she lived in a Romani neighborhood and alleged that she had suffered along with Roma, as a result of the discriminatory policy of CHEZ, the power company. The CJEU observed that the RED was not confined to a "particular category of persons"

40 *See D.H.*, 47 Eur. H.R. Rep. 59 (2007); AMNESTY INT'L, END INJUSTICE: ELEMENTARY SCHOOLS STILL FAIL ROMANI CHILDREN IN THE CZECH REPUBLIC (2010).

41 *EU Action Against Czech Republic for Discrimination in Schools Is a Victory for Rights, Justice, and Roma*, AMNESTY INT'L (Sept. 25, 2014), https://www.amnesty.org/en/latest/news/2014/09/eu-action-against-czech-republic-discrimination-schools-victory-rights-justice-and-roma/.

42 *European Commission Targets Slovakia over Roma School Discrimination*, OPEN SOCIETY (Apr. 29, 2015), https://www.opensocietyfoundations.org/press-releases/european-commission-targets-slovakia-over-roma-school-discrimination [https://perma.cc/H4HK-EPPF]; Answer Given by Ms. Jourová on Behalf of the Comm'n to the Eur. Parl. (Nov. 24, 2016), http://www.europarl.europa.eu/doceo/document/E-8–2016-007070-ASW_EN.pdf.

43 *Commission Probe Must Spell the End of Romani Segregation in Hungarian Schools*, EUROPEAN ROMA RIGHTS CTR. (May 26, 2016), http://www.errc.org/article/eu-commission-probe-must-spell-the-end-of-romani-segregation-in-hungarian-schools/4485 [https://perma.cc/N66H-5MBZ].

44 STINE ANDERSEN, THE ENFORCEMENT OF EU LAW: THE ROLE OF THE EUROPEAN COMMISSION (2012); CRAIG & DE BÚRCA, *supra* note 27, at 408–32.

45 *See* AMNESTY INT'L, THE CZECH REPUBLIC'S DISCRIMINATORY TREATMENT OF ROMA BREACHES EU RACE DIRECTIVE (2013) (resting its claims on the findings of national and international monitoring bodies).

46 *See, e.g.*, Richard Rawlings, *Engaged Elites: Citizen Action and Institutional Attitudes in Commission Enforcement*, 6 EUR. L.J. 4 (2000).

47 *CHEZ*, 2015 O.J. C 311/8. This marked the first time that the CJEU decided a Roma rights case. *See* Adam Weiss, *Can We Litigate Strategically in the Court of Justice of the European Union?*, EUROPEAN ROMA RIGHTS CTR., http://www.errc.org/news/can-we-litigate-strategically-in-the-court-of-justice-of-the-european-union (last accessed May 24, 2019).

but also protected persons who, though not themselves members of the category treated unfavorably, nevertheless suffered on account of the unfavorable treatment.[48] Nor did it matter that Bulgaria's implementing statute had defined "unfavorable treatment" as discrimination prejudicing "rights or legitimate interests." Although CHEZ tried to argue that there was no legitimate interest in electricity meters being at an accessible height, the treatment of customers in Romani neighborhoods was unfavorable in comparison to other neighborhoods.[49] This expansive notion of antidiscrimination was justified by the RED's purpose of ensuring "the development of democratic and tolerant societies" for all persons.[50] In short, the CJEU interpreted the goals of the RED broadly, equating antidiscrimination with the movement to build an inclusive democracy.

The expansive view of nondiscrimination in *CHEZ* echoes a reading of the Fourteenth Amendment's Equal Protection Clause. For many scholars of constitutional law, the Equal Protection Clause embodies an "antisubordination" or "group-disadvantaging" principle that prohibits the perpetual subjugation of any particular social group.[51] In this view, the Clause is a cudgel against the subordination of a group simply because the group lacks power; hence, a facially neutral law can fail equal protection analysis if the law perpetuates racial hierarchies.[52] Conversely, antisubordination would uphold race-specific policies such as affirmative action to redress historical subordination.[53] Naturally, given the conservative impulses that the Fourteenth Amendment had to thread during its passage, as well as the contemporary association of affirmative action with facially "discriminatory" law, there is a competing vision of equal protection: the antidiscrimination principle, which holds that the Clause merely limits the government's ability to classify, or discriminate among, individuals.[54]

These two visions fought for control over equal protection jurisprudence long before *Brown v. Board of Education*, the landmark school desegregation case from 1954 that is most analogous to *CHEZ*, and have continued to do so ever since.[55]

48 *CHEZ*, 2015 O.J. C 311/8, para. 56.

49 *Id.* paras. 66–68.

50 *Id.* para. 65. *See also* Julie C. Suk, *New Directions for European Race Equality Law:* CHEZ Razpredelenie Bulgaria AD v. Komisia za Zashitita ot Diskriminatsia, Anelia Nikolovai, 40 Fordham Int'l L.J. 1211, 1218 (2017) ("The main problem of discrimination as a subject for EU law is not the harm to any individual's rights or legitimate interests, but rather, the undermining of democratic and tolerant societies based on participation on equal terms.").

51 *See* Owen M. Fiss, *Groups and the Equal Protection Clause*, 5 Phil. & Pub. Aff. 107 (1976); Ruth Colker, *Anti-Subordination Above All: Sex, Race, and Equal Protection*, 61 N.Y.U. L. Rev. 1003 (1986); Laurence H. Tribe, American Constitutional Law 1515 (2d ed. 1988).

52 Colker, *supra* note 51, at 1007–08.

53 *Id.* at 1008–10.

54 *See, e.g.*, William Van Alstyne, *Rites of Passage: Race, the Supreme Court, and the Constitution*, 46 U. Chi. L. Rev. 775, 778 (1978). *See also* Fiss, *supra* note 51, at 108 ("the antidiscrimination principle embodies a very limited conception of equality, one that is highly individualistic and confined to assessing the rationality of means").

55 *See, e.g.*, U.S. v. Carolene Prods. Co., 304 U.S. 144, 152–53 n.4 (1938) (Stone, J.) ("Nor need we enquire ... whether prejudice against discrete and insular minorities may be a special condition,

Although both antisubordination and antidiscrimination proponents invoke *Brown*,[56] the case undeniably broke new ground in equal protection, overturning *Plessy* and expanding the types of evidence that could support legal arguments.[57] *Brown* provided federal courts with the precedent to wade into school desegregation and authorize injunctive remedies such as cross-district busing and reassignment of teachers.[58] Of course, by anchoring desegregation in the Fourteenth Amendment, the Supreme Court exposed antidiscrimination jurisprudence to generations of squabbling between the two camps over the meaning of equal protection. The camp that dominates any particular era ends up wielding outsized influence over profound questions, such as the legality of affirmative actions and minority set-asides,[59] as well as the viability of a disparate impact challenge to facially neutral laws.[60]

Institutionally, we find *Brown* and *CHEZ* to be suitable comparators because, in both decisions, the highest court in the federalist system invalidated a practice at the local level. At a time when each union was growing more comfortable with non-discrimination as a basis for racial equality and minority protections in constituent states, the top constitutional courts pushed antidiscrimination law even further. Thus, both cases played significant roles in refashioning the federalist design.

In Romani studies circles, however, the instinct has been to compare *Brown* to another case – *D.H. and Others v. the Czech Republic* (*D.H.*), a decision by the Grand Chamber of the European Court of Human Rights. In *D.H.*, the ECtHR (a COE rather than EU court) found that the Czech education system had discriminated against Romani schoolchildren by diverting them to special schools reserved for remedial students or students with disabilities.[61] *D.H.* relied heavily on statistics to show the disparate impact of facially neutral Czech education laws.

which tends seriously to curtail the operation of those political processes ordinarily to be relied upon to protect minorities, and which may call for a correspondingly more searching judicial inquiry."); Parents Involved in Cmty. Sch. v. Seattle Sch. Dist. No. 1, 551 U.S. 701, 748 (2007) (Roberts, J.) ("The way to stop discrimination on the basis of race is to stop discriminating on the basis of race."). *But see* Jack M. Balkin & Reva B. Siegel, *Fiss's Way: The Scholarship of Owen Fiss*, 58 U. Miami L. Rev. 9 (2003) (arguing that these two principles overlap rather than incessantly compete).

56 *Compare, e.g., Parents Involved in Cmty. Sch.*, 551 U.S. at 742–43 (Roberts, J.), *with id.* at 798–99 (Stevens, J., dissenting).

57 *See* Brown v. Bd. of Educ. of Topeka, 347 U.S. 483, 494–95, 492–93 (1954).

58 *See* Swann v. Charlotte-Mecklenburg Bd. of Educ., 402 U.S. 1 (1971). Of course, these Supreme Court decisions were slow and rare and soon backpedaled. Shortly after *Swann*, the Court struck down a multidistrict school desegregation program in Detroit, which presaged the resegregation of school districts. *See* Milliken v. Bradley, 418 U.S. 717 (1974).

59 *Compare* Wygant v. Jackson Bd. of Educ., 476 U.S. 267 (1986), *and* Metro Broadcasting, Inc. v. FCC, 497 U.S. 547 (1990), *with* City of Richmond v. J.A. Croson Co., 488 U.S. 469 (1989).

60 *Compare* Washington v. Davis, 426 U.S. 229 (1976), *with* Mobile v. Bolden, 446 U.S. 55 (1980). *See also* Griggs v. Duke Power Co., 401 U.S. 424 (1971); Ricci v. DeStefano, 557 U.S. 557 (2009).

61 The litigation arose during the mid-1990s in the Czech town of Ostrava, where 56 percent of special school students were Roma – even though the Roma comprised only 2.26 percent of schoolchildren. Statistically, a Romani child was twenty-seven times more likely to be placed in a special school than a non-Roma comparator. *D.H.*, 47 Eur. H.R. Rep. 59, at para. 18 (2007).

This maneuver supported the applicants' claim of indirect discrimination, which had not met with much success previously in the ECtHR.[62] In *Brown*, by comparison, it was the plaintiffs' social science evidence – famously, Dr. Kenneth Clark's doll studies[63] – that led the Supreme Court to find that segregation harms African American schoolchildren and, accordingly, to overrule *Plessy*.[64]

Read as school desegregation cases, *D.H.* and *Brown* are natural comparators: both cases struck down discriminatory and segregationist educational practices. *Brown* certainly shines brightly in the legal firmament. Other legal systems grappling with race have been transfixed by this inspirational beacon of U.S. Civil Rights, and the European human rights system is no different. In fact, the plaintiffs in *D.H.* were assisted by American legal consultants, including Jack Greenberg, a veteran of the NAACP Legal Defense Fund who litigated *Brown*.[65] Yet the ECtHR is a human rights court, not a constitutional court, so this comparison eschews federalism. The ECtHR allots a greater margin of appreciation to COE members than the CJEU to EU members.[66] Even if there is dissonance between the European Convention on Human Rights and EU law on minority protections,[67] the CJEU should be more exacting upon member states, a feature that heightens expectations for the current infringement proceedings.

Still, there is value in looking at *Brown* and *D.H.* side by side, because doing so illuminates the slow pace of change in the federal and supranational actors. During Civil Rights, federal law moved slowly, tempering African American expectations until massive resistance to desegregation provoked a response.[68] Gradualism was

62 *See* INTERRIGHTS, NON-DISCRIMINATION IN INTERNATIONAL LAW: A HANDBOOK FOR PRACTITIONERS 83 (2005); Hoogendijk v. The Netherlands, App. No. 58641/00, Eur. Ct. H.R. (2005); Zarb Adami v. Malta, App. No. 17209/02, 44 Eur. H.R. Rep. 3 (2006). *D.H.* ushered in a spate of indirect discrimination cases, several with Romani parties. *See* Sampanis v. Greece, App. No. 32526/05, Eur. Ct. H.R. (2008); Oršuš and Others v. Croatia, App. No. 15766/03, 52 Eur. H.R. Rep. 7 (2010); Horváth and Kiss v. Hungary, App. No. 11146/11, Eur. Ct. H.R. (2013).

63 *See* Gordon J. Beggs, *Novel Expert Evidence in Federal Civil Rights Litigation*, 45 AM. U. L. REV. 1, 9–16 (1995). *But see* Michael J. Klarman, Brown v. Board of Education*: Law or Politics?*, *in* FROM THE GRASSROOTS TO THE SUPREME COURT: *BROWN V. BOARD OF EDUCATION* AND AMERICAN DEMOCRACY 198, 203 (Peter F. Lau ed., 2004) (revealing that Justice Jackson "ridiculed the NAACP's brief as 'sociology,' not law").

64 Brown v. Bd. of Educ. of Topeka, 347 U.S. 483, 494–95, 492–93 (1954).

65 In fact, at least two lawyers at the ERRC who represented the plaintiffs were American-educated; among them was Jack Greenberg, a veteran of the NAACP Legal Defense Fund, who had argued *Brown*. *See* Jack Greenberg, *Report on Roma Education Today: From Slavery to Segregation and Beyond*, 110 COLUM. L. REV. 919 (2010); James A. Goldston, *Roma Rights, Roma Wrongs*, FOREIGN AFF., Mar./Apr. 2002 (under Goldston's byline).

66 *See* LILLA FARKAS, EUROPEAN COMM'N, REPORT ON DISCRIMINATION OF ROMA CHILDREN IN EDUCATION 9 (2014).

67 On the EU's tortuous path toward accession to the ECHR, see PAUL GRAGL, THE ACCESSION OF THE EUROPEAN UNION TO THE EUROPEAN CONVENTION ON HUMAN RIGHTS (2013); Daniel Halberstam, *"It's the Autonomy, Stupid!" A Modest Defense of* Opinion 2/13 *on EU Accession to the ECHR, and the Way Forward*, 16 GERMAN L.J. 105 (2015); Opinion Pursuant to Article 218(11) TFEU, Case C-2/13, ECLI: EU:C:2014:2454 (2014).

68 Michael J. Klarman, *Why Massive Resistance?*, *in* MASSIVE RESISTANCE: SOUTHERN OPPOSITION TO THE SECOND RECONSTRUCTION 21 (Clive Webb ed., 2005).

partially a result of the separation of powers in the American political process. Southerners dominated Congress for years, which impeded legislation.[69] In the face of overwhelming precedent to the contrary, the common law, too, changed slowly.[70] Thus, the White House had to be an early mover on integration, issuing executive orders that often preceded landmark legislation or court rulings.[71] However, executive action was uneven; if it was willing to act at all, the White House usually subsumed civil rights to the greater goal of winning the Cold War. It would take twenty years from the end of World War II, when African American servicemen returned home to segregation, to arrive at transformative civil rights legislation. In the EU, governance does not fit neatly with American preconceptions of separation of power among the legislative, executive, judicial, and administrative branches.[72] But, despite having the competence firmly in hand as a result of Article 13(1) EC and the RED, the Commission waited until 2014 to initiate proceedings against three CSEE states for violating EU antidiscrimination law by disproportionately directing Romani students to special schools. And there is no indication, five years on, that the proceedings are near conclusion.[73]

Contrary to the tendency to lionize *Brown*, and now *CHEZ*, the first movers on desegregation and Roma rights were not countermajoritarian courts or even lawmakers, but African Americans and Romani activists pressing for change (sometimes incremental) at the local level. In the decade before *Brown*, African Americans registered to vote and organized to end segregation of certain public spaces.[74] In the two decades before the fifth enlargement, Roma activists agitated for Roma rights during Communism, alongside political dissidents,[75] and founded NGOs afterward.[76] The campaigns of these advocates were buttressed by the historical contexts, namely, the prevalence of African American service during World War II,

69 Jackquelyn Dowd Hall, *The Long Civil Rights Movement and the Political Uses of the Past*, 91 J. Am. Hist. 1233 (2005).

70 Klarman, *Unfinished Business: Racial Equality in American History*, 93 Va. L. Rev. in Brief 249 (2008).

71 *See, e.g.*, Exec. Order No. 9981, 13 Fed. Reg. 4313 (July 26, 1948) (Truman desegregating the armed forces); Exec. Order. No. 10925, 26 Fed. Reg. 1977 (1961) (Kennedy eliminating racial discrimination in government contracting and establishing the precursor to the EEOC); Exec. Order No. 11246, 30 Fed. Reg. 12319 (1965) (Johnson forbidding discrimination in hiring government contractors).

72 Craig & de Búrca, *supra* note 27, at 31.

73 Slovakia and the Czech Republic have enacted some legislative reforms since the proceedings, but it is doubtful that these have equalized the access of Romani children to education. *See* Isabelle Chopin et al., European Comm'n, Roma and the Enforcement of Anti-Discrimination Law 15–16 (2017).

74 *See* Michael J. Klarman, *How* Brown *Changed Race Relations: The Backlash Thesis*, 81 J. Am. His. 81, 89 (1994).

75 *See* Kálmán Mizsei, *Reconstructing Roma Integration in Central and Eastern Europe: Addressing the Failures of the Last Quarter Century*, *in* Realizing Roma Rights 127, 131 (Jacqueline Bhabha et al. eds., 2017) (advocacy in Communist Hungary).

76 *See, e.g.*, *Short Presentation of Romani CRISS*, Romani CRISS (June 25, 2019), http://www.romanicriss.org/en/index.php?option=com_content&view=article&id=1737&Itemid=564 [https://perma.cc/K6S9-BE4G] (NGO formed during post-Communist Romania).

which imbued their demands with moral force, and the fall of the Iron Curtain, which enabled a renaissance of Romani civil society and the celebration of ethnic identity. Hence, strategic litigation before national and European human rights courts was the trailblazing of civil society where government would not act, though eventually government would follow. Even after the RED took effect and EU institutions could have forcefully stamped out anti-Romanyism, they sat back and let others fill in the interstices (as with the Decade) or resorted to nonbinding frameworks (as with the National Roma Integration Strategies). Ultimately, "landmark" cases such as *Brown* and *CHEZ* are hardly the vanguards of desegregation; rather, federal and supranational courts wait until there are glaring signs that the time is ripe for jurisprudence to shift.

There is one impediment to the RED that did not hobble U.S. civil rights laws in the same way. Because the RED is a directive, its implementation relies on EU member states, which exercise some freedom in the transposition of directives into national law.[77] Consequently, fulfillment of the letter and spirit of the RED is captured to an extent by national governments that might be hostile to Roma inclusion.[78] By contrast, during Civil Rights, the U.S. tried to federalize racial equality and oust states' jurisdiction – a strategy dating back to Reconstruction. In doing so, the federal government avoided sharing power with the states.[79] Compounding the sway of EU member states is the difficulty faced by individuals in getting before the CJEU. Under the preliminary reference procedure of Article 267 TFEU, national courts act as gatekeepers to the Court. It is the national court that refers a case to the CJEU; individuals do not have the right of appeal to the Court.[80] Thus, for a case such as *CHEZ* – a Roma rights case brought under the RED – to come to the CJEU, many stars had to have aligned, which explains why it took so long for such a case to appear.[81]

Stepping slightly farther back from *Brown* and *CHEZ*, we see that desegregation in the U.S. and the EU was made possible by even earlier developments, particularly periods when African Americans and Roma had to work and live alongside their majority compatriots – during World War II for the U.S. and under Communism for

77 On the parameters of this freedom, see Schütze, *supra* note 39; Craig & de Búrca, *supra* note 27, at 106.

78 Indeed, much of the criticism of the RED in particular revolves around weak implementation at the national level. *See, e.g.*, Hermanin & de Kroon, *supra* note 3, at 18–19. *See also* FRA, Race Equality Directive, *supra* note 36.

79 The justification is that, however federalism might balance federal and state power in other matters, the protection of racial minorities from discrimination is not one to be left to the states, which even federalists would seem to concede. *See, e.g.*, J. Harvie Wilkinson III, *Federalism for the Future*, 74 S. Cal. L. Rev. 523, 526 (2001) ("The Constitution does, of course, have its own set of strong national commands, among them the Fourteenth Amendment's ban on racial discrimination by state actors . . . .").

80 *See* TFEU art. 267; Craig & de Búrca, *supra* note 27, at 442–48.

81 The rareness of the opportunity might also explain why the Court used such strong, expansive language in characterizing the Directive.

CSEE. During World War II, African Americans served with whites as soldiers abroad and laborers at home, which lent credence to the need to dismantle Jim Crow. Just as importantly, the war effort helped whites and African Americans grow accustomed to cohabitation and collaboration. During Communism, when CSEE was embroiled in a war of a different sort, the Cold War, all citizens had to forsake ethnic identity, and in many settings Roma were integrated into society more thoroughly than ever before.[82] This abated mutual distrust and unfamiliarity and, just as importantly, educated and elevated a generation of Romani intellectuals who would become prominent after 1989.

Another notable difference between the evolution of American and EU antidiscrimination law, however, was the lack of popular support – or at least shifting societal attitudes – backing desegregation. Eurobarometers consistently show that majorities in CSEE, and at least pluralities across Europe, harbor anti-Romani sentiments.[83] This antipathy persists despite the passage of time and regardless of the country, inclusion initiatives, and how survey questions are asked.[84] In the U.S., there were wilder fluctuations. Opinion polls were neither as regular nor as systematic as the Eurobarometers, but they reveal two major trends. First, white support for desegregation was generally low and did not improve much after *Brown*; if anything, white resistance to integration hardened after *Brown*.[85] Second, public opinion shifted dramatically after white Southerners reacted violently to peaceful demonstrations, in other words, after massive resistance to integration caused the rest of the nation to recoil viscerally.[86] This is the "backlash thesis" of *Brown*: that the decision's major contribution is not so much that it revamped constitutional antidiscrimination jurisprudence, but that it provoked a white backlash that stirred the conscience of the entire nation, ultimately goading federal lawmakers to pass transformative legislation.[87] The backlash thesis finds corroboration in the pace of legislative change, as well as the platforms of political candidates who were winning elections. Civil rights legislation found congressional sponsors more during the immediate aftermath of World War II than the aftermath of *Brown*.[88] By contrast, political candidates in the South rode to victory on a popular wave against school desegregation, unseating moderates who had generally held office in the early and mid-1950s. These radical candidates, particularly in primaries for

82 *See supra* Chapter 2.

83 For example, Eurobarometer surveys show that non-Roma parents do not want their children to attend school with Romani students. *See, e.g.*, EUROPEAN COMM'N, SPECIAL EUROBAROMETER 437: DISCRIMINATION IN THE EU IN 2015 (2015), https://data.europa.eu/euodp/en/data/dataset/S2077_83_4_437_ENG.

84 *See supra* Chapter 3.

85 *See id. See also* Klarman, *supra* note 74, at 87.

86 Klarman, *supra* note 74, at 113.

87 *See id.* at 82–83.

88 *Id.* at 87.

governorships, conjured up racial threats and federal encroachment in school desegregation.[89] But when popular resistance to desegregation descended into massive, violent resistance, it stirred nationwide revulsion, and the pace of federal civil rights legislation picked up dramatically. In a reversal, the Kennedy administration accepted civil rights, and subsequently the Johnson administration shepherded through several laws in quick succession (the Civil Rights Act of 1964, the Voting rights Act of 1965, and the Fair Housing Act of 1968). To some extent, the RED also conforms to this theory: the Directive came on the heels of the Haider affair, which caused EU leaders to scramble to denounce xenophobia and pass a law whose recitals situate antidiscrimination alongside the highest aspirations of a united Europe.

Yet the larger disparities in popular opinion between the EU, where anti-Romanyism was mired in stasis, and the U.S., where integration enjoyed a remarkable upswing, would mean profound differences in how the reforms unfolded. Most obviously, Roma inclusion would garner less popular support than civil rights. Each new initiative, each court decision expanding antidiscrimination, would be more disconnected from the majority. Ironically, this predicament is compounded by the fact that contemporary Europe is making antidiscrimination law in a much more sophisticated environment than the U.S. in the 1950s, with more diverse tools and nuanced analysis. The ECtHR accepts statistical disparities as evidence of indirect discrimination, while the CJEU resoundingly endorses antidiscrimination as an integral part of democratic society. (On the other hand, the U.S. Supreme Court has gradually abandoned statistical evidence and disparate effects tests in racial discrimination cases while advancing a limited antidiscrimination vision of equal protection.[90]) Yet, against the grain of popular support, these legal advances in Europe threaten to be, or at least give the appearance of being, less democratic, less tethered to local and national realities, and therefore less legitimate.

Because nondiscrimination was often framed as a corollary of supranational citizenship, the misalignment of Roma inclusion and popular support means that over time the EU itself becomes less legitimate in pushing for integration. Along the way, Roma inclusion is tainted as a wholly EU project, and Roma themselves are viewed as a denationalized people, devoid of connection to CSEE societies. This has begun to happen already. As scholars have warned, because of the perception of Roma marginalization as an EU problem, national governments are content to sit back and let the EU take the helm.[91] And indeed, over time

89 *Id.* at 96–101.

90 *See, e.g.*, McCleskey v. Kemp, 481 U.S. 279 (1987); Washington v. Davis, 426 U.S. 229 (1976). At least in the early 2000s, antidiscrimination law and policy in Europe seemed ebullient, while in the U.S. it had been mired in retrenchment. *See* Gráinne de Búrca, *The Trajectories of European and American Antidiscrimination Law*, 60 AM. J. COMP. L. 1, 3–4 (2012).

91 *See, e.g.*, Peter Vermeersch, *Reframing the Roma: EU Initiatives and the Politics of Reinterpretation*, 38 J. ETHNIC & MIGRATION STUD. 1195, 1197 (2012):

Roma inclusion has lost some of its urgency. Prior to and immediately after accession, for instance, CSEE states defended de facto segregation with subtlety. The Czech government in *D.H.* deflected blame by pointing to anti-education attitudes among Roma; if it happened at all, segregation was happenstance, not intentional.[92] By the late 2010s, however, with right-wing populism hardening in CSEE, national governments openly baited Roma and stirred up centuries-old prejudices. National political leaders had cast off the veneer of respectability in arguing that segregation was accidental; now, they boldly pursued de jure segregation by building walls and tearing down Romani neighborhoods.[93] The resurgence of old prejudices is not likely to abate. Whole swaths of the economy have never fully recovered from the transition into capitalism, and now CSEE economies face the pangs of the financial crisis. These are not existential external threats that unify a nation, as the Cold War did the U.S.; rather, these are pressures that tend to cleave society and scapegoat its vulnerable segments.

While it is tempting to surmise that Roma inclusion languishes because of popular apathy, there is another way to view the relationship between nondiscrimination and public opinion. Social movements do not tend to draw popular support at their inception, but with careful planning they can galvanize support. As historians have pointed out, it was organizing by civil rights leaders that most directly spurred the viscerally repulsive violence that catalyzed legislation. Martin Luther King and his lieutenants saw from prior demonstrations that nonviolent protests attracted little attention if officials exercised restraint; however, they wagered that violent repression could provoke the nation's outrage.[94] Thus, they chose Birmingham and Selma for large-scale demonstrations; here, local officials were "constitutionally incapable" of restraint and lashed out against protestors with such brutality that Kennedy and Congress felt they had to respond with civil rights legislation.[95] For Roma rights, the real critique might not necessarily be that public sympathy has remained stagnant, but that nothing has been able to propel public attitudes out of stagnation. To be sure, throughout the post-Communist years conditions were ripe to ignite viscerally

> [T]he new tendency to single out the Roma as a *European* priority and a special *European* concern has also, rather paradoxically, opened up new opportunities for nationalist politicians to plead *against* new national measures to help the Roma. … [These politicians] have suggested that, while other citizens belong to the nation-states, the Roma belong to Europe, thus latching onto the alleged "Europeanness" of the Roma (and their alleged lack of national belonging) in order to exclude them symbolically from their own national space and frame them not only as "Europeans" without any attachment to any particular nation-state, but also as ethnic outsiders and cultural deviants.

92 *See D.H.*, 47 Eur. H.R. Rep. 59, at para. 26 ("The [Czech] Ministry of Education denied any discrimination and noted a tendency on the part of the parents of Roma children to have a rather negative attitude to school work.").

93 *See* Bernard Rorke, *The End of a Decade: What Happened to Roma Inclusion?*, OPEN DEMOCRACY (Sept. 29, 2015), https://www.opendemocracy.net/en/can-europe-make-it/end-of-decade-what-happened-to-roma-inclusion/.

94 Klarman, *supra* note 74, at 112.

95 *Id.* at 113.

abhorrent violence, from the race-baiting leadership of Mečiar (Slovakia) and Orban (Hungary) to vigilante killings to local initiatives to wall off Romani communities. Yet no Romani leader or group has emerged with the ability to organize the demonstrations that could touch off sustained, large-scale violence.

THE LIMITS OF ANTIDISCRIMINATION LAW

Antidiscrimination laws constitute the first generation of legal attempts at racial equality and minority protections. Though facilitating comparison between the U.S. and Europe, this label of "first generation" is not entirely precise. To be sure, the front line of discrimination has long been overt and intentional subjugation, for instance by way of segregation.[96] Hence, early efforts toward equality targeted these practices. Strategic litigation is a classic example; from *Brown* to the Roma rights cases before the ECtHR, these cases featured sympathetic plaintiffs challenging curated defendants under novel theories of law.[97] The RED and the Charter, too, stand as early EU prohibitions on discrimination, although there has been a dearth of case law under these frameworks (thereby directing comparativists to human rights cases under the ECHR).[98]

Second-generation discrimination, on the other hand, is subtler: it involves a structure of bias, exclusion, and subordination.[99] Often hiding behind race-neutral laws, its patterns reveal themselves only when large numbers of cases are assessed. Responding to these nuances, second-generation laws account for disparate impacts (more commonly known in Europe as indirect discrimination) and loosen the evidentiary burden for proving discrimination. Here, the generational labels unravel. In the EU, the RED features generous definitions and proof of discrimination,[100] and implementing legislation among the member states has also conceived of discrimination broadly.[101] Thus, the EU

96 *See* Susan Sturm, *Second Generation Employment Discrimination: A Structural Approach*, 101 COLUM. L. REV. 458 (2001).

97 *See* Lilla Farkas, *The Scene After Battle: What Is the Victory in* D.H. *Worth and Where to Go from Here?*, 1 ROMA RTS. J. 51, 52–53 (2008). *See also* EUROPEAN ROMA RIGHTS CENTRE, STRATEGIC LITIGATION OF RACE DISCRIMINATION IN EUROPE: FROM PRINCIPLES TO PRACTICE 79–82 (2004) (citing ease of proof, quality of domestic law, and potential to raise media attention among the considerations for pursuing strategic litigation).

98 Even earlier, conditionality itself might be thought of as first-generation antidiscrimination, given that it was the first time the EU seriously pursued Roma integration.

99 *See* Sturm, *supra* at 96, at 468–69.

100 Article 2(2)(b) of the RED defines indirect discrimination as "where an apparently neutral provision, criterion or practice would put persons of a racial or ethnic origin at a particular disadvantage compared with other persons, unless that provision ... is objectively justified by a legitimate aim and the means of achieving that aim are appropriate and necessary," while Article 8(1) shifts the burden of proof to respondents once a complainant has established facts leading to the inference of discrimination.

101 For example, the Bulgarian statute implementing the RED stipulated that the disadvantage of discrimination came from "any act, action, or omission which directly or indirectly prejudices rights or legitimate interests." *See CHEZ*, 2015 O.J. C 311/8, para. 14. This foundation allowed the CJEU to then define indirect discrimination broadly.

laws that grappled with racial and ethnic discrimination in the early 2000s recognized structural barriers to equality. This nuance is hardly surprising, since these laws were influenced by American civil rights legislation but had had time to mature into more sophisticated analyses.[102]

Nonetheless, loosely grouping minority protections temporally can help us discern their evolution as well as detect their limits. This first generation of antidiscrimination laws was constricted by structural, doctrinal, and institutional limits. Of these, the most daunting were the structural barriers to equality. Because the exclusion of African Americans and Roma is fused into the social fabric, nondiscrimination could never be enough to close the gaps separating these groups from the majority. Put differently, American and European legal systems could not integrate their way to full equality for African Americans and Roma.

Structural barriers tempered progress on school integration. After *Brown*, it took years to get school desegregation going. By the time remedies such as cross-district busing were at their peak in the 1970s, major demographic shifts had already been underway to neutralize the impact of integration. Since the Great Migration began in the early 1900s, African Americans had been leaving the South for cities in the North and the West; over time, they swapped sharecropping in the rural South for industrial jobs in urban centers.[103] Soon, cities became more ethnically homogenous but suffered the flight of industrial jobs abroad. Thus, by the 1970s, a significant percentage of African American students attended schools that were urban, majority black, and increasingly impoverished.[104] In this environment, antidiscrimination law proved ineffectual, since there were few white comparators in these areas; forced busing, too, became logistically more challenging, since schools had resegregated into districts tied to racialized maps.

Housing segregation was perpetuated by equally severe impediments. Whereas school integration could be more easily mandated and complied with (provided the political will for compliance existed), housing segregation was complicated by the interplay of several factors.[105] African Americans could not move into white neighborhoods, where home values were higher, partially because racially restrictive covenants prohibited white homeowners from selling to them and also because they earned less than their white counterparts.[106] Throughout the country, housing segregation was also perpetuated by government at all levels, through federal public

[102] *See* de Búrca, *supra* note 90, at 4 (noting the influence on EU antidiscrimination law of UK antidiscrimination laws from the 1970s, which had been influenced by American laws). For example, *CHEZ* and *Brown* were separated by sixty years.

[103] *See* The Great Migration in Historical Perspective: New Dimensions of Race, Class, and Gender (Joe William Trotter, Jr. ed., 1991); Isabel Wilkerson, The Warmth of Other Suns: The Epic Story of America's Great Migration (2010).

[104] *See* Halpern, *supra* note 10, at 10–11.

[105] *See* Richard Rothstein, The Color of Law: A Forgotten History of How Our Government Segregated America (2017).

[106] *See id.* at 77–85. *See also* Shelley v. Kramer, 334 U.S. 1 (1948).

housing programs that separated white and African American residents, federal insurers who refused to underwrite mortgages that broke with the racial uniformity of neighborhoods, and local zoning ordinances that demarcated white and African American housing stock.[107] Far from being an accidental confluence of factors, housing segregation was the intentional creation of law.[108]

In CSEE, Socialism and Communism had integrated Roma into the workforce crudely, as low-skilled laborers, but the post-Communist transition hit them especially hard. Newly unemployed and besieged by xenophobia, Roma often congregated in the rural outskirts or dense urban slums.[109] City officials walled off Romani neighborhoods, and police watched passively when Romani families were attacked.[110] These factors intensified housing segregation. Meanwhile, administrators piled Romani students into schools for the disabled on the basis of tests that were facially neutral but applied discriminatorily.[111]

Early laws barring racial discrimination were not drafted with Roma in mind. Adoption of the RED, for instance, was hastened by the reflexive outcry among EU elites against the generalized xenophobia, racism, and anti-Semitism of the Haider affair.[112] Its proponents envisioned antidiscrimination as an antidote to racism targeting Jewish populations or former colonial subjects of European empires rather than Roma.[113] Thus, EU institutions only recently applied antidiscrimination law to actions against Roma. Mostly, though, Roma integration in CSEE stumbled under the nondiscrimination paradigm because of the lack of meaningful implementation. During pre-accession, CSEE candidates readily agreed to the EU's conditions for Roma integration, but they stalled in compliance: the states funded initiatives insufficiently and failed to meaningfully implement the laws they had transposed.[114]

When Roma integration fell short, which happened frequently, the shortcoming was attributable not so much to structural barriers as to lack of political will.

107 *See* ROTHSTEIN, *supra* note 105, at 13, 30–34, 42–48.

108 *Id.* at xii–xv.

109 *See* DENA RINGOLD ET AL., WORLD BANK, ROMA IN AN EXPANDING EUROPE: BREAKING THE POVERTY CYCLE 15, 94 (2005).

110 *See, e.g.*, Moldovan and Others v. Romania, App. No. 41138/98 & 64320/01, Eur. Ct. H.R. (2005); Dan Bifelsky, *Walls, Real and Imagined, Surround Roma*, N.Y. TIMES, Apr. 2, 2010.

111 JULIA M. WHITE, PITFALLS AND BIAS: ENTRY TESTING AND THE OVERREPRESENTATION OF ROMANI CHILDREN IN SPECIAL EDUCATION (2012).

112 *See* Gabriel N. Toggenburg, *The Race Directive: A New Dimension in the Fight Against Ethnic Discrimination in Europe*, 1 EUR. Y.B. MINORITY ISSUES 231, 232 (2001–2002) (linking adoption of the RED to the Austrian affair); Cécile Leconte, *The Fragility of the EU as a "Community of Values": Lessons from the Haider Affair*, 28 W. EUR. POL. 620 (2005) (analyzing the failure of the same elites to adequately confront the affair, thereby sowing the seeds for future bouts of xenophobia).

113 *See* Andrew Geddes & Virginie Guiraudon, *Britain, France, and EU Anti-Discrimination Policy: The Emergence of an EU Policy Paradigm*, 27 W. EUR. POL. 334, 346–52 (2004) (detailing the influence of two paradigms toward antidiscrimination, the British and the French, on EU antidiscrimination policy). This pattern is reminiscent of the Copenhagen criteria's political conditionality, which was initially worried about refugees from and interethnic infighting in Southeast Europe, but not necessarily Roma themselves.

114 *See, e.g.*, HERMANIN & DE KROON, *supra* note 3; FRA, RACE EQUALITY DIRECTIVE, *supra* note 36.

Structural barriers certainly did exist, but at least antidiscrimination laws were broad enough to take care of indirect discrimination more readily than disparate-impact jurisprudence in the U.S. The infringement proceedings against Hungary, Slovakia, and the Czech Republic for school segregation, for instance, were premised primarily on indirect, systemic discrimination. Yet, for the most part, the Commission has pushed responsibility for Roma integration down to member states, who in turn have failed to act meaningfully.[115] As a directive, the RED is to be transposed into the national laws of each member state. National legislatures might have done so, but that process was prone to errors; further, national governments were slow to enforce the new legislations, and Roma did not know their rights thereunder.[116] The practical effect is that the enforcement and advocacy institutions were unwilling or unable to exorcise racial subordination. Thus, after *D.H.* school administrators might have integrated Roma into mainstream schools, but then they created "gifted" and "advanced" classes reserved for non-Romani students. Or parents and administrators built new schools in Romani neighborhoods catering to Romani students, or carved out non-Roma school districts from racially mixed neighborhoods, so that the schools were tied to Roma versus non-Roma districts.[117] Or, finally, parents created private religious schools catering to majority students.[118]

Lastly, antidiscrimination laws face doctrinal limitations. The Charter binds member states only when they are acting under EU law, a restriction rooted in the hesitancy to increase EU competences in human rights, extend the application of EU law, and augment the role of the CJEU.[119] For Roma rights, this limitation has not been particularly relevant, because segregation and anti-Roma discrimination fall within the scope of EU law (i.e., the RED). EU law permits some justifications for discriminatory treatment, which are narrower for direct than indirect discrimination.[120] Yet, in the context of racial discrimination, these justifications are either inchoate under existing case law or unavailable under the RED and case law.[121] By contrast, the doctrinal limitations would be much more consequential for civil rights in the U.S. context. In the decades after the Civil Rights movement, the

115 *See* EUROPEAN COMM'N, ROMA IN EUROPE: PROGRESS REPORT 2008–2010, 3 (2010).

116 *See id.* at 15.

117 *See* AMNESTY INT'L & EUROPEAN ROMA RIGHTS CENTRE, A LESSON IN DISCRIMINATION: SEGREGATION OF ROMANI CHILDREN IN PRIMARY EDUCATION IN SLOVAKIA 24–28 (2017); EUROPEAN COMM'N, A COMPARATIVE ANALYSIS OF NON-DISCRIMINATION LAW IN EUROPE 66–69 (2017).

118 *See* Eszter Neuberger, *Hungary's Highest Court Legitimizes Segregation in the Case of Religious Schooling*, BUDAPEST BEACON, Apr. 23, 2015.

119 *See* Gráinne de Búrca, *Beyond the Charter: How Enlargement Has Enlarged the Human Rights Policy of the European Union*, 27 FORDHAM INT'L L.J. 679, 694–95 (2004).

120 Justifications for direct discrimination include public security, public order, and public health; for indirect discrimination, they include affirmative action and the vague notion of "objective justification." *See* CRAIG & DE BÚRCA, *supra* note 27, at 900, 906–15.

121 The RED does not have a derogation for public safety like Article 2(5) of the Employment Equality Directive, 2000/78. Curiously, however, France invoked public safety in its expulsion of Roma in 2010. *See* SERGIO CARRERA & ANAÏS FAURE ATGER, CENTRE FOR EUROPEAN POLICY STUD., L'AFFAIRE DES ROMS: A CHALLENGE TO THE EU'S AREA OF FREEDOM, SECURITY AND JUSTICE (2010). In reality, these

Equal Protection Clause, which had anchored desegregation cases, would check the expansion of laws and policies designed to redress slavery and discrimination. The antidiscrimination principle would win out, ushering in a "color-blind" reading of the Constitution that struck down minority set-asides in municipal contracting and affirmative action as a remedy for historical mistreatment.[122]

TOWARD MULTILAYERED MONITORING AND ENFORCEMENT

Despite being beset by doctrinal and structural problems, could Roma rights at least benefit from the move toward multilayered monitoring and enforcement? This trend has accelerated in recent years and typifies the EU approach toward regulation; it has the potential to diversify the institutions that support Roma rights and backstop the abdication of enforcement responsibilities by national governments.

As Civil Rights and Roma rights unfolded, the U.S. and the EU relied on administrative agencies to monitor and enforce laws and integration policies, so that these tasks were not solely the responsibility of private litigants. In the U.S., variegated monitoring and enforcement occurred through the trilogy of civil rights legislation that has come to define the Civil Rights movement. The Civil Rights Act of 1964 outlawed discrimination in hotels, restaurants, and other public accommodations,[123] desegregated public schools,[124] barred discrimination in federally funded programs and activities,[125] and prohibited discrimination by covered employers.[126] The Voting Rights Act of 1965 prohibited racial discrimination in voting practices and procedures,[127] and the Fair Housing Act of 1968 outlawed discriminatory housing practices.[128] At least at their inception, these acts were focused exclusively on intentional discrimination; yet their drafters also realized that discrimination was a complex and dynamic problem.

To confront the endurance of discrimination, civil rights legislation bolstered the power of federal agencies. Title VII of the Civil Rights Act created the Equal Employment Opportunity Commission (EEOC) to enforce employment discrimination laws by issuing guidelines and investigating and mediating cases.[129] Title VI conferred authority on the Department of Health, Education, and Welfare (HEW), subsequently reorganized as the Department of Education and the Department of

expulsions were seen as triggering free movement and the Citizens Directive, 2004/38, more than discrimination and the RED. *See id.*

122 *See, e.g.*, City of Richmond v. J.A. Croson Co., 488 U.S. 469 (1989); Washington v. Davis, 426 U.S. 229 (1976); Ricci v. DeStefano, 557 U.S. 557 (2009).

123 Civil Rights Act, tit. II, 42 U.S.C. §2000a et seq. (2006).

124 *Id.* tit. IV, 42 U.S.C. § 2000c et seq.

125 *Id.* tit. VI, 42 U.S.C. § 2000d et seq.

126 *Id.* tit. VII, 42 U.S.C. § 2000e et seq.

127 42 U.S.C. §§ 10301–10314 (2014).

128 42 U.S.C. § 3601 (2006).

129 Sturm, *supra* note 96, at 550. *See also Overview*, U.S. Equal Emp't Opportunity Comm'n, https://www.eeoc.gov/eeoc/index.cfm (last accessed June 9, 2019).

Health and Human Services, to set guidelines for school desegregation.[130] Under Section 5 of the Voting Rights Act, the Department of Justice played a critical role in overseeing changes to the voting plans of states with a history of voter suppression.[131] Until this Section was eviscerated by the Supreme Court in 2013,[132] it operated as a powerful constraint against the ability of states, primarily in the South, to flout the Fifteenth Amendment. Finally, the Fair Housing Act directed the Department of Housing and Urban Development (HUD) to fight housing discrimination, which the agency does by investigating and filing claims.[133]

In moving from Civil Rights to Roma rights, the comparison crosses half a century, during which the monitoring and enforcement of minority protections became more multilayered and sophisticated. Since 1997, for example, the EU Agency for Fundamental Rights has conducted research and compiled handbooks for legal practitioners on racism, xenophobia, and minority rights.[134] Under the RED, the FRA supplements the Commission's reports on the application of the Directive; further, each member state has an equality body that assists victims in pursuing complaints, conducts surveys on discrimination, and issues reports and recommendations on discrimination.[135] These institutions supplemented the mechanisms that the EU had leaned on during eastern enlargement, such as funding, accession partnerships, and the Commission's monitoring reports. Even after accession, member states continued to receive EU funding for Roma inclusion initiatives, for instance through the European Social Fund.[136]

Of course, there were precursors to the EU's post-Communist embrace of Roma rights. In 1969, the COE adopted Recommendation 563 on the "Situation of Gypsies and other travellers in Europe." As the first text by a European institution on Roma, the Recommendation addressed the reception and rights of Roma in the COE member states, which at the time were located primarily in Western Europe.[137]

130 HALPERN, *supra* note 10, at 42–43.

131 52 U.S.C. 10304 (2014).

132 *See* Shelby County v. Holder, 570 U.S. 529 (2013).

133 *See* 42 U.S.C. § 3608. *See also* Robert G. Schwemm, *Overcoming Structural Barriers to Integrated Housing: A Back-to-the-Future Reflection on the Fair Housing Act's "Affirmatively Further" Mandate*, 100 KY. L.J. 125 (2012).

134 *See* FRA, RACE EQUALITY DIRECTIVE, *supra* note 36, at 7. In 2007, the FRA succeeded the European Monitoring Centre on Racism and Xenophobia, which had existed since 1997 to fulfill a slightly narrower mission. *See* CRAIG & DE BÚRCA, *supra* note 27, at 391–92.

135 RED Arts. 13, 17.

136 *See* European Comm'n, *Midterm Review of the EU Framework for National Roma Integration Strategies*, Communication from the Comm'n to the European Parl. and the Council (2017); Andzej Mirga, *Roma Policy in Europe: Results and Challenges*, *in* REALIZING ROMA RIGHTS 115, 118 (Jacqueline Bhabha et al. eds., 2017); Will Guy, *Anti-Roma Violence, Hate Speech, and Discrimination in the New Europe: Czech Republic, Slovakia, and Hungary*, *in* REALIZING ROMA RIGHTS 145, 160 (Jacqueline Bhabha et al. eds., 2017); Mizsei, *supra* note 75, at 135–36.

137 *See* JEAN-PIERRE LIÉGEOIS, THE COUNCIL OF EUROPE AND ROMA: 40 YEARS OF ACTION 33 (2012). The first EU text on Roma was the 1984 resolution of the European Parliament, titled "The situation of the Gypsies in the Community." *Id.*; Valeriu Nicolae, *Perfectly Equipped Failures: The European Union and Educational Issues Affecting the Roma*, 39 EUR. EDUC. 50 (2007).

Over the next several decades, the COE and other organizations, including the Organization for Security and Co-operation in Europe (OSCE),[138] the United Nations,[139] and the World Bank,[140] would take an interest in Roma rights, issuing a plethora of recommendations and reports. Where available, these organizations utilized enforcement mechanisms, such as litigation under the ECHR.

Because of the longstanding void in EU law to redress racial inequality and the EU's lassitude toward member states even after adoption of the RED, Roma have had to look to non-EU frameworks for recourse. This includes, most prominently, the ECHR, but also other human rights instruments such as the International Covenant on Civil and Political Rights, the International Convention on the Elimination of All Forms of Racial Discrimination, and, in the case of school segregation, the Convention on the Rights of the Child.[141] If CSEE states are signatories, then these instruments and their monitoring and enforcement bodies can fill in the gaps in EU law.

One discernable pattern in the evolution of these mechanisms, particularly in the EU's Roma rights and minority protection endeavors, is the pursuit of decentralized (as opposed to top-down), collaborative (as opposed to adversarial), and flexible (as opposed to rigid) governance. These are features of "new governance," the paradigm of multilevel integration, deliberation, and power sharing that characterized the EU as it shifted "from hierarchical governing towards more flexible forms of governance."[142] New governance inheres in the FRA, for example, which was conceived as fulfilling more of an advisory than a monitoring role.[143] The advisory capacity supplants a more adversarial approach to minority protections that pits

138 *See* OSCE Office for Democratic Institutions and Human Rights, *Roma and Sinti*, ORG. FOR SEC. AND CO-OPERATION IN EUR., https://www.osce.org/odihr/roma-and-sinti (last accessed Mar. 10, 2019).

139 *See United Nations Working Group on Roma*, U.N. OFFICE HIGH COMM'R FOR HUM. RTS., https://www.ohchr.org/EN/Issues/Minorities/Pages/UnitedNationsRegionalWGonRoma.aspx (last accessed Mar. 10, 2019).

140 *See* World Bank, *Conference Briefing Note: "Roma in an Expanding Europe: Challenges for the Future"* (2003).

141 *See* FARKAS, *supra* note 66, at 7, 9. Indeed, the ECtHR in *D.H.* also looked to a long list of international and foreign laws and principles for guidance. *See D.H.*, 47 Eur. H.R. Rep. 59, at secs. V, VI.

142 CRAIG & DE BÚRCA, *supra* note 27, at 161. For one of the classic works on new governance in the EU context, see Joanne Scott & David M. Trubek, *Mind the Gap: Law and New Approaches to Governance in the European Union*, 8 EUR. L.J. 1 (2002). For a succinct review of new governance, see Bradley C. Karkkainen, *"New Governance" in Legal Thought and in the World: Some Splitting as Antidote to Overzealous Lumping*, 89 MINN. L. REV. 471, 472–73 (2004).

143 *See* Bal Sokhi-Bulley, *The Fundamental Rights Agency of the European Union: A New Panopticism*, 11 HUM. RTS. L. REV. 683, 686 (2011). *See also* Gráinne de Búrca, *"New Modes of Governance" and the Protection of Human Rights*, *in* MONITORING FUNDAMENTAL RIGHTS IN THE EU: THE CONTRIBUTION OF THE FUNDAMENTAL RIGHTS AGENCY 25 (Philip Alston & Olivier De Schutter eds., 2005); Gráinne de Búrca, *EU Race Discrimination Law: A Hybrid Model?*, *in* LAW AND NEW GOVERNANCE IN THE EU AND THE US 97 (Gráinne de Búrca & Joanne Scott eds., 2006).

member states – and, in the context of Roma rights, CSEE member states – against the EU. For instance, an adversarial tone characterized political conditionality during the eastern enlargements, with its abundance of Commission monitoring reports.

Compared to civil rights legislation of the 1960s, the system of monitoring and enforcement for minority protections in the EU is more sophisticated, multi-layered, nuanced, and flexible – all benefits that came with the passage of time. Yet there were glimmers of proto–new governance as the Civil Rights regime evolved over time. In public enforcement, U.S. administrative agencies occasionally revealed themselves to be collaborative and flexible. Lacking formal enforcement and rulemaking power, some agencies have emphasized advisory over disciplinary functions. For instance, local offices of the EEOC, as well as the Office of Federal Contract Compliance Programs (which now reports to the U.S. Department of Labor), have experimented with outreach and education.[144] Federal protections of voting rights were even more nimble. For nearly two decades, the preclearance requirement under Section 5 of the Voting Rights Act was particularly effective in binding covered jurisdictions to then-current electoral practices; deviations in electoral policy and practice had to be approved by the Department of Justice. This helped federal enforcers respond as states and municipalities moved from poll taxes and literacy tests to subtler forms of voter suppression, such as gerrymandering and the submergence of minority voters in at-large districts.[145] But voting rights jurisprudence changed in the late 1970s, when, echoing the turn in equal protection, the Supreme Court required electoral changes to be retrogressive to violate Section 5; further, the Court required proof of invidious purposes to strike down electoral practices under Section 2, a part of the Voting Rights Act frequently used by minority plaintiffs.[146] In response, Congress amended the Voting Rights Act in 1982 to expressly prohibit electoral practices that result in the denial of equal opportunity (i.e., to supplant discriminatory intent with disparate impacts).[147]

At their best, the monitoring and enforcement institutions for civil rights and Roma rights advanced innovative solutions that followed open-ended standards rather than rules. Because the structural barriers to equality are multifaceted and ever evolving, they are better resolved through this flexible approach than with

144 *See* Sturm, *supra* note 96, at 550, 552–53.

145 *See* Richard L. Engstrom et al., *Louisiana*, *in* Quiet Revolution in the South: The Impact of the Voting Rights Act, 1965–1990 103, 116 (Chandler Davidson & Bernard Grofman eds., 1994).

146 *See* Beer v. U.S., 425 U.S. 130 (1976); Mobile v. Bolden, 446 U.S. 55 (1980). Section 2 echoed the Fifteenth Amendment but had been little used before the 1980s. *See* Thomas M. Boyd & Stephen J. Markman, *The 1982 Amendments to the Voting Rights Act*, 40 Wash. & Lee L. Rev. 1347, 1352–53 (1983). The Court's rejection of disparate impact in voting resembled its earlier decision in *Washington v. Davis*, 426 U.S. 229 (1976).

147 *See* Pub. L. 97-205, 96 Stat. 134 (codified at 42 U.S.C. § 1973(a) (1982)) (transferred to 52 U.S.C. § 10301); Samuel Issacharoff, *Polarized Voting and the Political Process: The Transformation of Voting Rights Jurisprudence*, 90 Mich. L. Rev. 1833, 1845–46 (1992).

narrowly tailored rules.[148] In bringing together a myriad of enforcers and norm-setting institutions, Civil Rights and Roma rights could tackle pressing racial problems from several dimensions. Of course, at their worst, a decentralized system of enforcement, pursuing open standards over clear rules, is prone to ambiguity and weak implementation, which can "dilute the law's normative impact."[149] Examples include the weakness of the FRA, which seemed preordained under EU law,[150] and the gutting or co-opting of the Office of Civil Rights.[151]

TOWARD STRUCTURAL SOLUTIONS FOR SYSTEMIC PROBLEMS

The emergence of multilayered enforcement and flexible standards in minority protection is consistent with a recognition that "second-generation" (structural) discrimination is protean and complex. Because the post-Communist Roma rights movement came half a century after Civil Rights, the EU was inevitably more cognizant of structural barriers to racial equality than the U.S. had been during Civil Rights. Compared to U.S. administrative agencies, the Commission has also committed itself more consciously to experimenting with forms of new governance.[152] In the sphere of Roma rights, the most notable example is the EU Framework for National Roma Integration Strategies up to 2020 (the "NRIS Framework"), a policy framework designed to prod national governments to devise tailored strategies for Roma inclusion.[153] The NRIS Framework focuses on Romani marginalization and exclusion,[154] and its method relies much more on "soft law" than does the RED, which seeks to advance the "hard law" of antidiscrimination.[155] As a policy framework, it is nonbinding but engages a panoply of actors adopting open-ended goals to inculcate the norms of Roma inclusion. Soon after its adoption, the NRIS Framework was supplemented by an EU

148 *See* Sturm, *supra* note 96, at 475.

149 *Id.* at 553. *See also* Päivi Gynther, Beyond Systemic Discrimination: Educational Rights, Skills Acquisition and the Case of Roma 220, 264–65 (2007).

150 *See* Gabriel N. Toggenburg, *The Role of the New EU Fundamental Rights Agency: Debating the "Sex of Angels" or Improving Europe's Human Rights Performance?*, 3 Eur. L. Rev. 385, 387 (2008).

151 *See* Charlie Savage, *Justice Dept. to Take On Affirmative Action in College Admissions*, N.Y. Times, Aug. 1, 2017; Halpern, *supra* note 10, at 85–91.

152 *See* Gráinne de Búrca & Joanne Scott, *Introduction: New Governance, Law and Constitutionalism*, *in* Law and New Governance in the EU and the US 1 (Gráinne de Búrca & Joanne Scott eds., 2006).

153 *See* European Comm'n, *An EU Framework for National Roma Integration Strategies up to 2020*, COM (2011) 173 final (Apr. 5, 2011).

154 In time, the NRIS also led EU institutions to fight anti-Gypsyism, which the Commission has recognized as "a specific form of racism against Roma and one of the root causes of Roma social exclusion and discrimination." European Comm'n, *supra* note 136, at 4.

155 On the distinction between the two in the context of EU governance, see David M. Trubek et al., *"Soft Law", "Hard Law" and EU Integration*, *in* Law and New Governance in the EU and the US 65 (Gráinne de Búrca & Joanne Scott eds., 2006). In short, soft law is a set of norms with no legally binding effect that can nonetheless shape behavior. *See id.* at 65. This is not to say that the RED is entirely hard law. *See* Búrca & Joanne Scott, *supra* note 152 (revealing how the RED blends elements of both norms and enforceable laws).

Council Recommendation,[156] and, beyond the Commission and member states, its implementation involves coordination with (i) the Roma Taskforce (to assess member states' use of EU funding for Roma integration), (ii) a network of national Roma contact points, and (iii) European and national platforms for Roma inclusion.[157] The pivot to a nonbinding framework is the EU's acknowledgment that nondiscrimination has been unable to secure social inclusion for Roma; consequently, the NRIS Framework calls on member states to devise comprehensive, multifaceted policies to integrate their Romani populations.[158] Remarkably, whereas the U.S. attempted to correct the failures of *Brown* and antidiscrimination jurisprudence by passing civil rights legislation, or more hard law, the EU resorted to norms and promises, sustained by a web of governments, monitoring organizations, and civil society.

The NRIS Framework was adopted in 2011 but, within the EU, discussions for such a policy structure started in 2007, after the accession of Bulgaria and Romania in the sixth enlargement.[159] Beyond the EU, the groundwork for the NRIS Framework was laid even earlier, through the Decade, launched at a 2003 conference in Budapest convened by the World Bank and the Open Society.[160] The Decade was a commitment by national governments of European countries to "eliminate discrimination against Roma and close the unacceptable gaps between Roma and the rest of society."[161] It sprang up from the realization, even before the fifth enlargement concluded, that all the transpositions of law and incorporation of the acquis were not improving the situation of Roma in CSEE significantly or quickly enough. Governmental and nongovernmental institutions therefore began to formulate policies to confront the structural and systematic nature of Roma exclusion. As a paragon of this structural approach, the Decade leaned on both state and nonstate participants, especially Roma rights NGOs,[162] marking a departure from the nebulous top-down mandates of conditionality. In fact, the Decade portended not only a shift from Roma *integration* to the more holistic Roma *inclusion*, but also a transformation in the most visible proponents of Roma rights from the EU to member states and civil society.

156 Council Recommendation of 9 December 2013 on Effective Roma Integration Measures in the Member States, 2013 O.J. (C 378) 1.

157 European Comm'n, *Effective Roma Integration Measures in the Member States*, Communication from the Comm'n to the European Parl., the Council, the European Econ. and Soc. Comm. and the Comm. of the Regions 6 (2016).

158 *See* European Comm'n, *supra* note 11, at 3.

159 *See* Stephan Müller, *European Framework for National Roma Policies and the Roma in the Western Balkans*, 10 EUR. Y.B. MINORITY ISSUES 397, 399 (2011).

160 RINGOLD ET AL., *supra* note 109, at vii, 184–85. *See also* World Bank, *supra* note 140.

161 *Frequently Asked Questions*, DECADE OF ROMA INCLUSION 2005–2015, *archived at* http://perma.cc/RJR5-JHRP. The Decade's site for the Decade was taken down shortly after the Decade ended; however, we have archived many of its pages at perma.cc.

162 *See* World Bank, *supra* note 140, at 2 (listing NGOs as among the most numerous participants at the conference). The dominance of NGOs, especially those with international funding, has prompted introspection about their authenticity. *See, e.g.*, AIDAN MCGARRY, WHO SPEAKS FOR ROMA?: POLITICAL REPRESENTATION OF A TRANSNATIONAL MINORITY COMMUNITY (2010).

The Decade aimed to reduce the gaps between Roma and majority populations in four key areas over its ten-year term: education, employment, health, and housing. While the consensus is that the Decade ultimately failed to deliver on this goal,[163] its methodical reports steered the inclusion movement toward measurable benchmarks and objective gauges of progress.[164] This systematic approach helped to compound the evidence that would spur other achievements such as the NRIS Framework.[165] True to its roots in development, the Decade and contemporaneous initiatives were couched not in the language of political ideals but of economic necessity. This, undoubtedly, was a lesson from conditionality: the diffusion of European norms into CSEE could not occur as heavy-handed, top-down mandates; the institutional drivers of Roma inclusion had to pursue more localized and narrowly tailored paths that appealed to the economic interests of national governments. The NRIS Framework, for example, begins with a recital of the economic benefits that would flow from lifting the Roma out of poverty.[166] The language of economic development also permeated progress reports of the Decade, which, after all, was sponsored by the world's premier development bank.

Rather than focusing singularly on discrimination, both the NRIS Framework and the Decade attempted to combat structural inequalities. Thus, they tackled inclusion in four key areas. Through the NRIS Framework and subsequent policy guidance, the Commission also encouraged national governments to collaborate with local and regional authorities and civil society, as well as to incorporate monitoring and evaluation, support national equality bodies, and coordinate with other member states on Roma mobility and best practices.[167] By contrast, U.S. civil rights legislation had failed to account for structural discrimination; during the period in which legislation was passed, the government was preoccupied with direct discrimination – actions invariably motived by discriminatory intent – and an understanding of structural barriers was just coming to light. As has been well-documented, enforcement mechanisms therefore struggled to

163 *See, e.g.*, DecadeWatch, Roma Activists Assess the Progress of the Decade of Roma Inclusion (2007) ("[D]espite some progress, the Decade has not reached the critical point that would guarantee success. Most governments think about Roma inclusion in terms of projects and sporadic measures but not programs or integrated policies.").

164 *See, e.g.*, DecadeWatch, Romania Report: Mid Term Evaluation of the Decade of Roma Inclusion (Iulian Stoian & David Mark eds., 2010) (methodical report on Romania's progress toward meeting its Decade goals).

165 On the link between the Decade and the NRIS Framework, see Bernard Rorke, *Somewhere Between Hope and Despair: Whatever Happened to Roma Inclusion Between 2005 and 2015?*, *in* A Lost Decade?: Reflections on Roma Inclusion 2005–2015 44, 46–48 (Bernard Rorke & Orhan Usein eds., 2015).

166 *See id.*

167 *See* Council of the European Union, Council Recommendation of 9 December 2013 on Effective Roma Integration Measures in the Member States, 2013 O.J. (C 378) 1; William Bartlett et al., European Parl., Evaluation of the EU Framework for National Roma Integration Strategies 22 (2015); European Comm'n, *supra* note 11, at 11–14.

keep pace as discrimination evolved into subtler, second-generation forms where intent was either difficult to discern or deliberately masked.[168]

Structural remedies for racial equality in the U.S. therefore arose after Civil Rights. They include affirmative action policies, particularly in hiring and education,[169] and reparations for slavery and economic exploitation of African Americans.[170] Some of these remain proposals and have not been implemented as policy. Here, parallels to Roma rights are limited: affirmative action has not been deployed for Roma as broadly (and therefore has not drawn the same intensity of controversy), and reparations for the *Porrajmos* have not been discussed as earnestly. There is also nothing built into the U.S. civil rights regime that resembles the complexity of the norm-setting scaffold of the NRIS.[171] As we look at how the comparators have experimented with second-generation -style reforms, then, the comparison becomes harder to sustain. And because the EU pushes so much of the work of inclusion down to its member states, the myriad of national approaches is difficult to summarize, leading to bland generalizations when monitoring agencies try to extrapolate broad themes.[172]

THE LIMITS OF STRUCTURAL SOLUTIONS AND MULTILAYERED MONITORING AND ENFORCEMENT

For all its thoughtfulness and complexity, the NRIS Framework has failed to dismantle the structural barriers to Roma inclusion. Implementation has been beset by problems, including a dearth of data and benchmarks, failure to integrate inclusion strategies, insufficient delineation of responsibilities, inadequate funding, and weak or nonexistent monitoring and evaluation.[173] This is despite the plethora of monitoring agencies, such

168 *See, e.g.*, Devon Carbado et al., *After Inclusion*, 4 Ann. Rev. L. & Soc. Sci. 83 (2008); Samuel R. Bagenstos, *The Structural Turn and the Limits of Antidiscrimination Law*, 94 Calif. L. Rev. 1 (2006); Sturm, *supra* at 96; Issacharoff, *supra* note 147.

169 For a compilation of writings on affirmative action through the decades, see Affirmative Action and the Constitution, vols. 1–3 (Gabriel J. Chin ed., 1998). Significantly, however, the U.S. Supreme Court has not viewed affirmative action as a remedy to "societal discrimination" or structural racism. *See, e.g.*, Regents of the Univ. of Cal. v. Bakke, 438 U.S. 265, 307 (1978); Wygant v. Jackson Bd. of Educ., 476 U.S. 267, 274 (1986).

170 *See* Ta-Nehisi Coates, *The Case for Reparations*, Atlantic, June 2014.

171 To be sure, in the U.S. scholars and advocates have moved beyond traditional legal processes in fighting for civil rights, resorting to broad political coalitions, community organizing, and grassroots activism. *See, e.g.*, Kevin R. Johnson & Bill Ong Hing, *The Immigrant Rights Marches of 2006 and the Prospects for a New Civil Rights Movement*, 42 Harv. C.R.-C.L. L. Rev. 99 (2007). Yet these moves have not occurred under the umbrella of a legal framework, such as the NRIS.

172 *See, e.g.*, European Comm'n, *supra* note 157, at 16, which summarizes assessments across member states and enlargement countries in typical fashion: "The assessment identified some positive trends . . . . However, efforts could not prevent further deterioration of the living conditions of Roma and widespread hostility of majority societies . . . . Member States should ensure a political recommitment to Roma integration . . . ."

173 *See* Bernard Rorke, Open Soc'y Roma Initiatives, Review of EU Framework National Roma Integration Strategies (NRIS) (2012); Farkas, *supra* note 66, at 8; Bartlett, *supra* note 167, at 8–9; European Comm'n, *supra* note 136.

as the FRA and the national Roma contact points, which might support data collection. Because data compilation must be done at the national level, if there is a lack of expertise or political will, monitoring agencies are rendered useless.[174] In fact, not only has the NRIS Framework fallen short in much the same way as the Decade, in many respects the Framework has not even meaningfully advanced the situation for Roma beyond the meager accomplishments of the Decade.[175] Hence, scholars and activists have invoked comparisons between Roma inclusion and Civil Rights to lament the lack of enforceability in Roma inclusion policies.[176]

However, this sentiment is misplaced: Roma inclusion has matured at a point in EU governance when, after the RED, the Union really did not want to develop more hard law on antidiscrimination, and certainly not on Roma inclusion. Instead, the EU opted to defer devising nonbinding norms to other institutions, from the development banks to national governments to civil society. Civil Rights, by contrast, was spurred in part by the Cold War, when the U.S. could not be seen by its allies and critics abroad as waffling on segregation. Thus, the U.S. had to desegregate its institutions quickly and unequivocally, which meant it had to mandate integration by law. Of course, the EU's choice of nonbinding norms such as the NRIS is not indefensible, given that the hard law of the RED had not improved the lives of Roma all that much. Further, having seen the regression of first-generation antidiscrimination in the U.S., the EU could not be faulted for trying to pay more attention to structural barriers and the flexible solutions that they demand.

Because of the vastly different historical contexts in which Roma rights and Civil Rights unfolded, the more fruitful comparison may to be assess how each fared on its own terms. For Roma inclusion, the EU's systemic approach was a disappointment. The NRIS, like its predecessor the Decade, has succumbed to the major flaw of new governance's dependence on norms: weak implementation, owing to the lack of enforceable law. Monitoring agencies can publish studies and best practices but are powerless to follow up with law. National governments quickly transpose the RED and sign onto the promises of the NRIS, but they do not follow through with enforcement or funding. Worse yet, national political elites might seize upon the "Europeanness" of Roma inclusion and openly resist inclusion policies as a badge of

174 *See, e.g.*, European Comm'n, Report on the Implementation of the EU Framework for National Roma Integration Strategies 6 (2014) ("Few Member States have provided information enabling comparison of the health of Roma with the general population."); Amnesty Int'l & European Roma Rights Centre, *supra* note 117, at 9 ("[T]he [Slovak] Ministry of Education does not compile ethnically disaggregated data with respect to schools and testing procedures and has no system in place to monitor or evaluate the implementation and effectiveness of the new 'SDE' testing system, which suggests a lack of engagement by the government with the objectives of the infringement proceedings.").

175 *See* Eben Friedman, *Education in Member State Submission Under the EU Framework for National Roma Integration Strategies* 18 (ECMI Working Paper No. 73, 2013).

176 *See, e.g.*, James A. Goldston, *The Unfulfilled Promise of Educational Opportunity in the United States and Europe: From* Brown v. Board *to* D.H. *and Beyond, in* Realizing Roma Rights 163 (Jacqueline Bhabha et al. eds., 2017).

Euroscepticism to win over domestic voters.[177] For their part, the institutions charged with honoring the NRIS fail even to gather the relevant data to assess the Framework's progress.

On its own terms, Civil Rights has given us a longer arc with which to assess its successes, but the record is mixed. In education, schools today are as segregated as they were in 1954, even though there was an interim period when cross-district busing and other remedies had achieved a modicum of integration.[178] In housing, the record has been more uniformly abysmal.[179] In voting rights, the last decade has been bitter: after the high-water mark of the 1982 Amendments, Section 2 claims became steadily more difficult to win, and in 2013 the Supreme Court gutted preclearance.[180] Equal protection jurisprudence has settled into a period in which disparate effects claims are usually unsuccessful and the antidiscrimination (as opposed to antisubordination) paradigm is supreme.[181] Above all, dual federalism has been resurgent, with federal powers to remedy discrimination dialed back in a number of cases.[182]

Administrative agencies have gyrated even more than equal protection or federalism jurisprudence. Because agency priorities change with the President, in certain administrations the agencies charged with civil rights enforcement have been reorganized, have lain fallow, or have taken on different priorities. Even in sympathetic administrations, when the Department of Justice actively filed suit its activity has been frenetic but without direction.[183]

Assessed on the terms of their comparators, the flaws of Roma rights and Civil Rights are even more apparent. Civil Rights has ignored structural racism, so that even if it has managed to root out intentional discrimination (or at least evidence of it), socioeconomic factors can create disparities that are effectively indistinguishable from the disparities of discriminatory intent. The EU has pursued a philosophy of Roma inclusion premised on a neoliberal vision of contribution to economic productivity.[184] This overlooks the most glaring issue for Roma: pervasive anti-Romanyism across the continent. When vigilantes burn Romani villages, police brutalize Romani communities, local leaders wall off Roma neighborhoods, and national politicians are elected on anti-Roma platforms, the obvious barrier to

177 On the temporal, utilitarian alignment of national elites with European integration and their tactical shift toward Euroscepticism, see Cécile Leconte, Understanding Euroscepticism 100–09 (2010). *See also* Vermeersch, *supra* note 91.

178 *See* Erica Frankenberg, UCLA Civil Rights Project, Harming our Common Future: America's Segregated Schools 65 Years after Brown (2019).

179 *See* Rothstein, *supra* note 105; Schwemm, *supra* note 133.

180 *See* Shelby County v. Holder, 570 U.S. 529 (2013).

181 Mark Tushnet, *The Return of the Repressed: Groups, Social Welfare Rights, and the Equal Protection Clause*, 2 Issues in Legal Scholarship 1 (2002).

182 E.g., City of Richmond v. J.A. Croson Co., 488 U.S. 469 (1989); *Shelby County*, 570 U.S.

183 *See* Halpern, *supra* note 10, at 187–89.

184 Goodwin & Buijs, *supra* note 19; Rorke, *supra* note 165, at 58.

inclusion is not integrating Roma into the market or reducing gaps in the four sectors. The obvious barrier is invidious intent.[185]

While Civil Rights has fallen short on many fronts, it has at least succeeded in driving invidious intent largely underground. Civil rights laws and equal protection jurisprudence did not do this by themselves. As revealed in a larger theme of this book, civil society led the way. Mainstream attitudes toward African Americans also changed along the way.

185 Rorke, *supra* note 165, at 59.

6

Filmic Representations

In mainstream culture, the marginalization of African Americans and Roma is reinforced through sign systems, or associations between images and ideas.[1] Stereotypes of both groups serve as signposts for an inability to become fully incorporated into the nation. This is hardly surprising: the prior Chapters of this book reveal how both groups have been excluded and marginalized for centuries, with weak recourse under law. Chapter 3 in particular shows how anti-Romani sentiment is deeply ingrained in CSEE societies. However, culture does not remain static; nor does the tug and pull between law and societal attitudes always yield predictable results.

Questions therefore abound. Have the depictions of Roma in the cultural products of CSEE changed over time? Have the signposts shifted? Has the sign system evolved? Answering these questions can help us gauge the efficacy of legal reforms and movement in society. Further, while the opinion polls and majoritarian resistance analyzed in Chapter 3 paint a bleak picture, there may still be subtle markers of change that portend more sweeping transformations.

To dissect the meanings that dominant culture has ascribed to portrayals of Roma, as well as to extrapolate broader patterns, this Chapter turns to film. Film is a cultural product whose images reflect what a society values, accepts, shuns, and disavows. Images, as cultural theorist Stuart Hall has observed, unconsciously reinforce in viewers the ideologies that are created and nurtured by societies.[2] Despite how images encode

[1] The idea of a sign system is based in the linguistics subfield of semiotics, which originated with the linguist Ferdinand de Saussure. The foundational ideas of semiotics uphold the notion that there is no inherent relationship between words and objects; rather, the meaning of a particular item is attributable to the culture that names it. The classic example is of the words "horse" (*equos* in Latin) and "tree" (*arbor* in Latin). There is no intrinsic relationship between the objects (the signified) and the words (signifiers) that we use for them. Rather, the meaning we give to words is constructed by factors beyond the objects themselves. In social semiotics, this relationship is extended, and explains how and why certain images, people, and concepts, among other things, are connected to an entire set of defining factors that are the result of culture, history, and experiences. For a discussion on semiotics and social semiotics in pop culture, see Bob Hodge, *Social Semiotics*, *in* The Routledge Companion to Popular Culture 36 (Toby Miller ed., 2016).

[2] *See* Stuart Hall, *Encoding/Decoding*, *in* Media and Cultural Studies: Key Works 163, 169 (Meenakshi Gigi Durham & Douglas M. Kellener eds., Blackwell 2006) (1980).

dominant constructs, critically decoding their meanings can stimulate "negotiated" interpretations that go beyond and subvert those constructs.[3] In that spirit, this Chapter traces the evolution of Romani characters in CSEE film through the comparative lens of the changing cinematic images of African Americans over time.

The hard-fought cinematic advances achieved by African Americans provide an interesting counterpoint to Romani representation. On screen, African American characters took on more nuance over time, especially after the Civil Rights movement. Yet the link between Civil Rights and filmic portrayals is not as straightforward as it might seem: the iconic African American figure in 1960s film was the "ebony saint," Sidney Poitier, but the disappointments of Civil Rights and the accompanying sanitized and flat images of African Americans ushered in blaxploitation in the 1970s, challenging the simplistic images of African Americans and offering instead characters challenging the social status quo.[4] Blaxploitation arose out of a confluence of realities: the inability of Civil Rights to produce meaningful inclusion despite its plethora of laws coincided with the deepening of black economic power and the growth of a black educated class that challenged traditional depictions. Hence, insurgent African American filmmakers could experiment with self-representation while playing to activists and an engaged viewing public.

A similar pattern is emerging in films from CSEE with Romani casts. We are entering a period in which depictions of Romani characters are diversifying, but also a period in which EU inclusion policies have not meaningfully improved the lives of most Roma in the region. The blaxploitation model would suggest that an ecosystem of filmmakers, viewers, and general post–Civil Rights frustration is needed to move cinema beyond established tropes. If the history of post–Civil Rights filmic images of African Americans can serve as a comparison – an assertion that we support – perhaps the continued persistence of diversity in African American images, despite the contemporary erosion of Civil Rights, can offer insight into the movement of Romani representations and inclusion into realist genres.

In contemporary representations, it is possible to locate nuanced images of African Americans and Roma. Of course, the recycling of stereotypes persists, but there are now increasingly realistic representations of African Americans and Roma in a multiplicity of genres, characters, and situations. By adopting this multiplicity, CSEE films featuring majority-Roma casts are now engaging with the EU's formulation of the "Roma Question," which has moved Roma inclusion from a human rights issue to a socioeconomic issue.[5] Realistic and complex portrayals of African Americans, by contrast, are a tradition that now spans decades, but this was not

3 *Id.* at 172–73.

4 Ed Guerro, Framing Blackness: The African-American Image in Film 21–31, 76 (1993).

5 *See* Márton Rövid & Angéla Kóczé, *Pro-Roma Global Civil Society: Acting for, with or Instead of Roma?*, *in* Global Civil Society 2012: Ten Years of Critical Reflection 110, 110 (Mary Kaldor et al. eds., 2012); Jacqueline Bhabha, *Realizing Roma Rights: An Introduction*, *in* Realizing Roma Rights 1, 21 (Jacqueline Bhabha et al. eds., 2017).

always the case. In fact, in attempting to trace a similar trajectory for the position of African Americans in film, we find a converse path, where economic concerns morphed into human rights during the Civil Rights movement.

This Chapter contextualizes the parallels between African American and Romani representation in cinema.[6] For both groups, the shift on screen from caricature to recognizable representations tracks the histories of the Civil Rights and Roma rights movements. We posit that the unsatisfactory Roma rights initiatives of the early 2000s set the stage for the progression of Romani depictions from predictable stereotypes and metonymic symbols to diversity by way of realistic portrayals. This shift is still nascent but, like blaxploitation, it constitutes a dialogue with the unfulfilled goals of a transformative rights movement.

This Chapter begins by laying the theoretical foundation for using film to gauge societal attitudes, relying on the work of Stuart Hall to illuminate the representation of black and "Gypsy" archetypes on screen. Then the Chapter briefly summarizes the shift in African American representation in films from the 1960s to the 1970s. Finally, it focuses on Romani representation in films with majority-Roma casts from CSEE after 2004. It is possible to see and track the movement from stereotypical portrayals linked to "Gypsy" archetypes to varied images of Roma in a manner similar to the way that stereotypical images of blacks moved to incorporate more nuanced and diverse portrayals in films in the U.S. The majority of these films about or focusing on Roma analyzed here are not made by Romani directors, but they nevertheless respond to external trends, namely, the EU's push for Romani economic and social inclusion. Interestingly, the production of rich films with majority-Roma casts by non-Roma directors parallels the dominance of non-Roma in the field of Roma rights more broadly.[7] In their own way, these directors push for social inclusion of Roma by employing realist narratives that reflect contemporary positionalities.

FRAMING DIFFERENCE: ENCODING/DECODING AND REPRESENTATION

Stuart Hall's reinterpretation of the communications model of encoding/decoding reveals how images are created for and processed by the viewing public, opening a space for individual interpretation beyond what is prescribed by dominant

[6] Numerous film scholars have addressed race and the cinematic representation of people of color. *See, e.g.*, Anikó Imre, *Screen Gypsies*, 44 FRAMEWORK: J. CINEMA & MEDIA 15 (2003); Nikolina Dobreva, *Constructing the "Celluloid Gypsy": Tony Gatlif and Emir Kusturica's "Gypsy Films" in the Context of New Europe*, 17 ROMANI STUD. 141 (2007); DINA IORDANOVA, CINEMA OF FLAMES: BALKAN FILM, CULTURE AND THE MEDIA (2001); DONALD BOGLE, TOMS, COONS, MULATTOES, MAMMIES, AND BUCKS: AN INTERPRETIVE HISTORY OF BLACKS IN AMERICAN FILMS (5th ed. 2016); GUERRO, *supra* note 4; Hall, *supra* note 2. However, to our knowledge, there has been no comparative work on filmic representations of African Americans and Romani peoples.

[7] Rövid & Kóczé, *supra* note 5.

constructs. Images work unconsciously to reinforce ideologies, and ideologies produce social consciousness (rather than the reverse), meaning that they can be "taken for granted" as true and appear on screen as natural.[8] Hall recognizes race as one such ideology, manifesting in both "overt" and "inferential" forms.[9] Overt racism happens when openly racist arguments are broadcast or racist policies advanced.[10] In contrast, inferential racism privileges unquestioned assumptions, which allow for sweeping statements about race that fail to account for intricacies.[11] This ideology applies language "impregnated with unconscious racism" and a hidden assumption that "*blacks* are the source of the problem."[12]

While race has profoundly shaped every aspect of the U.S. from its history to its culture and economic hierarchy,[13] in Europe race has not been interpreted as a dominant organizing principle since World War II.[14] However, for the reasons explored in Chapter 1, we refer to Roma as a "race," as opposed to the more regionally productive term "ethnicity," because of shared "mechanisms of racist exclusion" between the U.S. and Europe.[15] For Roma in particular, scholars are beginning to point out that race is an illuminating paradigm for analysis.[16] Race and racialization affect the position of Romani peoples from their daily interactions with majority populations who perceive them as outsiders to the EU's inclusion policies. Roma are viewed as visibly different even when that is not always the case, which suggests the deployment of a color line.[17] Moreover, discourses of Roma difference continue to be linked to migration narratives – real or imagined – of mythical travels from India to Europe. These perceived differences lay the groundwork for Romani racial formation, and racism and discrimination then become a "constant feature of [Romani] history."[18] Thus, filmic images of Roma as different contribute to a well-established system of racialized signifiers that position Roma outside the discourse and culture of the majority.

Film acts as a language that reinforces the ideology of African American and Romani difference; as a medium, it offers a setting "where these ideas are

8 *See* Hall, *supra* note 2, at 172.

9 Stuart Hall, *The Whites of Their Eyes: Racist Ideologies and the Media*, *in* Gender, Race and Class in Media: A Text-Reader 89, 91 (Gail Dines & Jean M. Humez eds., 2d ed. 2003).

10 *Id.*

11 *Id.*

12 *Id.*

13 *See* Michael Omi & Howard Winant, Racial Formation in the United States 106 (3d ed. 2014).

14 *See* Mathias Möschel, Law, Lawyers and Race: Critical Race Theory from the United States to Europe (2014).

15 Fatima El-Tayeb, European Others: Queering Ethnicity in Postnational Europe xxi (2011).

16 *E.g.*, Catherine Baker, Race in the Yugoslav Region (2018).

17 *See* Pina Batur, *Just a Link in the Chain: Global Racism and the Concept of "Blackness" in Russia*, *in* Racial and Ethnic Economic Inequality: An International Perspective 5 (Samuel L. Myers, Jr. & Bruce P. Corrie eds., 2006); Maja Mišković, *Roma Education in Europe: In Support of the Discourse of Race*, 17 Pedagogy, Culture & Soc'y 210 (2009).

18 Möschel, *supra* note 14, at 141.

articulated, worked on, transformed and elaborated."[19] Images and notions of race can constantly fluctuate, just as cultural imaginaries dictating the constructs of race can change. However, since film relies on recycled stereotypes and dominant discourses on African Americans and Roma, the medium tends to replicate the construction of difference and, in doing so, ensures the distance of these minority groups from the majority. Derogatory portrayals end up coding minorities as outside the structural mechanism of the majority, thereby cementing aspirational imaginings of the nation as homogenous.

This dialectic – the cultural construction of a homogenous nation with no space for racialized minorities – is buttressed in Europe and the U.S. by whiteness, which has historically functioned as an "unmarked category against which difference is constructed."[20] While whiteness has connections to power and access as well as imagined progress and humanism, the uses of whiteness in the U.S. and Europe, particularly in the CSEE states, varies.[21] In cinema from the U.S., the prevalence of whiteness codes long-standing social hierarchies that privilege dominant means of articulating the nation, leaving minimal expression for minorities and people of color. African Americans have contributed to the cinematic landscape since the early days of the form; nevertheless, the overwhelming visual difference of black characters offered an easily decodable signifier for the antithesis of whiteness, with little need for nuance.

Black characters in early films from the U.S. tended to fall into a few archetypes, according to Donald Bogle, such as the "Tom," the "Coon," the "Tragic Mulatto," the "Mammy," and the "Buck," all of which "entertain by stressing Negro inferiority." [22] These types have become so omnipresent through the course of history that their namesakes have been imbued with cultural capital. Mammy connotes a cantankerous, overweight, and desexed black woman; coon, an infantile ignoramus; and Tom, a sycophant willing to sacrifice himself for his master. Thus, these types persist even beyond the screen.

Importantly, these archetypes are typically gendered. Toms, coons, and threatening, oversexualized bucks are reserved for African American men, whereas mammies and sympathetic, sexual mulattos are portrayed by African American women. For the female characters, colorism plays an important role, too: the mammy typically possesses dark skin and the mulatto fair skin.[23] Hence, race, color, and gender all intersect in these characters.

[19] Hall, *supra* note 9, at 90.

[20] George Lipsitz, The Possessive Investment in Whiteness: How People Profit from Identity Politics 1 (rev. ed. 2006).

[21] *See* Charles W. Mills, The Racial Contract (1997); Anikó Imre, *Whiteness in Post-Socialist Eastern Europe: The Time of the Gypsies, the End of Race*, *in* Postcolonial Whiteness: A Critical Reader on Race and Empire 79 (Alfred J. Lopez ed., 2005).

[22] *See* Bogle, *supra* note 6.

[23] *See* Mills, *supra* note 21.

The origins of the Tom character lie, as expected, in Harriet Beecher Stowe's 1852 novel *Uncle Tom's Cabin*. The filmic Tom emerges in the earliest African American appearances on screen. Predictably, the Tom is a "socially acceptable Good Negro," ever ready to support the interests of his white companions, even his master.[24] The Tom is never disorderly or out of line; he is loyal and reliable. Accordingly, his appearance puts an audience at ease by reaffirming his inability to become angry, violent, or even frustrated at his unequal position in society.

The coon is an infantile buffoon who supplies a cache of stereotypes of African American inferiority. As a character, he is "unreliable, crazy, lazy, [and] subhuman," often presented stealing, gambling, eating watermelons, and speaking an exaggerated vernacular.[25] The coon emphasizes the inferiority and docility of African Americans, since actors in this typecast play roles devoid of higher reasoning, bound only by the basest of animal needs and desires. Well-known examples are the roles played by the actor Lincoln Perry, better known by his alter ego Stepin Fetchit, a ridiculous character whose speech was barely intelligible. Perry has been the subject of intense debate over whether divisive representation is preferable to no representation at all.[26] Some contemporary critics see Perry as pathbreaking because of his ability to open racial barriers in cinema, but others believe he merely made money by playing to the white imagination of black stereotypes. These two sides encapsulate the challenges of minority representation where it has unfolded in narrow confines.

The Tom and coon have analogues in the (tragic) mulatto and mammy, though the female characters possess a greater capacity to endear themselves to viewers. Still, both female archetypes illustrate inferiority, each in her unique way. The tragic mulatto is meant to evoke pity for her racial liminality: she is both African American and white, suggesting that life could have been kinder had she simply been one race or the other instead of both. She is the "victim of divided racial inheritance" and therefore sympathetic, relatable, and even overtly sexual, a feature not afforded to the mammy, the female counterpart to the coon.[27] The mammy is large and comically grouchy. As a type, she is closely related to Aunt Jemima, a variation of the Tom but religious, jolly, and attendant to white culture as she helps to reinforce its importance by accepting her lowered position, in the household specifically but also in society in general.[28] Aunt Jemimas, a variation of the mammy type, tend to be loveable caretakers who ensure that the household and its residents are functioning properly.

24 *See* BOGLE, *supra* note 6.

25 *Id.* at 5.

26 The character actor provides an interesting case of the challenges of minority representation because of the way black actors have been viewed historically.

27 *See* BOGLE, *supra* note 6.

28 *Id.* at 7.

The final character type is the brutal black buck, who first appeared as a white actor performing in blackface in the 1915 film *The Birth of a Nation*. This figure incited fear in the viewing public because he was so closely associated with sexuality and brutality. The buck falls into two subcategories: the black brute, a barbarian "out to raise havoc," and the black buck, an oversexed savage with a "lust for white flesh."[29] Bucks convey the need to suppress black males in general, lest they threaten the white race through acts of violence, both sexual and physical.

All of the above types provide a primary palette from which black characters are painted, fostering stereotypes that stymie any ideological dialogue about race because such dialogues are mired in flat portrayals of African American characters.

A similarly encoded difference in Romani representation can be found in films that date back to Communism and Socialism in CSEE. Dramas such as *I Even Met Happy Gypsies* (1967), *Who's Singing Over There* (1980), and *Radical Cut* (1984), as well as documentaries like *Gypsies* (1967), show how deeply entrenched the narrative of Romani difference is in the region. Compared against the archetypes explored above, we can see that, despite some legal and cultural inroads into dominant society, African Americans and CSEE Romani peoples remain marginalized in a process that is reproduced on screen.

Certain stereotypes and recurring motifs dominate the cinematic depictions of Roma, including a distance from whiteness and, therefore, the national imaginary that establishes power structures and determines belonging. As in the U.S., whiteness in the European context also builds the social hierarchies that define the nation. Yet whiteness takes on additional significance in Eastern Europe: because East Europeans are considered marginally European, and frequently see themselves as outside Europe, they reflexively tap into the transnational mechanisms of race to solidify their whiteness.[30] Consequently, dominant populations in CSEE adopt and apply racial formation to their minority groups.

Prior scholars, especially Anikó Imre, Dina Iordanova, and Nikolina Dobreva, have done extensive work in categorizing Romani filmic types. Imre highlights how Romani filmic portrayals default to "screen Gypsies": metonymic presentations of Romani peoples as uniform across the world. Screen Gypsies have souls "made of songs" and hearts "made of gold," living in "picturesque and photogenic poverty"; "their passionate temperament and indestructible vitality make them prone to violating the Ten Commandments and state laws."[31] These filmic Gypsies belie the diversity of real Romani communities.[32] Similarly, Dobreva analyzes representation of Roma as "celluloid Gypsies," and Iordanova argues that Southeast European films featuring Roma stand as allegories for the outsider status of the Balkans vis-à-vis

29 *Id.* at 10.

30 *See* Imre, *supra* note 21.

31 *Id.* at 90 (quoting Erzsebet Bori, *Vazonciganyok* [Screen Gypsies], 10 FILMVILAG 53 (1998)).

32 Imre, *supra* note 6.

Europe.[33] While these scholars converge broadly, they have tended to specialize in Romani portrayals tied to certain spaces: Iordanova focuses on filmic images originating from the Balkans, whereas Imre works primarily on Central European, especially Hungarian, cinema. The similarities in their findings suggest, however, that regional specificity need not constrain the analysis.

Portrayals of Romani peoples on screen are similar to those of African Americans; these representations perpetuate notions of the racialized internal Other, despite centuries of life in the lands where they hold citizenship and virtually no historical memory or cultural connection to their origins in West Africa and the Indian subcontinent. Yet diverse images of Roma are beginning to emerge on screen. Strikingly, this trend too resembles the rise of diverse African American images, facilitated by the historical, political, and legal battles of the Civil Rights era.

BLAXPLOITATION AND THE FAILURE OF CIVIL RIGHTS

In the early 1960s, during the concerted political activity of Civil Rights, African Americans forced the issues of race and freedom into the public fray.[34] These protests of "interpretive activism," where individuals fought against the negative images that could be interpreted from films featuring large African American casts,[35] were the result of advocacy by the National Association for the Advancement of Colored People (NAACP) pressuring Hollywood to "upgrade the cinematic image of blacks."[36] This generated a number of changes in representation, most notably in the portrayals of slavery.[37] The mid-1960s also saw the casting of Sidney Poitier in the role of "ebony saint," a favorable portrayal that had previously eluded black actors. Despite being well paid and in command of his own brand, Poitier embodied for many African Americans the superficiality of Civil Rights, which might have ushered in legal equality but failed to confer true integration for acceptance. Poitier's characters lacked depth and sexuality, and "the revolution in black consciousness very quickly rendered Poitier's saintly roles as laughably out of touch with the rising demand for assertive, realistic, black images on the screen."[38]

What followed, then, were more traditionally masculine and assertive roles for men and, eventually, women in the blaxploitation films of the 1970s. Melvyn Van Peebles brought forth a "new Black aesthetic" with his film *Sweet Sweetback's*

33 *See* Dina Iordanova, *Mimicry and Plagiarism: Reconciling Actual and Metaphoric Gypsies*, 22 THIRD TEXT 305 (2008); IORDANOVA, *supra* note 6.

34 GUERRO, *supra* note 4, at 29.

35 ELLEN SCOTT, CINEMA CIVIL RIGHTS: REGULATION, REPRESSION, AND RACE IN THE CLASSICAL HOLLYWOOD ERA 147–48 (2015).

36 GUERRO, *supra* note 4, at 29–31.

37 *See id.* at 35.

38 *Id.* at 76.

Baadasssss Song (1971), which asserted black "sexuality, violence, and freedom."[39] *Sweet Sweetback* was independent, directed by an African American, and created for an African American audience. It featured an African American lead in a powerful position, unafraid of the law and unapologetically black. The film proved groundbreaking; an independent film with minimal funding, it surpassed all expectations for profits. *Sweet Sweetback* responded to African Americans' desire to be heard and seen not simply as subjects but as individuals previously overlooked by white directors and studios.[40] Thus, in *Sweet Sweetback* the possibility of self-representation was realized, and what followed was nothing short of an explosion in self-representation that would come to be known as blaxploitation film. Blaxploitation would pave the way for a multiplicity of filmic representations of African Americans. The movement was known for its reinterpretations of genre films through powerful portrayals of masculine, testosterone-driven action and powerful, overtly sexual "black superwomen."[41]

Blaxploitation continues to provoke academic and popular debate over its utility and messages, but its lasting impact on filmic representation – notably, on propelling African Americans into the landscape of cinematic realism – is undeniable. The movement shows, counterintuitively, how self-exoticization and self-Orientalization garnered new possibilities for African American representation. In many blaxploitation films, stereotypes appear in tandem with retribution for structural and racialized violence directed at black bodies. Before we can utilize African American representation, particularly blaxploitation, as a window into the trajectory of Romani representation, we must first unpack the unabashed exploration of structural injustice and inequality in these films. There are hundreds of blaxploitation films spanning various genres. Many of these films are dismissed as extensions of the worse stereotypes associated with African Americans rather than a refutation of them. However, the cinematic portrayals of African Americans were empowering and enjoyable for some audiences, even if others recoiled at the association of African Americans with criminality, urban ghettos, drug activity, and deviant subculture.[42]

While blaxploitation films engaged in some of the worst stereotypes about African Americans, these Hollywood productions were open for broad consumption and helped propel African American cinema into the mainstream. However, this transition revealed that African Americans would be offered a place in mainstream cinema only if the actors and directors provided a framework that was familiar to diverse audiences. In other words, the images in blaxploitation cinema could be

39 Katherine Bausch, *Superflies into Superkillers: Black Masculinity in Film from Blaxploitation to New Black Realism*, 46 J. POPULAR CULTURE 257, 263 (2013).

40 *See id.*; PAULA MASSOOD, BLACK CITY CINEMA: AFRICAN-AMERICAN URBAN EXPERIENCES IN FILM (2011).

41 *See* BOGLE, *supra* note 6.

42 Critics taking the latter position included Civil Rights icons such as Jessie Jackson, the NAACP Congress of Racial Equality (CORE), and the Southern Christian Leadership Conference (SCLC). GUERRO, *supra* note 4, at 100–01.

decoded differently depending on the audience. The images created for black consumption relied on some of the most pernicious stereotypes projected on African Americans for generations: hypersexuality, violence, and criminality. Nevertheless, for African American audiences, blaxploitation films finally offered visual redemption for the oppression that their powerful white conationals had been inflicting on them for centuries. White audiences, however, saw in these films fantasies of triumph over oppressive power systems, visually represented through powerful white men such as the police, business owners, government officials, and even Klansmen. Of the 1971 blaxploitation film *Shaft*, for example, one critic wrote that it "provide[d] whites with a comfortable image of Blacks as noncompetitors, as people whose essential concern in life is making Mr. Charlie happy."[43] Similarly, John Semley argues that the films created an outlet for white filmgoers to enjoy visualized segregation, since the casts featured mostly, if not exclusively, black actors.[44]

Blaxploitation expression relied on a familiar trope of playing to expectations for a white ethnographic gaze that fulfilled stereotypes of the time, from the nonthreatening imbecile to the oversexed female to the brutal buck. Blaxploitation recycled these stereotypes, but within time and space frameworks relevant to its contemporary audiences. Following on the heels of Poitier, who fostered a new visual and caricaturized aesthetic for African American portrayals, blaxploitation allowed both black and white audiences to become accustomed to seeing African Americans on screen. In the 1970s, this was occurring in movies that were not part of the blaxploitation movement, such as *Lady Sings the Blues* (1972), *Boy and Man* (1971), *Sounder* (1972), *Black Girl* (1972), *Buck and the Preacher* (1972), and the screen adaptation of Sam Greenlee's *The Spook Who Sat by the Door* (1973). These films contrast greatly with the over-the-top aesthetics of blaxploitation films that were debuting alongside them, illustrating how the stereotypes created a pathway for more inclusion of African Americans into diverse genres, offering the potential for varied portrayals as well.[45] Arguably, this diversity in film would not have been possible without either Civil Rights, which combatted forms of black exclusion, or blaxploitation, which conditioned audiences to seeing African Americans on screen through narratives imagined as real and endemic to the black experience. These varied representations continued in the decades after the 1970s, giving birth to the New Black Realism of the 1990s in films such as *New Jack City* (1991), *Boyz in the Hood* (1991), and many Spike Lee films from the same time period.[46]

43 Clayton Riley, A *Black Critic's View of Shaft: Black Movie for White Audiences*, N.Y. TIMES, July 25, 1971.

44 John Semley, *Who's Bleeding Whom? Analyzing the Cultural Flows of Blaxploitation Cinema, Then and Now*, 80 CINEACTION 22 (2010).

45 *See* Bausch, *supra* note 39.

46 *Id.*

ROMANI SCREEN REPRESENTATION

Even before the fall of Socialism and Communism, films from CSEE featured Romani casts. The output from Czechoslovakia, Hungary, and Yugoslavia included *Gypsies* (1962), *I Even Met Happy Gypsies* (1967), *Who's Singing Over There* (1980), and *Radical Cut* (1983), among others. These films reflect a host of stereotypes connecting Romani characters to criminality, backwardness, rootlessness, and poverty. These racist depictions of Romani peoples emphasize their inferiority, enforcing the dominance and virtue of the majority. This process corresponds to transnational mechanisms of racial hierarchies based on articulations of visual difference, whether or not differences are in fact visible. In the case of Roma, as for African Americans, a constructed blackness maintains this positionality in opposition to whiteness (see Chapter 3).

The overlap of Romani and African American representation stems in part from a history of exclusion and marginalization, as well as legacies of the "posts": postcolonialism, post-Socialism, and post–minority rights. For all their differences, Civil Rights and Roma rights have tried to engage with Western mechanisms of power exercised through social and racial hierarchies. As prior Chapters explore, in Europe this unfolded recently as part of the post-Communist rounds of EU enlargement. In CSEE, the adoption of Western systems disrupted Socialist and Communist social orders, where the organizing paradigm avoided discourses of race and aimed to incorporate, even celebrate, ethnic diversity. In fact, this much-touted acceptance of diversity functioned as a counterpoint to discrimination in capitalist systems. With CSEE's embrace of Western structures, however, the rhetoric of racial equality was exposed as meaningless in light of the disparities, physical abuse, and social inequities faced by minorities and peoples of color.[47]

This "long shadow of discrimination and exclusion" continues to affect Romani communities and motivate Roma rights, an ongoing movement pushing for broad Roma equality and social and economic inclusion.[48] Eastward enlargement might have brought heightened attention to the dislocation and discrimination faced by Romani communities, prompting the EU, the Council of Europe, the Open Society Foundation, various NGOs, and even the World Bank to take action. Most agree, however, that for various reasons, these efforts have been largely unsuccessful.[49] Nevertheless, grassroots and international advocacy has forced EU policymakers to face the Romani community "on more equal terms."[50] But accommodation of this

47 *See* Maxim Matusevich, *Journeys of Hope: African Diaspora in the Soviet Society*, 1 AFRICAN DIASPORA 53 (2008); Imre, *supra* note 21; Bhabha, *supra* note 5.

48 Bhabha, *supra* note 5, at 3.

49 For more on the discussion concerning the failure of Romani inclusion, see Zeljko Jovanovic, *Why Europe's "Roma Decade" Didn't Lead to Inclusion*, OPEN SOC'Y FOUND. VOICES (2015), https://www.opensocietyfoundations.org/voices/why-europe-s-roma-decade-didn-t-lead-inclusion.

50 Bhabha, *supra* note 5, at 2.

parity must exist beyond the political and legal: representation, too, must relay equality so as to dismantle artificial differences.

Thus, filmic representations of Roma play off conflicting political, social, and cultural trends. Officially, the EU works to support its motto of "Unity in Diversity,"[51] but CSEE states are keen to assert their European bona fides through projections of whiteness. The challenge of filmmakers is to display inclusiveness while simultaneously encapsulating the distance of Roma from the majority. It is a delicate balance to maintain that hearkens back to blaxploitation, when African American directors employed stereotypes to quell white viewers and simultaneously satisfy black desires. There are, of course, differences between the images of Roma and those created for African Americans during blaxploitation, just as there are differences between Roma rights and Civil Rights. Nevertheless, the new images in CSEE films with large Roma casts are fostering empathy, which could facilitate inclusion in a manner similar to how Sidney Poitier helped white Americans become more comfortable with African Americans in their spaces. If the goal was integration, then Poitier was largely successful. In 1963 he became the first African American to receive an Academy Award for Best Actor, an honor not accorded to another African American male until 2001 when Denzel Washington won for his role in the film *Training Day*. The African American backlash that followed Poitier's sanitized portrayals came in the form of blaxploitation, a movement that did not shy away from stereotypes but presented a new way of confronting and using them. In contemporary CSEE cinema, the changes in Romani representation track the grassroots and EU attention to Romani inclusion strategies, and in these sympathetic and humanizing images the dialogues trickle down visually to viewers decoding the images for themselves.

The remainder of this Chapter will focus on post-2004 CSEE films that feature majority Romani casts. Though not directed by Roma, these films nonetheless fold in the goals of Romani inclusion, as well as the EU's articulation of those goals. The films do not address economic inclusion directly, but they respond to Roma social inclusion by employing realist narratives to convey contemporary Romani positionalities. While several films fit this mold, given space limitations we discuss only five: *The Shutka Book of Records* (2005), *Roming* (2007), *Just the Wind* (2012), *An Episode in the Life of an Iron Picker* (2013), and *Bravo!* (2015). These films span two distinct periods: pre- and post-EU expansion into CSEE. We selected these films because they illustrate the convergence of themes and characters in recent films from CSEE with majority-Roma casts, particularly in how Roma are depicted as racialized Others marked by their blackness. We look at the periods prior to and after the

[51] *The EU Motto*, Eur. Union, https://europa.eu/european-union/about-eu/symbols/motto_en (last accessed June 12, 2019).

fifth round of EU enlargement to gauge the effects of membership and the accession process.

If the activism of the 1960s reinvigorated stereotypes of African Americans as irascible, militant criminals, the image of Sidney Poitier helped to diffuse those fears. Subsequently, blaxploitation confronted those stereotypes and provided multiple ways of decoding their messages. The images of Romani characters in recent films navigate similar dynamics in a similar fashion, offering characters with whom non-Romani viewers can sympathize as they are denied basic human rights, equality, health, well-being, and education.

***The Shutka Book of Records* (Aleksandar Manic; Macedonia; 2005)**

The Shutka Book of Records premiered in the film festival circuit only a year after the fifth round of EU enlargement, when ten formerly Socialist and Communist nations entered the Union. This film takes place in the majority-Roma town of Shutka, Macedonia, and introduces residents as champions of various unusual things like fashion, old Turkish music collections, rock and roll music, sex, and graveyards.[52] Shot in documentary style, the film purports to offer an insider's perspective on the town's unique inhabitants and their unlikely experiences, personalities, and habits. Narration by a local resident enhances the film's verisimilitude. The interviewees include members of a Sufi order of dervishes, a vampire hunter, a boxer who trains young boys in the community, older men who engage in activities typically reserved for those much younger, dogfighters, and a pop singer.

The film pays homage to the town of Shutka and its residents, spinning a tale about the perplexing quandary of who gets to be a champion in a town where everyone is a champion of something. Narration by an insider ostensibly offers an unvarnished view of the town and its people, but the music score undercuts his trustworthiness. The background music is not the boisterous, energetic brass music traditionally associated with the region's Romani, or even the pop music highlighted in the stories about local musicians. Instead, the dominant score is redolent of circus music, with its whimsical, excessive brass. Compounding the carnival atmosphere are scenes with locals on a swing ride. Thus, the characters depart from being the subjects of a documentary and come to resemble circus acts.

Due to the way the film places these individuals on display, Mikhail Bakhtin's theory of carnival can elucidate the representation of Shutka and its Romani characters. For Bakhtin, carnival presents an opportunity to suspend normal behaviors and expectations.[53] It is liberating because it allows people an opportunity to escape the predictable doldrums of everyday life.[54] However, if *The Shutka Book of*

52 Residents obtain their title as "champions" either by self-proclamation or winning bizarre competitions.

53 For more on Bakhtin's idea of "carnival," see MIKHAIL BAKHTIN, PROBLEMS OF DOSTOEVSKY'S POETICS 122–23 (Caryl Emerson trans., Wayne C. Booth ed., 1984).

54 *Id.*

Records is supposed to simply record objective truths about the town, then its flirtation with carnival and the carnivalesque betrays an outside gaze that is judging the town against an extrinsic norm. Given the time period and focus of the film, this norm is likely Europe, more specifically the EU, which was wary of the accession of most of the Southeast European candidates. Films from the region dating to this period present the EU as aspirational, but incapable of aiding unfortunate, dislocated members of the community.

The West and the EU embody unrealizable desires, highlighted when the film opens in black and white with intertitles that state: "This film is the true and authentic story of a small town somewhere in the Balkans, on the edge of Europe." This message of Balkan distance from Europe hovers in front of the remnants of a stripped car, presumably the result of locals removing all the valuable metal. Following this, the film changes to color and features a dervish, Uncle Fazil, who says that he can travel to the U.S. without a visa because he can simply materialize there, which provides one bookend to the film: materialization. The conclusion of the film offers the Other the dream to dematerialize from Shutka and "fly far to the West."

This symbolic desire for Western inclusion afflicts not just the town of Shutka, but the region in general. Like Shutka, all of Macedonia and, by extension, the Balkans have been deemed unworthy, incapable of attaining the standards for European association (via EU membership). Roma, who are the very subjects of the film, stand in for a region deemed unassimilable. In fact, *The Shutka Book of Records* regularly defaults to established stereotypes for Roma, such as criminality, nonconformity, and sexual promiscuity. Yet the film exposes the complicated frames of Romani and Southeast European and Balkan difference, delving somewhat into structural hindrances for the community at large. Interestingly, perhaps contradictorily, the film shows Roma as exercising their own agency through the various lives, lifestyles, and means of survival in the town. Overall, however, despite introducing the complicated structural sources of poverty and dislocation, the film relies on familiar stereotypes of communal laziness, government dependency, universal poverty, and criminality to tell the story. As such, the film endorses the idea that it is impossible to discuss Roma without invoking old stereotypes, even if the film attempts to solve the mystery of why Shutka's inhabitants remain cut off from the outside world.

Roming (Jiří Vejdělek; Czech Republic, Romania, Slovakia; 2007)

Jiří Vejdělek's *Roming* premiered only three years after the fifth enlargement was complete in 2004. The movie marks a transition from stereotypical to nuanced Romani portrayals. *Roming* is an example of the road film genre, as it tracks the journey of the film's protagonists, Jura, Stanko, and Roman. It tackles stereotypes, but simultaneously reinforces them – a tension that both encourages and frustrates viewers. In engaging with contradictory images of Roma, *Roming* both supports and challenges the position of Romani people in the Slovak imagination as a broader metaphor for the relationship of Central and Eastern European to Western "Europe."[55]

The film recounts the story of two generations of a Romani family and their trip from the city to the country: the son, Jura; the father, Roman; and the father's old friend, Stano. The two generations contrast greatly. The father is an unemployed widower who depends on his son for financial support and is an amalgamation of Romani stereotypes: he is able-bodied but does not work, fond of drink, and a romantic dreamer. He pays the postman in refundable recyclable bottles instead of cash and turns off the lights in an act of solidarity with other Romani people who cannot afford electricity. Roman will prove his Romani credentials by penning a Romani epic structured around Somali, a Roma king whose story serves as a backdrop for the entire film. Throughout the film, Stano and Jura are at odds with one another: Stano claims to be a Gypsy and regularly challenges Jura to prove that he is a real Gypsy. Roman serves as a foil to Somali, but is otherwise a passive observer of events.

Jura provides an example of a character type that we would classify as an "educated Rom," but this privileged position comes by way of assimilation. Jura is introduced by extreme close-ups that show only his hands and a city skyline in the window that frames him. The camera then pans back to reveal Jura packing for his journey home. He is revealed first by books in his hands, his arms, and then his body as he packs his rucksack. Jura has been obfuscated and is then shown in reference to his girlfriend, who watches him pack. In the two early frames where Jura appears, he is defined by something (the city) or someone (his girlfriend Vera) else. Vera, like Jura, is significant not for who she is, but for what she is – a white woman. She also enters the film by way of extreme close-ups of her naked midsection, her hand, and the door. These scenes introducing Jura highlight the prevalence of whiteness in the film. Another example is an abundance of blonde hair as an assertion of Slovak Europeanness and whiteness. Further, Somali is the only Romani individual who is depicted working, and he does so in secret. Most shockingly, the well-known Slovak actor Marián Labuda and Czech actor Bolek Polívka are both white but play the characters of Stano and Roman in Gypsy face, or brownface.[56] The comedic portrayal of Roman and Stano centers on the inability of Roma to fulfill the cultural expectations of the majority and evokes other minstrel acts of brownface, echoing the long tradition of blackface in American cinematic history.[57]

The humor in the film derives from a notion of superiority of the majority culture and inferiority and ridiculousness of Romani culture. If being black or brown were

[55] *See* John McCormick, Europeanism 57 (2010).

[56] *See* Eva Woods Peiró, White Gypsies: Race and Stardom in Spanish Musicals (2012); Raúl Pérez, *Brownface Minstrelsy: "Jose Jiménez," the Civil Rights Movement, and the Legacy of Racist Comedy*, 16 Ethnicities 40 (2016).

[57] Pérez, *supra* note 56.

simply a matter of painting one's face, then the lives and experiences of "black" people are rendered irrelevant and unimportant, thereby reaffirming the dominance of the majority and the exclusion of the minority. Even if race itself exists by way of signifiers and structural imposition, those who are adversely affected by race will not explain daily racism as symbolic or constructed, so performing race is an act of cultural appropriation without the burden of having to face daily racism. In an interview, Polívka and Labuda joke about which one of them plays the "Romani spirit," insinuating that Romani lives, culture, and spirit can be performed, akin to a costume that you can put on and take off at will.[58]

There is a great deal more that could be said about this deeply rich film, but in considering the frames of Europeanness, the nation, and race, the film creates an overall space for Romani peoples to be incorporated into the nation, as all films referenced here do. What *Roming* promotes, however, is limited belonging based on the confines of the nation, Europe, and whiteness. Roman, Stano, and all others in the Romani cast cannot enjoy the benefits of incorporation as they are. In fact, Romani participation in the nation is categorically limited, and embodied by performativity such that it can be claimed only by those who are deeply assimilated, which is the case with Jura.

Just the Wind (Benedek Fliegauf; Hungary, Germany, France; 2012)

An Episode in the Life of an Iron Picker (Danis Tanović; Bosnia Herzegovina, France, Slovenia, Italy; 2013)

Bravo! (Radu Jude; Romania, Bulgaria, Czech Republic, France; 2015)

Two films that debuted after the sixth round of EU enlargement in 2007 and track the increased NGO and governmental interest in Roma are *Just the Wind* and *Bravo!* Both films mostly abandon broad character typologies of their Romani actors and opt instead for a dialogue with the past to offer commentary on the current state of Romani affairs by way of a categorization that we would define as the documented Rom. Documented Rom characters appear in films that are based primarily on historically accurate events or situations. They exist as a result of a generations-long struggle to be recognized as individuals and members of the nations in which they were born and live, and to be embraced by the mainstream. The Roma in *Roming* are presented as subjects worthy of pity, primarily because of expectations informed by human rights, as well as internal projections of the nation focused on European concerns and values. Members of the Romani community are primarily screened as cultural outsiders, working against endemic structural barriers and daily racism that seems to affect only them. The documented Rom tracks the ethnographic gaze projected on Roma and uses historical settings to comment on the present.

58 Tina Čorná, *Marián Labuda a Bolek Polívka – Umelci Rómskej Voľnosti* [*Maria'n Labuda and Bolek Poli'vka – The Artists of the Roma Freedom*], SME (Jan. 18, 2007), https://www.sme.sk/c/3099890/marian-labuda-a-bolek-polivka-umelci-romskej-volnosti.html.

Just the Wind is a docudrama that focuses on the personal narrative of one family to recount actual events from 2008, when Hungarian Romani families were the targets of horrific racist murderers. The film depicts the tragic lives of members of the community who are under attack simply because of their race. The narration revolves closely around the protagonists so that we empathize with their experiences and struggles for existence in the face of obstacles such as social ostracism, underemployment, general vulnerability, and social hostility. The film is shot in muted colors and, as in other films surveyed here, utilizes intertitles at the outset to convey the veracity of events while assuring viewers that the film is a fictionalized account and not a documentary.

The mise-en-scène provides a context for the drab, documentary feel of the film, positioning the protagonists as documented Rom. The movie is filmed primarily through medium and close-up shots to evoke feelings otherwise suppressed by the documentary-like quality. The close-up shots, paired with cool, drab colors, hint at the depth of feeling the film evokes. There is also an abundance of darkness that obfuscates details of the home setting and individual characters and their activities. This darkness suggests a universality of the experiences surrounding the lives of Roma. These features express the mood of the film, particularly in the final scenes, marked by virtual silence except for the sounds a mortician creates diegetically as he removes clothing and shoes from a rustling plastic bag and dresses the lifeless bodies of the murdered Romani family in preparation for their funerals.

There is little action in *Just the Wind*, save for the routine of daily life: the characters wake up, get ready for the day, and leave the house to make their long journeys to work and school. There is also little dialogue in the film, but when characters speak, it is frequently to remind each other of details, highlight community racism, and attempt to protect themselves. An example is when community members cleaning up a burned house stop the protagonist Mari to make sure she did not see or hear anything strange. Two scenes later, Mari is at school alone – presumably she arrives early because of her long commute – when her teacher tells her about computer equipment that was stolen. It is clear that the teacher believes Mari is guilty of the theft or may know something about it. This same teacher will harass Mari's mother, Anna, who works at the school, when he asks her if the room smells and remarks that the room smells better with a fan directed on her.

This racist expression surfaces throughout the film and, as in *Roming*, the symbols of power present a challenge to normal life. In one telling scene police officers are investigating a murdered family's home. While looking around, they eat a snack, showing their utter disregard for the setting. What's more, they are engaged in a conversation about how the killers killed the wrong Gypsies, and by killing "good Gypsies," they are "sending the wrong message" because it looks like a hate crime. One officer remarks that he knows which family they should have killed and recounts the various crimes he believes the family has committed.

Skillful camera work advances the film, and distinct play between the disorienting darkness that pervades the homes of the Romani family and the bright outdoors and school contrasts the two realities that the members of the family navigate daily. Inside the home, darkness obscures the characters. These scenes privilege the ear over the eye, which is rendered useless in the darkness. It is the pervasive darkness, in fact, that empowers the final scenes when the family is shot point blank. Viewers can hear but not see the chaos as Mari, Anna, and their family attempt to escape. The closest we get to confirming that we are witnesses to murder comes when the action shifts to outside the home, and we see the house windows light up with each shot. As the film ends with an undertaker dressing Mari, Anna, and the grandfather, one can assume that the storyline will repeat in the days that follow with different families.

The characters in Bosnian director Danis Tanovic's film, *An Episode in the Life of an Iron Picker* (2013), are also documented Rom, as the docudrama explores fictionalized accounts of actual events. In this film, the protagonist's wife nearly dies from lack of access to healthcare; the "actors" are the family to whom the horrific events actually happened. This verisimilitude personalizes their experiences, making their actions, experiences, and reactions to their settings universal, but the film's empathy is primarily a result of the symbolism of the Romani experience that is encoded by misfortune, evidenced by the examples above. In all of these films, the Romani characters have ceased to be the stereotypes of generations past, as the characters parallel trends in diverse representations and probes into historical settings to challenge flat narratives, much in the same way that directives, initiatives, and Roma rights organizations are insisting on dynamic narratives for the Romani people.

B*ravo!* is a black-and-white film from 2015 by Romanian director Radu Jude that blurs road, heritage, and Western film genres. Set in the nineteenth century, the film tells the story of a policeman charged with finding and returning a Roma fugitive slave who is guilty of having an affair with his master's wife. In *Bravo!* the focus is on the historical record. Discussing history and slavery, the film enters into a dialogue about the complicated roots of Romani difference and ostracism from Romanian society, as well as the distance of Roma from positions of power. By tracing the roots of the contemporary Romani positionality in Romania back to slavery, the film forces spectators to confront their own prejudices.[59] The self-critical view can be extended to the rest of the region to properly historicize the generational dislocation and de facto marginalization of Romani populations in Europe. That the fugitive slave is guilty of having sexual relations with the master's wife connects this film with reliable racial stereotypes of hypersexualization of racialized peoples.[60] This

59 Ileana Bârsan, *Mentalities and Historical (Re) Presentation in* Aferim! *by Radu Jude*, 1 CINEMATOGRAPHIC ART & DOCUMENTATION 5 (2016).

60 In Winthrop D. Jordan's book *White over Black* (1968), he systematically deconstructs the white perception of black sexuality as a byproduct of blacks being viewed as closer to beasts than humans. This association of black and brown bodies converges at this point whereby distance from whiteness makes one closer to blackness, which increases the association with beasts and, in turn, sexuality. For more on black associations with sexuality, *see id.* at 33, 35, 38, and 150.

provides the Romani slave character with depth: he is simultaneously worthy of pity since he is a slave and has no agency, but he has also committed what would be an irredeemable crime at the time.

Bravo! relates to contemporary Romani positionality via an exploration of slavery, a productive trope of African American dislocation that has long been historicized through portrayals on screen in the American context. In demonstrating the harsh reality for slaves in Wallachia, the film positions the status of the internal Other that Romani populations in CSEE occupy as directly related to Wallachian history. This dislocated position informs a contemporary reality, and properly historicizing Romani slavery in CSEE provides a context for understanding the distance of Romani populations from the majority. This approach in Romanian cinema was new; it offers a positive point to begin a dialogue about systemic inequality as a contributing factor to the contemporary marginalization of Romani peoples in Romania.

There are a number of American films with narratives centered on African American slavery in post–Civil Rights America, including *The Slaves* (1969) and *Roots* (1977). These early examples created pathways for important dialogues about race in the U.S. and helped establish a connection between African American marginalization and the history of slavery, similar to *Bravo!* These early forays into slavery and the connections that it has to African American cultural and national ostracism offer compelling counterpoints for exploring the role of a film like *Bravo!* in creating new narratives of the sources of Romani Otherness. In the American context, representations of slavery are too numerous to list, but some recent noteworthy examples include *Django Unchained* (2012) and *12 Years a Slave* (2013). Most recently, the television series *Underground* (2016) approaches slavery through discussions of escaping to freedom by featuring abolitionists and runaway slaves as protagonists, thus restoring slaves' agency in securing their freedom. This television show compares to *Bravo!* in that the storyline depends on a fugitive slave, but in *Underground* it is the slaves who advance the narrative, whereas the narrative in *Bravo!* focuses primarily on the slave capturer.

The importance of *Bravo!* to post-Communist Romanian new wave cinema cannot be overstated. Director Rade Jude has declared that "the topic of the film is not the past nor the present but the connection between them."[61] *Bravo!* is the first Romanian film to address the history of slavery and hint at its connection to contemporary Romani marginalization in Romania. In Romania, in contrast to the U.S., there is little formal recognition of the history of Romani slavery. It does not appear in textbooks, documentaries, or public discourse, so this film could be

61 Samuel Goff, *Chain Reaction: Meet the First Romanian Director to Tackle Roma Slavery Onscreen*, Calvert J. (Dec. 7, 2015), https://www.calvertjournal.com/articles/show/5109/chain-reaction-romanian-director-radu-jude-aferim-roma-slavery.

a catalyst not only for recognition of Romani enslavement but also for making connections with the structural roots of Romani marginalization.

When *Bravo!* is compared with African American films about slavery, it becomes obvious that there is an evolution in the treatment of the brutality and cruelty of slavery on screen that now aims to restore agency and narrative perspective to the slaves themselves. Early films about transatlantic slavery do not directly connect past to present in the same way that we can witness in *Underground*. This series fosters those connections by juxtaposing the historical setting, costumes, and subject matter with a score of contemporary music, typically hip-hop and rap, as nondiegetic sound. By shifting the background music from the traditional mellow and melancholic soundtracks of the past to the energized hip-hop of today, the series presses to move slave narratives from a narrative position of victimhood to one of resistance. *Bravo!* also taps into endemic sources of Romani dislocation; as a result, there begins a long path of recognition and reconciliation necessary for a collective understanding of the lingering effects of slavery on those who suffered under that system. That Romanian Roma have a history of slavery based solely on their difference further implicates Romanian Roma as affected by racialized hierarchies of superiority and inferiority based on race.

While the contemporary period does not directly correspond to the 1970s movement of blaxploitation, there are some compelling similarities. The Roma in these films are seen not by way of stereotypes or as the butt of a joke but rather as members of their societies. Both *Just the Wind* and *An Episode in the Life of an Iron Picker* focus on the injustice and everyday racism that the characters experience.[62] Because these stories are based on true events, one can assume that they represent the broad discrimination, ostracism, and racism that Roma face on a daily basis. These are simply the events that caught the attention of the press and, therefore, the filmmakers who chose to immortalize them. These films operate as a universal condemnation of the denial of human rights for Romani communities, much in the same way that films focusing on slavery functioned in the post–Civil Rights years and sparked a conversation about race and the American project of blaxploitation films.

What remains missing from this discussion, however, are examples of self-representation as a means to change the dialogue. In CSEE, Romani filmmakers are also using self-representation to challenge long-standing stereotypes and static images associated with Romani peoples. Clearly, there is much work to be done in facilitating diverse portrayals of Roma, but it is encouraging that some filmmakers are moving in that direction. In fact, within CSEE, Roma filmmakers Sami Mustafa, who is from Kosovo but based in France, and Katalin Bársony, who is from and works in Hungary, use their art to actively push back against Romani stereotypes. Mustafa runs FOCUS Roma Cinema Youth Project, which

[62] Perhaps the most significant recent development is the film *Genesis* (2018), directed by Hungarian-Rom director Arpad Bogdan. The film offers a pastiche of three individual stories woven together through the experiences of the protagonist of the film, a young Roma boy.

encourages young Romani filmmakers to create films actively challenging stereotypes and assumptions about the Romani community. One result of its work on Romani representation is the Roma Online Resource Center, an online database of 100 films by and about Roma that offers toolkits for film festival organization and classroom use.

Both Mustafa and Bársony have founded their own production companies, Romawood and Baxt Films, respectively, which produce documentaries and sponsor film festivals throughout Europe to showcase other Romani filmmakers. In addition, Bársony directs the Romedia Foundation, an NGO that works to push back against static stereotypes of Roma. Romedia has run an advertising campaign throughout CSEE countries to change the image of Romani women, trained young women to become filmmakers, and, through the program Mundi Romani, created documentaries showing the world "through Romani eyes." This work is promising, as it highlights the potential of a younger generation to contribute to a new cache of images and expectations regarding Romani communities. It shows what can be reaped from the struggles and sacrifices of the Roma rights movement. Romani filmmaking currently abounds in documentaries, so the movement is not simply an act of self-representation, but inclusion into realist aesthetics. In the NGO and European imagination, stereotypes continue to associate Roma with poverty and helplessness. Thus, documentary films mirror blaxploitation in that they respond to both an external ethnographic gaze and a desire for minority groups to be seen on screen. By taking control of the language of the documentaries, these Romani directors can encode their own images, paving the way for self-representation. If blaxploitation can be a model, Romani directors can and will use their racialized positions to advance dialogue and challenge their current positions through their filmmaking.

The 2018 feature-length film *Genesis* by Árpád Bogdán is one of only a few examples of a fictionalized filmic text of self-representation from this period and could indicate a shift from outside representation to "talking back," or resisting power through self-expression, in the form of Romani representation.[63] One review of the film notes that the film treats subject matter that had already been addressed in the 2012 film *Just the Wind*.[64] However, *Genesis* is not simply a reinterpretation of that film, or a retelling of the same events, but, rather, it is another example of talking back to challenge the narrative of the Roma murders from a Romani point of view. The film explores the 2008–2009 racist Romani murders that took place in Hungary through three interlocking story lines focused on three characters: Risci, Virag, and Hana. While each story builds on and relates to the others, it is the story of Risci that most deeply explores the unequal position of Roma in Hungary. Risci is a young boy who is at home with his family

63 Ian Hancock, Danger! Educated Gypsy: Selected Essays 42 (Dileep Karanth ed., 2010).

64 Alissa Simon, *Berlin Film Review: "Genesis,"* Variety (Feb. 20, 2018), https://variety.com/2018/film/reviews/genesis-review-berlinale-2018-1202704709/.

when a gang of men throw Molotov cocktails into their home and fire shots at anyone they see in the house. Risci loses his mother, his home, and his sense of security in this single night, and he is actually shot while trying to run away in response to his mother's final plea before she is shot. Risci's redemptive innocence, surprising ability to fight back when necessary, and use of restraint at other times, provide a rich counternarrative to the stereotypical image typically associated with Roma on screen. *Genesis* offers a reevaluation and reinterpretation of the Romani experience and a beginning or birth of Romani representation through ending the status quo by offering alternative images and exploring the negotiation of marginalization through the point of view of the one who has actually been marginalized. The dual meaning that can be interpreted based on one's subjective view, or dual address, surfaces in the tension between talking back through reclaiming a historical event and the negotiation of the marginalized position that those in the Romani community have in relation to the majority and the cultural negotiations that people of color must navigate daily.

Genesis, similar to other Romani and African American examples of filmic self-representation, illustrates the challenges that persist in the culture of a society irrespective of laws and movements that push for greater inclusion of any particular minority group. Although the list of films examined here is not exhaustive, when these films are considered collectively, they illustrate that being a person of color is a matter of mediating life between the poles of the majority and minority. The cinema reflecting the experiences of those excluded and disregarded by society will similarly be a balancing of poles and expectations coded between the two "norms." In the films analyzed above, the complications of being a minority of color play a powerful role in the form of social critique, illustrating the complicated gauntlet of daily life that Roma and African Americans must run. In calling attention to these difficulties, these films indirectly highlight the failures of American and European societies to meaningfully include Roma and African Americans, despite legal and structural changes focused on their inclusion in the period of Civil Rights and post-2004 EU eastern expansion. In confronting these contradictions, the films also present a powerful means of analyzing the failures of Civil Rights and Roma rights. They also illustrate the power of self-representation to effectively mediate the push and pull of the dominant and minority positions of belonging and the complicated ways in which minorities navigate those poles of existence.

Taking the movement of blaxploitation as an example, we posit, then, that the unsatisfactory Roma rights initiatives of the early 2000s have set the stage for the progression of Romani depictions from predictable stereotypes and metonymic symbols to diversity by way of realistic portrayals. The incorporation of Romani filmmakers framing their own images and telling their own stories has greatly advanced this project. This shift is still nascent but, like blaxploitation, it constitutes a dialogue with the unfulfilled goals of a transformative rights movement, particularly in films created by Roma directors eager to tell the various stories of the Romani experience. Much as the sympathetic portrayals of African Americans in the films referenced above provided a pathway to empathize with the African American experience, these Romani films by Roma directors can prime audiences for viewing Roma differently.

Conclusion

We first presented this project at Duke Law School in 2015. At the time, Barack Obama was ending his second term as President, and the U.S. had grown accustomed to seeing a person coded as "black" holding the country's highest political office. Obama's presidency seemed to hearken the unequivocal acceptance of African Americans into the cultural imaginary.[1] Meanwhile, Central European University (CEU) in Budapest was hosting the first in a series of conferences that would usher in the critical turn in Romani studies. CEU's 2015 conference adopted a comparative approach and took particular interest in mining U.S. civil rights for lessons while articulating points of commonality.[2] This approach echoed an emerging trend among scholars and advocates that viewed civil rights as a comparator, if not a model, for Roma integration.[3]

If there was any hubris in the comparison, any hint of civil rights exceptionalism, it vanished the following year. Even as the Obama presidency spurred conversations about post-raciality, it highlighted the deficiencies of the civil rights paradigm, which had not adequately addressed mass incarceration, voter suppression, racial inequality, and the endurance of school segregation.[4] The incongruence between the first African American President and everyday life for many African Americans

[1] *See* Ian Haney López, *Post-Racial Racism: Racial Stratification and Mass Incarceration in the Age of Obama*, 98 CALIF. L. REV. 1023, 1068 (2010) ("The power of race stems almost as much from its cultural meaning as its material impact, making the symbolism of a black presidential visage enormously forceful."). *See also* MICHAEL TESLER & DAVID O. SEARS, OBAMA'S RACE: THE 2008 ELECTION AND THE DREAM OF A POST-RACIAL AMERICA (2010); GWEN IFILL, THE BREAKTHROUGH: POLITICS AND RACE IN THE AGE OF OBAMA (2009).

[2] *Inside the Struggle: The U.S. Civil Rights Movement & the European Roma Rights Crisis*, Central European University (2015) [hereinafter *Inside the Struggle*], https://www.ceu.edu/event/2015–12-07/inside-struggle-us-civil-rights-movement-european-Roma-rights-crisis [https://perma.cc/3Z84-3YLE].

[3] *See, e.g.*, Jack Greenberg, *Report on Roma Education Today: From Slavery to Segregation and Beyond*, 110 COLUM. L. REV. 919 (2010); James A. Goldston, *The Unfulfilled Promise of Educational Opportunity in the United States and Europe: From* Brown v. Board *to* D.H. *and Beyond, in* REALIZING ROMA RIGHTS (Jacqueline Bhabha et al. eds., 2017).

[4] *See* López, *supra* note 1; ERICA FRANKENBERG, UCLA CIVIL RIGHTS PROJECT, HARMING OUR COMMON FUTURE: AMERICA'S SEGREGATED SCHOOLS 65 YEARS AFTER *BROWN* (2019).

was not lost upon the scholars who were drawing comparisons with Roma rights.[5] Ultimately Obama's two terms precipitated a backlash against the normalization of multiculturalism, highlighting what the racialized majority stood to lose if whiteness were no longer the dominant identity. In a rebuke to what Obama's presidency portended, the U.S. electoral college delivered a victory for Donald Trump in 2016. This reinforced the reality that the U.S. was as much an importer of sociopolitical trends as it was an exporter; the election came on the heels of Brexit and other right-wing populist victories and near misses.[6] If it can be said that democracy comes in waves,[7] then the same may be true of minority rights and xenophobic backlashes.

One pattern that the diachronic, transatlantic Roma rights–civil rights comparison illuminates is the cyclicality of racial equality and minority protections. For instance, grassroots agitation has reacted with external pressures such as the Cold War and refugee influxes to prompt political elites in the U.S. and EU to endorse equality; yet that support can recede if economic turmoil convinces the elites that it is more expedient to scapegoat racialized minorities. The cyclical nature of rights is also one lesson that comes from a broader historical comparison. For instance, to explain the limits of Civil Rights, U.S. scholars have looked increasingly to Reconstruction, whose gains faded into Jim Crow as whites re-exerted control over African American bodies.[8]

While Roma rights and civil rights have both undergone cycles, the crests and troughs of Roma rights have come with greater frequency and wilder swings over the last half century. In CSEE, Roma rights have had to contend with seismic social, political, and economic changes through Communism, post-Communism, EU accession, and xenophobic populism. Within fifty years, two wholly different paradigms of Roma rights have risen and fallen: Communism, with its emphasis on class struggle over ethnic identity, and EU-driven inclusion, with its emphasis on diversity and socioeconomic integration. In some countries, the history of Roma rights is as long and storied as the Civil Rights movement in the U.S.[9] In CSEE, however, post-Communist Roma inclusion is still young, as are many of its supporting institutions, from governmental equality bodies to NGOs. The federalism issues, with a supranational government imposing minority protections over local objections,

5 *See* Greenberg, *supra* note 3, at 977–78. *See also Inside the Struggle*, *supra* note 2 (featuring a panel on the "continuing challenges" of Civil Rights).

6 *E.g.*, the strong electoral showing in Austria by Norbert Hofer of the far-right Freedom Party, the victory of Rodrigo Duterte in the Philippines, and the resignation in Italy of Matteo Renzi, forced by the Five Star Movement.

7 Samuel P. Huntington, The Third Wave: Democratization in the Late Twentieth Century (1993).

8 *E.g.*, Henry Louis Gates, Jr., Stony the Road: Reconstruction, White Supremacy, and the Rise of Jim Crow (2019). *See also* Eric Foner, The Second Founding: How the Civil War and Reconstruction Remade the Constitution 169–75 (2019).

9 *See, e.g.*, Zentral Rat Deutscher Sinti & Roma, 45 Jahre Bürgerrechtsarbeit Deutscher Sinti und Roma (2017); Thomas Acton & Ilona Klímová, *The International Romani Union: An East European Answer to West European Questions?*, *in* Between Past and Future: The Roma of Central and Eastern Europe 157 (Will Guy ed., 2001).

really only came to the fore during pre-accession. It might even be argued that the most recent iteration of Roma rights has not undergone a full cycle: the gains have not been sufficiently meaningful enough for any retrenchment to register. The panoply of inclusion policies, from conditionality to the NRIS Framework, have been beset by weak data collection, vague benchmarks, and enforcement deficiencies.[10] Education stands as the single area where modest progress has been made,[11] perhaps because of pressures from litigation and infringement proceedings.[12] However, parents and school districts have reacted just as quickly to find new ways of excluding Romani schoolchildren.[13]

Ebbs and flows in minority rights come partly from the tug of war between popular sentiments and legal reforms. Since Reconstruction, for example, reforms in the U.S. have been driven principally by the federal government, often in the face of local and regional resistance, and federalism has mediated that tension. Roma policies have also changed each time the system of political governance was overhauled, for example from Nazi satellite states to Communism to post-Communism and EU enlargement. These overhauls were exogenous to Roma rights. In other words, Roma rights did not prompt these changes, as racial equality did Reconstruction or Civil Rights; instead, Roma rights were an afterthought to these transformations. Consequently, Roma rights cannot be said to have risen to a level of prominence sufficient to inspire systemic transformations.

Yet, over the longer sweep of history, Roma rights did coincide at points with revolutionary fervor. The reformist Hapsburg Emperor Joseph II abolished slavery in 1783, though his order was not evenly implemented at the local level. Later, in the parts of Wallachia, Moldavia, and Transylvania where Roma had been enslaved, their emancipation tapped into the energy of Romania's nation-building project of the mid-1800s. These differences presaged the variations in Roma policies that would cut across CSEE for the next two centuries. While some general patterns might be discerned, states typically pursued distinct policies toward their Romani communities. During World War II, some CSEE nations had succumbed to fascism while others waged full-throated resistance; these disparities determined whether Roma were persecuted more thoroughly or incorporated into antifascist partisans. Under Communism and Socialism, governments were more uniform in Roma policies, but national distinctions became particularly important in the post-Communist years before the EU took the helm on inclusion. In the early 1990s,

10 With conclusion of the NRIS Framework imminent, there is talk of another round of inclusionary efforts to follow up on NRIS, much as the NRIS had followed upon the Decade and the Decade had followed upon conditionality.

11 *See* European Comm'n, *Effective Roma Integration Measures in the Member States*, Communication from the Comm'n to the European Parl., the Council, the European Econ. and Soc. Comm. and the Comm. of the Regions 16 (2016).

12 Amnesty Int'l & European Roma Rights Centre, A Lesson in Discrimination: Segregation of Romani Children in Primary Education in Slovakia 9 (2017).

13 *See id.* at 24–28.

for instance, Hungary passed minority rights legislation, while Slovenia and Slovakia purged Roma of national citizenship.[14] Even after the EU reacted more forcefully to the failure of conditionality by passing the RED and launching the NRIS, implementation was pushed down to the member states. Disparities across CSEE endured.[15]

Whether construed narrowly or broadly, the Roma rights–civil rights comparison has its limits.[16] The U.S. cannot and need not be a comparator in all circumstances, especially given the variations within each comparator. To the extent comparisons can be made, civil rights serves as a cautionary tale: in times of progress, the full effect of legal and cultural shifts cannot be assessed until much later on, for there might be downturns and backpedaling.

Of course, it is not settled that Roma rights must undergo cycles at all. Minority rights and inclusion are the product of alignment between government and segments of society, as well as between law and culture. If those alignments are enduring, then rights and inclusion will last. If, on the other hand, legal advances are out of step with cultural attitudes and culture does not catch up, then enforcement may falter, and advances on the books will not be meaningful.

This comparison is as illuminating for the U.S. as it is for the EU. One of the insights from EU conditionality is that the U.S. has experimented with conditionality of its own, creating an incongruity between existing and aspiring states. While we have explored this dynamic in the Reconstruction Amendments, other scholars might choose to focus on minority rights at the member state level (e.g., comparing the Roma inclusion initiatives of EU member states with the civil rights initiatives of U.S. states).[17] Future

14 *See* Angéla Kóczé, *Political Empowerment or Political Incarceration of Romani? The Hungarian Version of the Politics of Dispossession*, *in* The Hungarian Patient: Social Opposition to an Illiberal Democracy 91, 92 (Péter Krasztev & John Van Til eds., 2015); Peter Vermeersch, The Romani Movement: Minority Politics & Ethnic Mobilization in Contemporary Central Europe 135 (2006); Jelka Zorn, *Ethnic Citizenship in the Slovenian State*, 9 Citizenship Stud. 135 (2005); Julia Sardelic, *Romani Minorities and Uneven Citizenship Access in the Post-Yugoslav Space*, 14 Ethnopol. 159 (2015).

15 The imprints of these disparities, too, might have been lasting. Lilla Farkas postulates, for example, that the Austro-Hungarian state left behind a familiarity with bureaucracies, so EU policies today are more easily implemented in the territories that had fallen under that empire (e.g., parts of Hungary, Romania, Slovakia, and the Czech Republic). By contrast, the territories under former Ottoman rule (e.g., the Balkans) did not acclimate to strong, centralized political institutions, Communism notwithstanding. Thus, in these areas, civil society must play a more active role in mediating between policies and the people. Interview with Lilla Farkas, former President of the Hungarian Equal Treatment Advisory Board and former Ground Coordinator for Race of the European Network of Independent Experts (June 1, 2019). *See also* János Ladányi & Iván Szelényi, Patterns of Exclusion: Constructing Gypsy Ethnicity and the Making of an Underclass in Transitional Societies of Europe (2006).

16 *See* Jacqueline Bhabha, *Realizing Roma Rights: An Introduction*, in Realizing Roma Rights 1, 8–10 (Jacqueline Bhabha et al. eds., 2017).

17 Or perhaps even by comparing laws and policies in cities or regions within states – a "federalism all the way down" comparison. *See* Heather K. Gerken, *Foreword: Federalism All the Way Down*, 124 Harv. L. Rev. 4 (2009).

scholarship might also contrast the influence of international law and norms upon the development of the minority rights regimes in EU versus the U.S., which tends to be more closed off. Such projects would be welcome additions to the Roma rights–civil rights comparative literature, which typically draws lessons from the U.S. experience rather than the other way around.

Beyond extrapolating academic lessons, another reason for comparing our two rights movements is to foster solidarity between Roma and African Americans. These two groups share a history of racialized exclusion, often reinforced by law and encompassing a cultural exclusion that pushes them out of the dominant narratives, despite the occasional cultural appropriation by the mainstream.

Civil society has tried to build this type of solidarity by emphasizing the commonalities between Roma rights and civil rights. As international Romani organizations sought to construct Romani nationalism in Europe after World War II, they emphasized the Romani identity as a defensive maneuver against racial construction.[18] When the ERRC, Open Society, and other groups fought for Roma rights in post-Communist CSEE, they started by adopting U.S.-style strategic litigation. As several of the Chapters show, civil society can concentrate the power and attention of otherwise diffuse peoples and push for rights and inclusion.[19] Further, civil society often molds legal and social realities. It acts where government has failed and can intervene to keep the government on task.[20]

Equally important, civil society organizations have supported artists, musicians, and cultural figures in their efforts to lift up Roma and African Americans from subaltern positions. In the early twentieth century, for example, Jack and Jill of America and Colored Women and Colored Girls clubs emerged as an alternative to mainstream social organizations that had been closed off to African Americans, especially African American women and mothers who sought to create a better

[18] *See* Nicolae Gheorghe & Thomas Acton, *Citizens of the World and Nowhere: Minority, Ethnic and Human Rights for Roma*, *in* BETWEEN PAST AND FUTURE: THE ROMA OF CENTRAL AND EASTERN EUROPE 54 (Will Guy ed., 2001).

[19] More specifically, the NAACP led an antilynching crusade that paved the way for Civil Rights, the Southern Christian Leadership Conference (SCLC) organized protests whose backlashes prompted the Civil Rights Act of 1964, and SCLC and the Student Nonviolent Coordinating Committee (SNCC) mobilized voter registration campaigns and protests that led to the Voting Rights Act. The ERRC's relentless litigation in national courts and international human rights courts provided the evidence of systemic discrimination that would draw the EU into infringement proceedings against CSEE states. Both the Decade and the NRIS Framework recognized that Roma rights NGOs had to be equal partners with governmental entities to spur meaningful inclusion.

[20] Despite the passage of civil rights laws and the NRIS Framework, for instance, organizations have sued the U.S. federal government and CSEE states to ensure compliance with the legal advances. *See, e.g.*, Adams v. Richardson, 356 F. Supp. 92 (D.D.C. 1973); *European Court Cases*, EUROPEAN ROMA RIGHTS CTR., http://www.errc.org/what-we-do/strategic-litigation/european-court-cases (last accessed June 20, 2019).

future for their children.[21] Similar organizations for Roma have had to straddle Europe's political and cultural boundaries, so, by comparison, they have served either diffuse interests or discrete local missions.[22] Or they have strived for unity out of utilitarian necessity, despite the thinness of cohesion.[23]

As scholars, we are particularly excited about the shift in knowledge production within Romani studies – a shift in the writings on Roma that is happening with the engagement of Roma themselves, not as subjects but as movers. Universities across CSEE are founding Romani studies programs, and the field is becoming a respected subject of critical inquiry. Some programs focus on linguistics, while others span disciplines and create international networks through institutional partnerships among Romani studies centers.[24] Because of the phenomenon of scholar-activists in the field, where scholars engage in advocacy work and consult on government-funded projects, these programs are becoming a focal point for academia and civil society to connect.[25] They can best be described as academic programs with a civic mission, training future generations of Romani academics while partnering with government, businesses, and civil society groups in the community.[26]

This trend, too, bears striking similarities to another development during and after Civil Rights: the establishment of black studies programs at U.S. universities in the 1960s and 1970s.[27] Black studies responded to student demands for curricula that promoted "positive self-images and racial pride" while engaging directly with African American communities.[28] The balance that such programs straddle – between academic inquiry and community activism – is hard, precarious work.

21 *See About Us*, JACK AND JILL OF AMERICA, INC., https://jackandjillinc.org/about-us/ (last accessed June 20, 2019); *Our History*, NAT'L ASS'N COLORED WOMEN, http://nacwc.org/history (last accessed June 20, 2019).

22 *See, e.g.*, *Joint Position of the Roma Civil Society on the 10th Annual EU Roma Platform Meeting*, 10TH MEETING OF THE EUROPEAN PLATFORM FOR ROMA INCLUSION 2 (2016) (125 NGOs signing onto the joint position); AIDAN MCGARRY, WHO SPEAKS FOR ROMA?: POLITICAL REPRESENTATION OF A TRANSNATIONAL MINORITY COMMUNITY 97 (2010) (counting hundreds of NGOs in Romania alone).

23 *See* Gheorghe & Acton, *supra* note 18.

24 *See, e.g.*, *Romani Linguistics at Manchester*, UNIV. MANCHESTER, https://romani.humanities.manchester.ac.uk/atmanchester/atmanchester.shtml (last accessed June 20, 2019); *Romani Studies*, CHARLES UNIV., https://kses.ff.cuni.cz/en/study/study-programmes/romani-studies-ba/ (last accessed June 20, 2019).

25 In 2017, for instance, CEU established the region's premier Romani studies program that aims simultaneously to prepare Romani students for graduate study, develop an infrastructure for critical research, and mobilize the community. *See About RSP*, CENTRAL EUROPEAN UNIV., https://romanistudies.ceu.edu/welcome-roma-access-programs1 (last accessed June 20, 2019).

26 In short, creating "a holistic approach to Roma community." Sunnie Rucker-Chang, *Challenging Americanism and Europeanism: African-Americans and Roma in the American South and European Union "South,"* 16 J. TRANSATLANTIC STUD. 181, 189 (2018).

27 *See id.*; Karen K. Miller, *Race, Power and the Emergence of Black Studies in Higher Education*, 31 AM. STUD. 83 (1990).

28 Miller, *supra* note 27, at 85, 89.

The Right accuses these programs of doing too much, while the Left accuses them of not doing enough.[29]

Romani studies and black or Afro-American studies programs do not merely connect scholars and activists, they also forge global solidarities. Over the decades, black studies became Africana studies at some schools, reflecting the diasporic presence of African peoples. And despite their relative youth, the new crop of Romani studies scholars and institutions have built global comparisons into their programming. Beyond U.S. civil rights, their conferences have explored connections with Dalit rights, among other things.[30] These explorations are a product of a field that has reflected more critically on its embedded assumptions, exorcising paradigms that have held firm for far too long. However hard xenophobic governments might push back against these nascent programs and Roma rights, the trend of critical, comparative thinking and building global ties is not likely to abate.

29 *Compare, e.g.*, Jonathan Lee, *CEU and NGO Crackdown: A Double Blow for Roma Inclusion in Hungary*, OPEN DEMOCRACY (May 5, 2017), https://www.opendemocracy.net/en/can-europe-make-it/ceu-and-ngo-crackdown-double-blow-for-roma-inclusion-in-hungary/ (Orbán and his Fidesz ruling party threatening to close CEU), *and* González v. Douglas, 269 F. Supp. 3d 948 (D. Ariz. 2017) (state of Arizona enacting a law to prohibit ethnic studies), *with* Ana Ivasiuc, *Introduction: Renewing Research and Romani Activism*, *in* ROMA ACTIVISM: REIMAGINING POWER AND KNOWLEDGE 129 (Sam Beck & Ana Ivasiuc eds., 2018) ("the pursuit of knowledge only for the sake of knowledge seems at best indecent"), *and* Miller, *supra* note 27, at 86 ("Activists labeled [Berkeley's black academics] "cowards, fair-weather opportunists, and middle class bourgeoise [sic] pigs.").

30 *See* Pardeep Singh Attriti, Digital Roma – Is Social Media/Internet a Game Changer for Roma?, Presentation at the 2019 Critical Approaches to Romani Studies Conference (2019) (on file with Central European University).

Select Bibliography

CASES

European Court of Justice

Bickel and Franz, C-274/96, 1998 E.C.R. I-7637.

CHEZ Razpredelenie Bulgaria AD v. Komisia za zashtita ot diskriminatsia, and Anelia Nikolava, and Darzhavna Komisia za energiyno i vodno regulirane, Case C-83/14, 2015 O.J. C 311/8.

Costa v. ENEL, Case 6/64, 1964 E.C.R. 585.

Defrenne v. Société Anonyme Belge de Navigation Aérienne Sabena, Case 43/75, 1976 E.C.R. 455.

Enderby v. Frenchay Health Auth. and Sec'y of State for Health, Case C-127/92, 1993 E.C.R. I-5535.

Internationale Handelsgesellschaft, Case 11/70, 1970 E.C.R. 1125.

Jenkins v. Kingsgate (Clothing Prods.) Ltd., Case 96/80, 1981 E.C.R. 912.

Nold v. Commission, Case 4/73, 1974 E.C.R. 491.

Opinion Pursuant to Article 218(11) TFEU, Case C-2/13, ECLI:EU:C:2014:2454 (2014).

Regina v. Sec'y of State for Emp't, *ex parte* Seymour-Smith and Perez, Case C-167/97, 1999 E.C.R. I-666.

Stauder v. City of Ulm, Case 29/69, 1969 E.C.R. 419.

Van Gend en Loos v. Nederlandse Administratie der Belastingen, Case 26/62, 1963 E.C.R. 1.

Zambrano v. ONEM, Case C-34/09, 2011 E.C.R I-01177.

European Court of Human Rights

D.H. and Others v. Czech Republic, App. No. 57825/00, 47 Eur. H.R. Rep. 59 (2007).

Hoogendijk v. The Netherlands, App. No. 58641/00, Eur. Ct. H.R. (2005).

Horváth and Kiss v. Hungary, App. No. 11146/11, Eur. Ct. H.R. (2013).

Moldovan and Others v. Romania (No. 2), App. No. 41138/98 & 64320/01, Eur. Ct. H.R. (2005).

Oršuš and Others v. Croatia, App. No. 15766/03, 52 Eur. H.R. Rep. 7 (2010).

Sampanis v. Greece, App. No. 32526/05, Eur. Ct. H.R. (2008).

Zarb Adami v. Malta, App. No. 17209/02, 44 Eur. H.R. Rep. 3 (2006).

National Courts

Bulgaria

ERRC v. Bulgarian Ministry of Education and Science (Sofia District Court 2007).

Hungary

Chance for Children Found. v. Town of Hajdúhadház, Legfelsöbb Bíróság, Pvf. IV. 20. 936/2008/4 (Hungarian Supreme Court 2008).

Romania

Stoica v. Romania, No. 42722/02 (Third Section 2008).

United States

Adams v. Richardson, 356 F. Supp. 92 (D.D.C. 1973).
Baker v. Carr, 369 U.S. 186 (1962).
Beer v. U.S., 425 U.S. 130 (1976).
Brown v. Bd. of Educ. of Topeka, 349 U.S. 294 (1955) (*Brown II*).
Brown v. Board of Education of Topeka, 347 U.S. 483 (1954) (*Brown I*).
City of Richmond v. J.A. Croson Co., 488 U.S. 469 (1989).
Civil Rights Cases, 109 U.S. 3 (1883).
Coyle v. Smith, 221 U.S. 559 (1911).
Dredd Scott v. Sandford, 60 U.S. (19 How.) 393 (1857).
Eisenstadt v. Baird, 405 U.S. 438 (1972).
Ex parte McCardle, 74 U.S. (7 Wall.) 506 (1868).
Ex parte Milligan, 71 U.S. (4 Wall.) 2 (1866).
Gideon v. Wainwright, 372 U.S. 335 (1963).
González v. Douglas, 269 F. Supp. 3d 948 (D. Ariz. 2017).
Griggs v. Duke Power Co., 401 U.S. 424 (1971).
Griswold v. Connecticut, 381 U.S. 479 (1965).
Heart of Atlanta Motel Inc. v. United States, 379 U.S. 241 (1964).
Johnson v. De Grandy, 512 U.S. 997 (1994).
Jones v. Alfred H. Mayer Co., 392 U.S. 409 (1968).
Lawrence v. Texas, 539 U.S. 558 (2003).
Loving v. Virginia, 388 U.S. 1 (1967).
McCleskey v. Kemp, 481 U.S. 279 (1987).
McLaurin v. Oklahoma State Regents, 399 U.S. 637 (1950).
Metro Broadcasting, Inc. v. FCC, 497 U.S. 547 (1990).
Milliken v. Bradley, 418 U.S. 717 (1974).
Miranda v. Arizona, 384 U.S. 436 (1966).
Mobile v. Bolden, 446 U.S. 55 (1980).
Obergefell v. Hodges, 135 S. Ct. 2584 (2015).
Parents Involved in Community Schools v. Seattle School District No. 1, 551 U.S. 701 (2007).
Plessy v. Ferguson, 163 U.S. 537 (1896).
Pollard's Lessee v. Hagan, 44 U.S. 212 (1845).
Regents of the Univ. of Cal. v. Bakke, 438 U.S. 265 (1978).
Reynolds v. Sims, 377 U.S. 533 (1964).
Ricci v. DeStefano, 557 U.S. 557 (2009).

Roe v. Wade, 410 U.S. 113 (1973).
Shelby County v. Holder, 570 U.S. 529 (2013).
Shelley v. Kramer, 334 U.S. 1 (1948).
Slaughterhouse Cases, 83 U.S. (16 Wall.) 36 (1873).
Swann v. Charlotte-Mecklenburg Board of Education, 402 U.S. 1 (1971).
Sweatt v. Painter, 399 U.S. 629 (1950).
U. S. v. Carolene Prods. Co., 304 U.S. 144 (1938).
U. S. v. Cruikshank, 92 U.S. 542 (1876).
Washington v. Davis, 426 U.S. 229 (1976).
Wygant v. Jackson Board of Education, 476 U.S. 267 (1986).

SELECTED EUROPEAN UNION MATERIALS

Treaties

Charter of Fundamental Rights of the European Union, 2000 O.J. (C 364) 1.
Arts. 21, 22.
Treaty Establishing the European Community, 2002 O.J. (C 325) 33 [EC].
Arts. 12, 13, 141.
Treaty of Lisbon, 2007 O.J. (C 306) 1.
Part Two ("Non-Discrimination and Citizenship of the Union").
Treaty on European Union, 2008 O.J. (C 115) 13 [TEU] (Lisbon Treaty amendments).
Arts. 2, 5, 6(1).
Treaty on European Union, November 10, 1997 O.J. (C 340) 145 [TEU] (Amsterdam Treaty amendments).
Arts. 6, 7, 49.
Treaty on European Union, July 29, 1992 O.J. (C 191) 1 [TEU] (Maastricht Treaty amendments).
Art. F.
Treaty on the Functioning of the European Community, 2012 O.J. (C 326) 47 [TFEU].
Arts. 2–4, 19–21, 258, 267.

Directives

2000/78, 2000 O.J. (L 303) 16 (EC).
2000/43, 2000 O.J. (L 180) 22 (EC) [Race Equality Directive].
79/7, 1979 O.J. (L 6) 24 (EEC).
76/207, 1976 O.J. (L 39), 40 (EEC).
75/117, 1975 O.J. (L 45), 19 (EEC).

Additional Materials

BARTLETT, WILLIAM ET AL., EUROPEAN PARL., EVALUATION OF THE EU FRAMEWORK FOR NATIONAL ROMA INTEGRATION STRATEGIES (2015).
CHOPIN, ISABELLE ET AL., EUROPEAN COMM'N, ROMA AND THE ENFORCEMENT OF ANTI-DISCRIMINATION LAW (2017).

Council of the European Union, Council Recommendation of 9 December 2013 on Effective Roma Integration Measures in the Member States, 2013 O.J. (C 378) 1.

European Comm'n, 35 Years of Eurobarometer: European Integration as Seen by the Public Opinion in the Member States of the European Union 1973–2008 (2008).

European Comm'n, Answer Given by Ms. Jourová on Behalf of the Commission to the European Parliament, June 19, 2015

European Comm'n, Answer Given by Ms. Jourová on Behalf of the Commission to the European Parliament (Nov. 24, 2016), http://www.europarl.europa.eu/doceo/document/E-8–2016-007070-ASW_EN.pdf.

European Comm'n, Bulgaria: 2005 Comprehensive Monitoring Report (2005).

European Comm'n, A Comparative Analysis of Non-Discrimination Law in Europe (2017).

European Comm'n, *Czech Republic: Accession Partnership*, 98/C 202/02 (1998).

European Comm'n, Croatia 2010 Progress Report (2010).

European Comm'n, *Effective Roma Integration Measures in the Member States*, Communication from the Comm'n to the European Parl., the Council, the European Econ. and Soc. Comm. and the Comm. of the Regions (2016).

European Comm'n, *An EU Framework for National Roma Integration Strategies up to 2020*, COM (2011) 173 final (Apr. 5, 2011).

European Comm'n, *Hungary: Accession Partnership* (1997).

European Comm'n, *Midterm Review of the EU Framework for National Roma Integration Strategies*, Communication from the Comm'n to the European Parl. and the Council (2017).

European Comm'n, *National Roma Integration Strategies: A First Step in the Implementation of the EU Framework*, Communication to the European Parl., the Council, the European Econ. and Soc. Comm. and the Comm. of the Regions (2012).

European Comm'n, Regular Report from the Commission on Bulgaria's Progress Towards Accession (2003).

European Comm'n, Regular Report from the Commission on Czech Republic's Progress Towards Accession (1999).

European Comm'n, Regular Report from the Commission on Slovakia's Progress toward Accession (1998).

European Comm'n, Regular Report from the Commission on Slovakia's Progress toward Accession (1999).

European Comm'n, Regular Report on Slovakia's Progress toward Accession (2000)

European Comm'n, Report on the Implementation of the EU Framework for National Roma Integration Strategies (2014).

European Comm'n, Roma in Europe: Progress Report 2008–2010 (2010).

European Comm'n, Situation of Roma in an Enlarged European Union (2004).

European Comm'n, Special Eurobarometer 393: Discrimination in the EU in 2012 (2012), http://ec.europa.eu/commfrontoffice/publicopinion/archives/ebs/ebs_393_en.pdf.

European Comm'n, Special Eurobarometer 437: Discrimination in the EU in 2015 (2015), https://data.europa.eu/euodp/en/data/dataset/S2077_83_4_437_ENG.

European Comm'n, Special Eurobarometer: Discrimination in the European Union (2006), http://ec.europa.eu/commfrontoffice/publicopinion/archives/ebs/ebs_263_en.pdf.

European Platform for Roma Inclusion, *Joint Position of the Roma Civil Society on the 10th Annual EU Roma Platform Meeting*, 10th Meeting of the European Platform for Roma Inclusion (2016).

European Union Agency for Fundamental Rights, *Introducing FRA: The EU Agency for Fundamental Rights*, European Union Agency for Fundamental Rights (May 2014), https://fra.europa.eu/en/publication/2014/introducing-fra-eu-agency-fundamental-rights.

European Union Agency for Fundamental Rights, The Racial Equality Directive: Application and Challenges (2012).
Farkas, Lilla, European Comm'n, Report on Discrimination of Roma Children in Education (2014).
Presidency Conclusions, Copenhagen European Council (June 21–22, 1993).

COUNCIL OF EUROPE MATERIALS

Eur. Parl. Ass., *Additional Protocol on the Rights of Minorities to the European Convention on Human Rights*, 22d Sess., Doc. No. 6742 (1993).
Framework Convention for the Protection of National Minorities and Explanatory Report (1995).

UNITED STATES MATERIALS

Constitutional Amendments

U.S. Const. amends. IV, XIII–XV.

Acts, Bills, and Statutes

Act of Apr. 20, 1871, ch. 22, 17 Stat. 13 (1871) [also the Enforcement Act of 1871 or Ku Klux Klan Act].
Civil Rights Act of 1866, ch. 31, 14 Stat. 27–30 (1866).
Civil Rights Act of 1875, 18 Stat. 335–337 (1875).
Civil Rights Act of 1964, Pub. L. No. 88-352, 78 Stat. 241 (codified as amended in scattered sections of 42 U.S.C.).
Civil Rights Act of 1968, tit. VIII, 42 U.S.C. §§ 3601–3619 [Fair Housing Act].
First Reconstruction Act, ch. 153, 14 Stat. 428 (1867).
Northwest Ordinance, Act of July 13, 1787, reenacted by Act of Aug. 7, 1789, ch. 8, 1 Stat. 50.
Southern Manifesto, 102 Cong. Rec. 4459–4461 (1956).
Voting Rights Act of 1975, 42 U.S.C. §§ 1973–1973aa-6 (transferred to 52 U.S.C. §§ 10301–10314).

Executive Orders

Exec. Order No. 9981, 13 Fed. Reg. 4313 (July 26, 1948).
Exec. Order. No. 10925, 26 Fed. Reg. 1977 (1961).
Exec. Order No. 11246, 30 Fed. Reg. 12319 (1965).

BOOKS, ARTICLES, AND OTHER PUBLICATIONS

Achim, Viorel, The Roma in Romanian History (Richard Davies trans., 2004) (1998), *originally published as* Ţiganii în istoria Românieri.
Ackerman, Bruce, 2 We the People: Transformations (1998).

Acton, Thomas & Ilona Klímová, *The International Romani Union: An East European Answer to West European Questions?*, *in* BETWEEN PAST AND FUTURE: THE ROMA OF CENTRAL AND EASTERN EUROPE 157 (Will Guy ed., 2001).

Ahmed, Tawhida, *The Treaty of Lisbon and Beyond: The Evolution of EU Minority Protection?*, 38 EUR. L. REV. 30 (2013).

Albert, Gwendolyn, *Education Policies in the Czech Republic*, *in* TEN YEARS AFTER: A HISTORY OF ROMA SCHOOL DESEGREGATION IN CENTRAL AND EASTERN EUROPE 179 (Iulius Rostas ed., 2012).

ALI, FATIMA, EUROPEAN OTHERS: QUEERING ETHNICITY IN POST-NATIONAL EUROPE (2011).

AMAR, AKHIL REED, THE BILL OF RIGHTS: CREATION AND RECONSTRUCTION (1998).

Amar, Akhil Reed, *The Case of the Missing Amendments*: R.A.V. v. City of St. Paul, 106 HARV. L. REV. 124 (1992).

AMNESTY INT'L, CZECH REPUBLIC'S DISCRIMINATORY TREATMENT OF ROMA BREACHES EU RACE DIRECTIVE (2013).

AMNESTY INT'L, END INJUSTICE: ELEMENTARY SCHOOLS STILL FAIL ROMANI CHILDREN IN THE CZECH REPUBLIC (2010).

AMNESTY INT'L, *EU Action Against Czech Republic for Discrimination in Schools Is a Victory for Rights, Justice, and Roma* (Sept. 25, 2014), https://www.amnesty.org/en/latest/news/2014/09/eu-action-against-czech-republic-discrimination-schools-victory-rights-justice-and-roma/ [https://perma.cc/26Z7-8P5P].

AMNESTY INT'L, *"We Ask for Justice": Europe's Failure to Protect Roma from Racist Violence*, AMNESTY INT'L (Apr. 8, 2014), https://www.amnesty.org/en/documents/eur01/007/2014/en.

AMNESTY INT'L & EUROPEAN ROMA RIGHTS CENTRE, A LESSON IN DISCRIMINATION: SEGREGATION OF ROMANI CHILDREN IN PRIMARY EDUCATION IN SLOVAKIA (2017).

ANDERSEN, STINE, THE ENFORCEMENT OF EU LAW: THE ROLE OF THE EUROPEAN COMMISSION (2012).

ANDERSON, BENEDICT, IMAGINED COMMUNITIES: REFLECTIONS ON THE ORIGIN AND SPREAD OF NATIONALISM (1983).

ANDERSON, CAROL, WHITE RAGE: THE UNSPOKEN TRUTH OF OUR RACIAL DIVIDE (2016).

Anderson, Karen S., *Massive Resistance, Violence, and Southern Social Relations: The Little Rock, Arkansas, School Segregation Crisis, 1954–1960*, *in* MASSIVE RESISTANCE: SOUTHERN OPPRESSION TO THE SECOND RECONSTRUCTION 203 (Clive Webb ed., 2005).

Andreev, Alexander, *Right-Wing Populist Appointed Integration Minister in Bulgaria*, DEUTSCHE WELLE (June 1, 2017), http://www.dw.com/en/right-wing-populist-appointed-integration-minister-in-bulgaria/a–39086764.

Ansley, Frances L., *Stirring the Ashes: Race, Class and the Future of Civil Rights Scholarship*, 74 CORNELL L. REV. 993 (1989).

ANTHIAS, FLOYA & NIRA YUVAL-DAVIS, RACIALIZED BOUNDARIES: RACE, NATION, GENDER, COLOUR, AND CLASS AND THE ANTI-RACIST STRUGGLE (2005).

APPADURAI, ARJUN, FEAR OF SMALL NUMBERS (2006).

Attriti, Pardeep Singh, Digital Roma – Is Social Media/Internet a Game Changer for Roma?, Presentation at the 2019 Critical Approaches to Romani Studies Conference (2019) (on file with Central European University).

Backer, Larry Catá, *The Extra-National State: American Confederate Federalism and the European Union*, 7 COLUM. J. EUR. L. 173 (2001).

Bagenstos, Samuel R., *The Structural Turn and the Limits of Antidiscrimination Law*, 94 CALIF. L. REV. 1 (2006).

BAKER, CATHERINE, RACE IN THE YUGOSLAV REGION (2018).

BAKER, CATHERINE, THE YUGOSLAV WARS OF THE 1990S (2015).

BAKHTIN, MIKHAIL, PROBLEMS OF DOSTOEVSKY'S POETICS (Caryl Emerson trans., Wayne C. Booth ed., 1984).

Balibar, Etienne, *Racism and Nationalism, in* RACE, NATION, CLASS: AMBIGUOUS IDENTITIES 37 (Etienne Balibar & Immanuel Wallerstein eds., 1991).

Balkin, Jack M. & Reva B. Siegel, *Fiss's Way: The Scholarship of Owen Fiss*, 58 U. MIAMI L. REV. 9 (2003).

BANCROFT, ANGUS, ROMA AND GYPSY-TRAVELLERS IN EUROPE: MODERNITY, RACE, SPACE AND EXCLUSION (2005).

BAPTIST, EDWARD E., THE HALF HAS NEVER BEEN TOLD: SLAVERY AND THE MAKING OF AMERICAN CAPITALISM (2012).

BARANY, ZOLTAN, THE EAST EUROPEAN GYPSIES: REGIME CHANGE, MARGINALITY, AND ETHNOPOLITICS (2002).

Barany, Zoltan, *Ethnic Mobilization and the State: The Roma in Eastern Europe*, 21 ETHNIC & RACIAL STUD. 308 (1998).

Bârsan, Ileana, *Mentalities and Historical (Re) Presentation in* Aferim! *by Radu Jude*, 1 CINEMATOGRAPHIC ART & DOCUMENTATION 5 (2016).

Bársony, János, *20th Century Roma History and the Pharrajimos, in* PHARRAIJMOS: THE FATE OF THE ROMA DURING THE HOLOCAUST 23 (János Bársony & Ágnes Daróczi eds., 2008).

Barten, Ulrike, *Minority Rights in the European Union after Lisbon*, 33 NORDIC J. HUM. RTS. 1 (2011).

BARTHES, ROLAND, MYTHOLOGIES (1975).

Batur, Pina, *Just a Link in the Chain: Global Racism and the Concept of "Blackness" in Russia, in* RACIAL AND ETHNIC ECONOMIC INEQUALITY: AN INTERNATIONAL PERSPECTIVE 5 (Samuel L Myers, Jr. & Bruce P. Corrie eds., 2006).

Bausch, Katherine, *Superflies into Superkillers: Black Masculinity in Film from Blaxploitation to New Black Realism*, 46 J. POPULAR CULTURE 257 (2013).

BECKER, GARY S., THE ECONOMICS OF DISCRIMINATION (2d ed. 1971).

Beckert, Sven & Seth Rockman, *Introduction, in* SLAVERY'S CAPITALISM: A NEW HISTORY OF AMERICAN ECONOMIC DEVELOPMENT 1 (Sven Beckert & Seth Rockman, eds., 2016).

Beggs, Gordon J., *Novel Expert Evidence in Federal Civil Rights Litigation*, 45 AM. U. L. REV. 1 (1995).

Bell, Derrick, Brown v. Board of Education *and the Interest-Convergence Dilemma*, 93 HARV. L. REV. 518 (1980).

BELL, DERRICK, SILENT COVENANTS: *BROWN V. BOARD OF EDUCATION* AND THE UNFULFILLED HOPES FOR RACIAL REFORM (2004).

BENEDICT, MICHAEL LES, A COMPROMISE OF PRINCIPLE: CONGRESSIONAL REPUBLICANS AND RECONSTRUCTION, 1863–1869 (1974).

Benedict, Michael Les, *Moments of Change: Transformations in American Constitutionalism*, 108 YALE L.J. 2011 (1999).

Benedict, Michael Les, *The Rout of Radicalism: Republicans and the Elections of 1867*, 18 CIV. WAR HIST. 334 (1972).

Bhabha, Jacqueline, *Realizing Roma Rights: An Introduction, in* REALIZING ROMA RIGHTS 1 (Jacqueline Bhabha et al. eds., 2017).

Biber, Eric, *The Price of Admission: Causes, Effects, and Patterns of Conditions Imposed on States Entering the Union*, 46 AM. J. LEGAL HIST. 119 (2004).

Bifelsky, Dan, *Walls, Real and Imagined, Surround Roma*, N.Y. TIMES, Apr. 2, 2010.

Bignami, Francesca, *Creating European Rights: National Values and Supranational Interests*, 11 COLUM. J. EUR. L. 241 (2005).

BILLIG, MICHAEL, BANAL NATIONALISM (1995).

Bjelić, Dušan I., *Introduction: Blowing Up the "Bridge," in* BALKAN AS METAPHOR 1 (Dušan I. Bjelić, I. & Savić Obrad eds., 2005).

BLACKMON, DOUGLAS A., SLAVERY BY ANOTHER NAME: THE RE-ENSLAVEMENT OF BLACK AMERICANS FROM THE CIVIL WAR TO WORLD WAR II (1992).

Bogdan, Maria et al., *Introducing the New Journal Critical Romani Studies*, 1 CRITICAL ROMANI STUD. 2 (2018).

BOGLE, DONALD, TOMS, COONS, MULATTOES, MAMMIES, AND BUCKS: AN INTERPRETIVE HISTORY OF BLACKS IN AMERICAN FILMS (5th ed. 2016).

Bori, Erzsebet, *Vazonciganyok* [Screen Gypsies], 10 FILMVILAG 53 (1998).

BORSTELMANN, THOMAS, THE COLD WAR AND THE COLOR LINE: AMERICAN RACE RELATIONS IN THE GLOBAL ARENA (2001).

Börzel, Tanja A. & Thomas Risse, *Who Is Afraid of a European Federation? How to Constitutionalise a Multi-Level Governance System, in* WHAT KIND OF CONSTITUTION FOR WHAT KIND OF POLITY? RESPONSES TO JOSCHKA FISCHER 45 (Christian Joerges et al. eds., 2000).

BOTTICI, CHIARA & BENOIT CHALLAND, IMAGINING EUROPE: MYTH, MEMORY, AND IDENTITY (2013).

Bourdieu, Pierre & Loïc Wacquant, *On the Cunning of Imperialist Reason*, 16 THEORY CULTURE & SOC'Y 41 (1999).

Boyd, Thomas M. & Stephen J. Markman, *The 1982 Amendments to the Voting Rights Act*, 40 WASH. & LEE L. REV. 1347 (1983).

Bradley, Curtis A., *Foreign Affairs and Domestic Reform*, 87 VA. L. REV. 1475 (2001).

Bratić, Ljubomir, *Romske organizacije i aktivisti sa područja bivše Jugoslavije*, Interview with Romani Activist from Vienna, MIGRAZINE (2012) [https://perma.cc/P7GF-FRF6].

Bridgewater, Pamela D., *Reproductive Freedom as Civil Freedom: The Thirteenth Amendment's Role in the Struggle for Reproductive Rights*, 3 J. GENDER RACE & JUST. 401 (2000).

Bringa, Tone R., *Nationality Categories, National Identification and Identity Formation in "Multinational" Bosnia*, 11 ANTHROPOLOGY E. EUR. REV. 80 (1993).

BROWN-NAGIN, TOMIKO, COURAGE TO DISSENT: ATLANTA AND THE LONG HISTORY OF THE CIVIL RIGHTS MOVEMENT (2011).

Brown-Nagin, Tomiko, *The Impact of Lawyer-Client Disengagement on the NAACP's Campaign to Implement* Brown v. Board of Education *in Atlanta, in* FROM THE GRASSROOTS TO THE SUPREME COURT: *BROWN V. BOARD OF EDUCATION* AND AMERICAN DEMOCRACY 227 (Peter F. Lau ed., 2004).

Búrca, Gráinne de, *Beyond the Charter: How Enlargement Has Enlarged the Human Rights Policy of the European Union*, 27 FORDHAM INT'L L.J. 679 (2004).

Búrca, Gráinne de, *EU Race Discrimination Law: A Hybrid Model?, in* LAW AND NEW GOVERNANCE IN THE EU AND THE US 97 (Gráinne de Búrca & Joanne Scott eds., 2006).

Búrca, Gráinne de, *"New Modes of Governance" and the Protection of Human Rights, in* MONITORING FUNDAMENTAL RIGHTS IN THE EU: THE CONTRIBUTION OF THE FUNDAMENTAL RIGHTS AGENCY 25 (Philip Alston & Olivier De Schutter eds., 2005).

Búrca, Gráinne de, *The Trajectories of European and American Antidiscrimination Law*, 60 AM. J. COMP. L. 1 (2012).

Búrca, Gráinne de & Joanne Scott, *Introduction: New Governance, Law and Constitutionalism, in* LAW AND NEW GOVERNANCE IN THE EU AND THE US 1 (Gráinne de Búrca & Joanne Scott eds., 2006).

Bulgarian Helsinki Committee, *Bulgarian Deputy PM Guilty of Anti-Roma Hate Speech*, LIBERTIES (Oct. 30, 2017), https://www.liberties.eu/en/news/valeri-simeonov-case-hate-speech/13328.

Bulgarian Nationalists Stage Anti-Roma Rally, AL JAZEERA (Oct. 1, 2011), https://www.aljazeera.com/news/europe/2011/10/2011101173254692117.html [https://perma.cc/2A4L-Z2QX].

Carbado, Devon et al., *After Inclusion*, 4 ANN. REV. L. & SOC. SCI. 83 (2008).

CARRERA, SERGIO & ANAÏS FAURE ATGER, CENTRE FOR EUROPEAN POLICY STUD., L'AFFAIRE DES ROMS: A CHALLENGE TO THE EU'S AREA OF FREEDOM, SECURITY AND JUSTICE (2010).

Carter, William M., Jr., *Race, Rights, and the Thirteenth Amendment: Defining the Badges and Incidents of Slavery*, 40 U.C. DAVIS L. REV. 1311 (2007).

Carter, William M., Jr., *A Thirteenth Amendment Framework for Combating Racial Profiling*, 39 HARV. C.R.-C.L. L. REV. 17 (2004).

Cass, Deborah, *The Word That Saves Maastricht? The Principle of Subsidiarity and the Division of Powers Within the European Community*, 29 COMMON MKT. L. REV. 1107 (1992).

Celik, Faika, Approaching Gypsies (Roma) in Early Modern Ottoman Balkans: Challenges and Prospects, Presentation at the Critical Approaches to Romani Studies Conference, May 25–26, 2017, Central European University, Budapest (unpublished manuscript) (on file with authors).

CENTER FOR REPRODUCTIVE RIGHTS, BODY AND SOUL: FORCED STERILIZATION AND OTHER ASSAULTS ON ROMA REPRODUCTIVE FREEDOM (2003).

Central European University, *Inside the Struggle: The U.S. Civil Rights Movement & the European Roma Rights Crisis* (2015), https://www.ceu.edu/event/2015–12-07/inside-struggle-us-civil-rights-movement-european-Roma-rights-crisis [https://perma.cc/3Z84-3YLE].

Chang, Felix B., *Roma Integration "All the Way Down": Lessons from Federalism and Civil Rights*, 1 CRITICAL ROMANI STUD. 62 (2018).

Charles, Guy-Uriel E. & Luis Fuentes-Rohwer, *Race, Federalism, and Voting Rights*, 2015 U. CHI. L.F. 113.

Chereseva, Maria, *Clashes at Anti-Roma Rally in Radnevo, Bulgaria*, BALKANINSIGHT (May 5, 2016), https://balkaninsight.com/2016/05/05/ethnic-tensions-provoke-violent-clashes-in-bulgarian-town-radnevo-05–05-2016/ [https://perma.cc/X8LQ-FX3E].

CHERNOW, RON, GRANT (2017).

Chin, Gabriel J., *Volume Introduction, in* AFFIRMATIVE ACTION AND THE CONSTITUTION: VOLUME 3, JUDICIAL REACTION TO AFFIRMATIVE ACTION, 1989–1997 1 (Gabriel J. Chin ed., 1998).

Choper, Jesse & John Yoo, *Wartime Process: A Dialogue on Congressional Power to Remove Issues from the Federal Courts*, 95 CALIF. L. REV. 1243 (2007).

Coates, Ta-Nehisi, *The Case for Reparations*, ATLANTIC, June 2014.

COENDERS, MARCEL ET AL., MAJORITIES' ATTITUDES TOWARDS MINORITIES IN WESTERN AND EASTERN EUROPEAN SOCIETIES: RESULTS FROM THE EUROPEAN SOCIAL SURVEY 2002–2003 (Report for the European Monitoring Centre on Racism and Xenophobia no. 4, 2005), https://fra.europa.eu/sites/default/files/fra_uploads/151-Report-4.pdf.

COENDERS, MARCEL ET AL., MAJORITY POPULATIONS' ATTITUDES TOWARDS MIGRANTS AND MINORITIES (Report for the European Monitoring Centre on Racism and Xenophobia Ref. no. 2003/04/01, 2001), https://fra.europa.eu/sites/default/files/fra_uploads/148-Report-1.pdf.

Colker, Ruth, *Anti-Subordination Above All: Sex, Race, and Equal Protection*, 61 N.Y. U. L. REV. 1003 (1986).

Collins, Patricia Hill, *The Tie That Binds: Race, Gender and US Violence*, 21 ETHNIC & RACIAL STUD. 917 (2010).

Common Mkt. Law Review Editorial Bd., *Fundamental Rights and EU Membership: Do as I Say, Not as I Do!*, 499 COMMON MKT. L. REV. 481 (2012).

Cooper, Belinda, *"We Have No Martin Luther King": Eastern Europe's Roma Minority*, 20 WORLD POL'Y J. 69 (2001/2002).

Čorná, Tina, *Marián Labuda a Bolek Polívka – Umelci Rómskej Voľnosti*, SME (Jan. 18, 2007), https://www.sme.sk/c/3099890/marian-labuda-a-bolek-polivka-umelci-romskej-volnosti.html.

Costache, Ioanida, *Reclaiming Romani-ness: Identity Politics, Universality and Otherness or, Towards a (New) Romani Subjectivity*, 1 Critical Romani Stud. 30 (2018).

Craig, Paul & Gráinne de Búrca, EU Law: Text, Cases, and Materials (5th ed. 2011).

Crenshaw, Kimberlé Williams, *Race, Reform, and Retrenchment: Transformation and Legitimation in Antidiscrimination Law*, 101 Harv. L. Rev. 1331 (1988).

Croon-Gestefeld, Johanna, *Reverse* Solange: *Union Citizenship as a Detour on the Route to European Rights Protection Against National Infringements*, *in* EU Citizenship and Federalism: The Role of Rights 665 (Dimitry Kochenov ed., 2017).

Crowe, David M., A History of the Gypsies of Eastern Europe and Russia (1996).

Cunningham, David, Klansville, U.S.A.: The Rise and Fall of the Civil Rights-Era Ku Klux Klan (2012).

Curtis, Michael Kent, No State Shall Abridge: The Fourteenth Amendment and the Bill of Rights (1986).

Daróczi, Ágnes & János Bársony, *Preface to the English Edition*, *in* Pharrajimos: The Fate of the Roma During the Holocaust ix (János Bársony & Ágnes Daróczi eds., 2008).

de Witte, Bruno, *Politics Versus Law in the EU's Approach to Ethnic Minorities*, *in* Europe Unbound: Enlarging and Reshaping the Boundaries of the European Union 137 (Jan Zielonka ed., 2002).

DecadeWatch, Roma Activists Assess the Progress of the Decade of Roma Inclusion (2007).

DecadeWatch, Romania Report: Mid Term Evaluation of the Decade of Roma Inclusion (Iulian Stoian & David Mark eds., 2010).

Defeis, Elizabeth F., *Human Rights, The European Union, and the Treaty Route: From Maastricht to Lisbon*, 35 Fordham Int'l L. J. 1207 (2012).

Delanty, Gerard, Inventing Europe (1995).

Delcourt, Christine, *The* Acquis Communautaire: *Has the Concept Had Its Day?*, 38 Common Mkt. L. Rev. 329 (2001).

Derrida, Jacques, Of Hospitality (2000).

Derrida, Jacques, The Other Heading: Reflections on Today's Europe (1992).

DeSantis, Vincent P., *Rutherford B. Hayes and the Removal of the Troops and the End of Reconstruction*, *in* Region, Race, and Reconstruction: Essays in Honor of C. Vann Woodward 417 (J. Morgan Kousser & James M. McPherson eds., 1982).

Dickens, Dienne, *Bulgaria: Anti-Roma Protests Continue After Alleged Romani Attacks on Teenagers*, Romea (July 4, 2017), http://www.romea.cz/en/features-and-commentary/reportage/bulgaria-anti-roma-protests-continue-after-alleged-romani-attacks-on-teenagers [https://perma.cc/5SDJ-R48E].

Dixon, Rosalind, *Toward a Realistic Comparative Constitutional Studies?*, 64 Am. J. Comp. L. 193 (2016).

Dobreva, Nikolina, *Constructing the "Celluloid Gypsy": Tony Gatlif and Emir Kusturica's "Gypsy Films" in the Context of New Europe*, 17 Romani Stud. 141 (2007).

Douglas-Scott, Sionaidh, *A Tale of Two Courts: Luxembourg, Strasbourg and the Growing European Union Human Rights* Acquis, 43 Common Mkt. L. Rev. 629 (2006).

Driver, Justin, *Rethinking the Interest-Convergence Thesis*, 105 Nw. U. L. Rev. 149 (2011).

Driver, Justin, *Supremacies and the Southern Manifesto*, 92 Tex. L. Rev. 1053 (2014).

Du Bois, W.E. Burghardt, The Souls of Black Folk: Essays and Sketches (A.C. McClurg & Co. 8th ed. 1909).

Dudziak, Mary L., Cold War Civil Rights (2000).

Dudziak, Mary L., *Desegregation as a Cold War Imperative*, 41 STAN. L. REV. 61 (1988).

EGERTON, DOUGLAS R., THE WARS OF RECONSTRUCTION: THE BRIEF, VIOLENT HISTORY OF AMERICA'S MOST PROGRESSIVE ERA (2014).

EL-TAYEB, FATIMA, EUROPEAN OTHERS: QUEERING ETHNICITY IN POSTNATIONAL EUROPE (2011).

Engstrom, Richard L. et al., *Louisiana, in* QUIET REVOLUTION IN THE SOUTH: THE IMPACT OF THE VOTING RIGHTS ACT, 1965–1990, 103 (Chandler Davidson & Bernard Grofman eds., 1994).

EQUAL JUSTICE INITIATIVE, LYNCHING IN AMERICA: CONFRONTING THE LEGACY OF RACIAL TERROR (3d ed. 2017).

European Roma Rights Centre, *Attacks Against Roma in Bulgaria: September 2011–July 2012*, EUROPEAN ROMA RIGHTS CTR. (July 31, 2012), http://www.errc.org/uploads/upload_en/file/attacks-list-in-bulgaria.pdf.

European Roma Rights Centre, *British Officials Continue Policy of Stopping Roma at Czech Airport; Czech Roma and ERRC Sue U.K. Government* (Nov. 7, 2001), http://www.errc.org/article/british-officials-continue-policy-of-stopping-roma-at-czech-airport%3B-czech-roma-and-errc-sue-uk-government/1289 [https://perma.cc/YHL2-3UUM].

European Roma Rights Centre, *Commission Probe Must Spell the End of Romani Segregation in Hungarian Schools*, EUROPEAN ROMA RIGHTS CTR. (May 26, 2016), http://www.errc.org/article/eu-commission-probe-must-spell-the-end-of-romani-segregation-in-hungarian-schools/4485 [https://perma.cc/N66H-5MBZ].

EUROPEAN ROMA RIGHTS CENTRE, STRATEGIC LITIGATION OF RACE DISCRIMINATION IN EUROPE: FROM PRINCIPLES TO PRACTICE (2004).

Fabbrini, Federico, *The Principle of Subsidiarity, in* OXFORD PRINCIPLES OF EUROPEAN UNION LAW, vol. 1, 221 (Robert Schütze & Takis Tridimas eds., 2018).

Farkas, Lilla, *The Scene After Battle: What Is the Victory in* D.H. *Worth and Where to Go from Here?*, 1 ROMA RTS. J. 51 (2008).

Fernández, Santiago Delgado et al., *Portugal and Spain in the Process of European Integration, in* IBERIAN ELITES AND THE EU: PERCEPTIONS TOWARDS THE EUROPEAN INTEGRATION PROCESS IN POLITICAL AND SOCIOECONOMIC ELITES IN PORTUGAL AND SPAIN 38 (Miguel Jerez-Mir et al. eds., 2015).

Fiss, Owen M., *Groups and the Equal Protection Clause*, 5 PHIL. & PUB. AFF. 107 (1976).

FONER, ERIC, RECONSTRUCTION: AMERICA'S UNFINISHED REVOLUTION, 1863–1877 (1988).

FONER, ERIC, THE SECOND FOUNDING: HOW THE CIVIL WAR AND RECONSTRUCTION REMADE THE CONSTITUTION (2019).

Foner, Eric, *The Strange Career of the Reconstruction Amendments*, 108 YALE L.J. 2003 (1999).

FONSECA, ISABEL, BURY ME STANDING (1995).

FOUCCAULT, MICHELE, DISCIPLINE AND PUNISH (2012).

FRANCIS, MEGAN MING, CIVIL RIGHTS AND THE MAKING OF THE MODERN AMERICAN STATE (2014).

François-Xavier Bagnoud Center for Health and Human Rights et al., *Accelerating Patterns of Anti-Roma Violence in Hungary* (Feb. 2014), https://cdn2.sph.harvard.edu/wp-content/uploads/sites/114/2017/12/FXB-Hungary-Report_Released-February-3–2014.pdf.

FRANKENBERG, ERICA, UCLA CIVIL RIGHTS PROJECT, HARMING OUR COMMON FUTURE: AMERICA'S SEGREGATED SCHOOLS 65 YEARS AFTER *BROWN* (2019).

FRASER, ANGUS, THE GYPSIES (1992).

FREDRICKSON, GEORGE M., WHITE SUPREMACY: A COMPARATIVE STUDY IN AMERICAN AND SOUTH AFRICAN HISTORY (1981).

Friedman, Eben, *Education in Member State Submissions Under the EU Framework for National Roma Integration Strategies* (ECMI Working Paper No. 73, 2013).

Garland, David, *Penal Excess and Surplus Meaning: Public Torture Lynchings in Twentieth-Century America*, 39 Law & Soc'y Rev. 793 (2005).
Gates, Henry Louis, Jr., Stony the Road: Reconstruction, White Supremacy, and the Rise of Jim Crow (2019).
Geddes, Andrew & Virginie Guiraudon, *Britain, France, and EU Anti-Discrimination Policy: The Emergence of an EU Policy Paradigm*, 27 W. Eur. Pol. 334 (2004).
Gerken, Heather K., *Foreword: Federalism All the Way Down*, 124 Harv. L. Rev. 4 (2009).
Gerken, Heather K., A *New Progressive Federalism*, Democracy J., No. 24, Spring 2012, at 37.
Gheorghe, Nicolae, *Origins of Roma Slavery in the Romanian Principalities*, 7 Roma 12 (1983).
Gheorghe, Nicolae, *The Social Construction of Romani Identity*, *in* Gypsy Politics and Traveller Identity 153 (Thomas Acton ed., 1997).
Gheorghe, Nicolae & Thomas Acton, *Citizens of the World and Nowhere: Minority, Ethnic and Human Rights for Roma*, *in* Between Past and Future: The Roma of Central and Eastern Europe 54 (Will Guy ed., 2001).
Gheorghe, Nicolae & Andrzej Mirga, *The Roma in the Twenty-First Century: A Policy Paper* (Project on Ethnic Relations Policy Paper, 1997), http://www.per-usa.org/1997–2007/21st_c.htm [https://perma.cc/8GP9-5Y85].
Ghodsee, Kristen, *Left Wing, Right Wing, Everything: Xenophobia, Neo-totalitarianism and Populist Politics in Bulgaria*, 55 Probs. Post-Communism 26 (2008).
Gillette, William, Retreat from Reconstruction: 1869–1879 (1979).
Gilroy, Paul, Postcolonial Melancholia (2005).
Gilroy, Paul, There Ain't No Black in the Union Jack (1987).
Ginio, Eyal, *Neither Muslims nor Zimmis: The Gypsies (Roma) in the Ottoman State*, 14 Romani Stud. 117 (2004).
Goff, Samuel, *Chain Reaction: Meet the First Romanian Director to Tackle Roma Slavery Onscreen*, Calvert J. (Dec. 7, 2015), https://www.calvertjournal.com/articles/show/5109/chain-reaction-romanian-director-radu-jude-aferim-roma-slavery.
Goldfield, David R., Black, White, and Southern: Race Relations and Southern Culture 1940 to the Present (1990).
Goldston, James A., *Roma Rights, Roma Wrongs*, Foreign Aff., Mar./Apr. 2002.
Goldston, James A., *The Unfulfilled Promise of Educational Opportunity in the United States and Europe: From* Brown v. Board *to* D.H. *and Beyond*, *in* Realizing Roma Rights 163 (Jacqueline Bhabha et al. eds., 2017).
Goodwin, Morag & Roosmarijn Buijs, *Making Good European Citizens of the Roma: A Closer Look at the EU Framework for National Roma Integration Strategies*, 14 German L.J. 2041 (2013).
Gragl, Paul, The Accession of the European Union to the European Convention on Human Rights (2013).
Greenberg, Jack, *Report on Roma Education Today: From Slavery to Segregation and Beyond*, 110 Colum. L. Rev. 919 (2010).
Grellmann, Heinrich Mortiz Gottlieb, *Die Zigeuner. Ein Historischer Versuch über die Lebensart und Verfaßung* (1783) (English ed., 1807).
Guerrero, Ed, Framing Blackness: The African-American Image in Film (1993).
Guy, Will, *Anti-Roma Violence, Hate Speech, and Discrimination in the New Europe: Czech Republic, Slovakia, and Hungary*, *in* Realizing Roma Rights 145 (Jacqueline Bhabha et al. eds., 2017).
Gynther, Päivi, Beyond Systemic Discrimination: Educational Rights, Skills Acquisition and the Case of Roma (2007).
Gypsy Politics and Traveller Identity (Thomas Acton ed., 1997).

Habermas, Jürgen, *Why Europe Needs a Constitution*, NEW LEFT REV. (2001), https://newleftreview.org/issues/II11/articles/jurgen-habermas-why-europe-needs-a-constitution.

Habermas, Jürgen & Jacques Derrida, *February 15, or What Binds Europeans Together: A Plea for a Common Foreign Policy, Beginning in the Core of Europe*, 10 CONSTELLATIONS 291 (2006).

Halberstam, Daniel, *The Bride of Messina: Constitutionalism and Democracy in Europe*, 30 EUR. L. REV. 775 (2005).

Halberstam, Daniel, *"It's the Autonomy, Stupid!" A Modest Defense of* Opinion 2/13 *on EU Accession to the ECHR, and the Way Forward*, 16 GERMAN L.J. 105 (2015).

Hall, Jackquelyn Dowd, *The Long Civil Rights Movement and the Political Uses of the Past*, 91 J. AM. HIST. 1233 (2005).

Hall, Kermit L., *Political Power and Constitutional Legitimacy: The South Carolina Ku Klux Klan Trials, 1871–1872*, 33 EMORY L.J. 921 (1984).

Hall, Stuart, *Encoding/Decoding*, *in* MEDIA AND CULTURAL STUDIES: KEY WORKS 163 (Meenakshi Gigi Durham & Douglas M. Kellener eds., 2006) (1980).

HALL, STUART, REPRESENTATION: CULTURAL REPRESENTATIONS AND SIGNIFYING PRACTICE (1997).

HALL, STUART, *The Whites of Their Eyes: Racist Ideologies and the Media*, *in* GENDER, RACE AND CLASS IN MEDIA: A TEXT-READER 89 (Gail Dines & Jean M. Humez eds., 2d ed. 2003).

HALPERN, STEPHEN C., ON THE LIMITS OF THE LAW: THE IRONIC LEGACY OF TITLE VI OF THE 1964 CIVIL RIGHTS ACT (1995).

HANCOCK, IAN, DANGER! EDUCATED GYPSY: SELECTED ESSAYS (Dileep Karanth ed., 2010).

Hancock, Ian, *Beyond Poverty, Beyond Europe*, 2 SAIS REV. 181 (2005).

HANCOCK, IAN, THE PARIAH SYNDROME: AN ACCOUNT OF GYPSY SLAVERY AND PERSECUTION (1987).

HANCOCK, IAN, WE ARE THE ROMANI PEOPLE (2002).

Harris, Cheryl I., *Whiteness as Property*, 106 HARV. L. REV. 1709 (1993).

Harrison, John, *The Lawfulness of the Reconstruction Amendments*, 68 U. CHI. L. REV. 375 (2001).

Havel, Václav, *The Future of Central Europe*, Speech to the Polish Sejm and Senate (Jan. 21, 1990), https://www.nybooks.com/articles/1990/03/29/the-future-of-central-europe/.

Hegreness, Matthew J., *An Organic Theory of the Fourteenth Amendment: The Northwest Ordinance as the Source of Rights, Privileges, and Immunities*, 120 YALE L.J. 1820 (2011).

HERMANIN, COSTANZA & EEFJE DE KROON, OPEN SOC'Y FOUNDS., THE RACE EQUALITY DIRECTIVE: A SHADOW REPORT (2013).

HIRSCHL, RAN, COMPARATIVE MATTERS: THE RENAISSANCE OF COMPARATIVE CONSTITUTIONAL LAW (2014).

HOBBS, ALLYSON, A CHOSEN EXILE: A HISTORY OF RACIAL PASSING IN AMERICAN LIFE (2014).

Hodge, Bob, *Social Semiotics*, *in* THE ROUTLEDGE COMPANION TO POPULAR CULTURE 36 (Toby Miller ed., 2016).

Horváth, Kata, *"Passing": Rebeka and the Gay Pride: On the Discursive Boundaries and Possibilities of Skin Colour*, *in* MULTI-DISCIPLINARY APPROACHES TO ROMANY STUDIES 123 (Michael Stewart & Márton Rövid eds., 2010).

Hughes, James & Gwendolyn Sasse, *Monitoring the Monitors: EU Enlargement Conditionality and Minority Protection in the CEECs*, 4 J. ON ETHNOPOL. & MINORITY ISSUES IN EUR. 1 (2003).

HUNTINGTON, SAMUEL P., THE THIRD WAVE: DEMOCRATIZATION IN THE LATE TWENTIETH CENTURY (1993).

IFILL, GWEN, THE BREAKTHROUGH: POLITICS AND RACE IN THE AGE OF OBAMA (2009).

IGNATIEFF, MICHAEL, THE WARRIOR'S HONOR: ETHNIC WAR AND THE MODERN CONSCIENCE (1998).

IGNATIEV, NOEL, HOW THE IRISH BECAME WHITE (1995).

Imre, Anikó, *Screen Gypsies*, 44 FRAMEWORK: J. CINEMA & MEDIA 15 (2003).

Imre, Anikó, *Whiteness in Post-Socialist Eastern Europe: The time of the Gypsies, the End of Race*, *in* POSTCOLONIAL WHITENESS: A CRITICAL READER ON RACE AND EMPIRE 79 (Alfred J. Lopez ed., 2005).

Inter-Parliamentary Union, *Bulgaria: Narodno sabranie (National Assembly)*, http://archive.ipu.org/parline/reports/2045_E.htm [https://perma.cc/SE3D-HAAJ].

INTERRIGHTS, NON-DISCRIMINATION IN INTERNATIONAL LAW: A HANDBOOK FOR PRACTITIONERS (2005).

IOANID, RADU, THE HOLOCAUST IN ROMANIA: THE DESTRUCTION OF JEWS AND GYPSIES UNDER THE ANTONESCU REGIME, 1940–1944 (2000).

IORDANOVA, DINA, CINEMA OF FLAMES: BALKAN FILM, CULTURE AND THE MEDIA (2001).

Iordanova, Dina, *Mimicry and Plagiarism: Reconciling Actual and Metaphoric Gypsies*, 22 THIRD TEXT 305 (2008).

ISIKSEL, TURKULER, EUROPE'S FUNCTIONAL CONSTITUTION: A THEORY OF CONSTITUTIONALISM BEYOND THE STATE (2016).

Issacharoff, Samuel, *Polarized Voting and the Political Process: The Transformation of Voting Rights Jurisprudence*, 90 MICH. L. REV. 1833 (1992).

Issacharoff, Samuel & Pamela S. Karlan, *Groups, Politics, and the Equal Protection Clause*, 58 U. MIAMI L. REV. 35 (2003).

Ivasiuc, Ana, *Introduction: Renewing Research and Romani Activism*, *in* ROMA ACTIVISM: REIMAGINING POWER AND KNOWLEDGE 129 (Sam Beck & Ana Ivasiuc eds., 2018).

Jameson, Fredric, *Reification and Utopia in Mass Culture*, 1 SOCIAL TEXT 130 (1979).

JOHNSON, JAMES WELDON, THE AUTOBIOGRAPHY OF AN EX-COLORED MAN (1912).

Johnson, Kevin R. & Bill Ong Hing, *The Immigrant Rights Marches of 2006 and the Prospects for a New Civil Rights Movement*, 42 HARV. C.R.-C.L. L. REV. 99 (2007).

JONES, MARTHA S., BIRTHRIGHT CITIZENS: A HISTORY OF RACE AND RIGHTS IN ANTEBELLUM AMERICA (2018).

JORDAN, WINTHROP D., WHITE OVER BLACK (1968).

Joris, Tony & Jan Vendenberghe, *The Council of Europe and the European Union: Natural Partners or Uneasy Bedfellows?*, 15 COLUM. J. EUR. L. 1 (2008/2009).

Jovanovic, Zeljko, *Why Europe's "Roma Decade" Didn't Lead to Inclusion*, OPEN SOC'Y FOUND. VOICES (2015), https://www.opensocietyfoundations.org/voices/why-europe-s-roma-decade-didn-t-lead-inclusion.

Kaczorowski, Robert J., *Federal Enforcement of Civil Rights During the First Reconstruction*, 23 FORDHAM URB. L.J. 155 (1995).

Kanev, Krassimir, *The Politics and Reality of Romani School Desegregation in Bulgaria*, *in* TEN YEARS AFTER: A HISTORY OF ROMA SCHOOL DESEGREGATION IN CENTRAL AND EASTERN EUROPE 145 (Iulius Rostas ed., 2012).

Karkkainen, Bradley C., *"New Governance" in Legal Thought and in the World: Some Splitting as Antidote to Overzealous Lumping*, 89 MINN. L. REV. 471 (2004).

Karlovic, N.L., *Internal Colonialism in a Marxist Society: The Case of Croatia*, 5 ETHNIC & RACIAL STUD. 276 (1982).

Kazin, Michael & Joseph A. McCartin, *Introduction*, *in* AMERICANISM: NEW PERSPECTIVES ON THE HISTORY OF AN IDEAL 1 (Michael Kazin & Joseph A. McCartin eds., 2006).

KELLEY, JUDITH G., ETHNIC POLITICS IN EUROPE. THE POWER OF NORMS AND INCENTIVES (2004).

KEYSSAR, ALEXANDER, THE RIGHT TO VOTE: THE CONTESTED HISTORY OF DEMOCRACY IN THE UNITED STATES (2000).

Klarman, Michael J., *Brown v. Board of Education and the Civil Rights Movement* (2007).

Klarman, Michael J., Brown v. Board of Education: *Law or Politics?*, *in* From the Grassroots to the Supreme Court: *Brown v. Board of Education* and American Democracy 198 (Peter F. Lau ed., 2004).

Klarman, Michael J., From Jim Crow to Civil Rights: The Supreme Court and the Struggle for Racial Equality (2004).

Klarman, Michael J., *How* Brown *Changed Race Relations: The Backlash Thesis*, 81 J. Am. Hist. 81 (1994).

Klarman, Michael J., *The Racial Origins of Modern Criminal Procedure*, 99 Mich. L. Rev. 48 (2000).

Klarman, Michael J., *Unfinished Business: Racial Equality in American History*, 93 Va. L. Rev. in Brief 249 (2008).

Klarman, Michael J., *Why Massive Resistance?*, *in* Massive Resistance: Southern Opposition to the Second Reconstruction 21 (Clive Webb ed., 2005).

Klein, Herbert S., The Atlantic Slave Trade (Cambridge Univ. Press 2010 ed.).

Kochenov, Dimitry, EU Enlargement and the Failure of Conditionality: Pre-accession Conditionality in the Fields of Democracy and the Rule of Law (2007).

Kóczé, Angéla, *Political Empowerment or Political Incarceration of Romani? The Hungarian Version of the Politics of Dispossession*, *in* The Hungarian Patient: Social Opposition to an Illiberal Democracy 91 (Péter Krasztev & John Van Til eds., 2015).

Kóczé, Angéla, *The Limits of Rights-Based Discourse in Romani Women's Activism: The Gender Dimension in Romani Politics*, *in* Romani Politics in Contemporary Europe: Poverty, Ethnic Mobilization, and the Neoliberal Order 135 (Nando Sigona & Nidhi Trehan eds., 2009).

Kóczé, Angéla & Martón Rövid, *Pro-Roma Global Civil Society: Acting for, with or Instead of Roma?*, *in* Global Civil Society 2012: Ten Years of Critical Reflection 110 (Mary Kaldor et al. eds., 2012).

Kóczé, Angéla & Márton Rövid, *Roma and the Politics of Double Discourse in Contemporary Europe*, 24 Identities 684 (2017).

Korb, Alexander, *Ustaša Mass Violence Against Gypsies in Croatia, 1941–1942*, *in* The Nazi Genocide of the Roma: Reassessment and Commemoration 72 (Anton Weiss-Wendt ed.) (2013).

Ladányi, János & Iván Szelényi, Patterns of Exclusion: Constructing Gypsy Ethnicity and the Making of an Underclass in Transitional Societies of Europe (2006).

Lake, Marilyn & Henry Reynolds, Drawing the Global Colour Line: White Men's Countries and the International Challenge of Racial Equality (2008).

Lampe, Robert, Yugoslavia as History: Twice There Was a Country (2000).

Leconte, Cécile, *The Fragility of the EU as a "Community of Values": Lessons from the Haider Affair*, 28 W. Eur. Pol. 620 (2005).

Leconte, Cécile, Understanding Euroscepticism (2010).

Lee, Jonathan, *CEU and NGO Crackdown: A Double Blow for Roma Inclusion in Hungary*, Open Democracy (May 5, 2017), https://www.opendemocracy.net/en/can-europe-make-it/ceu-and-ngo-crackdown-double-blow-for-roma-inclusion-in-hungary/.

Lemon, Alaina, *What Are They Writing About Us Blacks? Roma and "Race" in Russia*, 33 Anthropology E. Eur. Rev. 34 (1995).

Liégeois, Jean-Pierre, The Council of Europe and Roma: 40 Years of Action (2012).

Liégeois, Jean-Pierre, Gypsies and Travellers: Socio-Cultural Data (1987).

Linos, Katerina, *Path Dependence in Discrimination Law: Employment Cases in the United States and the European Union*, 35 YALE J. INT'L L. 115 (2010).

LIPSITZ, GEORGE, THE POSSESSIVE INVESTMENT IN WHITENESS: HOW PEOPLE PROFIT FROM IDENTITY POLITICS (rev. ed. 2006).

LOEWEN, JAMES, SUNDOWN TOWNS: A HIDDEN DIMENSION OF AMERICAN RACISM (2005).

López, Ian Haney, *Post-Racial Racism: Racial Stratification and Mass Incarceration in the Age of Obama*, 98 CALIF. L. REV. 1023 (2010).

LÓPEZ, IAN HANEY, WHITE BY LAW: THE LEGAL CONSTRUCTION OF RACE (2nd ed. 2006).

Luca, Ana Maria, *MEPs Vote for Romania and Bulgaria to Join Schengen*, BALKANINSIGHT (Dec. 11, 2018), https://balkaninsight.com/2018/12/11/meps-vote-for-romania-and-bulgaria-to-join-schengen-12–11-2018/.

MALTZ, EARL M., CIVIL RIGHTS, THE CONSTITUTION, AND CONGRESS, 1863–1869 (1990).

Maresceau, Marc, *Pre-accession*, *in* THE ENLARGEMENT OF THE EUROPEAN UNION 9 (Marise Cremona ed., 2003).

Marushiakova, Elena & Vesselin Popov, *European Policies for Social Inclusion of Roma: Catch 22?*, 3 SOC. INCLUSION 19 (2015).

Masoni, Marco, *The Green Badge of Slavery*, 2 GEO. J. ON FIGHTING POVERTY 97 (1994).

MASSIVE RESISTANCE: SOUTHERN OPPRESSION TO THE SECOND RECONSTRUCTION (Webb, Clive ed., 2005).

MASSOOD, PAULA, BLACK CITY CINEMA: AFRICAN-AMERICAN URBAN EXPERIENCES IN FILM (2011).

Matache, Margareta & Krista Oehlke, *Taking Stock of European Public Policy: The Impact of Roma Inclusion Strategies*, *in* REALIZING ROMA RIGHTS 97 (Jacqueline Bhabha et al. eds., 2017).

Matusevich, Maxim, *Journeys of Hope: African Diaspora in the Soviet Society*, 1 AFR. DIASPORA 53 (2008).

MAYALL, DAVID, GYPSY IDENTITIES 1500–2000: FROM EGIPCYANS AND MOON-MEN TO THE ETHNIC ROMANY (2004).

MAYERI, SERENA, REASONING FROM RACE: FEMINISM, LAW, AND THE CIVIL RIGHTS REVOLUTION (2014).

McAdams, Richard H., *The Origin, Development, and Regulation of Norms*, 96 MICH. L. REV. 338 (1997).

MCCORMICK, JOHN, EUROPEANISM (2010).

McFeely, William S., *Amos T. Akerman: The Lawyer and Racial Justice*, *in* REGION, RACE, AND RECONSTRUCTION: ESSAYS IN HONOR OF C. VANN WOODWARD 395 (J. Morgan Kousser & James M. McPherson eds., 1982).

MCGARRY, AIDAN, WHO SPEAKS FOR ROMA?: POLITICAL REPRESENTATION OF A TRANSNATIONAL MINORITY COMMUNITY (2010).

MCINNIS, MAURIE D., SLAVES WAITING FOR SALE: ABOLITIONIST ART AND THE AMERICAN SLAVE TRADE (2011).

MCMILLEN, NEIL, THE CITIZENS' COUNCIL: ORGANIZED RESISTANCE TO THE SECOND RECONSTRUCTION, 1954–64 (1994).

Merlingen, Michael et al., *The Right and the Righteous? European Norms, Domestic Politics and the Sanctions Against Austria*, 39 J. COMMON MKT. STUD. 59 (2001).

Merlino, Doug, *Roma v. Romania*, LEGAL AFF., Mar./Apr. 2006.

Miller, Darrell A.H., *The Thirteenth Amendment and the Regulation of Custom*, 112 COLUM. L. REV. 1811 (2012).

Miller, Karen K., *Race, Power and the Emergence of Black Studies in Higher Education*, 31 AM. STUD. 83 (1990).

MILLER-IDRISS, CYNTHIA, BLOOD AND CULTURE: YOUTH, RIGHT-WING EXTREMISM, AND NATIONAL BELONGING IN CONTEMPORARY GERMANY (2009).

MILLS, CHARLES W., THE RACIAL CONTRACT (1997).

Minow, Martha, Brown v. Board *in the World: How the Global Turn Matters for School Reform, Human Rights, and Legal Knowledge*, 50 SAN DIEGO L. REV. 1 (2013).

Mirga, Andzej, *Roma Policy in Europe: Results and Challenges, in* REALIZING ROMA RIGHTS 115 (Jacqueline Bhabha et al. eds., 2017).

Mirga-Kruszelnicka, Anna, *Romani Studies and Emerging Romani Scholarship, in* NOTHING ABOUT US WITHOUT US? ROMA PARTICIPATION IN POLICY MAKING AND KNOWLEDGE PRODUCTION 39 (Kieran O'Reilly & Marek Szilvasi eds., 2015).

Mišković, Maja, *Roma Education in Europe: In Support of the Discourse of Race*, 17 PEDAGOGY, CULT. & SOC'Y 210 (2009).

Mizsei, Kálmán, *Reconstructing Roma Integration in Central and Eastern Europe: Addressing the Failures of the Last Quarter Century, in* REALIZING ROMA RIGHTS 127 (Jacqueline Bhabha et al. eds., 2017).

MOLLOY, TOVE, NATIONAL MINORITY RIGHTS IN EUROPE (2005).

MÖSCHEL, MATHIAS, LAW, LAWYERS AND RACE: CRITICAL RACE THEORY FROM THE UNITED STATES TO EUROPE (2014).

MÖSCHEL, MATHIAS, THE RELEVANCE OF CRITICAL RACE THEORY TO EUROPE (2011).

Möschel, Mathias, *Towards a European Critical Race Theory*, 34 ETHNIC & RACIAL STUD. 1648 (2011).

Möschel, Mathias, *Color Blindness or Total Blindness? The Absence of Critical Race Theory in Europe*, 9 RUTGERS RACE & L. REV. 57 (2007).

Mudure, Mihaela, *Blackening Gypsy Slavery: The Romanian Case, in* BLACKENING EUROPE: THE AFRICAN AMERICAN PRESENCE 263 (Heike Raphael-Hernandez ed., 2004).

Mihaela Mudure, *From Gypsies to the African Americans*, 4 J. STUD. OF REL. & IDEOLOGIES 58 (2003).

Müller, Stephan, *European Framework for National Roma Policies and the Roma in the Western Balkans*, 10 EUR. Y.B. MINORITY ISSUES 397 (2011).

Murray, Rupert Wolfe, *Romania's Government Moves to Rename the Roma*, TIME (Dec. 8, 2010), http://content.time.com/time/world/article/0,8599,2035862,00.html.

NATIONAL ACADEMY OF EDUCATION, RACE-CONSCIOUS POLICIES FOR ASSIGNING STUDENTS TO SCHOOLS: SOCIAL SCIENCE RESEARCH AND THE SUPREME COURT CASES (Robert L. Linn and Kevin G. Welner eds., 2007).

Neuberger, Eszter, *Hungary's Highest Court Legitimizes Segregation in the Case of Religious Schooling*, BUDAPEST BEACON, Apr. 23, 2015.

NEUBURGER, MARY, THE ORIENT WITHIN: MUSLIM MINORITIES AND THE NEGOTIATION OF NATIONHOOD IN MODERN BULGARIA (2004).

Nicolae, Valeriu, *Perfectly Equipped Failures: The European Union and Educational Issues Affecting the Roma*, 39 EUR. EDUC. 50 (2007).

Nicolaïdis, Kalypso, *Trusting the Poles? Constructing Europe Through Mutual Recognition*, 14 J. EUR. PUB. POL'Y 682 (2007).

O'KEEFFE, BRIGID, NEW SOVIET GYPSIES: NATIONALITY, PERFORMANCE, AND SELFHOOD IN THE EARLY SOVIET UNION (2013).

OLZAK, SUSAN, THE DYNAMICS OF ETHNIC COMPETITION AND CONFLICT (1992).

OMI, MICHAEL & HOWARD WINANT, RACIAL FORMATION IN THE UNITED STATES (3d ed. 2014).

Open Soc'y Founds., *European Commission Targets Slovakia over Roma School Discrimination* (Apr. 29, 2015), https://www.opensocietyfoundations.org/press-releases/european-commission-targets-slovakia-over-roma-school-discrimination [https://perma.cc/H4HK-EPPF].

PANAGIOTAREA, ELENI, GREECE IN THE EURO: ECONOMIC DELINQUENCY OR SYSTEM FAILURE? (2013).

PEIRÓ, EVA WOODS, WHITE GYPSIES: RACE AND STARDOM IN SPANISH MUSICALS (2012).

Pérez, Raúl, *Brownface Minstrelsy: "Jose Jiminez," the Civil Rights Movement and the Legacy of Racist Comedy*, 16 ETHNICITIES 40 (2016).

Perić, Tanja, *Insufficient: Governmental Programmes for Roma in Slovenia*, EUROPEAN ROMA RIGHTS CTR., http://www.errc.org/cikk.php?cikk=1717 [https://perma.cc/T9LY-KFVF].

PERMAN, MICHAEL, REUNION WITHOUT COMPROMISE: THE SOUTH AND RECONSTRUCTION 1856–1868 (1973).

PINKUS, BENJAMIN, THE JEWS OF THE SOVIET UNION: THE HISTORY OF A NATIONAL MINORITY 212 (1988).

PIRRO, ANDREA L.P., THE POPULIST RADICAL RIGHT IN CENTRAL AND EASTERN EUROPE: IDEOLOGY, IMPACT, AND ELECTORAL PERFORMANCE (2015).

POTT, AUGUSTUS, DIE ZIGEUNER IN EUROPA UND ASIEN (1844).

PRESTON, CHRISTOPHER, ENLARGEMENT AND INTEGRATION IN THE EUROPEAN UNION (1997).

Prieto-Flores, Oscar, *Does the Canonical Theory of Assimilation Explain the Roma Case? Some Evidence from Central and Eastern Europe*, 32 ETHNIC & RACIAL STUD. 1387 (2009).

Rabinowitz, Howard N., *More Than the Woodward Thesis: Assessing the Strange Career of Jim Crow*, 75 J. AM. HIST. 842 (1988).

Rawlings, Richard, *Engaged Elites: Citizen Action and Institutional Attitudes in Commission Enforcement*, 6 EUR. L.J. 4 (2000).

Rehaag, Sean et al., *No Refuge: Hungarian Romani Refugee Claimants in Canada*, 52 OSGOODE HALL L.J. 705 (2015).

RESÉNDEZ, ANDRÉS, THE OTHER SLAVERY: THE UNCOVERED STORY OF INDIAN ENSLAVEMENT IN AMERICA (2016).

Rhodes, Matthew, *Slovakia after Mečiar*, 48 PROB. POST-COMMUNISM 3 (2001).

RICHARDSON, HEATHER COX, THE DEATH OF RECONSTRUCTION: RACE, LABOR, AND POLITICS IN THE POST-CIVIL WAR NORTH, 1865–1901 (2001).

RICHARDSON, HEATHER COX, WEST FROM APPOMATTOX: THE RECONSTRUCTION OF AMERICA AFTER THE CIVIL WAR (2007).

Riley, Clayton, *A Black Critic's View of Shaft: Black Movie for White Audiences*, N.Y. TIMES, July 25, 1971.

RINGOLD, DENA ET AL., WORLD BANK, ROMA IN AN EXPANDING EUROPE: BREAKING THE POVERTY CYCLE (2005).

ROEDIGER, DAVID R. WORKING TOWARD WHITENESS: HOW AMERICA'S IMMIGRANTS BECAME WHITE (2005).

Roithmayr, Daria, *Racial Cartels*, 16 MICH. J. RACE & L. 45 (2010).

ROMA MIGRATION TO AND FROM CANADA: THE CZECH, HUNGARIAN, AND SLOVAK CASE (Zsuzsanna Vidra ed., 2013).

ROMANI CULTURE AND GYPSY IDENTITY (Thomas Acton & Gary Mundy eds., 1997).

Rorke, Bernard, *The End of a Decade: What Happened to Roma Inclusion?*, OPEN DEMOCRACY (Sept. 29, 2015), https://www.opendemocracy.net/en/can-europe-make-it/end-of-decade-what-happened-to-roma-inclusion/.

Rorke, Bernard, *Somewhere Between Hope and Despair: Whatever Happened to Roma Inclusion Between 2005 and 2015?*, *in* A LOST DECADE?: REFLECTIONS ON ROMA INCLUSION 2005–2015 44 (Bernard Rorke & Orhan Usein eds., 2015).

RORKE, BERNARD, OPEN SOC'Y ROMA INITIATIVES, REVIEW OF EU FRAMEWORK NATIONAL ROMA INTEGRATION STRATEGIES (NRIS) (2012).

Rostas, Iulius et al., *Interview with Costel Bercus from Romania*, *in* TEN YEARS AFTER: A HISTORY OF ROMA SCHOOL DESEGREGATION IN CENTRAL AND EASTERN EUROPE 267 (Iulius Rostas ed., 2012).

Rostas, Iulius et al., *Interview with Ivan Vesely from the Czech Republic*, *in* TEN YEARS AFTER: A HISTORY OF ROMA SCHOOL DESEGREGATION IN CENTRAL AND EASTERN EUROPE 165 (Iulius Rostas ed., 2012).

Rostas, Iulius et al., *Interview with Rumyan Russinov from Bulgaria*, *in* TEN YEARS AFTER: A HISTORY OF ROMA SCHOOL DESEGREGATION IN CENTRAL AND EASTERN EUROPE 131 (Iulius Rostas ed., 2012).

Rostas, Iulius et al., *Interview with Viktória Mohácsi from Hungary*, *in* TEN YEARS AFTER: A HISTORY OF ROMA SCHOOL DESEGREGATION IN CENTRAL AND EASTERN EUROPE 197 (Iulius Rostas ed., 2012).

ROTHSTEIN, RICHARD, THE COLOR OF LAW: A FORGOTTEN HISTORY OF HOW OUR GOVERNMENT SEGREGATED AMERICA (2017).

Rucker-Chang, Sunnie, *Challenging Americanism and Europeanism: African-Americans and Roma in the American South and European Union* "South," 16 J. TRANSATLANTIC STUD. 181 (2018).

Rutherglen, George, *State Action, Private Action, and the Thirteenth Amendment*, 94 VA. L. REV. 1367 (2008).

Sampson, John, *On the Origin and Early Migration of the Gypsies*, 2 J. GYPSY LORE SOC. 156 (1923).

Sardelic, Julia, *Romani Minorities and Uneven Citizenship Access in the Post-Yugoslav Space*, 14 ETHNOPOL. 159 (2015).

SASSATELLI, MONICA, BECOMING EUROPEANS: CULTURAL IDENTITIES AND CULTURAL POLICIES (2009).

Sasse, Gwendolyn, *The Politics of EU Conditionality: The Norm of Minority Protection during and beyond EU Accession*, 15 J. EUR. PUB. POL'Y 842 (2008).

Sasse, Gwendolyn, *EU Conditionality and Minority Rights: Translating the Copenhagen Criterion into Policy* (European Union Institute Working Paper RSCAS No. 2005/16, 2005).

Savage, Charlie, *Justice Dept. to Take On Affirmative Action in College Admissions*, N.Y. TIMES, Aug. 1, 2017.

Schimmelfennig, Frank & Ulrich Sedelmeier, *Introduction: Conceptualization the Europeanization of Central and Eastern Europe*, *in* THE EUROPEANIZATION OF CENTRAL AND EASTERN EUROPE 1 (Frank Schimmelfennig & Ulrich Sedelmeier eds., 2005).

Schütze, Robert, *Direct Effects and Indirect Effects*, *in* OXFORD PRINCIPLES OF EUROPEAN UNION LAW, vol. 1, 265 (Robert Schütze & Takis Tridimas eds., 2018).

Schwartz, Mildred A., *Trends in White Attitudes toward Negros* (Report for the National Opinion Research Center No. 119, 1967), http://www.norc.org/PDFs/publications/NORCRpt_119.pdf.

Schwemm, Robert G., *Overcoming Structural Barriers to Integrated Housing: A Back-to-the-Future Reflection on the Fair Housing Act's "Affirmatively Further" Mandate*, 100 KY. L.J. 125 (2012).

SCOTT, ELLEN, CINEMA CIVIL RIGHTS: REGULATION, REPRESSION, AND RACE IN THE CLASSICAL HOLLYWOOD ERA (2015).

Scott, Joanne & David M. Trubek, *Mind the Gap: Law and New Approaches to Governance in the European Union*, 8 EUR. L.J. 1 (2002).

Sedelmeier, Ulrich, *After Conditionality: Post-Accession Compliance with EU Law in East Central Europe*, 15 J. EUR. PUB. POL'Y 806 (2008).

Semley, John, *Who's Bleeding Whom? Analyzing the Cultural Flows of Blaxploitation Cinema, Then and Now*, 80 CINEACTION 22 (2010).

Severance, Kristi, *France's Expulsion of Roma Migrants: A Test Case for Europe*, MIGRATION POLICY INST. (Oct. 21, 2010), https://www.migrationpolicy.org/article/frances-expulsion-roma-migrants-test-case-europe.

Shalhope, Robert, *Anticipating Americanism: An Individual Perspective on Republicanism in the Early Republic*, *in* Americanism: New Perspectives on the History of an Ideal 53 (Michael Kazin & Joseph A. McCartin eds., 2006).

Silverman, Carol, Romani Routes: Cultural Politics and Balkan Music in Diaspora (2012).

Simon, Alissa, *Berlin Film Review: "Genesis,"* Variety (Feb. 20, 2018), https://variety.com/2018/film/reviews/genesis-review-berlinale-2018–1202704709/.

Slovenia's "Erased People," Deutsche Welle (Nov. 27, 2004), https://www.dw.com/en/slovenias-erased-people/a–1408564.

Smith, Anthony D., Ethno-Symbolism and Nationalism: A Cultural Approach (2009).

Smith, Anthony D., Myths and Memories of the Nation (1999).

Smith, Karen E., *The Evolution and Application of EU Membership Conditionality*, *in* The Enlargement of the European Union 105 (Marise Cremona ed., 2003).

Smith, Tom W., *Changing Racial Labels: From "Colored" to "Negro" to "Black" to "African American,"* 56 Pub. Opinion Q. 496 (1992).

Snyder, Robert & Timothy J. White, *The Fall of the Berlin Wall: The Counterrevolution in Soviet Foreign Policy and the End of Communism*, *in* After the Berlin Wall Germany and Beyond 127 (Katharina Gerstenberger & Jana Evans Braziel eds., 2011).

Sokhi-Bulley, Bal, *The Fundamental Rights Agency of the European Union: A New Panopticism*, 11 Hum. Rts. L. Rev. 683 (2011).

Sokol, Jason, There Goes My Everything (1997).

Solonari, Vladimir, *Ethnic Cleansing or "Crime Prevention"? Deportation of Romanian Roma*, *in* The Nazi Genocide of the Roma: Reassessment and Commemoration 96 (Anton Weiss-Wendt ed., 2013).

Stein, Eric, *Lawyers, Judges, and the Making of a Transnational Constitution*, 75 Am. J. Int'l L. 1 (1981)

Stone, Jon, *EU President Invites Bulgaria and Romania to Join Borderless Schengen Area "Immediately,'* Independent (Sept. 13, 2017), http://www.independent.co.uk/news/world/europe/eu-brexit-bulgaria-romania-schengen-area-immigration-passportless-jean-claude-juncker-president-a7944196.html.

Stone Sweet, Alec, *Constitutional Dialogues in the European Community*, *in* The European Court and National Courts – Doctrine and Jurisprudence: Legal Change in Its Social Context 305 (Anne-Marie Slaughter et al. eds., 1998).

Stone Sweet, Alec & Wayne Sandholtz, *Integration, Supranational Governance, and Institutionalization of the European Polity*, *in* European Integration and Supranational Governance 1 (Alec Stone Sweet & Wayne Sandholtz eds., 1998).

Strumia, Francesca, *Individual Rights, Interstate Equality, State Autonomy: European Horizontal Citizenship and Its (Lonely) Playground from a Trans-Atlantic Perspective*, *in* EU Citizenship and Federalism: The Role of Rights 615 (Dimitry Kochenov ed., 2017).

Sturm, Susan, *Second Generation Employment Discrimination: A Structural Approach*, 101 Colum. L. Rev. 458 (2001).

Suk, Julie C., *New Directions for European Race Equality Law:* CHEZ Razpredelenie Bulgaria AD v. Komisia za Zashitita ot Diskriminatsia, Anelia Nikolovai, 40 Fordham Int'l L.J. 1211 (2017).

Surdu, Mihai, Those Who Count: Expert Practices of Roma Classification (2016).

Szep, Attila, *Some Aspects of Roma Migration from Slovakia*, *in* Social Networks in Movement: Time, Interaction and Interethnic Spaces in Central Eastern Europe 185 (Davide Torsello & Melinda Pappová eds., 2007).

Tesler, Michael & David O. Sears, Obama's Race: The 2008 Election and the Dream of a Post-Racial America (2010).

The Great Migration in Historical Perspective: New Dimensions of Race, Class, and Gender (Joe William Trotter, Jr. ed., 1991).

Theoharis, Jeanne F., *Introduction*, *in* Freedom North: Black Freedom Struggles Outside the South, 1940–1980 1 (Jeanne F. Theoharis & Komozi Woodard eds., 2003).

Todd, Tony, *France Opposes Border-Free Travel for Romania, Bulgaria*, France24 (Sept. 30, 2013), https://www.france24.com/en/20130930-france-against-romania-bulgaria-schengen-roma-europe-immigration.

Todorova, Maria, Imagining the Balkans (1997).

Todorova, Miglena S., *Race and Women of Color in Socialist/Postsocialist Transnational Feminisms in Central and Southeastern Europe*, 16 Meridians: Feminism, Race, Transnationalism 114 (2018).

Toggenburg, Gabriel N., *The Lisbon Treaty: A Rich Cocktail Served in an Only Half-Full Glass*, 5 Europäisches J. für Minderheitenfragen 78 (2012).

Toggenburg, Gabriel N., *The Race Directive: A New Dimension in the Fight against Ethnic Discrimination in Europe*, 1 Eur. Y.B. Minority Issues 231 (2001–2002).

Toggenburg, Gabriel N., *The Role of the New EU Fundamental Rights Agency: Debating the "Sex of Angels" or Improving Europe's Human Rights Performance?*, 3 Eur. L. Rev. 385 (2008).

Tölölyan, Khachig, *Rethinking Diaspora(s): Stateless Power in the Transnational Moment*, 5 Diaspora: J. Transnat'l Stud. 3 (1996).

Trehan, Nidhi & Angéla Kóczé, *Racism, (Neo-)colonialism and Social Justice: The Struggle for the Soul of the Romani Movement in Post-socialist Europe*, *in* Racism Postcolonialism Europe 50 (Graham Huggan & Ian Law eds., 2009).

Tribe, Laurence H., American Constitutional Law (2d ed. 1988).

Trubek, David M. et al., *"Soft Law," "Hard Law," and EU Integration*, *in* Law and New Governance in the EU and the US 65 (Gráinne de Búrca & Joanne Scott eds., 2006).

Tsesis, Alexander, The Thirteenth Amendment and American Freedom: A Legal History (2004).

Turda, Marius & Paul J. Weindling, Blood and Homeland: Eugenics and Racial Nationalism in Central and Southeast Europe (2007).

Turner, Ralph, *On the Position of Romani in Indo-Aryan*, 5 J. Gypsy Lore Soc. 145 (1927).

Tushnet, Mark, *Conclusion*, *in* Comparative Constitutional Federalism: Europe and America 139 (Mark Tushnet ed., 1990).

Tushnet, Mark, *The Return of the Repressed: Groups, Social Welfare Rights, and the Equal Protection Clause*, 2 Issues in Legal Scholarship 1 (2002).

United States Holocaust Memorial Museum, *Sinti and Roma: Victims of the Nazi Era*, *archived at* https://perma.cc/2D9N-H777.

Van Alstyne, William, *Rites of Passage: Race, the Supreme Court, and the Constitution*, 46 U. Chi. L. Rev. 775 (1978).

van Ham, Peter, The EC, Eastern Europe and European Unity: Discord, Collaboration and Integration Since 1947 (1993).

Vermeersch, Peter, *Ethnic Mobilisation and the Political Conditionality of European Union Accession: The Case of the Roma in Slovakia*, 28 J. Ethnic & Migration Stud. 83 (2002).

Vermeersch, Peter, *EU Enlargement and Minority Rights Policies in Central Europe: Explaining Policy Shifts in the Czech Republic, Hungary and Poland*, 14 J. Ethnopol. & Minority Issues in Eur. 114 (2015).

Vermeersch, Peter, *Reframing the Roma: EU Initiatives and the Politics of Reinterpretation*, 38 J. ETHNIC & MIGRATION STUD. 1195 (2012).

VERMEERSCH, PETER, THE ROMANI MOVEMENT: MINORITY POLITICS & ETHNIC MOBILIZATION IN CONTEMPORARY CENTRAL EUROPE (2006).

Vermeersch, Peter & Melanie H. Ram, *The Roma*, *in* MINORITY RIGHTS IN CENTRAL AND EASTERN EUROPE 61 (Bernd Rechel ed., 2009).

Visoka, Gëzim & Elvin Gjevori, *Census Politics and Ethnicity in the Western Balkans*, 29 E. EUR. POL. 479 (2013).

VUKSANOVIĆ-MACURA, ZLATA & VLADIMIR MACURA, STANOVANJE I NASELJA ROMA U JUGOISTOČNOJ EVROPI: PROKAZ STANJA I NAPRETKA U SRBIJI (2006).

Wechsler, Herbert, *Toward Neutral Principles of Constitutional Law*, 73 HARV. L. REV. 1 (1959).

Weinerová, Renata, *From East to West: The Roma Migration from Slovakia*, *in* SOCIAL NETWORKS IN MOVEMENT: TIME, INTERACTION AND INTERETHNIC SPACES IN CENTRAL EASTERN EUROPE 191 (Davide Torsello & Melinda Pappová eds., 2003).

Weiss-Wendt, Anton, *Introduction*, *in* THE NAZI GENOCIDE OF THE ROMA: REASSESSMENT AND COMMEMORATION 1 (Anton Weiss-Wendt ed., 2013).

Weiler, J.H.H., *Eurocracy and Distrust: Some Questions Concerning the Role of the European Court of Justice in the Protection of Fundamental Human Rights within the Legal Order of the European Communities*, 61 WASH. L. REV. 1103 (1986).

Weiler, J.H.H., *The Transformation of Europe*, 100 YALE L.J. 2403 (1991).

WELLS, IDA B., SOUTHERN HORRORS: LYNCH LAW IN ALL ITS PHASES (1892).

WEST, REBECCA, BLACK LAMB AND GREY FALCON (1941).

White, Gillian B., *How Money from Slave Trading Helped Start Columbia University*, ATLANTIC, Jan. 25, 2017.

WHITE, JULIA M., PITFALLS AND BIAS: ENTRY TESTING AND THE OVERREPRESENTATION OF ROMANI CHILDREN IN SPECIAL EDUCATION (2012).

White, Ronald C., AMERICAN ULYSSES: A LIFE OF ULYSSES S. GRANT (2016).

WHITMAN, JAMES Q., HITLER'S AMERICAN MODEL: THE UNITED STATES AND THE MAKING OF NAZI RACE LAW (2017).

Wiener, Antje & Guido Schwellnus, *Contested Norms in the Process of EU Enlargement: Non-discrimination and Minority Rights*, *in* LAW AND GOVERNANCE IN AN ENLARGED EUROPEAN UNION 451 (George A. Bermann & Katharina Pistor eds., 2004).

WILDER, CRAIG STEVEN, EBONY AND IVY RACE, SLAVERY AND THE TROUBLED HISTORY OF AMERICA'S UNIVERSITIES (2013).

WILKERSON, ISABEL, THE WARMTH OF OTHER SUNS: THE EPIC STORY OF AMERICA'S GREAT MIGRATION (2010).

Wilkinson, J. Harvie, III, *Federalism for the Future*, 74 S. CAL. L. REV. 523 (2001).

Willems, Wim, *Ethnicity as a Death-Trap: The History of Gypsy Studies*, *in* GYPSIES AND OTHER ITINERANT GROUPS: A SOCIO-HISTORICAL APPROACH 17 (Leo Lucassen et al. eds.,1998).

WILLIAMS, ANDREW, EU HUMAN RIGHTS POLICIES: A STUDY IN IRONY (2004).

Wilson, Woodrow, *Americanism and the Foreign Reborn*, *in* THE AMERICAN STUDIES ANTHOLOGY 127 (Richard P. Horwitz ed., 2001) (1915).

WOLFF, LARRY, INVENTING EASTERN EUROPE: THE MAP OF CIVILIZATION ON THE MIND OF THE ENLIGHTENMENT (1994).

World Bank, *Conference Briefing Note: "Roma in an Expanding Europe: Challenges for the Future"* (2003), http://documents.worldbank.org/curated/en/872391468749375351/pdf/26415.pdf.

WOODWARD, C. VANN, THE STRANGE CAREER OF JIM CROW (1955).

Zentral Rat Deutscher Sinti & Roma, 45 Jahre Bürgerrechtsarbeit Deutscher Sinti und Roma (2017).
Zietlow, Rebecca, The Forgotten Emancipator: James Mitchell Ashley and the Ideological Origins of Reconstruction (2018).
Zorn, Jelka, *Ethnic Citizenship in the Slovenian State*, 9 Citizenship Stud. 135 (2005).

FILMOGRAPHY

12 Years a Slave (Regency Enterprises 2013).
An Episode in the Life of an Iron Picker [Epizoda u Životu Berača Željeza] (SCCA 2013).
Black Girl (Cinerama Releasing 1972).
Boy and Man (Crean Films & Jemmin Inc. 1971).
Boyz in the Hood (Columbia Pictures1991).
Bravo! [Aferim!] (HI Film 2015).
Buck and the Preacher (Columbia Pictures 1972).
Circus [Цирк] (Mosfilm Studios 1936).
Django Unchained (Weinstein Co. & Columbia Pictures 2012).
Genesis [Genezis] (FocusFox 2018).
Gypsies [Cigányok] (Balázs Béla Stúdió 1962).
I Even Met Happy Gypsies [Skupljaci Perja] (Avala Film 1967).
Jaroka: Roma Immigration Is "Positive" for Countries, BBC (Feb. 20, 2014), https://www.bbc.com/news/av/world-europe-26273052/jaroka-roma-immigration-is-positive-for-countries.
Just the Wind [Csak a Szél] (Inforg-M&M Film 2012).
Lady Sings the Blues (Jobete Productions 1972).
Mister Twister (Soyuzmultfilm 1963).
New Jack City (Warner Bros. 1991).
Radical Cut [Radikalni Rez] (Barrandov Studios 1983).
Roming (In Film Praha 2007).
Roots (Wolper Productions & Warner Bros. 1977).
Sounder (Radnitz/Mattel Productions & Rainbow Group 1972).
Sweet Sweetback's Baadasssss Song (Yeah 1971).
The Shutka Book of Records [Knjiga Rekorda Šutke] (Aleksandar Manić 2005).
The Slaves (Slaves Company 1969).
The Spook Who Sat by the Door (Bokari 1973).
Underground (Get Lifted Film 2016).
Who's Singing Over There [Ko To Tamo Peva] (Centar Film 1980).

Index

www.ingramcontent.com/pod-product-compliance
Lightning Source LLC
LaVergne TN
LVHW011814200926
848484LV00005B/1186
9781107158368